JEFF DANBY

Day of the
PANZER

A Story of American Heroism
and Sacrifice in Southern France

CASEMATE

Philadelphia & Newbury

Published in the United States of America in 2008 by
CASEMATE
1016 Warrior Road, Drexel Hill, PA 19026

And in the United Kingdom by
CASEMATE
17 Cheap Street, Newbury, RG14 5DD

ISBN 978-1-932033-70-0

Printed in the United States of America

Typeset & design by Savas Publishing & Consulting Group

Book Club Edition

To all who served in the liberation of Southern France

Especially those of Company L and Cannon Company,
15th Infantry Regiment,

Company B of the 756th Tank Battalion,

and Company B of the 601st Tank Destroyer Battalion.

And particularly my grandfather, 1st Lt. Edgar R. Danby

"A country worth living in
is a country worth fighting for…"

— 1st Lt. Edgar R. Danby

CONTENTS

MAPS

ILLUSTRATIONS

A gallery of photos follows page 166

Preface
and Acknowledgments

The invasion of Southern France is the forgotten campaign of World War II. Nearly every other campaign and major battle in the European Theater has been well researched and described—especially those that took place in Northern France. Extraordinary accounts of combat on Omaha Beach, in Holland during Operation Market Garden, and at Bastogne during the Battle of the Bulge have been told and retold in everything from best-selling books to blockbuster movies. Yet few books have been written about the operations in Southern France. Most general histories mention it only in passing if they mention it at all. Even World War II enthusiasts are surprised to learn that fighting took place there. Although overshadowed by larger events, the campaign has been unjustly ignored—mainly because of the erroneous perception that the effort met with little or no resistance.

On a general level, the Southern France campaign appears to offer little excitement. The operation unfolded in a relatively blunder-free manner, was concluded one month later, and extracted far fewer Allied lives than planners originally feared. As a general rule, campaigns such as this rarely send historians scrambling for a typewriter. Some writers have derisively dubbed the operation "The Champaign Campaign," as if the massive operation during which many good men lost their lives was nothing more than a marching cocktail party. The moniker makes for a clever nickname, but it is also a most unjust characterization that dismisses the hardships and trials of thousands of men, many of whom were wounded or killed. The Southern France campaign does not offer historians something similar to those horrible initial hours on Omaha

Beach or the desperate fighting waiting in the hedgerow countryside beyond, but it is a rich and moving drama that deserves much more scrutiny than it has received.

*   *   *

An entire American army stormed the French Riviera one hot summer day in August 1944. Accompanied by British paratroopers and supported by a vast air force, the army was augmented with French infantry and armored divisions. A sweeping armada of 885 ships (with some 1,375 additional boats carried on the decks) set them ashore— 151,000 troops and 21,400 vehicles. Up until that moment, it was the second largest amphibious landing of the war. A German army and battle-hardened panzer division, skillfully resisted the inland Allied thrust with a spirited and skillfully conducted fighting retreat up the Rhône River Valley. When the battle for Southern France ended on September 15, more than 2,000 Americans were listed among the killed, captured, or missing, with another 2,500 wounded. Regular Free French forces suffered similar losses, and many other French Resistance irregulars and civilians perished. Estimates of Germans losses run as high as 7,000 killed and 21,000 wounded. For all of these unfortunate souls, Southern France was no "Champaign Campaign."

Despite the enormity of the operation, the landings were entirely upstaged by and sandwiched between two major events. That June, the critical landings at Normandy secured a solid foothold in Fortress Europe. Weeks of intense and bloody hedgerow fighting followed. The invasion of Southern France commenced after the Allies broke into the open and swept toward Paris. The news that the Allies had broken out of the Normandy region caught the attention of the world's press. Just after the operation in Southern France ended, the ambitious but ill-fated Operation Market Garden assault into Holland got underway. With both ends of France secure, the Allied armies merged quickly that autumn along a massive front and pressed toward Germany. Winter's arrival initiated larger and more pressing challenges in the Ardennes, the Hürtgen Forest, and Colmar. The memories and experiences in the south of France passed quickly off the stage against a backdrop of death and bad weather on an epic scale.

The war in Europe concluded the following spring. On its heels followed a spate of books on the war. To most observers, the Allied drive across Northern France provided a more appropriate and compelling framework for explaining the war on the Western Front. The more modest operation farther south was always intended to supplement the massive Normandy invasion. When measured against Omaha Beach and its immediate aftermath, the relative ease with which the American and French divisions achieved their objectives lessened the campaign's appeal. This unfortunate oversight continues to this day.

No one involved in the Southern France operation expected the grand success that resulted. Winston Churchill feared another Anzio-like stalemate and had lobbied long and hard against the effort. The combat veterans of the Italian campaign prepared for the worst and fully expected their leaders were about to deposit them into another corner of Hell. How could they have thought otherwise? The entire push up the boot of Italy had been one long grueling and bloody struggle against an imaginative, resourceful, and competent enemy whose steely defensive resolve frustrated the Allies at nearly every turn. Every Italian town, hill, and field wrested from their German adversaries, thinned Allied rosters.

Although Churchill's fears of another Anzio failed to materialize, the German defenders managed stiff resistance in many places. These deadly clashes took place mostly at small unit levels. World War II has often been called a "Lieutenant's War," and for good reason. The battle orders originated with men sporting crisp star-pinned collars, but it fell on the unwashed and sleep-deprived captains, lieutenants, and sergeants to inspire their teenage recruits and execute the plans under rapidly unfolding and often chaotic circumstances. The character and improvisational ability of men in front line companies, platoons, and squads led to the success or failure of the larger operational plans and always involved on-the-spot life or death decisions. Each of these men were flesh and blood individuals with names, personalities, and unique hopes and dreams. Some made the ultimate sacrifice and left behind families, friends, and unrealized aspirations. Others hurled themselves into situations of extreme danger and inexplicably survived. Like every campaign in every war, the true drama of the campaign that unfolded across the south of France Campaign unfolded at the small unit level. By retracing the footsteps of the infantryman and the tanker one discovers the campaign was not as easy and effortless as those who have so long ignored it would lead us to believe.

The Day of the Panzer details a large-scale operation, but its core is based upon the experiences of one infantry company during the first two weeks of the campaign. L Company was one of three rifle companies in 3rd Battalion, 15th Infantry Regiment, 3rd Infantry Division. L Company and 3rd Battalion were supported by a platoon of "Sherman" medium tanks from B Company, 756th Tank Battalion, tank destroyers from B Company, 601st Tank Destroyer Battalion, and self-propelled howitzers from 15th Infantry Regiment's "Cannon Company." A rifle company was but one small part of an advancing infantry force, and could not fight well or successfully without plenty of support.

I did not set out to write this book. The path to its writing began when I began researching a few basic details about the war service of my long-departed grandfather. My quest took me to a website on the Society of the Third Infantry Division, where I quickly made contact with some of my grandfather's associates. Through a nascent network of sources, a combat story emerged, one that became more fascinating with each revelation. Every answer produced a new set of compelling questions. Even knowing as little as I did then about the operations in Southern France, I was surprised at how little I could find on the subject. Before long I was thoroughly hooked.

Because the details I sought were not conveniently found in the standard histories of the war, I was forced to look elsewhere. The task of reconstructing what these men endured and achieved was a painstaking one that required laborious research in a thousand scattered sources. My journey took me to Southern France (twice), Fort Knox, Kentucky, the Military History Institute in Pennsylvania, and the National Archives in Maryland, where I spent endless hours spread across multiple visits. I recreated rosters to help me locate and interview living veterans— particularly of L Company of the infantry and B Company of the tanks. With the additional help of surviving families and friends of others, and the French civilians who witnessed and/or participated in the fighting, other fascinating details were uncovered. After five and a half years of research, it became obvious that if anyone was going to write about these events, I would have to do it. The final story—their final story— demanded the permanence of ink and paper.

Although I have tried my best to present the facts as accurately as possible, I am always mindful that I was not present during the events described in these pages. Despite my best efforts, parts of the story will remain incomplete or sketchy. Even those men who were there only witnessed their own small personal slice of the history of the Southern France operation. Sixty-three years have elapsed since the guns fell silent. The young men are now old, their memories faded or conflicting; many particulars have been forgotten completely. As a consequence, parts of the record will forever be open to speculation. Wherever gaps or conflicts appeared, I asked for the opinions of the participants and offered the most informed interpretation of what had transpired. I identify these occasions and offer additional explanation in the notes.

*   *   *

Many people have selflessly helped me with the book and I wish to thank them—particularly the American combat veterans I interviewed. They survived horrendous events, returned home, and did their best to put the past behind them and move on with their lives. Six decades later I called upon them to remember and relive a dark segment of their young lives all over again. I deeply appreciate their patience and grace, and can't thank them enough for their assistance. Above all, they've taught me that the capacity to endure and triumph through any trial is within each of us, and that every life is like the finest wine—meant to be nurtured, savored, and appreciated. The flames of war consumed many young men before they were allowed to fully age. We'll never know what richness they might have added to this world.

The contributors to this book are listed in the "Interviews, Contacts and Contributors" section. Nevertheless, some deserve special mention for without their help, *The Day of the Panzer* could never have been written:

David Redle offered boundless patience and indispensable assistance. I have asked him every possible question and he always endeavored to provide me with an honest and complete answer. A more serene and giving man an author could not hope to find.

George Burks offered candor, encouragement, and good humor. He is a brave and deeply caring soul whose tenure in command of L Company was much too short. He represents all the best qualities found within the American soldier.

John Shirley offered me his guidance and wisdom, and graciously tossed many good leads my way. John led men through terrible combat during World War II. He remains the embodiment of the "Can Do" spirit.

George Polich has a magnificent memory and boundless generosity. He encouraged me to trust my conclusions—even where his opinions and mine differed. I can't thank him enough.

Rudy Jantz shared his excellent combat and leadership insights. Rudy began his distinguished twenty-five year military career in L Company, so his descriptions and experiences offer an especially valuable perspective.

Ed Olson warmly welcomed me into the 756th Tank Battalion Association family. It was Ed who first suggested I write this book. I hope he is still happy he made the recommendation once he finishes reading it.

Michel Seigle responded to my e-mail inquiry in September 2000, and generously assisted me at every opportunity thereafter. The warm hospitality of Michel and his wife Marie-Thérèse transformed Allan from a distant foreign village into my adopted French hometown.

Maurice Martel for keeping a wartime journal and publishing a 1947 book about his beloved village of Allan. Without his work, I'd be lost.

Lucien Martel, Maurice's son, helped me see the aftermath of the battle at Allan through his eyes and his photographs.

All the people of Allan helped me in many ways, large and small. I would like to especially mention Jean Pic, Jean Rozel, Michel Imbert, Jean Dessalles, and Robert Borne, witnesses and survivors of the combat in their town and now my friends.

Robert Ramirez helped me reconstruct the events of August 23, 1944, around his hometown of Vitrolles, France, and shuttled me around the old battlefield in his beautifully restored WWII-era GMC 2½-ton U.S. Army truck. If I had had a helmet and carbine with me, I would have been fully lost in time!

Kenneth Schlessinger not only dispensed invaluable advice and answered all my National Archives questions with patience and professionalism, but made me feel like a V.I.P researcher. Alonzo Bouie obtained my Morning Report requests from the National Personnel Records Center promptly, courteously, and enthusiastically. Thank you both.

Richard Heller maintained the Society of the Third Infantry Division website, where my search began. It has remained my "Grand Central Station" ever since.

I would like to thank my publisher Casemate, and especially David Farnsworth and Steven Smith, for accepting my manuscript for publication.

Onno Onneken located, obtained, and translated every piece of surviving German Nineteenth Army documentation he could find. He took a deep interest in my research, and I thank him for that.

Amy Rule reviewed my French document translations and interview tapes for accuracy and any missing details.

Russell Danby-Jones, my father, served as my informal research assistant and sounding board. It was a pleasure to work with him on this book.

Becky Linebrink watched the kids when my research took me out of town.

I would be remiss if I did not mention my especially supportive wife Melinda, who endured ad nauseam five years of non-stop jabbering every time I uncovered a new detail. Now she can read everything in one place at her leisure while I find something else to talk about!

Jeff Danby
Granville, Ohio
March, 2008

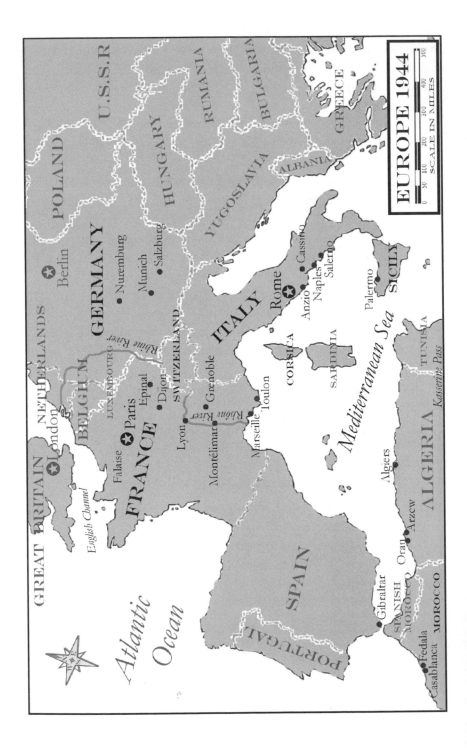

Introduction

3rd Infantry Division and Operation Anvil

On December 7, 1941, Imperial Japan launched a surprise attack against the U.S. naval base at Pearl Harbor. Four days later, Japan's two Axis allies, German and Italy, declared war against America. Wholly unprepared to fight a conflict on a global scale, America set about to develop and project its military power abroad. Other than minor air operations and submarine warfare, however, fighting on a significant scale would have to wait. America, Great Britain, and the Soviet Union, meanwhile, decided the best course to victory over the Axis powers was to hold in the Far East, defeat Nazi Germany and Italy, and then turn decisively against Japan.

With Great Britain and the Soviets locked in combat at sea and across large swaths of Europe and North Africa, the Americans finally joined the fighting on land in August of 1942 when U.S. Marines landed on Guadalcanal, a small patch of land in the Solomon Islands. The campaign was designed to slow Japanese expansion while providing a base of operations for American involvement in the Far East. A few months later on the other side of the globe, the Americans launched an entirely different operation.

On November 8, 1942, Allied forces landed in North Africa. The initial landings pitted Americans against French defenders. It was an odd beginning on the road to the end, but it was a beginning nonetheless. The massive invasion, code-named Operation Torch, involved the amphibious landings of British and American troops in three places along the Moroccan-Algerian coastline. American contribution to the operation included a pair of armored divisions and three infantry divisions.[1] One of the later was 3rd Infantry Division. Attached to 3rd Division was 756th Tank Battalion—a "light" tank battalion. Its M5 tanks were small and fast, but lightly armed and thinly protected compared to their German armor counterparts.

3rd Division and 756th Tank Battalion made up the bulk of General George S. Patton's "Western Task Force" landing near Casablanca. They fought French colonial forces obliged under the terms of the 1940 Armistice to resist Allied attacks. Fortunately, the defenders quickly recognized there was no long term benefit fighting Allied soldiers trying to free France of German occupiers. Capitulation ended the resistance within two days. At first, the Americans didn't understand this initial French "honor" resistance, but were grateful the fight was short and that French colonial forces realigned with them. The next few months were spent working together, training together, and sharing food and drink. The preparations and planning between the two former adversaries increased their mutual respect and admiration for what each side brought to the greater struggle confronting the free Western world.

In the spring of 1943, 3rd Division traveled by rail 500 miles east to Arzew on the Mediterranean to undergo additional amphibious training. Weeks of mock beach landings and practice pillbox assaults followed. That July, the division (less the recently detached 756th Tank Battalion) participated in the invasion of Sicily, moved with lightning speed through the mountains, and captured the key city of Palermo. In September, the 3rd Division landed at Salerno, Italy, with General Mark Clark's Fifth Army. The fighting on the Italian peninsula was of the bitter attrition variety, a mile by mile slugfest northward on the drive toward Cassino. On November 17, 1943, the division was pulled from the line for some long overdue rest and to prepare for its fourth amphibious operation: Anzio.[2]

Attached to 34th Infantry Division, 756th Tank Battalion drove north on the drive toward Cassino. In December 1943, 756th was upgraded to a "Sherman" medium tank outfit. M4 "Sherman" tanks were an improvement over the lighter M5s, but still inferior in head-to-head matchups against nearly every piece of German armor. The tankers of 756th had to find ways to coax advantages out of their new tanks. Cassino was their bloody proving ground.

By January 1944, stiff German resistance along the Gustav Line, a series of powerful defensive positions bisecting the Italian peninsula into its northern and southern halves, stopped the advance of the U.S. Fifth Army and the British Eighth Army. Unable to punch through, the Allies sought a more creative way to break the impasse. The plan settled upon was codenamed Operation Shingle, an amphibious end-around that would land troops behind the Gustav Line at Anzio. Planners believed the Germans would have but little choice other than to draw back their forces in response. The landings went smoothly, with thousands of Allied soldiers disembarking on the beaches at Anzio during the early morning hours of January 22, 1944. By that evening, 36,034 troops and 3,069 vehicles[3] from the British 1st Division, the U.S. 3rd Infantry Division, and three battalions of "Darby's Rangers"[4] were firmly ashore. In forty-eight hours, the beachhead had expanded seven miles inland.[5] Pleased thus far, the Allies knew better than to venture deeper into Italy until reinforcements arrived. The inability to punch deeply into enemy territory exposed the plan's serious flaw. Operation Shingle didn't put enough troops or firepower on the ground during those crucial first days, to take advantage of surprise and sustain a breakout. Reinforcements took another week to arrive and assemble. The respite gave the Germans plenty of time to react. Their decision-making was helped significantly when a copy of Operation Shingle plans fell into German hands on the very first day of the landings.[6] Despite early success and promise, Anzio quickly degenerated into a second stalemate.

Stalemate at Anzio, however, was only one rung on the ladder above abject failure. The Germans stubbornly held along the Gustav Line at Cassino, where with each passing day the battlefield shifted back and forth over the same muddy riverbanks and hilly terrain, through the same ruined buildings, and the same rain-filled shell holes. The "modern war" of the 1940s imitated the macabre landscapes of World War I. Fallen soldiers lay scattered and decomposing for weeks—covered, uncovered, and covered over again with each exchange of artillery fire. A mule carcass, blown into the air by a large shell, came to rest upended through a ruined farmhouse roof. A broken soldier drooped like a discarded rag doll in the splintered boughs of an apple tree.[7]

In an effort to break the horrendous stalemate, the Allies shifted to a heavy aerial bombing campaign. On February 15, the ancient abbey at Monte Cassino was leveled. The decision was controversial during its own time and still questioned today, but the move was prompted by Allied intelligence that the Germans were using the monastery as an artillery observation post. The Geneva Convention prohibited the use of cemeteries, churches, or monasteries for military purposes. More heavy air bombings followed until the Gustav Line was finally cracked in early May.

When the Gustav Line began to disintegrate, the go-ahead was given to the Allied forces farther up the coast at Anzio to strike out. On May 23, 1944, the penned-up forces attacked, and 3rd Infantry Division paid an especially high price. The assault cost the division 995 men in killed, wounded, or captured within the first twenty-four hours of the breakout. It was the largest single-day casualty count for a U.S. Army division in World War II.[8] While the price was indeed appalling, the breakout succeeded. Rome fell two weeks later on June 4 as the Germans scurried northward behind a series of new defensive lines. For the Germans, the loss of much of Italy and the fall of Rome, was the first of two serious strategic blows, the second falling just two days later when the Allies opened another front in Europe with the D-Day landings in Normandy, France. For the Allies fighting in Italy, however, the fall of Rome was lost in the triumphant headlines generated by the Allied landings in France.

By mid-June 1944, 3rd Division was finally pulled from the front for R&R (rest and relaxation) after months of nearly unending battle. The break barely lasted two weeks. The collapse of the Gustav line, the Anzio breakout, and the fall of Rome presented new possibilities for the Allies to exploit in the Mediterranean theater. One promising opportunity was the invasion of Southern France. 3rd Infantry Division was reassigned to the Seventh Army, marched to Naples, and given a new assignment that was starting to grow old: more amphibious training.

Finely tuned after supporting the French during the drive on Rome, 756th Tank Battalion rejoined 3rd Division. No one knew with any certainty the next destination, but everyone suspected Southern France was a good possibility. Because of the significance of the operation, even Allied military leaders weren't sure where the invasion would be mounted until the very last minute.

An Allied invasion along the southern coast of France had been planned for the better part of World War II under the code name Operation Anvil. However, the timing, scope, and even the necessity for the operation were constantly debated among Allied decision makers.

Originally, Anvil was supposed to coincide with the Normandy invasion, but landing ships were limited and the Allies did not have the means to undertake both simultaneously. Operation Overlord (the invasion of Normandy) took precedence and "Anvil" was postponed. The difficulty of the Italian campaign also made launching "Anvil" more problematic because defeating the tenacious Germans at Cassino drew vital supplies and materials away from "Anvil" preparations.

British Prime Minister Winston Churchill and his military staff were consistently opposed to an invasion of Southern France. As they saw it, the plan offered little strategic advantage and would only weaken the already difficult ongoing campaign in Italy. Instead, Churchill called for redoubling military efforts in Italy, with the ultimate hope of seeing British, American, and French forces striking Germany through a new front in the Balkans. Churchill was thinking ahead to a postwar Europe and feared (justifiably, as events transpired) that Eastern Europe would fall under Russian domination. The downside of Churchill's argument was that military planners projected ruinous Allied losses. The Americans—especially President Roosevelt in an election year—did not want to see any loss of American lives beyond what was absolutely necessary to win the war, and were open to more conservative alternatives that had a chance of winning the war.

In the end, logistics resurrected Anvil. As the weeks passed, it became clear there was a pressing need for additional seaports on the western front. The massive preparations for Overlord strained English seaports with ships, men, equipment, and supplies to the breaking point. The situation would only worsen once the invading Allied forces pushed deeper into Northern France. The south of France offered two large waterfront gems in the established seaports at Marseille and Toulon. Anvil looked even more attractive because the Germans neglected their southern coastal defenses in France to bolster the Atlantic Wall in the north. German preoccupation in the northern part of the country increased once the Allies established a firm foothold in Normandy. Stretched thin on several fronts, the Germans cannibalized men, tanks, and supplies from Southern France to bolster defenses elsewhere to prevent a breakout behind the Normandy beachhead. By mid-summer 1944, an invasion of Southern France was beginning to look too good to pass up.

As the summer of 1944 rolled on, General Dwight D. Eisenhower agreed that invading Southern France was a good idea. President Roosevelt also liked the plan. Both men believed the benefits far outweighed the risks. After the two prime Mediterranean ports were secured, the southern Allied armies could push northward and rendezvous with the Normandy armies cutting across the northern part of France. The plan not only opened up a vital new supply line to feed Allied armies in Europe, but also offered a strategic augmentation of force into the Western Front. The logistics of invasion no longer looked insurmountable. The landing ships used at Normandy were available for another operation, and plenty of troops and supplies were already in the Mediterranean Theater. Allied High Command expected that a major shift in resources to the south of France might slow down the Italian Campaign, but Anvil offered a viable method for ending the war more quickly, which was always the overall goal.

The French, of course, loved Anvil because it meant the direct liberation of their homeland. The Russians were in favor of the plan because it opened up another major front without interfering with their own long-term designs. Churchill, however, remained adamantly against Anvil. Even as an invasion fleet assembled in the Mediterranean a few days prior to the landings, Churchill was chewing Eisenhower's ear in an effort to forestall the thrust into Southern France in favor of one of his own ideas. He finally acquiesced and the plan received his final blessings—but not before he had the operation's codename changed from "Anvil" to "Dragoon" because he believed he had been "dragooned" into supporting it. Despite his misgivings, Churchill was a team player. As the main convoy of transports departed Naples, Italy, for Southern France on August 13, 1944, astonished and cheering troops jammed the decks to watch Churchill buzzing about in a small harbor boat, cigar in hand while flashing his famous "V" for victory hand sign.

The responsibility for carrying out Operation Dragoon fell to the United States Seventh Army under the command of Lieutenant General Alexander Patch. The force included American, Free French, and British forces. The heart of Seventh Army was Major General Lucian Truscott's VI Corps. Truscott's command was comprised of three battle-hardened American infantry divisions: 3rd, 45th, and 36th—all steeled by months of fighting in Italy. This experience made these three divisions natural choices to spearhead the invasion. The battle plan called for them to

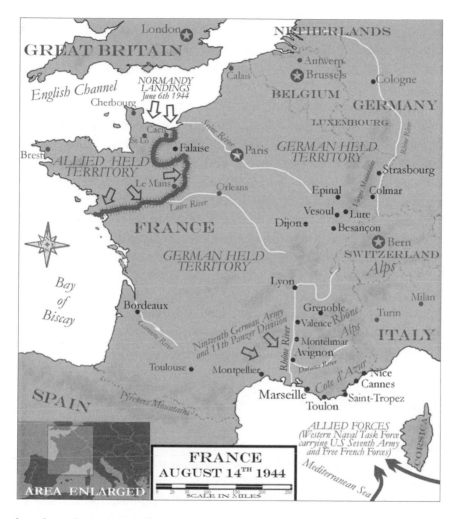

beach at three separate locations along sixty miles of French coastline, smother and conquer enemy defenses, and expand quickly into the interior to meet up with Allied paratroops airdropped twenty miles inland. If all went according to plan, the Free French forces would follow immediately behind, breaking westward along the coast to attack the all-important seaports of Marseille and Toulon.

36th Infantry Division Landing had orders to land on the right (eastern) flank of the thrust near the coastal town of Saint-Raphael just west of Cannes. After securing the beachhead, it would strike northward through the mountains to guard against any German reinforcements or counterattacks west from Italy. 45th Infantry Division's landing zone was in the middle of the attack near Sainte-Maxime. Its task was to secure territory to the northwest while 3rd Infantry Division landed and seized the left flank, storming two separate beaches on the Saint-Tropez peninsula.

The landing beaches were amenable to amphibious operations, and offered smaller local ports to facilitate the influx of shipboard men, equipment, and supplies in the days and weeks to follow. Direct attacks against the main ports of Marseille and Toulon from the sea were not pursued because the cities were well defended with garrisons and heavy coastal guns. Operation Dragoon avoided the main ports until a firm beachhead was established and a breakout accomplished. A successful beachhead, followed by a breakout, would seal off the two ports from the north. So long as they fell before the weather turned unfavorable in mid-October, the planners believed Operation Dragoon could be achieved with a minimal loss of life.

More so than the other two divisions, 3rd Infantry's role was vitally important to securing Marseille and Toulon. Its job, under the aggressive leadership of Major General John "Iron Mike" O'Daniel, might best be described as a wide left-hook across miles of hilly terrain north of Toulon and Marseille. In addition to sealing off the ports from the north, the thrust would put the 3rd in a position to thwart any counterattack by the German Nineteenth Army.

The Nineteenth Army, the core of Army Group G, faced a nearly impossible task: the defense of Southern France at all costs. Many of its essential elements were no longer with the Army. The Allied landing in Normandy prompted a division of the defending force in the south, with parts of Nineteenth stripped away and rushed north to help contain the Normandy invasion. Still, Nineteenth Army remained a formidable force, with the experienced 11th Panzer Division providing a solid veteran armor component and it was the whereabouts and intentions of 11th Panzer Division that kept Allied planners up at night. On the eve of the invasion, intelligence provided by FFI (French Forces of the Interior) operatives indicated 11th Panzer was too far west of the invasion area to directly threaten the landings or spearhead a counterattack in the immediate days to follow. That was welcome news, and if true would leave 3rd Division the freedom to focus on the immediate task at hand—securing a beachhead on the Saint-Tropez peninsula and striking out as far as possible before the Germans and their panzers could react in strength.

3rd Infantry Division hailed from a proud heritage. Nicknamed "Rock of the Marne" for its tenacious combat skills during the World War I, the men of the 3rd Division proudly carried forward its tradition into World War II—so much so that the Germans called them the "Blue and White Devils"[9] out of respect for the diagonally-striped divisional sleeve patch and the soldier who wore it. 3rd Division was a mini-army of roughly 18,000 men in both infantry and supporting roles.[10] The division's core comprised three regiments: 7th, 15th, and 30th. Each regiment fielded approximately 3,200 men, only about half of which were combat infantrymen. Each regiment, in turn, was comprised of three fighting battalions: the 1st, 2nd, and 3rd. Each battalion contained about 800 troops organized into five companies: three rifle companies, one "heavy-weapons" company, and a headquarters company. A regimental supply company, a towed gun "anti-tank company," and a "cannon company" of self-propelled howitzers could be called upon for support. A regimental headquarters company managed the deployment of the three battalions and the support assignments of the anti-tank and cannon companies. Divisional artillery was also available to the regimental commanders.

For armor punch, one company of tanks and one company of tank destroyers was assigned to each regiment. A tank company normally fielded three platoons of five M4 "Sherman" tanks each, and a tank destroyer company had three platoons of four M-10 tank destroyers apiece. A tank destroyer (or TD for short) was essentially a 3-inch naval gun mounted in an open-top traversing turret on a lightly armored medium tank chassis. The gun was more powerful than the tube carried by a Sherman tank, but the chassis and turret were not as heavily armored. A crew of five manned both the Sherman and M-10 tank destroyer. In 3rd Division, these companies came from 756th Tank Battalion and the 601st Tank Destroyer Battalion. The armor companies were considered "attached" to the regiments. Though they remained at the disposal of the infantry regiment and battalion commanders, they technically maintained their own independent chain of command.

The idea of "farming out" armor companies to infantry regiments was a relatively new practice born of necessity rather than design. The idea was tried as early as the Casablanca landings, but evolved from the combat experiences gleaned in North Africa and Italy. During the early part of the war, American military planners envisioned European battlefields with vast waves of tanks roaming the fields in giant clashes of armor. This thinking was inspired by the stunning success of the 1939-1940 German Blitzkrieg into Poland and France. Understandably, American armor crews were trained to maneuver and fight as elements of larger tank groups. This style of combat was well suited to the vast desert expanses of North Africa, but was completely impractical in the tight little towns and narrow mountain roads of Italy. The challenge encountered on the Italian peninsula was not smashing hordes of German panzers sweeping across a map, but knocking out stubborn pillboxes, hidden machine gun nests, or solitary German tanks hidden in the rubble of a small village. These were modest infantry problems in need of modest armor answers, and the standard solution was to break up the tank units so smaller infantry units could use them effectively.

The practice did not always work well. Very few infantry commanders knew anything about how to utilize tanks, and many did not understand their technical limitations. As a result, tankers soon grew hesitant about taking orders from infantry officers they did not know. Initially, tank-infantry teams were improvised short-lived arrangements without the time to develop familiarity and trust. The ideal solution was to keep the combinations together as long as possible, but there were not enough tanks to support every infantry need for armor.

For Southern France, the practical solution to this dilemma was to assign each infantry regiment a tank company and a tank destroyer company. Most regimental commanders decided to assign one tank platoon and one tank destroyer platoon to each of their three infantry battalions. This provided individual battalion commanders with some armor flexibility, and the tankers some degree of familiarity with the infantry officers with whom they were teamed.

This new approach would receive an immediate trial with 3rd Battalion / 15th Infantry Regiment of 3rd Infantry Division. The battalion and its three rifle companies I, K, and L were slated to hit the beaches of Saint-Tropez in the first wave. Assisting them would be 3rd Platoon of B Company / 756th Tank Battalion in specially outfitted amphibious Sherman tanks.

Military intelligence expected moderate combat resistance on the beaches at Saint-Tropez, and invasion planners believed thorough planning and careful execution would quickly reduce the German defenses. In order to establish the beachhead successfully, minefields, barbwire, obstacles, pillboxes, and anti-tank guns had to be destroyed. The landing infantry and tanks could not accomplish this alone. The Twelfth Air Force stationed out of Corsica and heavy naval guns in the ships escorting the invasion convoy, would bombard the beach in advance of the landings—but only during the final hours before the landings. Some element of surprise was still necessary for success. The Germans knew the invasion was coming, but like D-day the previous June, did not know where the assault would land.

*　*　*

"Our days started with a frightening similarity—brushing one's teeth and attacking." — *First Lieutenant George Burks, Executive Officer of L Company / 15th Infantry Regiment*[1]

"Tankers didn't sleep unless there was nothing going on, and there was always something going on." — *Captain David Redle, Commander of B Company / 756th Tank Battalion*[2]

"The funny thing about war is this: the 'right' thing to do in one situation is not the 'right' thing to do another time in the exact same situation." — *Sergeant Roy Anderson, Tank Commander in B Company / 756th Tank Battalion*[3]

"Whatever you learned at Fort Knox, you better forget it and listen to me." — *Staff Sergeant Haskell Oliver, Platoon Sergeant in B Company / 756th Tank Battalion, to Private Frank Cockerill, a replacement member of his crew*[4]

"It was almost as if the Germans were saying, 'Up until now, you have had it easy. From this point on—no more.'" — *First Lieutenant Lloyd Cotter, Platoon leader in Cannon Company / 15th Infantry Regiment, describing the fighting at Allan in southern France*[5]

Chapter One
L Company

irst Lieutenant George Burks thought life aboard U.S.S. *Henrico* was heaven. Although the 492-foot attack transport was crammed full of men and equipment, Burks welcomed this shipboard claustrophobia over the misery he and L Company had endured only three months earlier on the Anzio beachhead.

Anzio had been a wretched existence, trapped among cramped and clammy foxholes awaiting the next terrifying salvo of German artillery. On *Henrico,* he was dry and comfortable. He could remove his boots and sweaty socks, massage his feet, and put on a dry pair without risking his life. He could take a shower and fall asleep in a warm clean bunk. Three hot meals each day filled his belly, and each was deliciously prepared. Coffee constantly flowed in the officers' wardroom. What's more, the stuff was served in china cups with saucers. These were grand luxuries to any infantryman. Best of all, aboard this great grey ship, there were no heart-in-the-throat night patrols, "screaming meemie" rocket attacks[6], or the tormented cries in the night for a medic. Burks could get used to Navy life. What was he doing in the Army anyway?[7]

Unfortunately, this relative paradise came with a price. For an infantry officer, the downside was reading through reams of material in preparation for the impending invasion of southern France.[8] Burks was a naturally inquisitive and thorough officer, and he did not find the task too daunting. Despite the lack of meaningful sleep, the plan's particulars were not hard to absorb—especially since the Navy kept fresh hot coffee percolating in the officers' wardroom. Burks was motivated by thoughts that the more he could retain, the better chances his men had for success and survival. That night's letter home to his young wife and nine-month old son would have to wait.

The twenty-four year old officer viewed the impending invasion with a mix of apprehension and anticipation. This would be his first amphibious landing—not counting, of course, the dozens of practice landings near Naples the division had undertaken over the summer. He was used to the lively streets of New York City, so he could not help but see a bit of adventure in every danger. The rigorous summer of training left him in the best shape of his life—six feet tall and 185 pounds without a single ounce of fat.[9] Every man in L Company was in the same tip-top condition and primed for the mission like taut bowstrings.

L Company, along with the 3rd Battalion of the 15th Infantry Regiment, began loading up on *Henrico* at Naples Harbor on August 8, 1944. For the next few days, they jammed the vessel with nearly 1,000 combat infantrymen, plus all their equipment, vehicles, weapons, ammo, and rations. The undertaking was an enormous logistical miracle repeated over hundreds of ships anchored throughout Naples harbor. *Henrico* departed Naples mid-afternoon of August 13, as part of Commodore Edgar's ALPHA attack force, which was but one small section of an 800-ship invasion fleet.[10]

The voyage thus far had been surprisingly uneventful. The weather was calm, clear, and warm. No German planes, subs, or patrol boats harassed the ships. The only shipboard problem arose about a day and a half into the journey. The voice of *Henrico's* captain broke over the PA to announce that a number of infantry weapons had turned up missing. Apparently, some sailor pilfered them as souvenirs. Burks couldn't believe some heartless idiot would steal an infantryman's weapon and leave him to wade ashore defenseless under enemy fire. The ship's captain demanded the return of the weapons to their rightful owners and gave his promise that no questions would be asked. He warned his crew that the ship had a limited number of hiding places, and that if the weapons were not promptly returned the man caught with the goods would be "run up the ship's mast." The weapons magically reappeared almost immediately.[11]

The impending August 15 landings would mark Burks' fifth full month in L Company. He was positively ancient under the compressed time standards of war. Surviving a single day of frontline combat was a milestone. A week of combat made him a grizzled veteran. There weren't many old-timers left in L Company or 3rd Battalion. Nearly half of the fresh faces milling about *Henrico's* crowded decks were replacements brought in immediately after the horrific losses sustained three months earlier during the bloody Anzio breakout.

Burks was also a replacement, joining the outfit two months before the breakout. He reported fresh from the States to L Company on March 15, 1944—roughly six weeks after the initial landings at Anzio.[12] He and another first lieutenant by the name of Americus Covello, reported for duty together under cover of darkness—the only time that sort of movement was advisable. Both were taken to the ruins of an Italian farmhouse. One of the rooms, still intact, was being used as the L Company command post (CP). All windows, doors, and cracks had been meticulously covered to black them out from German observation. Once inside the dimly lit and smoke-filled room, the two young officers were introduced to L Company's commander, 1st Lt. James "Red" Coles. Coles had recently taken over after Captain Andrew Leaming was severely wounded in a German artillery attack.[13] Leaming wasn't expected back, and Coles was awaiting his captain's bars to complete the command transition. His promotion was only days away from becoming formal.[14]

Coles was a towering man with broad shoulders and huge bear paws for hands. He looked like a running guard straight off a college gridiron.[15] The origin of his nickname "Red" was obvious. Everything about the man's appearance was red, from his coarse hair and ruddy weather-beaten face, to a body covered with freckles.[16] When the big company commander spoke, he was blunt and to the point, completely unconcerned with diplomatic niceties. Although he was rough around the edges, an immediate and inimitable confidence set him apart.[17]

The gruff lieutenant greeted his new officers by asking them for their promotion dates to first lieutenant. Burks outranked Covello by one month, so Coles told Burks that he was the company's new executive officer. Covello took command of one of the four platoons. The manner Coles handled the assignments was Burks' first indication that "Red" was not a man who liked to fool around.[18]

Coles offered a brief lecture on his philosophy for suppressing fear— a talk Burks sensed had been recited many times before. He cautioned them that obsessing about the prospects of being wounded or killed was completely futile. The odds were fifty-fifty of becoming a casualty, so worrying about it was an absolute waste of time. Even if you get hit, he cautioned, the odds were another fifty-fifty that the wound would be superficial, so again, there was no point worrying. If by chance you were badly wounded, you would be shipped stateside, out of the war and right back where you wanted to be anyway—in which case, you were an idiot for worrying. Finally, if you were killed through some stroke of bad luck, all your worries were over![19] With that, Coles dismissed the new lieutenants. Burks would never forget that introduction to life in a combat zone. He didn't know it at the time, but the big burly officer would turn out to be one of the most unforgettable men he would ever meet.

It did not take long to discover that the new captain practiced what he preached. Anecdotal chatter and firsthand observation of Coles confirmed as much. Burks did not, however, hear Coles talk of himself. He never boasted about his own abilities.

Coles was one of the few L Company "originals" left over from the Casablanca, Africa, landings of November 1942.[20] As a boy growing up in El Paso, Texas, Red attended military school with his older brother before moving west, where he enlisted in the California National Guard. After the Japanese attack on Pearl Harbor, Uncle Sam called him up and sent him to infantry Officer Candidate School (OCS) at Fort Benning, Georgia. He graduated as a thirty-year old 2nd Lt. and shipped out with the 3rd Infantry Division, where he flourished as a platoon leader in L Company.[21] Coles trained with the outfit in North Africa and fought across the island of Sicily, receiving a Bronze Star in the process. In Sicily and Italy, Coles began to shine as a combat officer, earning the growing admiration and respect of his men and superiors alike. He was as fearless as they came, with a fighting confidence that was infectious to those around him. With a slew of battlefield challenges a daily reality, Coles' reputation grew quickly into near-legendary proportions.[22]

After arriving in Italy, Coles led his platoon on a mission to take a vital mountain pass on September 22, 1943. The infantry school motto was "Follow Me," and Coles took that simple phrase to heart. As a platoon leader, he always led by walking ahead of his men. When Coles approached the well-defended pass, German riflemen opened fire on him. Rather than take cover, he dodged forward. Even though a German machine gun joined the fusillade, he rushed them like a rampaging bull— tossing grenades and firing off his pistol while yelling at the top of his lungs. Witnesses had just observed one of his hallmark maneuvers. He knocked out the machine gun and crew, but a second one opened up on him and his platoon. Coles went after them with the same primal display. This time, the Germans cut and ran out of panic, leaving the machine gun, ammo, bewildered pack mules, and the now unoccupied pass, behind. The platoon leader earned a Silver Star for his bravery.[23]

Such feats were quite common for Coles, and although his instincts sometimes had him "going places he shouldn't,"[24] the enlisted men simply loved him. Coles' aggressive style never crossed into recklessness, and he never asked his men to do anything he hadn't done before, or wasn't willing to do himself. Most enlisted GIs were young men starving for a hero. They simply wanted someone who could show them how to carry out the mission and survive the war. Coles fit the bill perfectly.

Though he was always serious about fighting, Coles was not uptight like so many other officers, and delighted the guys with his brand of irreverent humor. One time he called the company together to pass along an order regarding the treatment of prisoners. The Army wanted to put an end to the "looting" of prisoners for war souvenirs. Coles read the general directive aloud, and then tossed it aside to move on to the company's immediate business. In his next sentence, he deadpanned: "I want the next patrol to bring me a wrist watch."[25]

Coles also earned the respect of his men by simply showing them trust. He was usually quite liberal with the granting of short leaves— whether official or unofficial. Invariably, when there was a break in fighting his men approached him for permission to do a little unofficial patrolling or to check out a nearby town. Coles knew they were after girls, booze, fresh food, or all three. He granted the requests with a certain time when they were expected back.[26] Most young men needed some distraction and entertainment away from the endless pressure of combat, and Coles certainly wasn't above drinking and raising hell himself.[27] Without some release, the morale and fighting ability of everybody in the company would suffer.

Along with that trust went accountability. Coles expected a punctual return and did not want to hear of trouble. His demands for basic responsibility went far beyond simple R&R behavior. In L Company, a man was expected to do his job. If anyone failed that or took advantage of Coles' trust, the big man didn't hesitate to dish out hell at a personal level, and he wasn't afraid to use his fists from time to time to underscore his point. Even so, some were still foolish enough not to heed his instructions.

Each evening, Coles set out to personally check the outposts along the company perimeter. The men paired off for guard duty at every outpost. One guy would sleep while the other remained awake and alert for any sign of enemy encroachment. It was absolutely essential that the perimeter guards remained awake at their outposts—the safety and survival of the company was in their hands. One evening, Coles found a guard asleep who should have been awake. He woke the kid and beat the crap out of him.[28] The kid didn't fall asleep on duty again.

On another night, as Coles approached one outpost, an overly anxious rifleman began shooting at him through the darkness at almost point blank range. The kid gave no warning "halt" or call sign challenge as required—just a hail of bullets. Coles hit the ground while the kid emptied a full clip of ammo wildly in his direction. By miracle or sheer incompetence on the guard's part, he had escaped every bullet. Before the kid could reload, the steaming mad officer rushed him, seized him with his big hands, and beat the living daylights out of him, too.[29]

Under U.S. military code, striking a soldier under one's command was usually looked upon as inappropriate discipline. However, the few who received Coles' brand of authority rarely complained and received little sympathy from their buddies. Most understood their captain was either acting out of concern for the welfare of the company, or to correct some fool who required a serious attitude adjustment. Certainly, no one wanted to see Coles removed. They feared landing some incompetent replacement who preferred issuing "chicken shit" orders and commanding death for others while sitting safely in the rear. The Army had plenty of those types. Coles was not the perfect officer—he could be blustery, argumentative, and hot headed—but fairness, battle smarts, and fearlessness definitely made him a keeper.[30] Nearly everyone in L Company was proud of Coles and would have followed him into Hell if he asked them to go.[31]

That pride was palpable to the other company commanders in the battalion. I Company commander, a capable and courageous officer himself, unconsciously emulated Coles whenever they were together—right down to his infectious swagger.[32]

Coles' admirers stretched far up the command chain. For example, General John W. O'Daniel, the division commander, always called him by his nickname "Red" whenever he stopped in to visit.[33] None of this attention or admiration, however, made Coles aspire for anything beyond his company command. He had absolutely no interest in promotion, and seemed to enjoy life right where he was—tackling the thrills, challenges, and dangers of combat.[34]

Naturally, Lieutenant Burks wanted to know what made such an extraordinary soldier so successful. Strangely, Coles showed no interest in befriending any of his subordinate officers. At times, this disinterest bordered on appearing nothing short of contempt. This was odd because Coles got along extremely well with officers outside his command, and fabulously with the enlisted men—particularly those who had proved themselves in combat. But with the five lieutenants assigned to him, Coles was downright difficult. Perhaps he had an attitude carryover from his enlisted days in the California National Guard. Perhaps Coles felt the officers directly responsible to him were more prone to try taking advantage of his friendship. Maybe he just didn't want to get to close to someone whose corpse he might one day have to yank out of the mud. The reasons for his attitude were impossible to know. He didn't talk about it.

But one thing was certain; if a lieutenant didn't measure up to Coles' expectations he wasn't kept around for long. Coles didn't hesitate to test a man or bust a man immediately. While at Anzio, a new lieutenant left for a daylight patrol with a platoon sergeant and a radioman to try to locate the source of enemy fire. The platoon sergeant, Staff Sergeant (S/Sgt.) Ben Thompson, was a levelheaded and experienced soldier. The radioman was Private First Class (Pfc.) Rudy Jantz, a recent replacement assigned to the company. Jantz looked like the all-American kid with a fresh face and a great smile. He was also a combat rookie. The trio crawled forward more than 200 yards to a roadside ditch, where they got a clear look at the offending German mortar position. If they could visually establish the mortar location, they could use Jantz's radio to call in return fire, and adjust accordingly until the mortar was knocked out. S/Sgt. Thompson raised his binoculars and immediately spotted the telltale puffs of smoke. He told the lieutenant he could clearly see the German mortar crew firing from a barn loft, and it was time to call in the artillery. As Thompson lowered his binoculars, Jantz looked over just as the bullet from a German sniper hit the staff sergeant squarely between the eyes. The binoculars fell and the dead man slumped to the ground.

Stunned, Jantz turned to the lieutenant for guidance. Without saying a word, the new lieutenant jumped up and ran back toward the rest of the company, leaving Jantz to fend for himself.

The lieutenant's action was appalling on so many levels, not the least of which included a complete dereliction of his duty. The mission failure forced Coles to pull back a large section of his company from the area receiving the mortar fire. An abandoned Pfc. Jantz, though alone and burdened with a thirty-five pound radio strapped to his back,[35] was able to return—but only after L Company support positions threw down some covering fire for him. The thoroughly agitated Jantz let loose with a slew of choice words for the lieutenant.

In such moments Coles showed a fatherly, compassionate side—particularly toward the enlisted men in whom he saw potential. He pulled Jantz aside and calmed him down. Jantz was particularly upset over witnessing his first man killed in action. Once Coles learned Jantz's side of the story, he organized a second patrol to retrieve the dead staff sergeant before the Germans could pilfer anything of military value from his body. Jantz was also nervous about cussing the lieutenant out—another military "no no"—but Coles assured him that he was in no trouble.

Eventually, Jantz was sent over to First Sergeant (1st Sgt.) Byron Jay, who counseled him on how to handle similar situations in the future. Jay calmly explained that the dead man's weapon, maps, wallet, and one of his dog tags should have been removed before returning. As the second patrol was retrieving the items, the panicked lieutenant was relieved of his command and sent away.[36]

Coles did not tolerate incompetence or any "yellow streak" in his lieutenants. Burks was given his share of tests, and always passed. Despite the incident—or perhaps because of it—Jantz spent most of his time within arm's length of Captain Coles, toting the heavy SCR-300 radio around on his back. Coles told him he didn't want to ask for a radioman when he needed one.[37] Jantz stuck to him, and Coles appreciated his dependability.

The company had two SCR-300 radios capable of communication with the battalion and with each other. In tactical situations, one radio remained near the captain while the other traveled with the assault platoon. This way the captain could remain in contact with the company's advance elements. The radios were temperamental but vital to the fighting effectiveness and survivability of the company. The other radioman was Pfc. Harold Noble. Out of fairness to Noble, the two radiomen would occasionally switch assignments. Still, Coles seemed to prefer having Jantz near him.

Hanging with Captain Coles did have its hazards. The division and regiment were in constant need of fresh intelligence, which could only be gained through nightly patrols. Often, these patrols set out to study German defenses or test response and reaction times. Coles liked to lead them. One night, he asked Jantz and several others to go with him on patrol. Their aim was to scout out a particular enemy outpost and report their findings.

Coles' group nearly reached their objective when the night suddenly erupted in pandemonium. Rifle and machine gun fire fractured the cool night air. Flares ignited overhead and mortars exploded around them. They had been detected. Coles indiscriminately grabbed dark figures by the arms and yelled for them to get in line and retreat to safety. Coles shoved one of the men into Jantz. The light was too dim to see the man, but the uniform didn't feel right—nor did it smell right. Jantz caught the unmistakable odor of heating tablets used to cook rations—German heat tablets.

"Krauts!" Jantz yelled over to Coles, who was still shoving shadowy figures in line.

Their patrol had run into a German patrol moving the opposite direction, and Coles was grabbing the wrong guys! Through sheer luck, Coles and his men scrambled away and returned to camp without losing anybody. Afterward, Coles had a good laugh over the affair and wrote Jantz up for a Bronze Star. In keeping with his custom for mystery, he never explained his reasons for recommending the medal to Jantz—he just did it.[38] Whatever his thinking, the compliment was huge. Coles had a very stingy reputation for recommending medals.[39]

In addition to the two SCR-300 radios, the company had six smaller SCR-536 radios.[40] These were hand-held devices with an extremely limited range, and could only be used effectively for communication at the platoon level.[41] Though the heavier SCR-300 was far from perfect, it was worth its weight in gold. Often, the SCR-300 was a company's only way of calling for help from the battalion.

One day Coles called Burks over and pointed to an SCR-300 radio. "Take care of that radio and keep it with you at all times. If you have to dig in, dig it in with you. If you don't do those things, some day it could mean your ass," Coles stated with his usual brevity.[42]

Burks understood that his captain was imparting important advice. Though he was tough and demanding of his lieutenants, Coles could be quite generous about sharing his combat lessons and practical experience.

On the other hand, Coles was also generous about delegating non-combat responsibilities. He had an obvious distaste for any chores unrelated to combat, and Burks became his favorite recipient. After Burks mastered the usual executive officer duties—which included overseeing the company headquarters, maintaining communications with the battalion, and solving any problems that might affect unit efficiency—Coles passed on to him most of the other administrative duties customarily reserved for the captain.[43] Burks felt this extra work wasn't fair, but accepted it without complaint.

Initially, Burks was more irritated and confused by his captain's reclusive habits. After a long day of fighting, Coles often turned the company over to Burks and simply withdrew from the world. Burks wouldn't see him again until the next morning. He often wondered if the captain even liked him. But by virtue of the extra responsibilities, Burks presumed he was doing something right. Still, if Coles was grooming Burks for the day he would eventually lead his own company, he sure had an enigmatic way of going about it.

Nothing was more mysterious than Coles' personal life. His non-army past remained a virtual unknown to Burks and most others. He really had nothing to hide, but simply preferred to keep his private life private. Coles was married to a beautiful woman who had been his wife for nearly ten years. She and two young daughters lived in Encinitas, California. She also worked as an office manager at Camp Pendleton, and would occasionally mail him whiskey.[44] The marriage was suffering some strain, and may have been one reason why Coles was mum.[45] Perhaps he did not wish to confront these pains on top of the tremendous pressures of combat leadership. Perhaps he was afraid of showing weakness to his men. Maybe there was something he feared after all.

Prior to the war, Red operated a gas station in Encinitas.[46] For a man with a very ordinary background to quickly become such a tremendous soldier might seem strange, but he was not alone. America had rapidly assembled a vast army of average Joes who were accomplishing incredible things in Europe and the Pacific. It was only fitting that Coles was just another average Joe.

Although his men noted that Coles never shed a tear over those who fell—even those whom he knew well—few ever saw the inner man. There was a side Coles only dared to reveal to his widowed mother, and he confided to her that being surrounded by death bothered him deeply, and he struggled to find a way to cope with it all. "The sight of someone being killed used to give me sleepless nights. Now I look on worse things as just another incident," he later explained. "We have to be that way to keep mentally healthy." Coles wrote late in 1943, "I don't feel very different after having been in the middle of so much death, horrors of battle and suffering. I just trust in God and don't let the ugly things make an impression on my mind."[47]

Coles decided his best chance at survival was to banish mortal fear from his soul and wage war with a single-minded zeal. Once the day's fight was over, he either played hard with equal fervor, or disappeared like a hermit into a foxhole. Coles led, inspired, and succeeded. He was beloved and admired by many, yet befriended few. Though married with children and a business back home, he fought like there was no tomorrow. Simply put, Captain James "Red" Coles was born to lead men in battle.

For most men, the four-month deadlock at Anzio was a cruel test for finding an individual's breaking point. Aside from the terrifying tit-for-tat frontline skirmishes and heart-in-the-throat night patrols, L Company and the rest of the 3rd Division had to endure round-the-clock harassment from German artillery.

The "screaming meemie" rockets were the worst. The Germans called them Nebelwerfer—which translated innocently as "fog thrower." Originally, these were heavy mortars used for laying smokescreens, but the Germans converted them into fearsome and deadly weapons. For maximum psychological impact, the Germans drilled holes into the projectile fins to make them scream as they rained down from the sky. Some of the rounds weighed nineteen pounds; others were upwards of seventy-seven pounds or more. No matter what size they were when they were fired, every one ended in a blast of tiny razor-sharp fragments sprayed out at a high velocity in every direction.[48] These rockets were fired electrically from each six-sleeved launcher in successive pairs.[49] After the first pair howled in and exploded, those on the receiving end scrambled for cover and waited for the remaining pairs to follow. Fear gnawed at the mind—whispering that the next blast would be the one to finally get you.[50] A fair share of men simply went crazy from the constant stress. It was often a big risk just getting in a chow line. German artillery spotters prized troop concentrations—especially around kitchens—and they would hammer them without mercy.[51]

Germans also taunted the Anzio beachhead through means less deadly, but equally unnerving. One time, some of the men from L Company were playing a game of volleyball on the beach. Later that night, "Axis Sally" the notorious German radio propagandist, reported the exact score of the game.[52]

In mid-April, 1944, L Company was pulled off the line for a few days of R&R. "Rest" began with a nighttime march several miles back to a bivouac area among the beach dunes. The "relaxation" area was a series of covered trenches and foxholes used by other units that rotated in and out for the same purpose. Though it was a welcome break from the front lines and the direct observation of German spotters in the Alban hills, it was certainly no escape from nightly Luftwaffe bombing runs or attacks from larger German artillery pieces such as the dreaded "Anzio Express"—a colossal 280mm railroad gun that could toss 550-pound shells from twenty-five miles away.[53]

1st Sgt. Byron Jay had transferred over to K Company, leaving L Company to await the assignment of its new first sergeant.[54] As the highest-ranking enlisted man in the company, the first sergeant was, more or less, the right-hand man to the captain—sort of like a fighting office manager, human resources director, and shop foreman all rolled into one. A good first sergeant was priceless. No company commander wanted to be long without one, and the rank and file were always a little anxious to see what new sort of character they were going to have to put up with.

After the march away from the front, L Company settled into the old foxholes to try to catch some of that "rest." Dawn was but a few hours away, and the men craved sleep. At 5:30 that morning, Burks woke to the sound of a whistle. He hadn't heard a whistle since he was stateside. "Who was blowing a whistle and why?" Burks wondered to himself. "At Anzio of all places! Whoever he was had to be nuts!"

Burks stumbled to his feet, shook off his grogginess, and tried to locate the source of the regular whistle blasts. With the sky still dark and fog rolling in off the Mediterranean, the task was not easy. Finally, his eyes zeroed in on the offending figure. He was the company's new top non-commissioned officer (NCO)—1st Sgt. Walton Works.

"What the hell are you doing?" Burks asked incredulously.

With complete naivety, Works replied that he was waking the company for first formation. Burks instantly set him straight with a warning that if he wanted to see another day—let alone the end of the war—he should never ever blow that whistle again.[55] Works nearly swallowed the thing off its lanyard. He had probably made the worst first impression of any first sergeant in the war. The entire company wanted to string him up that morning. Works never blew that whistle again. However, after starting off in a very deep hole that morning, he turned out to be an outstanding leader. No one showed greater pride in L Company than 1st Sgt. Works.[56]

By mid-May of 1944, the Allied forces in the south of Italy had finally pierced the German "Gustav Line." After a long winter of frustrating siege, the enemy defensive front disintegrated like a collapsing dam. The Allies moved through and contended with stiff resistance in places, but steadily advanced northward toward Rome.[57] The time was ripe for the 3rd Infantry Division and its comrades (two British and five American divisions)[58] holed-up on the twenty square miles of Anzio beachhead, to join in the drive. The naturally swampy ground surrounding Anzio had become dry enough for the tanks to move forward. Nevertheless, any breakout was not going to be an easy task. The attackers would have to pierce through lines of elaborate German defenses.

The first half of May had been spent training under the intermittent harassment of German artillery.[59] In one sense, the drills were similar to live fire exercises—except with the real enemy providing the ambiance. Infantry-tank assault teams assembled using the tanks of the 751st Tank Battalion, pillbox mock-ups were attacked, and all the men of the 3rd Division underwent vigorous physical conditioning.[60]

General O'Daniel took the infantry-tank team concept one step further through the use of experimental sleds pulled in two columns behind a moving Sherman tank. Each sled carried a prone soldier and was daisy-chained together so that an entire squad could be towed along the tank tracks, avoiding mines and keeping a low profile until the right moment arrived to bust out of them. The idea was a bit unorthodox, but

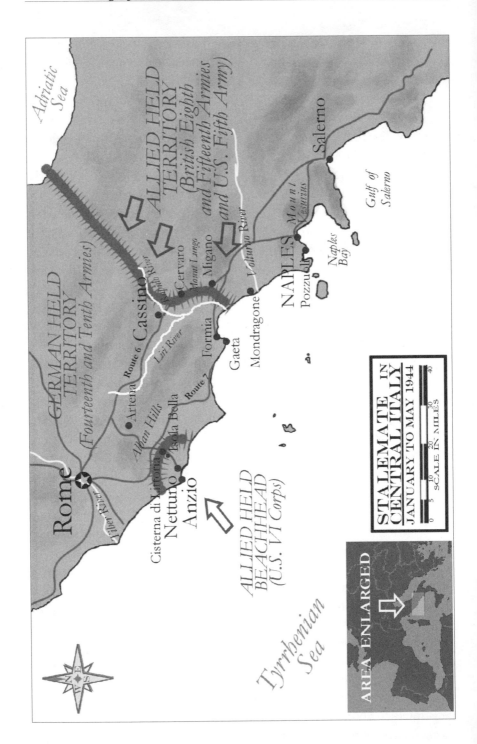

O'Daniel was always looking for battlefield advantages no matter how crazy an idea seemed. Five twelve-man sled teams were created by borrowing riflemen from each of the division's three regiments. One of those teams was assembled with men from I Company of the 15th Infantry Regiment.[61] The sled teams were supposed to be top secret, but that didn't stop Axis Sally from mocking them in her daily broadcasts.[62]

The 3rd Division's main objective was Cisterna di Littoria—a village long since reduced to piles of stone rubble. This job was given mainly to the 7th and 30th Infantry Regiments on the left.[63] To the right, the 15th Infantry Regiment had orders to bypass Cisterna and seize heavily defended enemy positions along Highway 7, the main road heading northwest toward Rome.[64] The terrain was mostly flat with tall fields of grass and wheat, broken occasionally by a shallow ditch, an artillery-battered tree, or the ruins of a concrete farmhouse.[65] Concealed among the pastoral landmarks were also more sinister surprises prepared by the Germans during the prior four months. These consisted of elaborate trenches, pillboxes, barbed wire, minefields, and machine gun "kill zones."

The 3rd Battalion was selected to spearhead the regimental attack and L Company was placed on point. The plan called for a 6:00 A.M. jump off on May 23, 1944. As dawn was breaking and the final ten minutes ticked down, German mortar and artillery began exploding all around them. Despite the rude send off, L Company set out on time— bolting from a field ditch about 1,000 yards east of Isola Bella and storming toward the objective, a road junction 500 yards farther east. The German response redoubled immediately with a blizzard of fire from small arms, machine guns, and tanks. As the men scrambled to find whatever cover was available, some trapped in the maelstrom groaned and crumpled to the ground amid snapping bullets, while others were blown to pieces by exploding shells.

The advance slowed to an agonizing crawl as the company absorbed a horrific toll. Toward the rear of the advance, Burks and the men of the company headquarters section and Weapons Platoon, hugged the ground—waiting and praying for the next respite and the opportunity to move forward another few yards.[66] Ahead, Burks could see the company's three rifle platoons being chewed apart man by man as they attempted to inch forward. He grew increasingly distressed over the lagging support from the battalion. For some reason, K and I Companies and the tanks with the battle sleds were being withheld. Burks couldn't understand the delay. L Company seemed alone and forsaken with no future beyond a few more minutes, or at most, an hour.

Burks grabbed the handset of the SCR-300 radio and screamed into the phone for the battalion to release the tanks, to no avail. Whatever grand plan the higher-ups had in mind, somebody felt the time was not ripe to release the armor. Burks slammed the receiver back down in frustration and waited for complete annihilation.[67]

Despite the heavy fire, Captain Coles kept pushing his three rifle platoons, exhorting the men to shoot their way through the nearby drainage ditches and wheat fields. More men dropped, two wounded here, another killed there. At long last the TDs from the 601st Tank Destroyer Battalion joined in support—blasting targets ahead of L Company's advance from hidden positions back behind the jump off point.[68] The shock provided cover enough for L Company to move in a series of rushes and overtake two ruined houses along the eastern road. They managed to claw out patrols to two more houses 100 yards distant, but sacrificed more men in the process.

In the thick of it all, moving about as though fixed within the eye of a hurricane, was Coles, hollering above the din for his men to keep moving. He stepped past Pfc. Arthur Schrader who was lying useless on the ground with his leg split open from a gunshot. Schrader looked up in disbelief at this inspiring—almost ethereal—display of courage. His captain was truly a man devoid of fear. Coles turned, still barking out commands. Schrader looked into his freckled face. Coles was smiling. The man actually enjoyed combat.[69]

At this point, L Company had managed to tough out several hours of fierce battle, but was losing its cohesion and effectiveness. The company jumped off with approximately 180 men,[70] but by mid-morning had been reduced to only thirty or forty scattered haphazardly along a loose skirmish line. The attack was stalling. The Germans knew it too, and decided to up the ante by opening up with heavy artillery from "Chateau woods," 1,000 yards distant.[71]

Finally, Lieutenant Colonel (Lt. Col.) Frederick Boye—the tall and composed commanding officer (CO) of the 3rd Battalion—ordered K and I Companies to press forward through L Company's advance position. This new offensive included the tank-sled teams. As the tanks and infantry arrived, the remaining L Company effectives joined in the revitalized attack.

The new push forward attracted another intense round of German mortar attacks. S/Sgt. Michael W. Cormanick,[72] a recent Silver Star recipient[73] and a young squad leader in Weapons Platoon, hit the ground about ten feet ahead of Burks. Cormanick was fortunate enough to reach a ditch—or so Burks thought. As the volley slowed, Burks called for Cormanick, but he did not respond. Burks scampered over to him. A piece of shrapnel had pierced the staff sergeant's backpack and driven deeply into his heart. The only outward sign of the wound was a tuft of white stuffing fluffed out of a hole in his backpack. The poor kid was killed instantly. Burks left him where he lay and moved on.

The battalion seized the crossroads and pushed beyond into tenaciously-defended zigzagged trenches and wheat fields. Near one of the trenches, the Germans placed an American GI helmet atop a staked human skull. The intent was to induce fear, but the effect was the opposite. The American doughboys seethed with anger at the ghoulish totem and channeled their fury into taking out the defenders.[74]

The combat descended into intensely personal fighting, including hand-to-hand confrontations, and lasted several more hours until the German defenses collapsed. Nearby "Kraut Woods" was overwhelmed, as were a few more remaining farmhouses, out buildings, and small pockets of resistance.[75] The 2nd Battalion captured the more distant "Chateau Woods" and the intolerable German artillery assault of the immediate area finally fell silent.[76]

The first day of the breakout had been terribly costly to the 3rd Battalion in general and L Company in particular. Most of Coles' men were gone.[77] Twenty-three were dead and another sixty-nine wounded, many seriously.[78] Some who could still fight had become separated from the company in the chaos and were fighting with other units. Others were separated and still scattered among the ditches, churned up fields, and rubble piles awaiting orders from officers and NCOs long gone. With night approaching and the situation tenuous and confusing, they didn't dare go anywhere.

The small portion of the company still functioning as a unit barely qualified as a platoon. They remained together, held up at what they believed was a support position and began digging in for the night. The day's chaos thrust Coles and Burks side by side with the SCR-300 radio between them.[79] Ideally, the captain and the executive officer were supposed to maintain some distance in battle to prevent the loss of both from a single explosion or ambush. The "rules," however, were often chucked the way of the battle plans after the first shot.

The two surviving officers spent the early evening hours digging foxholes side-by-side. After a short time, Coles quit and lay down even though his hole was still quite shallow. Burks urged him to keep at it, but Coles growled that he was "too damned tired" to keep digging. As night descended, both men settled in for some uneasy sleep—Burks nestled in his deep hole and Coles curled in his shallow one.

As dawn was breaking, the two awoke to the sound of a German tank engine rumbling a short distance away, accompanied by German voices, clattering equipment, and rustling footsteps. Burks and Coles looked at each other in quiet astonishment. They thought they had dug in at a support position. The Germans were not supposed to be this close.

Someone on the American side chose this most inopportune moment to visit a nearby bush and take a pee—apparently believing he would remain unobserved in the lifting darkness. He was wrong. The Germans saw him, and the morning peace was shattered by an instant cacophony of small arms and tank fire. L Company responded, and a firefight raged for the next several minutes. One of the tank rounds burst very close to Burks and Coles—showering both with dirt and stones. Burks heard Coles exhale with a loud grunt and saw him lie motionless.

"Ready or not, I'm now the commanding officer of L Company," Burks' mind flashed with apprehension and resignation. "Coles should have dug deeper."

Once the action let up a bit, Burks scampered out of his hole to check on Coles. To his relief he found the captain alive, but the big man was clutching his side in severe pain and breathing with great difficulty. With some effort, Burks rolled him over and checked beneath his shirt. His torso showed no blood or any evidence of an entrance wound. Burks deduced that the tank blast must have thrown a good-sized rock into Coles' chest and cracked some ribs. Whether he had sustained internal damage was impossible to know.

The two officers sensed that the company's position was becoming unsustainable. While gritting out the pain, Coles told Burks to order the company to fall back through those same wheat fields they had taken at such a high price the previous morning and to reposition along a line of old German trenches. The L Company remnant fell back and managed to hold their new position for the remainder of the day. Once darkness descended and movement was safer, Burks had Coles evacuated to the battalion aid station.[80]

Burks assumed temporary command of L Company. Out of six company officers, he was the only one not killed, seriously wounded, or missing during the breakout. Of the 180 or so enlisted men who jumped off as an experienced combat unit less than forty-eight hours earlier, Burks' "Company" now comprised a rag-tag assortment of fifteen men.[81] Despite their exhaustion and alarm, Burks and his surviving band felt a remarkable and palpable pride that they still stood as L Company.[82]

Over the next few days, a few stragglers filtered into the company. Among them were 1st Sgt. Works, Pfc. Jantz, and a couple of wire layers—all that was left of headquarters.[83] The survivors' numbers barely formed a platoon, so Burks' men were temporarily attached to I Company until replacements could be brought in to reconstitute the company. On May 29, thirty-six replacements arrived. Twelve more were assigned the following day for a total of forty-eight.[84] Although these replacements could not yet be properly integrated into platoons or squads and the company remained severely undermanned, L Company was back—at least on paper.[85]

By May 31, the 3rd Division had pushed out twelve miles from Cisterna and prepared to attack Artena. Although L Company and the rest of the 3rd Battalion were relegated to supporting roles for that operation, they still endured another heavy round of casualties. During the battle of June 1-2, two men from L Company were killed and another eighteen wounded, mostly from enemy artillery attacks.[86] The road to Rome, however, was blown wide open.

Two days later, the Allies marched into the city virtually unopposed.

★ Chapter Two

Respite and Preparations

After the liberation of Rome, L Company established camp approximately a half mile away from the ancient Coliseum.[1] The entire division was finally given a break from the fighting and a new assignment helping to guard the city. At first, concerns circulated about possible sabotage by Fascist malcontents, but the threat never materialized.[2] The guard duty assignments proved easy, as most of the Italian population was overjoyed and welcoming of the Allied soldiers. Captain Coles returned after two weeks of hospitalization. Though he was still pale and had lost a bit of weight, he was his same old self—looking to either fight or raise hell at a bar. After Anzio, everybody wanted to cut loose and forget the war for a while. For the first time in more than six months, L Company was enjoying some well deserved R&R.

During the break, more replacements arrived for assimilation. Through them, 1st Sgt. Works began to put his stamp on L Company. Like Coles, Works was a no-nonsense individual. He was twenty-seven years old[3] but already rich in life experiences after working every depression-era job under the sun—from picking apples to tending bar.[4] He was worldly, streetwise, and nobody's fool.[5] Though Works was much smaller than Coles physically, he was every bit as tough with an even meaner edge.[6] His amateurish whistle-blowing mistake when he first arrived was already a distant memory. Works had become a battle-tested survivor of Anzio, an experienced manager, and the perfect compliment to Captain Coles.

Like all good first sergeants, Works maintained strict discipline throughout the company. He took great pride in his job and was personally offended if any of his men screwed up. He found the best method to prevent screw-ups was to get into the heads of the replacements early, while they were still green and receptive. Whenever a new batch of newcomers arrived, Works lined them up and howled out a short, stern introduction. His presentation was a mixed bag of threats designed to scare everybody, but with one clear message; no one would shirk his duties or go AWOL (absent without official leave). Works warned that any violators would not be court-martialed. Instead, he promised to personally "kick the shit" out of any slacker. For his grand finale, Works threw down this challenge: "Anyone who doesn't think I can do it...step forward right now!"

No one ever stepped forward. But a few days after the camp in Rome was established, Works' authority was tested by a couple of long-standing troublemakers.[7]

The two had been with the company long before Works' arrival and had already amassed notorious reputations for repeatedly going AWOL. Their most recent stunt was their most egregious, and essentially amounted to desertion. The two took off just before the company jumped off at Anzio—at the precise time they were most needed. Their actions had nothing to do with fear, and garnered little sympathy from anybody. Everyone was scared. These two screw-ups simply had a history of not giving a damn about anyone other than themselves.

After their desertion, the two men wandered back to the beach and stole a jeep. Somehow they managed to convince sailors that they belonged aboard an LST (Landing Ship Tank) departing for Naples. They arrived in town and ran with a couple local girls for nearly two weeks before MPs (Military Police) hauled them in. Once their true unit assignment was learned, they were shipped all the way back to L Company in Rome.[8]

1st Sgt. Works was the first to "welcome" them home. For a little privacy, he escorted the two around to the back of a shed. "Where have you been?" he demanded.

Their responses were less than forthcoming, and Works wasn't in the mood for wasting time. He ordered them to start digging six-foot by six-foot holes until told to stop. The ground was hard clay. Neither deserter looked particularly pleased about the assignment, and stood in obstinate silence.

Works was not a man of great patience. "If you don't like it," he hissed with a scowl, "let's settle it right now."

One of the men who happened to outweigh Works by a good thirty pounds, leaned forward. Before the fool could fully plant his first step, Works landed a punch with the compact force of a recoiling 155mm howitzer. The man crumpled to the ground like a tower falling in slow motion, and began gasping in pain. His buddy remained in place, wide-eyed and absolutely still.[9]

For the rest of the day the two deserters dug six-by-six holes in the hard earth. After each hole was completed, Works would carefully inspect and critique their handiwork for form and function. If satisfactory, the scowling first sergeant would snatch the ever-present cigarette butt dangling from his lip and flick it into the hole. Then he would tell them to fill it up and dig another a few yards away.[10]

When Works thought the two deserters had finally completed the perfect hole, he presented them to Lieutenant Burks at the company headquarters (HQ). Burks had just returned from posting guards in Rome and was surprised to see how bloody, battered, and filthy Works' diggers appeared.

The lieutenant gave the pair a quick once over. "What happened to them?"

Works shrugged. "They must have had an accident while riding up from Naples."

Of course, Burks knew his top NCO was dishing up a shovel full of pure bull crap, but let the explanation slide. He also knew Works was never going to confess to beating them up—and Works never did. Even though plenty of witnesses had circulated around the hole-digging spectacle throughout the afternoon, no one in the company admitted to seeing anything.

The two men viewed their harsh treatment as some universal injustice and formally complained to the division. A chaplain was dispatched to investigate. When he could not obtain testimony from anyone, the matter was dropped for lack of evidence. The rest of the company completely ostracized the deserters. Works' rough welcome was a final appeal for repentance and they blew it. Any chance to salvage some honorable future in the U.S. Army was also gone. For the sake of everyone involved, the two were ultimately turned over to the Provost Marshal—where they were confined while awaiting court martial.[11]

Burks deeply appreciated Works because he always found a way to get any job done. Burks had long learned that he didn't have to know how Works did it; just that it always got done. Works never let the lieutenant down and proved to be 100% reliable both on and off the battlefield. Burks also found Works to be far more personable than Coles, and struck up a lasting friendship with his first sergeant. Works had a very engaging philosophical outlook forged from his harsh and multifaceted life.[12] Beneath the gruff layers, Burks caught glimpses of an exceedingly decent man. Some only saw Works for his ugly side, and others absolutely hated him. If you crossed him, Works could be a relentless SOB.[13] It mattered little to him if a man loved him, hated him, or avoided him altogether.[14] What mattered most was that every man carried out his duties and responsibilities in L Company.

The company bivouacked on the outskirts of Rome for nearly two weeks, and the men enjoyed the relaxation. One common pastime was to have personal photos taken by traveling Italian photographers. Everyone fantasized about an early end to the war. Some passed the days chasing girls, drinking alcohol, or visiting the historic sites of Rome. Others developed more innovative ways to pass the time.

Pfc. William W. McNamara, a very popular and witty BAR (Browning Automatic Rifle) man in the 1st Platoon, unfurled a blanket on a hill near the Coliseum, covered it with a bunch of his accumulated trinkets, and held a sale. Beaming with his trademark "Cheshire Cat" grin[15] and barking like a bombastic auctioneer with a thick New York City accent, McNamara prattled about the virtues of his junk to every passerby—much to the delight of his buddies.[16] McNamara was the unofficial company performer and had enlisted two of his squad buddies, Pfc. Arco Ciancanelli, a fast talker from Chicago, and Pfc. Joseph Leithner, a quiet handsome fellow from Pennsylvania to be his partners in various entertainment schemes.[17] As a kid, McNamara attended every matinee Broadway show he could afford and memorized the song and dance numbers.[18] He passed on some of those routines to Ciancanelli and Leithner, and the trio enjoyed a lively little side career performing street shows for the local Italians. The shows weren't simply for fun—they sought payment in fresh eggs.[19]

The three actors were also proven combat soldiers. Although they had rowdy downtime reputations, when the time came to fight they were all business. Before the Anzio breakout, Coles called upon the trio many times for patrol duty and was never disappointed with their accomplishments. Now that the company was at rest, Coles figured they were ready to assume a new level of responsibilities. He asked them to take fifteen new replacements on a twenty-four hour conditioning march, and gave them some general verbal guidelines. Before they departed, Coles added, "And no funny business."

The trio marched the replacements about five miles into the hills before spotting a valley town. Unable to resist temptation, they told the recruits to stop and camp for the night on the hillside. Then the three veterans ran down to town and had a good time. They returned the next morning and marched the replacements straight back to L Company. As they returned to camp, they told the recruits to act as though they'd been pounding their boots all night long. Coles wasn't a fool and the ruse did not trick him even for a minute. He called the three in for a visit. "You didn't go the whole way, did you?" Coles queried them with some disappointment.

The three knew they had been caught, and weren't about to become liars on top of the misdeed. "Well, Captain" McNamara responded sheepishly, "You don't want to wear them out before they go into combat!"

Coles cut them some slack and let the incident slide,[20] but if he was auditioning them as the next generation of sergeants, they hadn't shown themselves to be quite up to the task.

With the Germans pressed well north of Rome, the 3rd Division was safely outside the range of German artillery. As a result, the kitchens were up and running again and hot food was served regularly to the GIs. Near L Company's kitchen, starving Italian kids appeared early every morning in search of scraps and handouts. Army orders forbade cooks from passing out anything to the kids directly, but no rules prohibited individual soldiers from taking pity on the locals. Although most soldiers had skipped breakfast in the past, a massive turnout occurred every morning in Rome, and the cooks made sure they served up a big breakfast. As the kids politely waited in lines by the garbage pits, the American soldiers would walk down to them bearing full plates. Powdered eggs, grits, and toast were piled into tin cans and other makeshift food holders so the children could run home and provide their families with something to eat.

One particular replacement joined only a few days earlier but had already earned a company-wide reputation as the consummate "pisser and a moaner." Private (Pvt.) William F. Hawkins, a tall hillbilly from Tennessee and a crack-shot rifleman, grew quickly tired of the guy's chronic complaints. The man shuffled ahead of Hawkins in the chow line, bitching ad nauseam about the food or anything else that came to mind. Doing his best to ignore him, Hawkins sat down with the others and tried to enjoy his meal. The grumbler finished early and continued to complain aloud as he walked downhill to wash his utensils at the hot water station next to the garbage dump. The Italian kids had already lined up at the dump, waiting patiently for scraps.

One undernourished nine-year-old girl named "Maria" proudly stood first in line. Maria's family lived about a quarter mile away. The little girl had become a favorite to many L Company members—reminding them all of younger sisters or nieces they left back home in the States. The complainer passed Maria, cursed at her, and threw his leftover food in her face. Hawkins witnessed the whole incident from the mess tent and went ballistic. Like an olive green flash, Hawkins shot downhill and closed fast on the jerk, who was now lumbering up a slight hill. Hawkins grabbed the guy by the throat and punched him squarely in the face. The stunned man stumbled back, grasping his jaw and spitting out teeth between long strands of blood. The two men were taken to Coles' tent by MPs.

Captain Coles and Lieutenant Burks eyed both men without saying a word. Neither looked too happy about the interruption to their breakfast. After a couple long quiet minutes standing at attention, Hawkins began to worry. Was he in deep trouble? Coles finally spoke up and asked Hawkins to explain himself. Hawkins gave a complete and honest account of what happened. When he was finished, Coles turned to the replacement.

"Is this true?"

The replacement unabashedly admitted his role. As he added additional details of the incident, he called Maria a "damn little Italian bitch."

Coles stepped forward and landed a punch of his own across the replacement's tender jaw, knocking the kid to the ground. "Get that piece of shit down to Naples," Coles ordered. "I don't want to ever see him again!"

As the stricken soldier was being hauled off, Coles turned to face Hawkins. "Take some men over to Maria's family and apologize. Dismissed."

Word of the incident traveled all the way up to the regimental commander, Colonel Richard Thomas. As the day unfolded, Hawkins grew concerned that both he and his popular captain were in serious trouble. But the matter was never raised again by anyone, probably because of Coles' reputation. The ill-tempered replacement was never heard from again.[21]

Nearly a month after the hellish breakout from Anzio, L Company was finally beginning to operate again like a well-trained infantry outfit. Most of the replacements were assimilating well. Veterans wounded during the breakout or the march on Rome returned to find their old platoons filled with dozens of new faces. Many were handed promotions, pay raises, and Combat Infantry Badges. Although new combat challenges surely lay ahead, the survivors could celebrate living to see the summer of 1944. Though their experiences at Anzio were forever haunting, they were among the living. The simple joy that came from watching a pretty Italian woman in a sun dress walk by, or from sharing a few carefree laughs and good-natured ribbing with buddies, took on an almost spiritual dimension. News of the successful Normandy landings and overall progress of the war also did wonders for morale. If the Army could ever claim "halcyon days," these were it. Some even dared to hope and talk openly about an early end to the war.

One day, however, all of war's horrors were made painfully real again for Lieutenant Burks. Graves Registration units had the thankless task of identifying and removing the remains of battle fatalities. Out of respect for the dead and to preserve the morale of the living, Army policy called for the removal of the dead as soon as possible. Sometimes this was accomplished quickly, but other times the condition of the battlefield made collection slow and problematic. Army engineers often had to sweep areas of mines and booby traps before others could safely enter and remove the fallen. Sometimes weeks passed before the dead could be gathered. Nevertheless, most American and German war dead retained "dog tag" necklaces or had pocket bibles, letters, or papers that helped to make identification a fairly straightforward process.

Men from a Graves Registration unit had been systematically working the fields where L Company lost many during the morning of

May 23, but were frustrated with the large number of unidentifiable bodies. Most remains were reasonably intact, but had been pilfered by local Italians of everything from weapons and clothing to personal identification. The scene was absolutely ghastly. Many Italians suffered severe deprivation as a result of the war, but this sort of desecration was beyond the comprehension of their American liberators. To help identify the remains, Graves Registration asked for someone from L Company who had survived that battle to come and help them.

Captain Coles—the man who often dared to stare death in the face—wanted nothing to do with the job. He delegated the thankless task to Burks.[22] After the twenty-mile road trip, Burks returned to the trampled wheat fields, ditches, and artillery craters to walk among the breakout's silent fallen. Several weeks of merciless summer sun had hastened the steady decomposition process. The stench was unbearable. Despite the constant impulse to gag and recoil, Burks drew upon his profound sense of duty to his fallen men and their loved ones to sustain him. He walked solemnly for hours with Graves Registration personnel, helping where he could and seeing what he wished he hadn't seen.

During the course of that unforgettable afternoon, Burks happened upon the remains of S/Sgt. Cormanick. The young man lay exactly where he had fallen. His clothing had been thoroughly rifled, and his feet had been yanked from the calf bones and lay on the ground several feet away. Some Italian wanted the dead man's boots so badly he tore off Cormanick's feet to get them, tossing them aside like garbage. Burks' disgust turned into a seething anger as he struggled to maintain his cool.

A few moments later, a small muffled explosion rocked a nearby field. A woman appeared shouting and crying hysterically in Italian. Although mines had been marked by small fluttering flags, not every explosive device had been located. Her husband had just stepped on a live one. The blast ripped him to pieces. A sergeant fluent in Italian approached Burks for advice on what to do for the poor woman, but the macabre sight of Cormanick's desecration left Burks in no mood for sympathy. He clenched his teeth and quietly replied: "Tell her I'm sorry, but there is nothing I can do about it."

Later that evening, Burks returned to L Company. He did his best to forget the horrible experience and all the foul feelings it drew from within him.[23]

Throughout the second half of June, L Company worked its way south in fits and starts in preparation for its next assignment. On June 15, the men left Rome and were trucked seventeen miles southwest to reestablish camp near the coastline. A week later, they piled on trucks again. This time they logged a twenty-seven mile journey to encamp on the outskirts of Anzio—a homecoming of sorts. Finally, on June 24, the company loaded up on LCI-1040 in Anzio Harbor and set sail for Naples.[24] Ten hours later they arrived on the outskirts of Pozzuoli and established a more permanent bivouac beneath a canopied grove of chestnut trees.[25]

For the next several weeks, L Company and the entire 3rd Division underwent a new round of intensive amphibious assault training. With Mount Vesuvius billowing ominous clouds of ash in the distance, the men practiced and re-practiced beach landings day and night in all types of weather and sea conditions.[26] When they didn't practice, they marched in obligatory parades and troop reviews.[27] No one could divulge to them what their ultimate objective was, but rumors swirled between southern France, northern Italy, and the Balkans. Axis Sally told them in her propaganda broadcasts they were destined for southern France.[28] The training was relentless, exhausting, and far more demanding to be just some busywork holding pattern. The troops knew they were heading somewhere important.

Late in July, word of the near miss "bomb plot" against Hitler caused an exuberant buzz throughout the division, so much so that General O'Daniel circulated a letter among the ranks warning against being too overly optimistic.[29]

During the first week of August, the 15th Infantry Regiment crammed in additional training covering demolition work, communications, compass use, and physical conditioning. The conditioning included twenty-five mile hikes and five mile "speed marches."[30] At long last, the men of L Company loaded their gear onto trucks and rode eight miles from Pozzuoli to Naples harbor. Along the way, they passed a makeshift prison compound with a long barbed wire fence running parallel to the road. Propped along the inside of the fence lingered the two Anzio deserters 1st Sgt. Works manhandled two months earlier. As the convoy rolled past, the recognition between the passing men and the two deserters was instant. After several silent seconds elapsed, one of the deserters shouted, "So long, suckers!" A drum roll of clicking gun bolts immediately erupted throughout the departing convoy, but no one pulled a trigger.[31]

At Naples, the men of L Company loaded aboard the U.S.S. *Henrico* along with the entire 3rd Battalion. Once underway, the soldiers were finally told the purpose for the long summer of training and the vast armada of ships: in three days they would attack along the coast of southern France. Axis Sally was dead on the mark again.

The evening before the landings, 3rd Battalion commander Lt. Col. Frederic Boye gathered his company officers for a final review of the invasion's particulars. Lieutenant Burks, Captain Coles, and the commanders of I, K, and M Companies crowded into Boye's tiny wardroom to review maps, schedules, and objectives.

The overall responsibility of the 3rd Infantry Division was to secure the Saint-Tropez peninsula the first day, and to move swiftly inland on the second day. The landings would take place on two separate beaches approximately five miles apart. The 7th and 30th Infantry Regiments would land on "Red Beach" at the Bay of Cavalaire to the southwest section of the peninsula. The 15th Infantry Regiment would strike "Yellow Beach" at the Bay of Pampelonne on the eastern side. The 1st and 3rd Battalions of the 15th would be the first in—storming the beach at an 8:00 A.M. "H-hour." Four tanks from the 756th Tank Battalion would join that first wave. The 3rd Battalion would attack the center of the beach and the 1st Battalion would land to the south. Both battalions needed to reduce all beach defenses as quickly as possible to maintain the ambitious invasion schedule and insure the successful landing of subsequent waves.

"Yellow Beach" was a crescent-shaped sandy beach roughly two miles long, situated along a north-south bearing. The beach's shallow water approach was ideal for an amphibious assault. The Germans saw that same potential and constructed defenses along the shoreline, including extensive minefields augmented with a few concrete pillboxes, machine gun positions, and anti-tank guns. Military intelligence classified the overall German defenses as "moderate."[32] In other words, they expected a successful landing . . . but at a price.

Beyond the beach, grassy bluffs and scrub pines receded into highland hills a mile or two inland. Numerous farms, vineyards, pine forests, and olive groves dotted the countryside, and a narrow coastal road ran parallel to the beach approximately 200 yards from shore. The

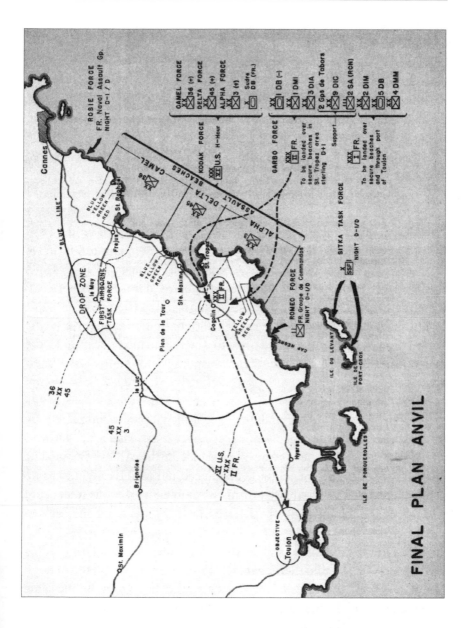

goal of the 3rd Battalion was to seize that road after neutralizing the beach defenses. Once this was accomplished, the 2nd Battalion arriving in a subsequent wave had orders to pass through the 3rd Battalion to seize the town of Saint-Tropez three miles to the northwest. Saint-Tropez was the division's prime objective for the day. The town had a small but serviceable harbor vital to sustaining the overall Allied invasion in the days to come. Nothing could happen, however, until the 3rd Battalion took that beach in the first wave.

Lieutenant Colonel Boye was an invasion veteran. His experience stretched back to the first landings at Casablanca in November 1942.[33] This was his fifth amphibious landing, and he wanted it to be the best. Boye's greatest concern was that his men might disembark too far from the beach. During the Anzio landings in January 1944, Boye accompanied the assault wave under cover of darkness. His LCVP (Landing Craft Vehicle Personnel—also known as a "Higgins boat") hit a sandbar. Though well short of the beach, the coastguardsman lowered the ramp. Boye and his men stepped off into water up to their necks and were forced to wade ashore with their weapons held high above their heads—an extremely vulnerable and ineffective way to attack an enemy position.

Fortunately, the Anzio landings caught the Germans completely by surprise and initial resistance was exceedingly light. This time, surprise and the cover of darkness were not factors in the Allies' favor. The invasion of southern France, to be conducted in broad daylight, was no secret to anyone. Boye stressed to his assembled officers to make sure that the coxswains piloting the LCVPs took the boats all the way to shore.[34]

The meeting adjourned. The officers dispersed along the ship's narrow corridors to hold their own last minute meetings with the platoon commanders and sergeants of their companies, who in turn did the same with their squads. Though Lt. Col. Boye did not spell out exactly how his officers would insure that the LCVPs got ashore, Coles had a solution for his men. He told them that if any coxswain tried to pull up short, the senior NCO on each boat was to seize control and drive it in.[35] Each LCVP carried three coastguardsmen and forty infantrymen armed to their necks with every conceivable weapon. Coles saw no reason why his men couldn't convince their pilots to drop them off where they were supposed to go.

At long last, the men of L Company and the 3rd Battalion settled into their bunks for a few hours of sleep. Combat veterans and replacements alike, lay awake and alone with only their thoughts and prayers for comfort. Many wondered if 8:00 A.M., August 15, 1944, would mark the last few minutes of their young lives.

Chapter Three

Yellow Beach

In the calm early hours of August 15, 1944, the transport ships and support vessels of Naval Task Force 84 emerged like grey ghosts in the pre-dawn haze, to drop anchor ten miles southeast of the Bay of Pampelonne.[1] Once the ships were in their assigned positions, general quarters sounded and a mad scramble ensued. The clocks on the bulkheads showed the time as precisely 4:36 A.M.[2] D-Day in Southern France was officially underway.

In the cramped recesses of U.S.S. *Henrico*, the men of the 3rd Battalion were roused from bunks stacked five and six high, after a sleepless night of trepidation.[3] They lined up for one last coffee and shipboard meal before assembling their gear and heading topside.[4] The early morning was already warm, and the Mediterranean was eerily placid.[5] Each infantryman was handed a gas mask, a set of K and D rations, and carbon dioxide capsules for his life preserver. The rations included two packs of cigarettes, a bottle of salt tablets, and a bottle of Halazone tablets for water purification.[6] In addition to weapons and a helmet, each man carried a field pack, canteen, shovel, extra grenades, and ammunition bandoleers.[7]

With workmanlike precision, *Henrico's* sailors prepared the wooden Higgins boats for the assault.[8] Each thirty-five foot long craft was lowered by davits and tethered to the side of *Henrico*. Netting with wooden footholds was draped over the sides of *Henrico* down to the boats dipping and swaying twenty feet below.[9] Each man, fully laden with heavy combat gear and supplies, slowly descended the netting to waiting boats below. The process was dicey: an accidental slip and fall into the water or a swell that pushed the bobbing vessels apart at just the wrong moment, would send a soldier straight to the bottom.

Technical Five (T/5) Herman Cogdell carried a BAR and was a squad leader in the 1st Platoon of L Company. He was from a South Carolina farming family and joined the Army in 1939. Although a longtime veteran of L Company and an Anzio survivor, the guys knew him best for his farming skills. Many in the 1st Platoon were city kids and didn't know the first thing about milking a cow. For Cogdell, it was second nature. In Italy, he delighted the men by taking fresh milk and a chocolate bar ration and heating them together in a helmet to create chocolate milk. Afterward, the guys were constantly looking for a cow so Cogdell could make more.[10] As Cogdell led his squad down the rope ladder that morning, chocolate milk was the furthest thing from his mind. He moved with extra care until he reached the last rung, where he paused and jumped three feet into the bobbing LCVP. He hit the deck with a sigh of relief.[11] One by one, Cogdell's squad mates joined him and assisted each other until everyone was safely aboard.

Farther along the top deck of *Henrico*, Lt. Burks took one last look around. He was going to miss this big ship and all its cramped amenities.[12] He checked his gear, adjusted his helmet with a white officer bar painted on the back,[13] and descended with his men down the rope ladder to another awaiting LCVP. Captain Coles and the remaining men of the company boarded three other LCVPs assigned to L Company, while Companies I and K filled their respective boats. The long summer of repetitive training and physical conditioning drills had paid its first dividend; no one leaving *Henrico* was lost.[14]

By 5:30 A.M., the first boats of the assault wave gathered a short distance away at the predetermined "Queen" position in the bay, still ten miles from the beach. They circled restlessly, waiting for the other boats to load and join them for a coordinated assault.[15] Pfc. Robert Tyler and his best buddy, Pfc. Robert Seegitz, found the wait long and nauseating. The diesel exhaust from the circling Higgins boats hung in the thick morning air and the circular pattern forced them to breathe the same noxious fumes over and over again.[16] They weren't alone. Others soldiers were using their helmets as catch basins to collect their vomit.[17] The beach assault itself was beginning to look like a welcome change.

The men were told to sharpen their bayonets, so many passed the time doing so.[18] Some told jokes to cut the tension. Others quietly prayed, fidgeted with talismans, or compulsively checked and rechecked their equipment. The GIs were ready to go, but the 8:00 A.M. "H-hour" was still more than two hours away.

Approximately forty Higgins boats loaded for the first assault wave. The plan called for twenty of those boats to line up on the left side and carry members of the 1st Battalion and the 3rd Recon Company to the southern section of the beach. From there, the 1st Battalion would attack inland and take the walled town of Ramatuelle. The other twenty boats would line up on the right side and carry the 3rd Battalion and the 15th Infantry Regiment's "Battle Patrol" to the middle of the beach.

While this first wave of infantry loaded and assembled for the assault, preparations were underway aboard LCT-1015 to launch four specially outfitted Sherman tanks. These tanks were made amphibious by fitting them with a high inflatable canvas wall around the sides and by outfitting dual propellers off the back.[19] They were called "Duplex Drive Tanks" or "DD-tanks" for short. The DD-tanks were designed to float and move under their own power, and were scheduled to hit the beach two minutes ahead of the first wave.[20] At 6:10 A.M., LCT-1015 began moving from "Queen" to a new position less than a mile off the beach.[21] Because of their instability, the DD-tanks had to be dropped off as close to shore as possible.

The twenty men crewing the four tanks were from the 3rd Platoon of B Company of the 756th Tank Battalion. Two months of intensive training prepared them for this operation. The work was extremely dangerous. While at sea, most of the tank was submerged below the water surface like an open-topped caisson. The waterline splashed dangerously close along the top of the canvas wraparound, making the 33-ton tank unwieldy and difficult to maneuver. Any wave larger than two feet could swamp the vehicle and send it quickly to the bottom of the Mediterranean.[22] As a safety precaution, each of the five DD-tank crewmen wore special underwater breathing devices called "Momsen Lungs" originally designed for submarine escapes.[23] Even with these, escape from a sinking tank was problematic. At best, the crew had but a few seconds to exit through three narrow hatches—two down front above the driver and bow gunner, and one up top for the turret crew. A crew member clearing a hatch still had to avoid entanglement in the cage of supports welded to the tank deck to secure the canvas wraparound. If snagged, he would plummet into the murky depths along with the tank.

The B Company DD-tank crews trained extensively over the summer in the Bay of Naples at an area similar to the beaches of Southern France. Training required 100% battle accuracy, so the DD-tanks carried a complete stock of live ammo and a full tank of gas in order to maintain the proper buoyancy. The 753rd Tank Battalion, assigned to the 36th Infantry Division, held their DD-tank rehearsals south near Salerno. The area was also where the 756th Tank Battalion's A Company DD-tank crews were rehearsing at the time. One of the 753rd DD-tanks swamped during training and immediately sank sixty-five feet to the bottom of the bay. Despite all the precautions, including the Momsen lungs, one crew member drowned.[24] The story traveled fast among the DD-tank crews of both battalions.

The tank commander was particularly vulnerable to wounding or death. He was required to stand behind the tank turret on a welded steel platform no larger than a sheet of paper, completely exposed to all hazards—including small arms fire.[25] While in this position, he steered the twin propellers with a tiller until the vehicle reached shore. Once there, the tank driver inside took over and the commander—if still alive—would climb inside the turret for cover.[26] Lieutenant Colonel Glenn Rogers, the CO of the 756th Tank Battalion, fully expected to lose all of his DD-tank commanders if enemy beach resistance proved heavier than expected.[27]

Second Lieutenant (2nd Lt.) Andrew Orient commanded the B Company DD-tank platoon. Orient was a recently married thirty-two year old Pennsylvania farmer who had volunteered for service soon after the war broke out. He qualified for OCS, and like most tankers trained at Fort Knox, Kentucky. He was assigned to B Company of the 756th as a replacement officer during the drive on Rome.[28] Although the fight lasted barely a week beyond his arrival, Orient proved a capable combat officer and swiftly became very popular with his men. He looked out for them, and put their needs above his own—to the point where he did not eat until they ate.[29] Over the summer Orient's platoon trained together, forging a deep camaraderie in the process.

The other three tank commanders were Sergeant (Sgt.) Roy Anderson, Sgt. Lloyd Stout, and S/Sgt. Haskell Oliver. Oliver was the platoon sergeant and second in command after Lt. Orient. Oliver was a savvy, experienced tanker who distinguished himself in the hellish fighting for Monte Cassino. He had been a member of the 756th since

1941, when the battalion was formed as a light tank outfit and stationed at Fort Lewis, Washington.

Prior to becoming a tank commander, Sgt. Anderson had been Oliver's tank driver at Cassino. Anderson was a tall man with mid-western common sense and an ironic wit. Sgt. Stout was a shorter, dark haired kid from Michigan recently promoted after serving as a long-time tank gunner in the company. During the march on Rome, Stout was shot in the neck. He fully recovered and returned to the company on July 2 in time for training.[30] Stout's brother was also a member of the 756th and served in A Company.[31]

Prior to the summer of 1944, none of the 3rd Platoon tankers had ever heard of a "DD-tank," but after six weeks of training and dozens of mock landing drills, the Army considered them battle ready. Now they were heading into combat as submariners in the Army.

By 6:15 A.M.,[32] the warships supporting the Yellow Beach invasion began churning up the beach with their heavy guns. The intent was to soften up German defenses in advance of the assault waves. Blasting away at the beach were the fifteen-inch guns from the British battleship H.M.S. *Ramillies* and the smaller guns from six cruisers and six destroyers.[33] The show was spectacular and fearsome. As big explosions tossed sand, soil, and foliage skyward, naval minesweepers transited back and forth in the waters between the ships and shore. Adding to this choreographed pandemonium was the launch of nine "AJAX" drones. These unmanned Higgins boats were jammed with high explosives and controlled by radio signals—a rudimentary guided missile of sorts. These nautical bombs detonated in the shallow water at the shoreline to set off submerged mines before the assault waves accidentally found them.

Finally, at 6:50 A.M., all first wave Higgins boats were in position. With dawn breaking, they broke from their circular holding patterns at "Queen" to form two separate attack wings for the assault run. On the left, the 1st Battalion boats maneuvered into position; the 3rd Battalion boats did likewise on the right side. At 7:05 A.M., the coxswains opened up the diesel motors and kicked up cool salty spray into the air to commence the ten-mile journey toward shore. As they departed, additional Higgins boats carrying support teams of engineers, artillery, and the 2nd Battalion of the 15th Infantry Regiment assembled at "Queen" for the second and third waves. During the approach, heavy naval guns continued to pound the beach mercilessly. Every staggering flash and boom kicked up additional sand, dust and smoke, to mix with the morning haze. And then, without warning, the naval shelling stopped.

Moments later, waves of Allied planes from the Twelfth Air Force based out of Corsica, passed overhead and rumbled toward the beach. From 7:10 A.M. to 7:35 A.M., they saturated the landing site with yet another spectacular series of bombings. Everything from big B-17s and B-26s to smaller single engine P-51s and P-47 Thunderbolts took part.[34] Once the aerial bombing slowed to a trickle, the AJAX boats arrived one after the other along the beach and exploded. Six of the nine detonated as planned.[35]

By 7:40 A.M., the assault wave began to assemble into "V" formations as they approached the smoky beach.[36] Over the rising and falling front ramps, the nervous riders strained to discern threats from the haze silhouetted beach and highland hills. The boat crews did their best to remain on target, but found the task a Herculean challenge as dust, smoke, and fires obscured most of the designated landmarks. Other than a few German artillery shells lobbed ineffectively at the AJAX control boat crews, the enemy response was only enough to show that someone was there.[37]

At the same time, LCT-1015 reached her set position ahead of the assault wave. The craft commander told the tankers they were 1,000 yards out—the distance required by the invasion plans. The tankers thought the distance was more like 2,000 yards and immediately questioned the assessment. Sgt. Anderson thought the Navy skipper must have been new to his command and nervous about the dangers of dropping them in close.[38] Nevertheless, the LCT commander's word was the final one and the front bow ramp dropped open. The four DD-tank crews began inflating the sidewalls of the canvas and bracing the support struts in place.[39]

The driver of the first DD-tank cranked up the engine and slowly eased the heavy machine down the ramp toward the water. As the tank's canvas bow began to plunge into the calm Mediterranean, the LCT's helmsman gently nudged the ship into reverse, a move that allowed the DD-tank to gently lift off the deck, right itself, and achieve implausible buoyancy. The DD propellers engaged, the motor revved, and the crazy machine plodded off in a puff of exhaust and idled a short distance away—waiting for the others to join. One by one, they followed until all four DD-tanks were bobbing in a line approximately seventy-five yards from each other. Anderson had the extreme right position. Oliver and Stout idled next to him on the left, while Orient pulled up on the far left. Once set, they began creeping toward shore at a top speed of five miles per hour. A faster pace risked tearing the front canvas in two and sinking the tank. The commanders working on top of each contraption tried to avoid excessive maneuvering with the tiller and did his best to keep the improbable boat moving straight and true.[40]

With H-hour only ten minutes away, the Navy let loose one final eight-minute barrage. Over 3000 hissing rockets were launched from four British LST(R)s positioned to the rear of the floating task force.[41] LST(R)s were 350-foot long flat-decked ships with nearly 800 five-inch rocket tubes[42] honeycombed together on the deck. The rockets were launched in rolling fashion to limit the effects of the exhaust on the deck. Even so, the heat was so intense that the deck crew wore asbestos suits. Waves of these rockets sailed high over the DD-tanks and infantry assault boats and hit the shore—exploding like giant rolls of firecrackers. Some rockets fell short, either slicing the water as duds or exploding around the approaching LCVPs. The near misses added to the anxiety of the men aboard, but miraculously no one was hit.[43] At two minutes to eight, the deafening rocket attack ceased, and the moment arrived for the ground forces to take over.

The first wave hit the beach at precisely 8:00 A.M. To the south, the three rifle companies of the 1st Battalion landed exactly where planned. Farther north, however, the haze and smoke from the rockets prevented the coastguardsmen from properly aligning with beach landmarks. As a result, they approached about 1,300 yards south of their target zone, with no time to alter course.[44]

The five L Company boats held the center of the attack formation while Captain Hahn's five K Company boats pressed in at the left and Captain Stuart's five I Company boats held the right.[45] On the extreme right of the wing, Battle Patrol was riding on four additional LCVPs.[46]

Captain Coles was rolling and pitching along with thirty of his men in one of the lead Higgins boats. He didn't like the speed of approach. Over the roar of the diesel motor, Coles hollered for the coxswain to kick up the throttle. With the beach approaching, Coles' restless infantrymen faced toward the front ramp, waiting for the door to drop at any moment. To help them keep their focus, Coles barked some last minute instructions and encouragement to them.

He finished with particular emphasis: "Be sure you have your helmets on!"[47]

Those still without their helmets sheepishly threw on their steel pots and returned to ready positions. The seconds ticked down like hours. Coles still didn't think the boat was moving fast enough. Unwilling to gamble his men's lives on protocol, he shoved the coxswain out of the way, grabbed the wheel, and threw open the throttle.[48] The commandeered boat crunched hard against the sand and the front ramp fell open. Coles' men jumped out onto dry sand, tore off across the beach, and found cover among the nearby dunes and beach grass. Coles abandoned the wheel and scrambled ashore with the last men off, M1911A1 pistol in hand and fiery red hair gleaming in the morning sun. He reached his men among the dunes and took a quick head count. Everyone made it. Coles was discussing how best to move toward the beach road when he noticed his men smiling and staring back at him. He felt the top of his head and grinned back. He left the LCVP without his helmet![49]

The remaining boats of Company L men beached nearby. The confident pilot of 1st Lt. Burks' boat took the craft clear onto the beach. As the ramp fell, Burks felt his heart pounding in his throat.[50] Ahead he could see roughly 100 yards of sand, beyond which stretched a barbed wire fence. Strangely, nobody seemed to be shooting at them. Burks' team stormed off the boat onto dry land, fanned out, and sprinted toward the barbed wire fence. Burks could see a small sign posted about twenty-five yards away with words written in plain English: "DANGER: MINES."

"Where the hell did that come from?" Burks wondered as he pulled up, hollering and gesturing for his men to avoid the area.

He figured that FFI operatives had covertly placed the signs during the night, and gave some quick mental thanks for their assistance as he darted into a sheltered dune area.[51]

The men on T/5 Herman Cogdell's LCVP promised their coxswain they would help push the boat back to sea if he put them on dry sand. The coxswain set them squarely ashore. Cogdell and a few others remained behind momentarily as the ramp was raised to help shove the boat back into the surf.[52]

Once away, Cogdell raised his BAR and splashed out of the knee-high water. With extra ammo clips and grenades clanking about his waist, he chased down the others just as they began to disappear into a smoky and hazy vineyard off the beach. As Cogdell ran, he noticed that most of the men had already ditched their bulky and cumbersome gasmasks.[53] Cogdell didn't want to be weighed down with any unnecessary items either, so he also ditched his mask.

Scattered among the beach debris were "pole charges," which had been distributed to some of the men before the landings. These were eight-foot poles with TNT strapped on one end for use against pillboxes. Once the boat ramps dropped, there were few pillboxes left that had survived the bombardment. No one wanted to carry extra weight, so the men ditched the heavy pole charges, too. One of the guys even tossed his flamethrower overboard when he hit the beach. Since he saw no immediate use for it, he wasn't about to run around with a big bomb strapped to his back.[54]

As Cogdell reached the vineyard, he understood why they were told to sharpen their bayonets. A tangled field of vines and wire stood between them and their beach road objective a few hundred yards inland.[55] The vineyard was heavily mined, but the charges had been planted for so long that the dirt and sand around them had weathered away. Many telltale detonators sat completely exposed in the glinting sunlight.[56] Cogdell and the others gingerly negotiated through the field, surveying the ground for mines while casting nervous glances ahead for German riflemen or machine gun nests. One unlucky man stepped on a mine, which flashed and popped loudly. The man collapsed to the sand while his boot and foot sailed high into the air.[57]

Once through the vineyard, a German soldier unexpectedly appeared ahead with his hands in the air. As he walked toward Cogdell, more Germans popped up from behind him. Each signaled a willingness to surrender. One of the last men to rise shouted in perfect English, "Wait for me!" Cogdell thought he was hallucinating. He had seen many strange things during his long stint with L Company, but this was the first time he had ever heard a German eager to surrender and speaking in English![58]

Elsewhere, another squad of L Company men cautiously approached the rear of an armored turret positioned near the beach. The gun could only fire seaward and was incapable of traversing inland. With Americans preparing to blow off the back door, the gun crew wisely surrendered.[59]

Only one of the five L Company LCVPs failed to discharge the men on dry land. The boat ferrying McNamara, Ciancanelli, and Leithner's "unruly squad" snagged a sandbar and dropped short. Rifle grenadier Pfc. Arthur Schrader was also aboard after recovering earlier in the summer from the gunshot wound to his leg during the Anzio breakout. The men jumped off in waist-high water, scrambled ashore, and struck out across the dunes and vineyards to catch up with the rest of the company.[60] A solitary German sniper hidden in a tree not nearly high enough or far enough away was idiotic enough to shoot at them. He was quickly killed by one the BAR men.[61]

A few hundred yards north of the 3rd Battalion landing area, Sgt. Anderson was carefully negotiating his DD-tank through a series of wooden posts spaced fifteen to twenty feet apart in the water. Some were clearly visible, but others were hidden below the waterline. Despite the earlier explosions of the Apex boats, Anderson could see that a few posts still had live mines attached to them. He did his best to steer clear without upsetting his tank's unstable buoyancy. Anderson noted with relief, at least, that no one seemed to be shooting at him.

Through the smoke and haze, Anderson could barely make out the beach ahead. The place appeared deserted—none of the doughboys had yet arrived. At two o'clock right, his trained eyes focused on the grey outline of a pillbox perched upon a beach bluff. As he neared the beach, Anderson discerned a long barrel sticking out from the roughly square shape. It looked to him like a big 150mm gun, but there was nothing he could do about it until the DD-tank hit shore and dropped the canvas. The tank's gun was inoperable while the canvas was up. Anderson took some comfort in that gun barrel was pointed away from him and not moving, but watched constantly for any sign of movement. He wondered to himself why the gun crew hadn't noticed a solitary American tank approaching their otherwise empty beach. Perhaps the Germans figured Anderson and his crew were crazy and had either laughed themselves silly or were taking pity on them.

Suddenly, Anderson felt something below the waterline bump and scrape along the tank hull. Anderson held his breath and waited for an explosion that never occurred. He looked back in the wake and saw they had brushed a post. Luckily, it had no mine. As they closed within fifty feet of shore, the tank treads began to drag against the sandy bottom and skidded to a stop. Anderson raised the props and signaled via intercom to the driver T/5 Emil Tikkanen to deflate the canvas. Tikkanen cracked opened the valves and the two front struts dropped automatically. Anderson jumped down from his turret platform to release the remaining side struts on the tank deck, all the while stealing glances toward the big 150mm gun on shore. Though it remained eerily silent, Anderson knew he would feel a lot better once his turret gun was operational.

While Anderson bounded hastily about the deck freeing struts, a Higgins boat pulled to the beach to drop off a smoke-laying crew. Anderson was happy to finally see company, but the coxswain was either nervous or in a hurry—and completely unaware of the DD-tank's vulnerability to high waves. Once the chemical team departed, he jack-knifed the boat around behind Anderson and hightailed back to sea. Anderson watched helplessly as the boat wake washed over his partially deflated canvas and spilled down into the tank's rear engine compartment. The batteries instantly shorted and the engine sputtered into dead silence. The tank could not be restarted without a maintenance team. All the summer training and the long slow cruise in from LCT-1015 ended as the result of some jumpy American coxswain. Anderson and his tank had been reduced to nothing more than a simple pillbox stranded a few yards off the beach in four feet of surf. He looked up at the long gun of his beach counterpart. Fortunately, it remained motionless.

S/Sgt. Oliver's tank pulled in and stopped about fifty yards left of Anderson's position. The muscular platoon sergeant was fast at work popping down struts and lowering his canvas. Anderson surveyed the area. He was sure they were where they were supposed to be, but aside from the one LCVP that came and went, no other infantry boats could be seen. Anderson figured they had to be around somewhere in the haze. He grabbed his radio microphone and hollered over to his platoon sergeant:

"Well Ollie, it looks like we're the only ones here!"

Oliver switched on his own set and nodded his head in agreement: "Yep!"

No operation ever went as planned.

Anderson informed Oliver he was dead in the water and would have to wait for help. All Oliver could do was to wish him luck. Moments later, the agile staff sergeant dropped down into his commander hatch, his head and shoulders sticking above the rim as he adjusted his helmet. From this position, he had a clear field of vision and could swivel the hatch plate halves around to protect his head against enemy sharpshooters and machine gunners.[62] Once set, Oliver's tank lurched forward out of the water. The driver shifted gears and the machine charged across the beach kicking up twin plumes of sand as they disappeared into a cloud of smoke and dust. The flapping canvas wrap made the tank look more like a runaway carnival stand then some fierce weapon of war.

For the next twenty minutes, Anderson and his crew sat anxiously in the gently rolling surf wondering what happened to their infantry support. Anderson wasn't aware at the time, but he and Oliver had indeed landed in the right place, while the entire 3rd Battalion beached three-quarters of a mile south of the rendezvous point.[63] Once the third landing wave pulled in around Anderson's stalled tank twenty minutes later, the five tankers were no longer alone. While the doughs scurried to secure the beach, cool seawater seeped into the tank leaving T/5 Emil Tikkanen and the bow gunner sitting in about two feet of it. Anderson, his gunner Corporal (Cpl.) Steve Vargo, and the loader Pvt. Dual Dishner were high and dry in the turret, but the cramped conditions were hot and uncomfortable. The crewmen began asking when they could leave the tank, but Anderson told them to stay put until the infantry cleared the area. As long as the big pillbox gun remained still, Anderson did not think there was a safer place than inside the tank.

Later that morning they vacated the tank without incident. The big German pillbox gun never moved—either the crew was dead or they had abandoned it during the early morning naval and aerial barrage.[64]

The other two 3rd Platoon DD-tanks landed safely farther down the beach. Lt. Orient and Sgt. Stout joined up with the 1st Battalion for the push toward Ramatuelle. Oliver's tank, however, threw a track while plodding toward the 3rd Battalion area and was stranded on the beach.[65]

At the 3rd Battalion landing zone, the men of L Company stormed the fence, cut the barbed wire and advanced toward the beach road running parallel to the shore. Getting to the fence was not easy. The bombardment had churned up the entire area, tossing about many unexploded land mines everyone sought to avoid.[66] And yet, despite the blasts, weathering, and the FFI's helpful warning signs, thousands of other mines remained untouched and hidden below the soil. A soldier moving near Lt. Burks stepped on one, setting off the sickening "POP!" that shredded his foot.[67] A mine tripped by another rifleman blasted into his legs and private parts.[68] As both men writhed in agony, medics rushed in to attend them.[69] A few local French farmers came out of hiding to help the Americans negotiate their way through to the road.[70]

Even with the minefield difficulties, the morning was unfolding far more quickly and smoothly than anyone imagined. German resistance along the beach was virtually non-existent—which came as a huge surprise to everyone. With no serious concentration of enemy to stop them, L Company and the 3rd Battalion reached their first objective in only a half hour. Clearing the way to the beach road was supposed to take the better part of the morning. No one complained about the speed of events.

After the men of L Company secured their section of road, a contact platoon moved south to remain in touch with the 1st Battalion. Other L Company members returned to the beach to safely guide the subsequent landing waves through the minefields.[71] But in keeping with the plan to seize as much territory as possible, the bulk of L Company began to fan out and move northward toward a forested area some distance from the beach.

A contingent from the 1st Platoon moved left toward a small patch of wooded hills along the main road. Though they lacked the guidance of an officer or NCO, Pfc. William W. McNamara boldly led the team ahead. Just as they arrived at a road bend, bullets began snapping and popping all around them. The eleven Americans immediately dove into the left ditch for cover. About thirty yards ahead on the right side of the road were three German riflemen positioned in the ditch. McNamara lifted his head slightly to survey the situation and made a decision. He jumped out of the left ditch toting his BAR, scurried over the road, and dropped just as quickly on the other side. The three Germans opened fire on him, but missed. McNamara caught a quick breather before charging straight up the right ditch with his BAR blazing from the hip. The incident was over in seconds. The remaining ten 1st Platoon men dashed out of the left ditch to catch up with McNamara. They found him standing over two dead Germans and a third, mortally wounded enemy.

McNamara and his men set out again, but after advancing only a dozen yards found themselves again the objects of unwanted attention. This time the gunfire was much heavier, raining down from a wooded hill along the road about 100 yards on the right. As machine gun and rifle fire cracked against the dirt shoulder and bounded off the hot asphalt road, McNamara's men scrambled for the ditch a second time. Approximately two dozen Germans appeared to be holding the hill, but it was difficult to tell with certainty because they were well camouflaged and dug in. They also had a distinct defensive advantage because they held the high ground.

McNamara's men formed a skirmish line along the ditch and returned fire. During the exchange, Pfc. Schrader exhausted all of his rifle grenades in a vain attempt to dislodge the Germans from the hillside. The counter fire accomplished little. McNamara asked for a volunteer to accompany him up the hillside to take it to the Germans. The idea sounded suicidal. Schrader couldn't go. He was now a rifle grenadier without grenades, and so not much use to anyone. The other nine men remained silent. McNamara counted out his BAR clips. He had eight. He borrowed eight more from another BAR man in the group, strapped them on, and took off alone.

Astounded, McNamara's buddies watched him work his way along a shallow ravine leading to the hill. As he approached within forty yards of the base, a German rifleman hidden behind a bush fifteen yards from McNamara nervously fired his Mauser rifle—but somehow missed the advancing blonde American. McNamara turned and cut the man down with a quick burst from his BAR. A few yards from the fallen man, a second German rifleman stepped forward with his hands up.

"Kamerad!" ("Comrade!") He shouted.

McNamara cautiously stepped forward to disarm the man, but a third rifleman suddenly appeared with his rifle leveled at McNamara. He fired at point blank range and also missed. When it became clear to McNamara the "surrender" was nothing but a dirty trick, he sprayed a clip of bullets across the midsections of both Germans and angrily continued moving up the ravine. Gone was his "Cheshire grin." No longer the entertainer, the jokester, or the trinket salesman, McNamara was now a one man army on a mission.

The Germans defending the hill had fixed their undivided attention on the crazy American BAR man advancing toward them. As McNamara continued moving up the shallow but steep ravine, the Germans sent a spattering of small arms his way that ripped through the leaves and grass around him. Sometimes McNamara was fully concealed as he moved, but at other times his head and shoulders were plainly visible and he had to dash from tree to tree to avoid the flurry of German machine gun and rifle fire tracking him.

When McNamara achieved a vantage point slightly above the German hill positions, he took a few moments to study the deployment of the enemy. The enemy was spread out among simple "prone shelters," shallow holes only deep enough to protect a soldier lying down. McNamara counted them up, devised a plan of attack, and rushed downhill firing his BAR into the nearest German positions. The Germans spun around and answered with a waist high concentration of machine gun and rifle fire. McNamara bounded forward, firing and reloading his BAR as he zigzagged from tree to tree. Bullets chipped off the nearby tree bark as he closed in. The Germans resorted to tossing their "potato masher" stick grenades to no avail. When McNamara found cover close enough to toss in a few grenades of his own, the explosions panicked a few of the Germans, who scrambled out of their holes and fled for the bottom of the hill. McNamara's stationary buddies along the skirmish line picked them off one at a time as they appeared.

After a few more minutes of chaos, the German hill positions fell silent. Pfc. Schrader, Pfc. Ciancanelli, and the rest of the guys at the skirmish line strained to see what had become of their friend. They naturally assumed the worst. Suddenly, McNamara appeared in a clearing on the hill, waving emphatically to his friends below to join him.

"Get the hell up here!" he shouted.

McNamara's men left the ditch and scurried up the hill. They found McNamara standing among the shallow holes with nine dead or dying Germans lying around him. Thirteen others stood silently in a line, weaponless, their hands firmly folded behind their heads. McNamara pointed his BAR squarely at their midsections in case they tried another "kamerad" stunt. No one did.

One of McNamara's squad mates stepped forward and took custody of the prisoners. With a Tommy gun pointed at their backs, he marched the captured Germans toward the beach for interrogation. McNamara, still juiced with adrenaline, headed farther into the woods in search of more Germans. By that time, a second group of L Company men joined up with them.

The entire episode consumed only twenty minutes. During that brief time, McNamara had personally killed fifteen Germans and captured thirteen more.[72] His feat was an astounding display of single-minded courage in action, for which he was awarded the Distinguished Service Cross. Those who witnessed it never forgot it.

★ Chapter Four
On to Saint-Tropez

As amphibious landings go, the operation on the southern coast of France clicked on in nearly text book fashion. The remaining first wave of LCVPs carrying I and K Companies as support for L Company's flanks also managed to place most of the infantrymen onto dry land. Lt. Col. Boye's concerns about his men being dropped in the water turned out to be largely unfounded. The coastguardsmen did a magnificent job.

The men of I Company stormed the beach just to the north of Coles' men with a similar mission; clear the beach of any resistance and secure the main road running north to Saint-Tropez. Like L Company, a few men were lost to land mines during the initial push forward, but I Company drove ahead and secured its segment of the road in short order. Once the initial objective was in hand, the men turned north along the beach and began working their way up into the highlands.

Battle Patrol beached farther north of I Company and began moving along the coastline toward Saint-Tropez, where its members were ordered to rejoin the battalion. Along the way, they encountered an elaborate—and thankfully abandoned—German defensive network. Their job was to clear out all such places along the shoreline. Inside, they discovered several cases of sardines packed in peanut butter. The men took the opportunity to load up on a few cans.[1] This method of clearing out enemy positions was definitely preferable over what they had trained for and expected.

K Company landed on L Company's left flank, crossed the beach, and secured another segment of the main road. Once there, its men established a roadblock and set up security at the assembly point for the four DD-tanks and two tank destroyers supporting the first wave. As L and I Companies began moving north, K Company followed behind in reserve.

The remainder of the 3rd Battalion, consisting of Headquarters Company plus the heavy machine gun and mortar crews of M Company, arrived ten minutes behind the first wave and unloaded on the beach. Lt. Col. Boye set up his battalion command post, while the men of M Company remained at the ready in case the advancing rifle companies needed more firepower.

A naval liaison was assigned to the 3rd Battalion HQ just in case Boye required help from the Navy's big guns. Divisional artillery was not scheduled to land for another hour.[2] Neither was needed. The dawn naval bombardment had silenced or driven away most of the German beach defenders. Though relatively quiet, occasional explosions went off inside the 3rd Battalion beach area; another unlucky soldier had just set off a mine. Boye's men set off red smoke canisters and fired red rifle grenades as a signal to the subsequent LCVP waves that the beach was secure.[3] Everyone was tremendously relieved. The real beach landings proved a lot easier then the ones they had practiced all summer long near Naples.[4]

At 8:20 and 8:30 A.M., the second and third waves placed the 2nd Battalion south of the 3rd Battalion. They assembled on the beach and awaited word on the progress of the 3rd Battalion.[5] 2nd Battalion scouts quickly discovered that their area was not heavily mined. They soon found out why when they discovered crates of unused German S-mines a short distance from the beach. These were the dreaded "Bouncing Betty" type. Most of the buried mines they had encountered up to that point were of the smaller "shoe mine" variety. "Shoe mines" were made of wood and difficult to detect, but held only enough explosive charge to wound or maim. A soldier unlucky enough to step on one usually lost a foot or leg. "Bouncing Betty" mines were far more destructive. They were about the size of an oil quart can and filled with buckshot. When triggered, the mine jumped about six feet high and sprayed the steel pellets everywhere.[6] A Bouncing Betty could take down an improperly dispersed infantry squad. Evidently, the Germans did not have time to plant these more destructive mines.

The 2nd Battalion, however, did not take their section of the beach unscathed. At 8:45 A.M., two German artillery shells screamed down from hills and exploded one hundred yards from the shoreline. The 2nd

Battalion men scrambled for cover. About a minute later, two more exploded in the same vicinity. The sudden attack snuffed out the lives of two enlisted men from F Company.[7] Both died instantly when hot razor sharp shrapnel whizzed through the air and ripped into their bodies. The harassment continued for another forty-five minutes as Army spotter planes crisscrossed the skies above seeking the source.

This incident marked the only artillery fire the Germans were able to place on the middle section of Pampelonne beach.[8] The effort was pointless, for by this time the invasion could not be turned back. By 9:30 A.M., the troublesome guns fell silent. Perhaps they were knocked out or maybe the crew ran off to seek safety in the highlands. 2nd Battalion, still far ahead of schedule, advanced to the beach road and followed behind 3rd Battalion's northward push on Saint-Tropez.[9]

As a bright beautiful morning sun arose over Pampelonne and burned off the haze, wave after wave of Higgins boats and DUKWs (amphibious trucks) beached in fifteen or twenty minute intervals.[10] The cyclic spectacle of arriving and departing boat waves underscored a message of inevitability. Most vessels reached shore without a problem. A few momentarily lodged on underwater obstacles before continuing on. Miraculously, none fell victim to underwater mines. Combat engineers and support personnel swarmed the dunes and fields, roping off the minefields and building makeshift roads. Others prepared the beach for the stockpiles of artillery, gasoline, jeeps, and trucks still waiting on larger ships in the bay. Additional engineering teams busily prepared the bay to allow the larger equipment-bearing vessels to anchor closer to the beach.

During the remaining morning hours, 3rd Battalion pushed steadily up the beach road and into the highlands overlooking Saint-Tropez. L and I Companies led the drive along opposite sides of the road—L on the left and I on the right. The road was free of mines, which made for a faster advance. Along the way, some enthusiastic FFI fighters volunteered to serve as guides and also helped to speed the advance.

A patrol scouting ahead of the L Company encountered a small but dangerous pocket of resistance along the road. Two enemy machine guns crews with supporting riflemen opened fire, sending the patrol scrambling for the ditch. The L men returned shots but with little results. One of the well protected enemy machine guns was positioned in a culvert.

Sgt. Melvin Singer, the patrol leader, ordered his men to remain in place and return fire. Singer circled around to the side of the German gun positions. Doing his best to stay low and undetected, he bypassed the first machine gun and worked his way toward the second. Once Singer reached a point where he could no longer move unobserved, he placed his M-1 rifle on his hip and bolted across 100 yards of open ground toward the second machine gun position— moving in leaps and bounds while firing for effect. An attack from such an unexpected direction momentarily stunned the Germans. Panicked, they swung the machine gun around and fired wildly at the lone American. Fortunately for Singer, the Germans were unable to zero in on him. The best they could manage was to kick up dirt and sand around his fast moving feet. Singer raised his rifle high and squeezed off a quick series of shots that killed three Germans outright and wounded two more. Fearing that more Americans might swarm in from another unexpected direction, the remaining Germans promptly surrendered to the sergeant, whose men by this time were racing forward to assist him. Both machine guns were captured intact, together with twenty-four additional prisoners who were sent back to the beach for interrogation.[11]

The 3rd Battalion encountered several additional pockets of resistance in the morning push toward Saint-Tropez, but most were small and uncoordinated. Two strong points displayed some tenacity. Company I ran into a network of German machine-guns within an hour of the landing. The defenses were overcome without the death of a single I Company member, but a platoon lieutenant's arm was nearly severed from a burst of sub-machine gun fire.[12] In another engagement, the 3rd Battalion's anti-tank platoon encountered two stubborn German machine gun positions hidden in the foothills and had to use bazookas to knock them out.[13]

The veterans of the 3rd Battalion realized early on that they were not facing the best soldiers of the German Army. Their defensive tactics were sloppy and the machine gun positions poorly chosen. Most of the defenders were quick to surrender.[14] Many didn't even look German. A good portion were Azerbaijani Russians captured and impressed into German military service or had been anti-Bolshevik volunteers from the early days when Germany's invasion of the Soviet Union seemed more like liberation than conquest.

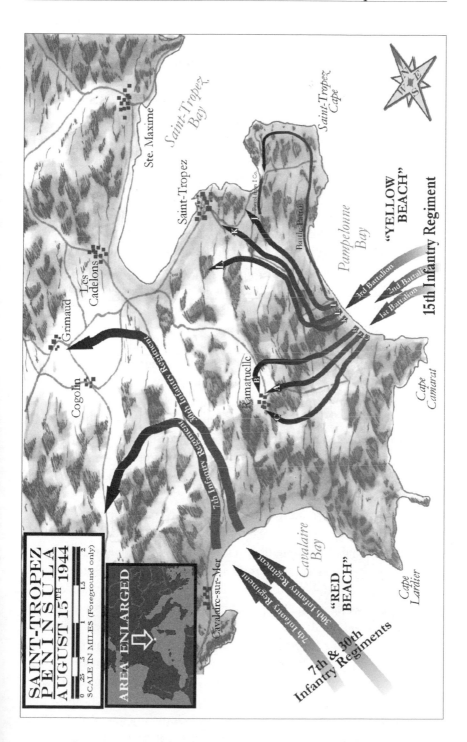

Aside from a single prisoner, no one spoke English. Those who spoke German reported that they were from the 807th Ost ("East") Battalion. Three months earlier, their battalion was reassigned the "4th Battalion" to the 765th Grenadier Regiment of the 242nd Division, and placed along the beach.[15] Although they wore gray German uniforms, they were sorry representatives of the Fatherland. Many were in poor physical and fighting condition, and happily surrendered their weapons with bright and in some cases, toothless smiles. Their hearts were obviously not in the fight.[16] Some gave up as soon as their German officers surrendered, while others bitterly complained that their officers abandoned them.[17] They made docile prisoners, and most of them were relieved they had survived the horrifying dawn bombardment and were now permanently out of harm's way. They were also overly appreciative when they received a small bite to eat or a cigarette. Even the toughest GI couldn't help but feel some sympathy for these hard-luck Osttruppen (Eastern Troops).

By early afternoon, L Company established roadblocks in the hills overlooking Saint-Tropez. In the process, they captured another collection of soldiers with little fight left in them. This small group was composed of German engineers and a barbwire-laying team.[18] During the operation, an odd assortment of about a dozen FFI fighters slipped past L Company, evidently on some secret mission of their own. Each of the fighters was properly mannered, impeccably dressed, but somewhat elderly. Pfc. Patrick "Joe" Rodger, an L Company rifleman, commented that they "looked like a bunch of squires."[19]

Seven American paratroopers emerged from the nearby woods to join up with the L Company grunts for a short time. Part of the 509th Parachute Infantry Battalion, they had been scattered over the area prior to dawn twenty miles south of their intended drop zone. Some of their buddies touched down in Saint-Tropez Bay and drowned. The paratroopers were not a happy bunch. The airdrop error left them disorganized and out of communication with the rest of their unit. They told of surviving the horrific beach bombardment and a nasty shoot out with a German patrol. They got the best of that patrol, they boasted, pulling out plenty of souvenirs to prove it.[20] Relieved to see other Americans, they tagged along with L Company until others from their unit were located. On L Company's right, I Company made contact with Battle Patrol east of Saint-Tropez, taking eight more prisoners in the process. The way was now clear for the 2nd Battalion to make a final push on the town of Saint-Tropez itself. According to some of the prisoners, only eighty German soldiers held the town.[21]

By mid-afternoon, the 2nd Battalion passed through L and I Company positions on the way toward town. In advance of the attack, the Navy began shelling Saint-Tropez at 3:15 P.M.[22] A brief but sharp fight at on old lighthouse west of town erupted before F Company reached the town proper.[23] Once there, they learned from French civilians that most of the Germans left to defend the place had fled across the harbor by boat the evening of August 13th.[24] To their surprise, they also discovered that American soldiers were already in the town. A rag-tag group of about 250 paratroopers from the 509th Parachute Infantry Battalion and the 463rd Parachute Artillery were already securing the town with the assistance of the local FFI.[25]

The paratroopers accidentally dropped around Saint-Tropez numbered in the hundreds, and were part of the First Airborne Task Force. They were supposed to land twenty miles north and help secure the key regional crossroads at Le Muy. Most of the First Airborne hit their objective, but some of the C-47 pilots became disoriented by low cloud cover in the night. With dawn approaching and fuel running low, the paratroopers jumped over Saint-Tropez. Captain Jess Walls, commander of C Company of the 509th, organized the remnants and made contact with the local FFI. Based upon their recommendations, Walls decided to move into Saint-Tropez with the men he had on hand. By the time F Company arrived, part of the town was already under the control of Walls' men and the FFI. F Company assisted in clearing out some German snipers and machine gunners holed up in a large hotel building in town.[26] By 5:30, the main part of town was scoured and deemed enemy-free.[27]

One last group of Germans stubbornly held out within a walled sixteenth century citadel east of town. Captain Walls contacted Colonel Thomas of the 15th Infantry Regiment and asked for more assistance in taking the old fortress. Colonel Thomas ordered K Company to join the attack. While K Company and a single tank destroyer moved in from the south, paratroopers and partisans attacked from the west. Once the heavy mortars of the 15th Infantry Regiment joined in the siege, the fortress fell in one hour.[28] The defenders raised a white flag up the main mast at 6:30 P.M., and sixty-seven German Marines walked out with their hands held high.[29] With their surrender, the port of Saint-Tropez was officially liberated.

Later that same afternoon, the full complement of "land" tanks for B Company of the 756th disembarked from several LCTs at Pampelonne Beach. All seventeen tanks were ferried in close to shore, where the LCTs could drop their front ramps in three feet of water. One by one, each tank drove off into the surf and plodded ashore under its own power.[30] The transfer went well, but a few of the tanks were swamped after hitting a hidden trench below the surf; B Company mechanics helped get them ashore.[31]

Captain David Redle, commander of B Company, stepped ashore on French soil for the first time. He would not miss Italy. Redle had been a member of the 756th Tank Battalion since September 1941, and was a veteran of most of the battalion's battles. After Captain Charles "Wilkie" Wilkinson was captured early in the fighting at Cassino, Redle was promoted from B Company's executive officer to its CO.[32] He guided the company through the Cassino breakout and many smaller battles along the road to Rome. After eight months as CO, Redle was adapting to fundamental shifts in how the infantry employed his tanks.

Cassino was one of the last times B Company fought together as a unit. Trained to fight together, tankers naturally preferred to operate with the strength and protection of numbers. An entire company or battalion of tanks attacking en-masse brought an enormous shock value to a battlefield. The effect was similar to the days when a mass of heavy cavalry fell upon a line of enemy infantry. In fact, much of the "armor doctrine" taught to the tankers at Fort Knox Kentucky, had its foundation in cavalry experience. General George S. Patton, a former cavalry officer, preferred to wield large tank concentrations across a battlefield like a giant ax. General Eisenhower, however, hailed from the more methodical and deliberative infantry school. The war in Europe was under Ike's control, meaning the tanks moved with the infantry.

The infantry preferred having the tanks close by. Experience showed that the troops advanced more aggressively when they had tank support.[33] An M4 Sherman provided the infantry with moving cover from small arms fire. Its 75mm gun also made short work of any pillbox, machine gun nest, or foxhole of snipers along the way. To get the foot soldiers their tanks, a typical infantry division such as the 3rd Division, was usually assigned a single tank battalion with fifty-four medium tanks and seventeen light tanks.[34] The tanks were then "farmed out" in small units so that every infantry company could have access to them.

This "farming out" solution may have made the infantrymen more aggressive, but the doctrine gave the tankers serious concern. The Sherman was a practical wonder of American mass production, but it was also a weak battle tank. German medium or heavy tanks were on the whole far superior, boasting thicker armor and far more powerful guns. In a one-on-one match, M4s were at a distinct disadvantage. Even from point blank range, an M4 could not penetrate the frontal armor plate of either a German Panther or Tiger tank. In stark contrast, either German model could drive a projectile through the front of a Sherman from as far as 2,000 yards.[35] American tankers learned to knock out German panzers by ganging up on them the way a pack of wolves might take down a moose. Sherman crews utilized numerical strength to outflank and kill a German tank by striking its thinner armor along its sides or rear. For these reasons, American tank crews did not like operating alone or in sections smaller than a platoon. Upcoming operations in Southern France would soon put their concerns to the test.

Captain Redle's B Company was assigned to the 15th Infantry Regiment, and each of his three M4 platoons was further dispersed to each of the regiment's three battalions. At that level, the tank platoon was used at the discretion of the infantry battalion commanders. Some deployed the five-tank platoon as a unit, while others sent smaller sections or individual tanks into battle. Redle didn't like the practice, but couldn't do much about it other than to try and educate infantry officers on the capabilities and the limitations of his tanks.

This arrangement shifted his responsibility from that of the company's tactical leader to a role more akin to mother hen. With his platoons distributed all across the countryside, Redle's regular challenge was to make sure his men received the rations, ammunition, and gas they required. While operating this way during the drive on Rome, Redle maintained his command post near the front at an equidistant point from his three platoons. This way, he could monitor the communications of the crews in battle and quickly respond to their needs.[36] Usual re-supply trips took place after dark, which resulted in many nerve-wracking "lights-off" jeep rides and nights without sleep.

Captain Redle remained remarkably resilient throughout the dizzying challenges confronting his command. His men admired him for his approachability, sincerity, and impeccable honesty. Redle grew up in a large Catholic family in Sheridan, Wyoming. While earning his degree in chemistry at Creighton University, he enrolled in the ROTC (Reserve Officer Training Corps), graduated in 1941, and was assigned to Fort Lewis, Washington, with the newly formed 756th Tank Battalion. At the time, the battalion was a "light" tank outfit without any tanks, and most battalion members had yet to be issued pistols or rifles.[37] The U.S. had only begun to build up its military arsenal to catch up with the out-of-control events of the world. After the Japanese attack on Pearl Harbor later that year, the 756th was rushed to Montesano, Washington (still without tanks) to defend against a possible Japanese invasion.[38] Redle liked to joke that he was a tanker before tanks.

Redle was slight of build—just over five feet eight inches tall and very thin, but had a steadfast and rock solid spirit.[39] His best friend, 1st. Lt. Roger Fazendin, was seriously wounded in Italy. "In that small fellow there was a lion's heart," Fazendin later wrote of Redle.[40] Redle drew great strength from a quiet and profound religious faith. One of his sisters was a nun who prayed constantly for his safety. Every bit helped.

In the field, Redle dressed down like a regular GI and maintained such a low-key bearing that he virtually melted away among any crowd of soldiers. However, he was always engaged, always learning, and always processing. His sharp mind absorbed and recalled every detail he took in—no matter how miniscule—with the firm belief that any tidbit might someday prove to be the difference between life and death.

Redle also had a reputation for being extremely lucky, so much so that at Cassino a dark joke circulated through the battalion to avoid standing by Redle in combat situations. The joke went that if someone was going to get hit, it wasn't going to be him. One cold wet night, a German artillery barrage sent everyone scrambling for cover. Captain Robert Rydman, another battalion officer, dove beneath a nearby tank. To his chagrin, if not to his horror, he discovered Redle already taking cover there. Rydman started swearing until both men burst out laughing. Redle was quite aware of the joke, too.[41]

Redle may or may not have led a charmed life, but he was certainly not carefree. He constantly fretted over the welfare of his men. Being out of contact with his three tank platoons drove him to distraction. From time to time, he had to live without knowing what was going on with the crews he cared for so deeply. August 15, 1944 was one of those times.

The evening before, Redle slept on the open deck of the LST transporting the bulk of B Company for the invasion. From there, he could observe the predawn bombardment of the shoreline and watch the general assault unfold. His DD-tanks were prepared on a separate vessel much closer to the action. The smoke and haze along the shoreline made their deployment impossible for Redle to observe.[42] Because of the distance and limitations of the FM radios aboard the DD-tanks, Redle was also unable to monitor the communications between the DD-tank commanders throughout the morning and early afternoon. Although nearly eight hours had passed since the landings, Redle still had no clear idea what had happened to them.

Once Redle arrived ashore with his small headquarters section, he established a command post and asked 1st Sgt. Alvin Nusz to radio Lt. Orient. After a few moments, Orient's voice crackled in response and informed Nusz and Redle of the platoon's disposition. Despite the early tank problems for Anderson and Oliver, all the men were safe and well. The news washed over Redle in a wave of relief.

Throughout the sweltering day, the tanks of Lt. Orient and Sgt. Stout supported the 1st Battalion at the southern half of the peninsula. They encountered beach and terrain remarkably similar to the Italian practice areas between Gaeta and Formia, and the hills near Mondragone.[43] Two tank destroyers from B Company of the 601st Tank Destroyer Battalion also joined that drive.[44] After the 1st Battalion secured the southern section of the beach, they moved west into the hills toward the old walled town of Ramatuelle. After a brief but vicious fight, the town of Ramatuelle fell around 2:00 P.M. and large groups of prisoners were rounded up and marched back to the beach.[45] Patrols were dispatched farther west to "Red Beach" to establish contact with the 7th and 30th Infantry Regiments.

American casualties were somewhat higher at Red Beach than they were at Yellow Beach. During the 8:00 A.M. assault, two Higgins Boats from the 7th Infantry Regiment hit underwater mines. The resultant blasts blew apart the boats and those unlucky enough to have been onboard.[46] Four DD-tanks from the 756th Tank Battalion's A Company attacked with the first wave. As with Lt. Orient's platoon at Pampelonne, the A Company DD-tanks rolled into the water approximately 2,000 yards out and plodded toward shore while Navy rockets soared overhead. One of the rockets careened out of control and exploded into a shower of shrapnel above the DD-tank piloted by Sgt. Norman Fuller. The explosion killed the sergeant instantly, earning him the unfortunate distinction of being the first battle death in southern France for the 756th Tank Battalion. Fuller's crew valiantly pressed ahead, only to strike a mine. Fortunately, the four remaining crewmembers were able to bail out before the tank plummeted to the bottom. Another Company A DD-tank commander was shot in the stomach by enemy gunfire.[47] By comparison, Lt. Orient's tankers had been extremely fortunate.

With the seventeen "land" tanks of B Company ashore, arrangements were made to replace the four DD-tanks with the original tanks of their platoon. No one intended to use the DD-tanks beyond the first day. Sgt. Anderson was the only one to get his "land" tank right away. Orient and Stout had traveled too far inland and would have to make their exchanges later.[48] Oliver's regular tank arrived off the LCT with mechanical problems, so a maintenance crew repaired the thrown track on his DD-tank. Once fixed, Oliver moved off to join the others in the highlands.[49]

During the late afternoon and evening hours, the 2nd and 3rd Battalions cleared out a few remaining pockets of resistance in the hills and along the shoreline west of Saint-Tropez. At 8:00 P.M., the 2nd Battalion captured twenty-seven prisoners from blockhouses along the southwest highway out of Saint-Tropez.[50] They were among the last taken captive that first day.

The day was spectacularly successful—far better than anyone imagined it would be. In a little over twelve hours, the entire peninsula was under the control of the 15th Infantry Regiment with the 7th and 30th Infantry Regiments securing additional territory to the west. During the same time period, the 3rd Division captured more than 1,600 prisoners, with the 15th Infantry Regiment alone responsible for 822 taken in the Yellow Beach sector.[51]

Across the Côte d'Azur, the concurrent landings of the 45th and 36th Infantry divisions met with similar success. Despite the scattered early morning drop, paratroopers of the 9000-strong First Airborne Task Force accomplished their mission of capturing key road junctions around Le Muy.[52] A firm beachhead had been established across the coastline with minimal resistance. "We broke a very thin crust", was the succinct summary analysis of one American officer.[53]

Thin or not along the coast line, no one seriously believed that one good day was a harbinger of things to come. The coastal forces encountered so far were not the best the Wehrmacht had to offer. German armor was conspicuously absent. Evidently, their fearsome panzers and best troops were being withheld to fight for another day. The obvious reason would be for a counterattack.

Indeed, the Seventh Army planners were expecting one. Eight months earlier, the first day of the Anzio invasion also went remarkably well. However, not enough men and material were put ashore to sustain an immediate breakout. The Germans had several days to react and counterattack, erecting a stout defense that ground the invasion to a stalemate. That initial Allied delay ultimately extracted the high price of a very costly breakout on May 23rd, or four months after the first troops landed at Anzio. Allied planners were determined to avoid repeating that mistake. Operation Dragoon planners provided everything necessary to expand the beachhead right away. To ensure this, extra artillery was packed aboard the supply ships, even at the expense of gasoline.

With dusk descending, all three battalions and attached armor of the 15th Infantry Regiment assembled at the small town of Cogolin in the hills immediately west of the landing zone.[54] As soon as a column moved forward, the men began a march that would last all night and into the following morning.

Chapter Five

Across Southern France

The morning of August 16 dawned, promising another scorcher of a day. As the sun rose, the beach at Pampelonne erupted into a beehive of Allied activity. Large transport vessels pulled in close to the shoreline to drop off enormous stockpiles of equipment, including field artillery, anti-aircraft guns, additional tank destroyers, supplies, and of course, more men. Once empty, these ships withdrew quickly to make room for sister ships disgorging similar manifests. Army and Navy engineers cleared beach roads with bulldozers and laid steel mesh for a makeshift airfield. Minefields had been meticulously roped off, and steely-nerved engineers were delicately probing the sand with bayonets and digging up every deadly box they could find.

Twenty miles to the west and northwest, the three regiments of 3rd Division were pushing inland as fast as their vehicles, legs, and the blazing heat would allow. As the 7th Infantry pushed west along the coast toward Toulon, the 30th and 15th Infantry regiments drove northwest to seize the main highways threading through the region.

The men of the 15th Infantry Regiment and both B Companies to the 756th Tank Battalion and the 601st Tank Destroyer Battalion, had enjoyed little rest since the landings. The assembly at Cogolin the preceding evening lasted only a few hours, barely enough time to clean guns, re-supply the tanks, and catch a few minutes of well-deserved sleep.

The march lasted all night long and continued well into the morning. The tired men pounded out more than twenty-three miles along a tight winding road through a rough, hilly terrain peppered with pine and cork oak forests. Though picturesque, the grueling march was particularly uncomfortable because the men were still wearing their hot, heavy, and

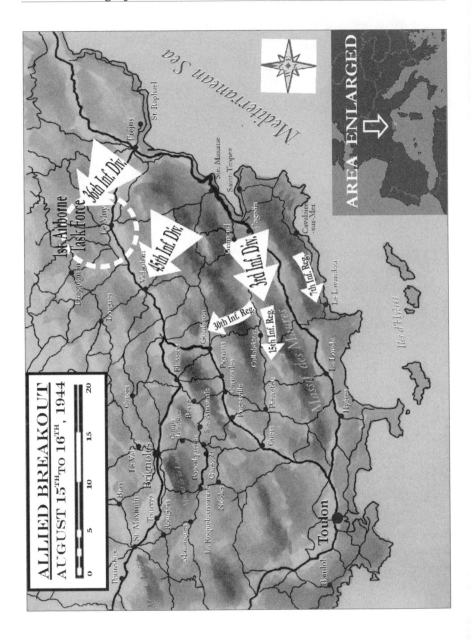

abrasive cool weather olive drab uniforms (ODs).[1] The lighter cotton uniforms had not arrived in time for the invasion.

The march was the classic "Truscott Trot," a grueling march regimen conceived by General Lucian Truscott when he commanded 3rd Infantry Division earlier in the war. Before the invasion of Sicily, Truscott had his men train vigorously under the hot North African sun and expected them to march five miles in one hour, four the next hour, and three in each remaining hour, all while carrying full equipment.[2] Those who couldn't cut it were shipped out of 3rd Infantry Division. General Truscott's soldiers also trained in water discipline, restricted to what they had in their canteens as they performed their strenuous maneuvers. This "skill" was also practiced during the Italian campaign.[3]

Despite Truscott's best efforts, the training didn't keep the equipment from feeling progressively heavier than it was as the day wore on. With the oppressive sun hanging high in the late-morning sky, some gave into temptation by dumping a spare box of ammunition or a heavy mortar stand along the roadside in order to continue forward a few pounds lighter. Later, a quartermaster truck retraced the route to recover the discarded equipment.[4]

The march was a particular challenge for those rotating in and out on the "flank patrols." These patrols were composed of infantry squads responsible for protecting the march. They fanned out and reconnoitered along either side of the column, making sure the enemy was not planning a surprise attack against the vulnerable flanks of the snaking column. Just maintaining the same pace as the rest of the column in the rough and hilly terrain was an exhausting task. Every now and then, flank patrols tangled with enemy snipers and machine gun positions burrowed into the brush.[5] Some Germans surrendered peacefully, but others refused and were killed.

Lt. Orient's four-tank platoon moved with the long infantry column, the individual tanks interspersed up and down its length. The doughboys took turns clinging to the turrets and tank decks to rest their aching feet. Inside, the crews were hot and stuffy but otherwise happy to be spared the marching. Tank hatches were latched open for fresh air, and Orient and his three commanders spent every second they could surveying the landscape for any hidden dangers. Every bend in the jagged road and every small hamlet presented an opportune location for a dreaded German anti-tank gun. Orient's men strained to stay alert for fear of meeting a fate similar to that suffered in Italy by so many tankers. Experience was a ruthless teacher.

Three of the DD-tanks had been replaced with regular M4s. Only S/Sgt. Oliver and his crew weren't able to make the exchange. After only one day of use, the canvas skirt and inflatable wraparound of Oliver's DD-tank had taken a beating. Torn flaps were hanging and dragging along the hot asphalt. It looked like a slow-moving elephant pulling along a khaki circus tent.

Sgt. Anderson and his crew were pleased to be back inside their old tank. The steel box had been theirs since the Cassino days, and by now, after so much, felt like home. But like all the men, Anderson was far from home. The tanker hailed from southern Illinois, where he grew up on a farm. When he was old enough to work, he took a job at Alcoa Aluminum. Twenty-one and single when the war broke out, Anderson was quickly snatched by the draft and dropped into the Army. He trained first with an infantry anti-tank unit at Camp Wheeler in Georgia, where he learned every possible way to kill a tank, from 37mm anti-tank "cannons" to Molotov cocktails. The instructors knew every way to exploit a tank's many vulnerabilities. The training taught Anderson a lesson; anyone who volunteered for tank service had to be out of his mind. Once graduation day arrived, Anderson and about a dozen others traveled to Fort Dix, New Jersey, where they joined their new unit before shipping overseas. In typical Army fashion, instead of being assigned to an anti-tank unit, Anderson and his buddies were assigned as tank crewmen in the 756th Tank Battalion. Some of Anderson's friends went AWOL when they found out.[6]

Like so many others, Anderson learned "on the job" how to be a soldier—or in his specific case, a tanker. In time, he became a driver—and a darn good one. Teamed up with Oliver, Bert Bulen, Ed Sadowski, and George Davis, they became a close-knit team, fighting and surviving through very tough times. His actions during the bloodshed of Cassino earned Anderson a promotion to sergeant and the command of his own tank. Oliver stepped up as platoon sergeant and was assigned a new driver to his crew.

S/Sgt. Haskell Oliver or "Ollie" was a sincere, soft-spoken Arkansan three days away from his twenty-ninth birthday. Though prematurely balding, Oliver had matinee-idol looks and a muscular build. In battle, he proved creative, aggressive, and 100% reliable. His many months of combat experience gave him a shrewd survivor mentality and an uncanny sixth sense for danger. Some men grew arrogant with experience, but Oliver remained just the opposite. He was more like a kindly elder brother—particularly attentive to any new replacement joining the platoon. Everyone who met Oliver couldn't help but love him. Captain Redle offered Oliver a battlefield commission more than once, but he turned it down each time. He was eminently qualified, but was either too humble to accept the promotion or simply following that sixth sense he possessed. He had watched as many lieutenants came and went, usually minus a dog tag. Oliver was a first class soldier, but he also wanted to return home alive.

George Davis was Oliver's Texan bow gunner who doubled as the crew's comedian and morale booster.[7] Oliver's gunner was Oklahoma native Bert Bulen.[8] Though on the small side, Bulen was blessed with exceptional reflexes, and had garnered a reputation as one of the best gunners in the company.[9]

The team's muscle came from loader Ed Sadowski, a big Pennsylvania steel worker[10] and a bull of a man who used to swim rivers as a kid.[11] Sadowski often seemed unaware of his own strength. Whenever he'd give a kindly slap on the back or shake a hand, he'd come close to breaking bones.[12] As loader, Sadowski was responsible for seating seventeen-pound 75mm rounds in the gun chamber. The job required agility, strength, and concentration, all particularly tricky to execute together under the pressures of battle. To arm the main gun, Sadowski cradled the bottom of a round with the left hand and with one swift motion, drove the shell into the chamber with the top part of the right fist. Because the same movement also automatically closed the breechblock, one slight misstep could lead to severed fingers or a broken hand or arm. After the gunner fired, the breechblock swung open and ejected the hot casing onto the turret floor so the gun would be ready to reload. Sadowski had to be prepared for the tank commander to call out one of three shell choices: "HE" for high explosive, "AP" or "shot" for armor piercing, and "smoke" for white phosphorus.[13] Normally Sadowski kept some of each at arm's length along the perimeter of the turret.

No other loader came close to matching Sadowski's speed for reloading the main gun. He could have it ready to re-fire almost as soon as the casing was ejected. One day at Cassino, Oliver's crew had the unenviable task of knocking out a German Mark IV tank hidden in the town ruins. The Mark IV had heavier armor and a gun with twice the muzzle velocity of Oliver's Sherman. Oliver's crew had the advantage of knowing where the Mark IV was, and of course, they had Sadowski. Oliver's tank spun around a street corner to confront the Mark IV, with Sadowski pumping rounds into the chamber as fast as Bulen could fire them. The rounds struck the German tank one after the other, destroying it before it could even return fire. Later that evening, some of the Germans prisoners taken from the ruins that day kept asking to see the "automatic loading Sherman."[14]

Because of the Sherman tank's glaring design deficiencies, American tankers learned to rely more heavily on teamwork, initiative, and intelligence. The four tank crews in Orient's platoon were close-knit "families," each with unique and complementary qualities that gave the platoon a special edge. Captain Redle thought they had the best *esprit d' corps* he'd ever seen in a tank platoon.[15] Although Orient's platoon was usually shortchanged a tank (four rather than the full compliment of five), the men never bitched about their lot or handicapped themselves. They simply did their best regardless of the circumstances.

By the early afternoon of August 16, Orient's tanks and the exhausted 3rd Battalion infantry arrived at the small town of Collobrères. Fortunately, the long march from Saint-Tropez involved no major encounters with the Germans. Most had cleared the area ahead of the American advance. The townsfolk of Collobrières turned out with enthusiasm to greet their liberators. Similar scenes of civilian gratitude would be repeated many times in the days to come.

The division arranged for water trucks to arrive soon after, and the men were able to refill their canteens and stave off dehydration.[16] With a few free hours, they were also finally able to secure some meaningful rest. Most pulled off their boots, swapped wet socks for dry ones, and found shady places to rest.[17]

Some welcome news filtered down from General O'Daniel; for the next few days, the 15th Infantry Regiment would follow in reserve behind the advance of the 7th and 30th Infantry regiments. On the offensive, American infantry units usually moved in the form of an inverted triangle. This tactical concept was employed from the army level down to squad level. As a division moved, two forward regiments attacked abreast of one another on left and right flanks while the third regiment followed behind them. Regiments periodically rotated to give everyone a break from frontline combat. The reserve regiment had the responsibility of cleaning out any remaining pockets of resistance while remaining ready to reinforce either assault regiment. Obviously, most GIs preferred the less demanding tasks of a reserve unit to the challenges of being in front.

Pfcs. Ciancanelli, Leithner, and McNamara used the down time to try out their song-and-dance routines on the locals and catch up on some reading and letter writing. Ciancanelli thumbed through a GI newspaper and saw an article about the Baby Ruth Company shipping thousands of boxes of free candy to the guys at the front. With great indignation, he flashed the article to his buddies. No one in L Company received any of this candy. Ciancanelli figured the rear echelon boys must have pilfered their allotment. Still steamed, he wrote a letter to the Baby Ruth Company. No one thought Ciancanelli had a snowball's chance in Hell of hearing back, but the energetic Chicagoan remained undaunted. If anything, his action was one of hope. First, that the candy bar company would respond to his request for a special delivery; and second, that he would be around to receive it.

Pfc. Earl V. Potter was a runner and an assistant to Communications Sgt. Luther Dillie in company headquarters. An eighteen-year-old Michigan kid, Potter stood five feet six inches tall and barely tipped the scales at 115 pounds.[18] He'd been with 3rd Division Reconnaissance before contracting yellow jaundice in December 1943, an illness that demanded hospitalization for several months.[19] He joined L Company at the end of May as one of the many replacements brought in to refill the ranks after the Anzio breakout.[20] Though he had spent the entire summer working alongside Captain Coles in the company headquarters, the captain was forever confusing him with another small guy in the company named Pvt. Patrick McEldowney.[21]

While near Collobrières, L Company HQ was established in a building that had once served as a restaurant and bar before the German occupation. Potter and some of the other HQ personnel took seats at the old dusty bar. Coles sat across the room, conducting business at one of the tables. Potter had just purchased a fancy brown leather belt from a local. Deciding to show a little individual flair, he replaced his olive drab army-issue belt with his newfound treasure.

A few moments later, Coles sounded off from across the room, "Hey, Mack." Nobody responded at first. No one in the room had that nickname. Coles growled again, only louder this time. "Hey, MACK!"

One of guys elbowed Potter and gestured for him to turn around: "I think the captain's talking to you."

Suddenly, Potter registered the connection: Coles called McEldowney by the nickname of "Mack," and he was confusing the two of them again.

Potter turned around abruptly and stood at attention. "Yes, sir!"

Coles pointed to Potter's waist. "Where did you get that belt?"

Potter stammered, "I don't know . . . back up the road . . ."

"It's not regulation." Coles cut in. "Get if off and report to 3rd Platoon."

The fact was that too many men were assigned to headquarters, and Potter had just gave his captain a reason to move one of them out. Disappointed with himself, Potter replaced the belt and reported to S/Sgt. Sam Badalamento in the 3rd Platoon. With a newly issued Tommy gun, Potter's recon days had suddenly returned.

About an hour after reporting, 3rd Platoon and a tank moved out to reconnoiter a small town. They arrived and found the place completely free of Germans. The townspeople welcomed them warmly, and soon all were partaking in a wonderful celebration that lasted well into the evening. Though the retreating Germans confiscated most of the town's food, the Americans and French organized a bountiful fish fry by tossing concussion grenades into a nearby millpond. Maybe the transfer out to 3rd Platoon wasn't such a bad thing after all, mused Potter.[22]

After dark, some of the guys from 1st Platoon discovered a cow tied up inside a nearby house. One of them tracked down Cogdell and asked him to serve up some chocolate milk. Cogdell arrived, set down his BAR, and took off his helmet to use as a bucket. He shined a small light under the animal to locate the udder and hesitated for a second or two. A broad grin greeted the expectant faces waiting in the room. "I can't help you," Cogdell told them, "but you are sure welcome to try it yourself." The cow was a bull.

"You have to know the difference first," Cogdell chuckled. He flipped his helmet back on his head, grabbed his BAR and headed back out the door, laughing at all the sad-faced city sophisticates in the room.[23]

Southern France had begun well for L Company, but the men knew their luck couldn't last. The other two regiments were pushing ahead and encountering serious pockets of resistance, and other companies in 15th Infantry Regiment were still busy cleaning up some of the leftovers. Late in the afternoon of August 16, G Company of 2nd Battalion, Battle Patrol, and the tanks of 2nd Platoon were sent eight miles west of Collobrières to the town of Pierrefeu. The 2nd Battalion of the 30th Infantry Regiment took the town earlier and was preparing to move out. Nevertheless, when the men of the 15th arrived in relief, they encountered a by-passed pocket of resistance on a ridge southeast of town. A firefight broke out for some time until twenty-nine Germans surrendered. Throughout the evening, G Company and its support maintained the roadblock with wide-eyed vigilance.[24]

Twenty miles to the northeast, the paratroopers from 1st Airborne Task Force landing near Draguignan and Le Muy had wreaked havoc all day. After landing and organizing, they cut all communication wire in sight, and isolated and captured the German LXII Armeekorps headquarters. Though the Germans were still reeling from the shock of the invasion, the Americans fully expected them to quickly regroup and bite back hard.

On the morning of August 17, the bulk of 15th Infantry Regiment fanned out northwest of Collobrières in the textbook inverted triangle formation. 1st Battalion, along with tanks of 1st Platoon and TDs of 2nd Platoon of B Company / 601st Tank Destroyer Battalion, set out shortly before 6:00 A.M. The march was along a wickedly jagged mountain road that wound its way through the Pignans Forest. The men and vehicles moved as the regimental "right" flank while 2nd Battalion moved on the left toward Pierrefeu. 1st Battalion passed through Pignans and Carnoules, but met little opposition along the way. The battalion stopped about noon at Besse to avoid getting too far ahead of everyone else. The long sweaty march covered another twenty-five miles, but the terrain was finally becoming easier on the feet and lungs.[25] The men had crossed the Massif Des Maures, the craggy mountain chain separating the Saint-Tropez peninsula from the interior farmland of provincial France. The sharp hills had softened into beautiful green rolling countryside dotted with serene medieval hamlets and timeless fieldstone farms topped with gleaming roofs of burnt orange tile. Picturesque southern France was simply too beautiful a place to be fighting a war.

A few hours later, 3rd Battalion accompanied by a platoon of towed 57mm antitank guns, Lt. Orient's tanks, and the TDs of Lt. William "Bones" Finley's 3rd Platoon, retraced the same route. Because they served as the regiment's reserve battalion, they held up at Pignans momentarily as 1st Battalion secured Besse. In terms of military encounters, the move was rather uneventful, but the march itself never lacked for excitement. Joyful civilians appeared everywhere to shower the arriving Americans with gratitude and press gifts of wine, bread, and fresh fruit into their passing hands.[26] Many types of food were scarce in southern France, and the GIs were amazed at what the French were willing to share with them. Although the U.S. Army tried to discourage the men from accepting food beyond what was officially served up, the policy was impossible to enforce and almost universally ignored.[27]

The French were astonished to see so many young, smooth-faced American soldiers. They'd grown accustomed to an occupation force of older German soldiers—from dour middle-aged administrators to beleaguered Russian Front veterans matured beyond their years by the hard fighting and reassigned to the Riviera to mend their broken spirits.[28] Americans, the French quickly discovered, were infectiously happy by way of comparison. They whistled, joked, and smiled. Though in a constant hurry, they always found a spare moment to stop and distribute such luxuries as chewing gum and candy to wide-eyed French children, and cigarettes to the adults. One of the B Company tank platoon leaders taught his men how to sing the La Marseillaise phonetically—which thrilled the masses as the tankers passed by singing from their hatches.[29] The energizing American presence assured them that France's long national nightmare was nearly over, and that a wonderful bright future had arrived on their shores. The threat of combat and death was always waiting beyond the next hill or road bend, but the synergetic moments of French hospitality and youthful American enthusiasm made the war seem half a world away on that August day.

On the left flank near Pierrefeu, 2nd Battalion was still experiencing sporadic action. Pierrefeu was only twenty miles northeast of Toulon and close to where 7th Infantry Regiment and newly landed French units were pressing south along the coastline. That pressure was stirring up German activity throughout the area. Before midnight the previous evening, Companies E, F, and H of 2nd Battalion, the remaining 2nd Platoon tanks and 1st Platoon tank destroyers, scrambled west to

Pierrefeu to shore up G Company's positions and establish more roadblocks. At 2:00 A.M. and again at 4:00 A.M., several rounds of flat trajectory artillery landed near an E Company roadblock.[30] No one was sure if the attacks marked the opening salvos of a larger German plan, or whether it was just mild harassment. French civilians and FFI members in the area reported seeing more Germans lurking in the hills west of town, and as dawn approached two F Company men manning an outpost along a nearby ravine were nabbed by a stealthy German patrol. A larger American patrol moved as far west as Cuers to investigate and attempt a rescue of the missing men, but returned empty-handed.[31]

2nd Battalion continued to encounter harassing fire and scattered resistance throughout the day. The situation remained unstable as elements of the 7th Infantry Regiment arrived as relief later that afternoon. Even as 2nd Battalion troops boarded trucks headed north, French partisans were tangling with another group of twenty German soldiers on the outskirts of Pierrefeu.[32]

The day began sunny and hot, but clouds rolled in by the late afternoon and a heavy rain blanketed the entire region.[33] At first, the cool down-burst was welcome and refreshing. The clean rain rinsed sweaty faces and cooled the sun-baked steel of the tanks. But the deluge lasted until 9:00 P.M. By the time it was over, everyone was soaked down to their drawers and stank of wet heavy wool.

Back at Besse to the northwest, the civilian rail stationmaster warned a Cannon Company officer that 1,500 Germans were digging into the high hills north of town with the intent of trapping and knocking out any U.S. troops emerging north of Besse. The same Germans previously warned French civilians that they had until 7:00 P.M. to get out of town. The threat was taken seriously, and 3rd Battalion was ordered immediately up from Pignans to augment 1st Battalion positions already established near Besse.[34]

To everyone's relief, the attack never materialized. Either the threat was an idle one, or the Germans had become preoccupied with 30th Infantry Regiment's move behind them from Flassans toward Brignoles.

The city of Brignoles was crucial to both sides. Control of the Brignoles Valley meant control of National Route 7, the main east-west artery of southern France. For the Allies, Brignoles opened the way for seizing the regional communication hub of Aix and outflanking the Germans in Toulon and Marseille. If the Germans held any hope of containing and launching a counterattack against the beachhead, they had to hold Brignoles. Whether the Germans had the manpower to do it was an open question. They certainly did not have the armor within a hundred miles. 11th Panzer Division was still well east of the Rhône River and moving at a snail's pace. Because of the Allied control of the skies, the panzers could only move at night, and had to contend with blown bridges and constant FFI harassment.[35] The situation was a vexing challenge for even the most experienced German commanders.

The Germans proved masters of rearguard combat on the Italian peninsula, but southern France presented the Axis occupiers with far more difficult operational conditions. Chief among them was the U.S. Twelfth Air Force, which bombed the enemy with near-impunity because the Luftwaffe was virtually non-existent in that part of the country. Most German aircraft had been scrambled north to defend Normandy. Units from the German Nineteenth Army moved north for the same reason, including one of the three panzer battalions of the 11th Panzer Division. This and other examples of cannibalized units triggered dark humor within the ranks of Nineteenth Army. A standing German joke at the time was that the 11th Panzer Division was an armored division without any armor.[36]

The French population grew increasingly unmanageable for their German occupiers—particularly as news of the Allied landings swept through southern France. Emboldened FFI operatives, FTP partisans (communist-led resistance), and other freelance groups sabotaged German activities every way they could. German communication lines were cut as quickly as they were strung. If a bridge offered a throughway for a moving German column, operatives blew it up. If two or three German soldiers wandered away from their unit, they often disappeared forever. The Germans saw little about the French Resistance to joke about. Many Germans were more afraid of the French irregulars roaming the countryside armed with rifles and patriotic vengeance than they were of the Americans with all their planes, tanks, and artillery. Unlike Italy, the German defense of southern France had quickly become tenuous and problematic.

General Friedrich Weise of the German Nineteenth Army held some hope of halting the Allied advance at Brignoles, but the loss of the LXII Armeekorps to paratroopers was a tremendous setback to his plans. The burden of establishing a defense at Brignoles fell upon the only remaining corps HQ of the Nineteenth Army, LXXXV Armeekorps under the command of Lieutenant General Baptist Kniess.[37] Kniess hastily moved elements of the German 338th and 242nd divisions toward Brignoles in an effort to shore up the badly battered 244th Division and establish some semblance of a defensive line.

The showdown for Brignoles shaped up rapidly. With 30th Infantry Regiment driving in from the east, 15th Infantry Regiment found itself in an ideal position to take up the southern flank in the attack. In the early evening hours, 3rd Battalion passed through 1st Battalion positions at Besse and pushed out into the high hills west as the regimental spearhead—methodically working along either side of the road running from Besse to the country town of Sainte-Anastasie. Beyond Sainte-Anastasie was Forcalqueiret, a crossroad town about six miles to the south of Brignoles. Forcalqueiret was designated "Phase Line Chicago." 3rd Battalion's orders were to reach and secure Forcalqueiret that evening.

*   *   *

Captain Coles was restless. Two days had passed since the beach landings and L Company had yet to see any real action. As his men fanned out along the road and eyed the hills, Coles buzzed back and forth in his jeep encouraging them to pick up the pace westward.[38] Darkness was fast approaching and they still had one town and about five miles waiting between them and Forcalqueiret.

A series of short-burst automatic fire barked out from woods on a hillside near the road. No one was hit, but the sudden disruption sent the L Company doughs scrambling for the cover of ditches and tree trunks. Coles was not at all pleased with the delay. He dispatched a 2nd Platoon squad to investigate and eliminate the problem. The squad maneuvered up the hill until it located the source of trouble; a German machine gun nest manned by four soldiers. The American squad rapidly outflanked and overran the nest, leaving two Germans dead and the other two wounded. Satisfied the area was clear, the squad leader sent a runner to Coles to report the situation and obtain orders on what to do with the two wounded prisoners.

The runner returned a short time later, though without clear instructions on how to handle the custody of the two slightly wounded prisoners. Coles was more intent on avoiding further delays and seemed uninterested in their fate. Some FFI fighters tagging behind the squad offered to take the prisoners. The young Americans agreed to the transfer, thinking the FFI would escort the two men back to the nearest prisoner stockade. Instead, to their horror, the French irregulars marched the wounded men some distance away, shot them, and stripped them of everything of value. It was only then the Americans realized the FFI was fighting a completely different war.[39]

L Company and 3rd Battalion continued moving until they reached Sainte-Anastasie at dusk. Near the town, they encountered another group of fifty Germans. Shots were exchanged but the Germans had nothing beyond their standard Mauser rifles and Schmeisser machine pistols to counter the American advance. The brief skirmish ended with a German withdrawal.[40]

Lt. Col. Boye sent K Company ahead to reconnoiter Forcalqueiret from the nearby hills under cover of darkness. As a key crossroads town, he expected the place to be crawling with Germans. At the very least, he believed, they would spot a German roadblock near the village placed to protect the southern flank of their Brignoles position. A platoon of M8 howitzers from Cannon Company moved forward with 3rd Battalion in anticipation of a minor battle.[41] K Company worked a platoon up in the hills near Forcalqueiret to covertly observe the quiet village below. To the surprise of many, the place appeared absolutely quiet and serene.

K Company sent more patrols down into the village to confirm that the town was free of Germans. It was. The stunning news was sent to the battalion HQ. Boye took the gift and ordered both K and L Company to immediately occupy Forcalqueiret and establish roadblocks around the perimeter.

Rumors abounded of large numbers of Germans holding the high hills to the northwest between Forcalqueiret and Brignoles. Another K Company platoon trudged off into the darkness to investigate, but found nothing. Additional patrols probed beyond the town of Garéoult approximately two miles to the west, but still no Germans were observed.[42]

As Forcalqueiret fell without a shot, 2nd Battalion completed its move as reserve battalion from Pierrefeu to a new bivouac area along the road between Carnoules and Pignans.

Elsewhere that day, 7th Infantry Regiment made similar gains to the south, but at a heavier cost, securing the coastal town of La Londe on the push toward Toulon. To the northeast, 2nd Battalion spearheaded the advance of 30th Infantry Regiment. The battalion reached the outskirts of Brignoles at dusk, ran into some heavy resistance, and lost an M8 scout car and a tank destroyer to a German anti-tank gun.[43] The regiment held up outside the city for the evening and prepared to renew the attack at first light.

Farther northeast of the 3rd Division zone, 45th and 36th Divisions were also pushing rapidly into the interior of southern France, expanding the beachhead at a dizzying rate. Because of this early success, General Truscott ordered a special expeditionary unit dubbed "Task Force Butler" to assemble near Le Muy and strike toward Grenoble in the early morning hours. Task Force Butler was comprised of reconnaissance, motorized infantry, and armor from 36th Infantry Division.[44] Its mission was to drive fast and deep through the mountainous north with the aim of cutting off any German retreat into Germany. The plan was audacious and daring, but carried with it the tantalizing prospect of trapping an entire German army.

In the space of twenty-four hours, General Weise's response options had dramatically altered, not so much because of the advance of the U.S. Seventh Army or FFI sabotage, but as a result of events far beyond southern France. The Allies in the northern part of the country had broken out of the Normandy peninsula and were threatening to annihilate two entire German Armies in a huge snare called the Falaise Pocket.[45] Weeks earlier, the German High Command had warned Hitler that holding France would prove futile. They pressed for an immediate withdrawal to the Rhine, where they could prepare a far more formidable defense of the Fatherland in time for winter. Hitler dismissed the idea with his customary and notorious stubbornness. Now he had no choice but to double back on that decision.

On August 16, the order for the general withdrawal from France was dispatched to all German units. However, General Weise did not receive his order until late in the day on August 17. His orders were to withdraw immediately north to Dijon, though he was to leave the garrisons in Marseille and Toulon in place. Hitler's personal directive demanded that those garrisons fight to the death.[46]

The new orders simplified the challenges for General Weise and his Nineteenth Army. Released from the burden of defending a huge swath of territory, Weise could now fully concentrate on the survival of his army. Unfortunately for the German general, the Allies had decoded those same orders through ULTRA,[47] and Lieutenant General Patch of the U.S. Seventh Army was fully aware of Wiese's new instructions.[48]

★ Chapter 6
Toward Marseille

August 18 dawned with another warm clear morning. At sunrise, when a rested and geared up 30th Infantry Regiment resumed its westward drive into Brignoles, the Germans of 757th Infantry Regiment / 338th Division responded with spirited resistance. 30th was forced to make a more deliberative daylong attack in which 1st Battalion endeavored to outflank the defenders by maneuvering through the northern hills overlooking town.

To support 30th Infantry Regiment's advance on the center of the city, 3rd Battalion of 15th moved out and secured positions west and northwest of Forcalqueiret. At 11:00 A.M., I and K Companies, along with Orient's tanks and two TDs, pushed through Garéoult toward the towns of La Roquebrussanne and Mazaugues.[1] Their orders were to secure these towns, head north to Route 7 on the western edge of Brignoles, and prevent the German defenders from receiving reinforcements. As they approached La Roquebrussanne, they began meeting scattered resistance.

L Company remained behind in the town of Garéoult awaiting relief from A Company of 1st Battalion. With 3rd Battalion moving out, 1st Battalion took over at Forcalqueiret as reserve battalion.[2] Around the same time, 2nd Battalion set out on trucks from Carnoules, passing through Besse and Sainte-Anastasie, and finally through Forcalqueiret. From there, it continued north toward Camps-la-Source on the southeastern outskirts of Brignoles. This regimental right flank attack was designed to coincide with 3rd Battalion's northward attack on the left.

By noon, Companies I and K secured La Roquebrussanne and started out of town along the main road north.[3] Captain Warren Stuarts' I Company took the lead. Their next objective was a large hill known locally as the "Montagne de la Loube" rising ahead on the east side of the road. By gaining the north face of the heights, the battalion would have a clear view of Route 7. As Stuart's men pressed 1,500 yards out of town, a sudden hail of small arms fire erupting from the south side of Loube forced them to drop for cover. Stuart met the challenge with his usual deliberate and methodical approach. He ordered his men to fan out over the high ground east of the road and dismantle the opposition piece by piece. They spent the early afternoon systematically driving back the defenders.

By 2:30 P.M., however, as they neared the base of the hill, the Germans upped the ante by tossing in heavier fire from a network of machine gun nests. Beyond these defenses, a convoy of enemy vehicles was spotted moving along the road. Stuart called in the big guns of the tank destroyers, which promptly rolled forward and fired about twenty rounds of high explosive into the hillside. The machine guns fell silent, and two Germans surrendered. Stuart's men swept through the abandoned positions and tried to locate the German vehicles they had seen earlier, without success.[4]

At 3:00 P.M., Company L rejoined 3rd Battalion at La Roquebrussanne after being relieved at Garéoult by A Company, and assumed a reserve position behind K Company. I Company began investigating the slopes of the Montagne de la Loube, but encountered only a few infrequent rifle shots. The hill was huge, rising nearly 2,750 feet above sea level. It took four hours to survey it. By 8:50 that evening, the hill was theirs. The reward was a spectacular twilight view of the valley with Brignoles and Route 7 in the distance. The privilege came at the price of one dead and five wounded Americans.[5] Night was falling when a German high velocity gun zipped a few parting rounds in the direction of 3rd Battalion, though without effect.[6] Undaunted, I Company successfully dispatched a patrol to the town of Tourves on Route 7, six miles to the northwest.

Late that same afternoon, 2nd Battalion met with particularly stubborn resistance just north of Forcalqueiret. With F Company leading, the battalion attacked along the road south of Camps-la-Source toward its objective, a smaller hill dubbed "551." At 5:00 P.M., F Company stumbled into a heavy concentration of mortar, small arms, and high-velocity fire coming from a well-entrenched group of Germans on the hill.[7] The ferocity of the German reaction caught F Company off guard, and they initially suffered heavy casualties. The company remained pinned down until roughly 8:00 P.M., when G Company and three 2nd Platoon tanks from B Company moved forward to reinforce F's embattled position and regain the initiative.[8]

The reinforcements were not enough. The Germans—estimated to be a battalion or more—stubbornly clung to the hillside. The fighting intensified, and the entire 2nd Battalion was forced into a vicious and confusing engagement lasting well into the night.

A panzerfaust (a German anti-tank rocket fired by an infantryman) slammed into S/Sgt. Hamilton A. Smith's tank, killing Pvt. Walter F Smith and seriously wounding the driver, T/5 Albert Jaksys.[9] Smith and his gunner, Cpl. Donald LaDue, abandoned the wounded vehicle and sought refuge in a nearby ditch, where an incoming mortar round a few minutes later killed them both.[10] Word of their deaths was radioed back to Captain Redle, who was monitoring tank communications at his CP southwest of Forcalqueiret. These were his company's first losses in southern France. Smith was 2nd Platoon sergeant and a Silver Star recipient from the battle at Cassino.[11] The short, energetic, and humorous man and had been with B Company since the Fort Lewis days. LaDue was a tall, slender artist from Vermont with a kind, quiet temperament. Both would be sorely missed.

Losses were always tough on Redle, but they hit 1st Sgt. Alvin Nusz particularly hard.[12] Nusz had the responsibility of completing all the required paperwork for battle deaths, including notifying next-of-kin and sending home the personal belongings of his company's deceased tankers. These men were often long-time friends—as was S/Sgt. Smith and Cpl. LaDue. Nusz would laugh with them one day over a cigarette while making his mail rounds, and mourn them the next. He had the emotional task of identifying their bodies, which were often blown apart by shell fire. He had to sift through bloody pockets to locate letters, money, and Bibles . . . anything that might have sentimental value or bring tiny comfort to the dead man's family. Nusz also had to write that letter home to the mother, the father, the wife, or the sweetheart, informing them that a big empty hole had just been ripped in their lives that would never be filled.

Nusz was drafted about a year before the attack on Pearl Harbor at the age of twenty-one.[13] The son of a German immigrant farming family, he dropped out of school during the Great Depression to help support his family. He managed to finish high school just before he was drafted. Assigned to 756th Tank Battalion, Nusz landed with them at Casablanca, and was a tank commander by the time the unit reached Salerno, Italy, in late 1943.

One cold and wet day, Nusz's tank was rolling down a narrow mountain road with Nusz standing halfway out of the commander's hatch watching out for any difficulties. Suddenly, a mule-drawn wagon with an elderly Italian man at the reins emerged from beyond an upcoming road bend. Realizing his driver would not be able to stop in time, and wishing to avoid killing the civilian and his mule, Nusz yelled into his throat mike for his driver to make a hard right turn into the grade of the mountain. The split-second decision saved the Italian, his wagon, and his mule, but overturned Nusz's tank, pinning him backward against the muddy side of the mountain. If not for the turret machine gun mount, the accident would have killed the commander. As it was, he suffered a serious back injury that precluded him from ever returning to his beloved tank. After an extended hospitalization and once he regained some mobility, Nusz returned to B Company as first sergeant.[14]

Nusz made a fine first sergeant. He had flawless character, a flair for organization, and commanded the respect of all the men. Above all, he made Captain Redle's job a whole lot easier. Redle could concentrate on the battlefield and the tactical needs of his tank crews while Nusz handled the administrative details.[15] Unfortunately, those details included experiencing the very real, very personal costs of war in a way no one else did. To everyone else, S/Sgt. Smith, Cpl. LaDue, and Pvt. Smith were there one day and gone the next. Nusz was reminded of their deaths over and over again through the footlockers they left behind, the Graves Registration paperwork he had to complete, and the letters from loved ones that trickled in over the following weeks that he had to return marked "Deceased."

Meanwhile, near La Roquebrussanne, Lt. Col. Boye called upon Coles to dispatch a contact patrol to 2nd Battalion area of operation on the right.[16] Coles asked Sgt. Edmund Rovas, a squad leader from 3rd Platoon, to lead that patrol. To carry out the task, Rovas was given one of the two company jeeps, a driver, and a machine gunner named Farmer who was responsible for manning the .50-caliber machine gun mounted at the center. The three men set out immediately after sunset.

After ten minutes of cautious driving, they passed two shadowy figures walking by the roadside in the opposite direction. Although the two made no threatening moves, Rovas was suspicious and wanted a second, closer look. He told the driver to stop and back up. As they rolled within pistol range of the figures, Rovas motioned again for the driver to stop and the jeep skidded to a standstill. Rovas vaulted out and crouched with one knee on the ground. With his Tommy gun pointed and ready, he shouted out the call sign with a clear voice and waited for a response.

For several tense seconds, nothing happened.

When Rovas heard the unmistakable click of a German Schmeisser machine pistol being readied for action, he and the two Germans simultaneously opened fire on one another. A split second later, Farmer joined in from the jeep with the big .50-caliber M2. Tracers and sparks of lead bounded off the dark asphalt like an out-of-control Fourth of July fireworks show. Rovas felt one of the German bullets slam into right front side of his helmet with a metallic rap. The outburst lasted a few more seconds before Rovas and Farmer realized they were no longer being fired upon. When they took their fingers off the triggers, both men were certain the two Germans were either dead or had run away in the darkness. The firefight had alerted any other Germans in the area to their presence, so they weren't about to go chase anyone down or hang around and search for bodies. Rovas called off the patrol and started back for L Company.

As the adrenaline subsided during the ride back, Rovas suddenly realized he was bleeding from the right forehead. Only then did he recall that a bullet had slammed into his helmet. He pushed his hand up under the sweatband and tentatively felt his head, relieved when he did not find a bullet wound. When he took off the helmet, he discovered a hole blown through the side and the rear strap severed completely in two. The German bullet had missed his head by a mere half-inch. Shrapnel bits from his own helmet had pierced his right forehead, but did not penetrate to the bone. It was a very close call.

When Rovas and the jeep crew returned to L Company headquarters, company medic "Doc" Lefevre picked out the shrapnel from Rovas' forehead and dressed his wounds.[17] Lefevre wanted Rovas to rotate back to the Evac Hospital as a precaution, but the tough sergeant declined. He didn't believe that the wound was serious enough to justify any time away from his squad.

The next morning, Farmer and the jeep driver drove back to the site of the encounter and found the bodies of a German officer and an enlisted man. Both were riddled with .50-caliber bullet holes. They later told Rovas of their discovery. Although they were the enemy and one had nearly shot Rovas' head off, he considered their deaths a senseless waste. Why didn't they simply surrender?[18]

Brignoles fell to 30th Infantry Regiment on the night of Rovas' short jeep patrol. Most of the Germans retreated under the cover of darkness westward toward Aix, leaving behind a few defensive pockets to stall for whatever additional time they could. The retreat was so rapid that 3rd Battalion of 15th Infantry Regiment never had the opportunity to seal them off west of the town. Nevertheless, the short stand at Brignoles cost the Germans dearly. Almost the entire 757th Regiment of 338th Division was beaten, broken up, and killed or captured. The fall of Brignoles also ended the Germans' last best hope for halting the Allied breakout. 3rd Division was now free to rapidly advance on Aix and the suburbs of Marseille.

On the morning of August 19, as 30th Infantry Regiment mopped up the remaining resistance in Brignoles, 15th Infantry Regiment prepared to leap ahead in westward pursuit as the regimental spearhead. Before it could, however, it had to attend to some unfinished business. Southeast of Brignoles, 2nd Battalion of 15th Regiment was still trying to break the Germans holding Hill 551 north of Forcalqueiret. At dawn, Colonel Thomas called in a sustained artillery barrage upon the hillside to dislodge them once and for all. The heavy shelling stopped at about 7:50 A.M. and Companies F, G, and the remaining tanks of 2nd platoon rushed forward into the smoldering positions. Though weakened and shell-shocked, the German defenders managed to hold off the Americans for nearly two more hours before finally relenting at 9:30 that morning. The entire episode was a sobering reminder of the German soldier's fighting spirit and tenacity.

In the end, approximately 150 prisoners were rounded up, including two captains. Most were members of II Battalion to the German 757th Infantry Regiment. With the battle finally over, 2nd Battalion moved to La Celle on the southern outskirts of Brignoles to reorganize and take a needed turn as reserve battalion.[19]

Throughout the same morning, 3rd Battalion remained north of La Roquebrussanne awaiting word on 2nd Battalion's situation. Colonel Thomas wasn't about to allow 3rd Battalion to move ahead until Hill 551 was taken. The I Company patrol dispatched northwest to Tourves the previous evening returned in the early morning hours and reported seeing large groups of German soldiers and vehicles escaping via Route 7. The lack of action and the morning delay were particularly frustrating for action-minded Captain Coles.[20] Relief units from the French Army were already beginning to catch up with 3rd Battalion's rear positions between Forcalqueiret and La Roquebrussanne. When word finally came down that 2nd Battalion had seized the hill, 3rd Battalion was unleashed at 11:06 A.M. with instructions to take Tourves and drive after the retreating Germans.[21] If they had any hope of catching them, a lot of territory had to be covered in a hurry.

By now, the Allies held a swath of southern France fifty miles wide and roughly thirty miles deep. In only four days, U.S. Seventh Army had liberated nearly five hundred square miles—with no sign of stopping. Free French Army forces following the American assault had already pressed to within ten miles of the key port of Toulon. The Germans were ceding territory far faster than the invasion planners ever imagined. The fall of Toulon and Marseille was now considered achievable in only a matter of days instead of the weeks or even months originally envisioned. Sheer numerical superiority dictated the outcome. Still, not all the news was good. Allied ships along the Riviera were unloading untold numbers of crates of artillery shells for a tough and bloody breakout that was never going to happen. The invasion planners had pre-loaded those shells at the expense of fuel. With the Germans falling back, a vigorous pursuit was called for. Pursuits, however, are impossible without gasoline—a lot of gasoline.

Much of the invasion's success was due to the invaluable and dangerous work of the FFI. The FFI was a general acronym used to describe a loose collection of resistance groups working throughout France. Some were more viable and better organized then others. These disparate groups ran the political gamut, from hard-line communists of the FTP to far right nationalists, and were often at odds with each other in one way or another. However, all the groups shared the same goal, the expulsion of the Germans and the restoration of a free France.

Joining an FFI group was a supreme act of self-sacrifice. France was a nation of close-knit communities and extended families where trades passed from generation to generation. To join the FFI, a fighter had to completely renounce all prior social connections—including family.

British and American intelligence worked closely with many French resistance groups in southern France long before the landings. Daring intelligence officers such as Major Francis Cammaerts of the British SOE parachuted into France early in the war to help strengthen and coordinate the Resistance.[22] Periodic airdrops of guns, ammunition, and other vital supplies followed. In return, the FFI began making life very difficult for their German occupiers and provided priceless intelligence to Allied invasion planners.

Once the invasion of Southern France was on, the FFI stepped up all manner of operations. Their efforts created such havoc that the Germans often preferred to simply vacate an area rather than to contend with them. As a result, American forces often found towns free of Germans. Instead of being greeted by enemy soldiers, rag-tag FFI units poured out sporting homemade armbands, wide smiles, and bottles of wine. The contributions of the FFI, often gained at the cost of their members' own blood, saved hundreds and perhaps thousands of American lives and helped ensure the success of the landings.

The American soldiers appreciated and admired the dedication of the FFI. Nevertheless, they preferred to keep them at arms' length. Some FFI intelligence "rumors" resulted in nothing more than wild goose chases. On other occasions, the Americans were suckered into the middle of intrigues simmering between differing agendas of rival FFI groups. Some of the FFI's methods of retribution filled American soldiers with discomfort and alarm—such as the shooting of prisoners and the public humiliation of the captured girlfriends of Germans soldiers. As the Americans saw it, the FFI was well suited for intelligence and reconnaissance work—the eyes and ears of the countryside. Much of their information was dead accurate and proved extremely useful. For an American infantry company on "point" ahead of everyone else, raw unsubstantiated local observations were always better than nothing at all, and the help of FFI volunteer guides was rarely refused.

*   *   *

With a blazing midday sun above and a baking asphalt road beneath their feet, 3rd Battalion set out for Tourves as the regimental point. In times like these, Lt. Col. Boye preferred putting L Company and Captain Coles in the lead. Coles was like a star running back who always wanted the football. I Company followed closely behind L along a ridge on the left side, with K Company bringing up the rear.[23] Joining the advance were Lt. Orient's tanks[24] and two TDs from Lt. Finley's platoon.[25]

Within forty-five minutes, L Company reached the outskirts of Tourves. As its men drew near the place, a few shots of resistance rang out and a small firefight erupted.[26] Caught out front as the bullets began to fly was 3rd Platoon's newest scout, Pfc. Earl Potter. After a short time the Germans withdrew, but for Potter, who was uncomfortably cramped while seeking cover, the retreat seemed to take forever. As Coles' men spilled into town, twenty-five FFI members rushed over to greet them. All were eager and enthusiastic to join the fight, but the only problem was that they didn't have any weapons![27] As L Company prowled the narrow streets of town amidst swarms of happy townspeople,[28] I Company combed the surrounding high ground and dispatched a patrol north to the small town of Bras.

With the day's first objective met in a fraction of the expected time, Lt. Col. Boye contacted regimental HQ for updated instructions. At 1:38 P.M., the new instructions came through; push farther west along Route 7 to Saint-Maximin with 2nd Battalion trailing. 30th Infantry Regiment would bring up the rear. L and I Companies were still finishing up in Tourves, so Boye ordered K Company, a TD, and two of Orient's tanks to pass through and take the lead. To gain an early indication of what might lie ahead, one of the K Company platoons moved five hundred yards in advance of the battalion column. Before mid-afternoon, the battalion was on the move again.[29]

With sweat dripping down from their helmets and stinging their tired eyes, the men of 3rd Battalion left Tourves. To escape the heat, many unbuttoned the fronts of their wool shirts and rolled up the sleeves. This was contrary to regulations, but no one said anything. Some carried wine instead of water in their canteens. This was also prohibited, but clean water wasn't always available and no one wanted to get sick drinking bad water. The wine also tasted better and offered certain "medicinal" benefits that helped one temporarily forget the pounding pain in his cramped and blistered feet.

The lucky GIs hitched rides on the tanks and TDs or piled in every possible way aboard the few jeeps, trailers, and trucks belonging to the battalion. After a spell, their sergeants would order them to hop back onto the pavement so others could get relief from marching.

Life in the tanks was not much more comfortable. Sherman tanks were not designed for comfort at any level. Inside, it was noisy, stuffy, and intolerably hot—even with the hatches open and the ventilators running. The turret loader had the worst position. His only "hatch" was a small "pistol port" side door roughly eight-by-eight inches square, which he used to eject the spent shell casings from the main gun. The loader was not only isolated from fresh air but usually the last one out of the tank in an emergency. His only means of escape was through the commander's hatch on the opposite side of the turret. Because the inside of the turret was so cramped and crowded, he could leave only after the commander and the gunner had escaped.

One interesting quality about the American combat soldier was how he convinced himself that things could be always be worse. The infantry, the tankers, and the TD crews independently believed they had it better than the other guys. The last place on earth an infantryman wanted to be was fighting from inside a tank or TD. He knew armor on a battlefield attracted the immediate attention of the enemy. If the Germans spotted a Sherman tank surrounded by a dozen infantrymen, the first thing they went after was that Sherman. Once hit, tankers often said, a tank lit up like a "Ronson lighter." No infantryman in his right mind wanted to be inside a rolling crematorium. The average foot soldier was more than content with taking his chances out in the open, where he could rely on his wits, some degree of anonymity, and had a wide choice of places where he could dive for cover.

The tankers had a similar view of things from their own unique perspective. The vehicles offered TD and tank crews protection from all forms of small arms fire. They took comfort in the fact that they didn't have to worry about being cut in half by machine gun fire or forced to hug a slender tree to avoid a sniper. They didn't get blisters on their feet from marching, either.

The TD guys took pity upon their M4 tanker friends. They looked upon them as virtual "submariners," trapped inside gloomy turrets with only one small escape hatch to serve three men. The M10 tank destroyer's open-top turret allowed the entire turret crew to escape at once. The M10s burned diesel, so they didn't usually explode in flames like the gasoline burning Sherman tank. And an M10's gun was better. TDs weren't normally called upon to perform the dangerous close infantry support the more heavily armored M4 was designed to do.

On the other hand, Sherman tankers saw their closed turrets as a positive attribute. It offered them overhead protection from German "air burst" artillery, mortar fire, or from a "potato masher" grenade tossed down from a second floor window or dropped from a waiting grenadier's hand after he scrambled up onto the tank. Everyone had his own method of counting blessings. Seeing the undignified poses of dead German soldiers sprawled out on a baking highway was one way everybody could feel fortunate.

During the six-mile march on Route 7 to Saint-Maximin, 3rd Battalion found the road strewn in places with destroyed German vehicles, some reduced to unrecognizable twisted frames. Most hulks were charred and silent, while others still smoldered and smelled of death.[30] Dead German soldiers were scattered about the wreckage, already bloating from a sun that showed no respect for the departed. Their bodies were as disfigured, broken, and twisted as the vehicles upon which they had been riding. The small column had been part of the larger troop exodus from Brignoles the previous day. Their destruction came at the claws of P-47 Thunderbolts, part of the Twelfth Air Force. Some of the troops instinctively looked skyward as they walked, nervously gripping the yellow smoke canisters they carried with their gear. Air power was devastating to an army moving during daylight, and from several thousand feet up, the distinction between Allied and Axis troops and vehicles often depended on which showed the yellow smoke. The signal wasn't foolproof. Many of the men remembered only too well the terror that had coursed through their veins when their own planes strafed them on the long road to Rome.[31]

The route was partially blocked in places, and the jeeps, trucks, and tanks of 3rd Battalion had to move off road several times to avoid striking the wreckage. One of Orient's tanks was carrying some doughboys from I Company. The driver was trying his best to avoid debris while keeping his riders securely on the deck and maintain the pace of the column. He missed seeing the body of a dead German, and the track ran squarely over the man's head. The popping sound was something none of them ever forgot.[32]

The roadway cleared again and the column continued on unimpeded. At 3:30 P.M., the advance platoon from K Company reached Saint-Maximin and radioed back that the town was clear. Another large contingent of accommodating FFI—this time well-armed—was there to greet them. Other than that, the advance platoon had nothing further to report.[33]

At roughly the same time, regimental HQ informed Lt. Col. Boye of a change in plans. 3rd Battalion was ordered to hold up short of Saint-Maximin for a few hours and allow 2nd Battalion to pass through its position. Boye's men had orders to scout the high ground about a mile southeast of Saint-Maximin in an area identified on the maps as "La Defenos."[34] At 7:25 P.M., 2nd Battalion passed through on quartermaster trucks,[35] waving as they rode toward the front. 3rd Battalion marched on to La Defenos, where it settled in for the evening. Lt. Orient's tank platoon moved six miles farther south of Saint-Maximin to the town of Rougiers to relieve 1st Platoon tanks so they could return to Forcalqueiret for overdue maintenance.[36] S/Sgt. Oliver celebrated his twenty-ninth birthday by manning a 1st Battalion roadblock. If his wish was for a quiet and safe evening, someone granted him his wish.

It had been four days since its entry into southern France, and during that short time 3rd Battalion had been very fortunate. It had yet to see serious battle, and losses thus far had been surprisingly light.[37] Since the landings, only three men in the entire battalion had been killed, all I Company men.[38] Another man was missing in action,[39] and twenty-six others fell wounded.[40] For a battalion steeled by dreadful battles across Sicily and the Italian peninsula, the light resistance was a welcome change.

Captain Coles, on the other hand, grew tired of marching and riding day after day, only to have his men pat down a few surrendering German stragglers here and there, or exchange a few shots with shadows that quickly disappeared into the hills. Coles wanted action, and it was his turn for the night's patrol. If he had to go out and find action himself, so be it.

At dusk, Coles rounded up a BAR man and a few riflemen, including Pfc. Albert Whisnant. The group piled aboard both L Company jeeps and bounded down the road. Whisnant was riding in Captain Coles' jeep watching the scowl on his commanding officer's face grow with each passing minute. Every so often Coles checked his maps and directed the driver accordingly, but the Germans were no where to be found. The futile patrol continued into the deep hours of night without encountering so much as a single enemy soldier.

"I believe they left the whole damned country!" Coles spat out, unable to hide his exasperation.

He was ready to call it quits for the night and head back when an anti-tank gun flashed in front of them, illuminating the jeeps like a giant strobe light. A high-velocity round whooshed just above their heads with a shockwave that cracked the evening air. Everyone froze for a split-second before Coles, with an almost comedic sense of timing, exclaimed, "I believe we found them!"

Nobody laughed. Coles didn't either.

"Get the hell out of here!" he ordered with his next breath.

The jeeps spun 180 degrees on the road shoulder as several German machine guns opened fire, chattering loudly in the darkness. The drivers shoved the accelerators to the floor, leaving behind a cloud of exhaust and fading gunfire. They were gone before the German anti-tank gun had time to reload.

Coles wanted to find and kill Germans, but he was not suicidal. A BAR, a few rifles, and a jeep-mounted machine gun didn't have a prayer against an anti-tank gun.[41] Although Coles couldn't fully discern what he ran into in the darkness, in all probability it was a rearguard position sporting an anti-tank weapon.[42] Whatever the situation, the problem would have to wait until morning. Coles ordered the patrol home.

Earlier that same evening, 2nd Battalion continued by truck along Route 7 west of Saint-Maximin. It passed a few more charred wrecks of German vehicles, eerily silent in the featureless twilight.[43] The men jumped off the trucks at Pourcieux and marched unopposed all the way to Trets—a full twelve miles west of Saint-Maximin—where they settled in for the evening.[44] During the march, the men of 2nd Battalion watched explosions of German ack-ack (anti-aircraft fire) in the skies above Aix.[45] Despite the day's rapid advance, the Germans remained well west of 3rd Division. As evidenced by the ack-ack, only the Twelfth Air Force was landing the punches.

Ten miles to the southeast, 1st Battalion holed up at Rougiers for the evening. It had marched a parallel course south of Route 7 from Néoules through La Roquebrussanne and Mazaugues before arriving at Rougiers, but was unable to make contact with the enemy.[46]

Despite the successful advances of the day, no one was about to let his guard down. Captain Coles and many others had clear memories of how the Germans unexpectedly counterpunched in Italy—particularly while retreating. Rumors began circulating about German armor massing to the west. Twelve Mark IV tanks were spotted west of Aix. Twenty more tanks—possibly the monstrous sixty-ton "Tigers"—were seen north of Aix just across the Durance River.[47] Sketchy sightings like these drove battlefield planners crazy. They were too vague for action, and yet too serious to ignore.

Captain Donald H. Lieb, the regimental S-2, feared an old familiar pattern was beginning to emerge. In his S-2 report for August 19, he summarized the day's action as follows: "Resistance was composed chiefly of infantry elements and prisoner of war identifications indicate that he is assembling miscellaneous units into fighting organizations as they become available, in a manner similar to his build up at Anzio."[48]

Whether Lieb's concerns were real or remote, no one wanted to relive anything similar to Anzio.

For the time being, 3rd Infantry Division accepted whatever territory the Germans vacated, but kept up a vigilant guard.

The arrival of August 20 presented opportunities for General O'Daniel's men that were supposed to arise weeks after the invasion began, not less than a week after the first GI boot touched southern French soil. The hub city of Aix-en-Provence and all the northern roads leading out of Marseille were within striking distance. Their seizure would allow 3rd Division to seal off most of the German garrison's escape routes out of Marseille, while French Forces along the coast moved in for the kill. With this in mind, 30th Infantry Regiment moved northwest to take Aix, while 15th Infantry Regiment moved to clear out the areas south of Aix and establish roadblocks in and around Gardanne.

After a quiet evening, 2nd Battalion of 15th Infantry Regiment set out on foot at 8:00 A.M. from Trets heading southwest toward Gardanne.[49] The trek covered fifteen-miles through hilly country. Around the same time, 3rd Battalion began marching toward Trets. As usual, the weather was clear and hot. Roughly an hour into the march, the quartermaster trucks caught up with 3rd Battalion column and the men happily grabbed hold of the railings and piled into the cargo beds. The convoy proceeded through Trets and then southwest to Peynier, where the men were dropped off to again tread the pavement in the direction of the magnificent Chaîne de L'Etoile Mountains. Just beyond lay Marseille.

By the early afternoon, 3rd Battalion reached the day's objective and established roadblocks southeast of Gardanne near the towns of Saint-Savournin and Cadolive at the eastern base of the mountain chain. Patrols slipped into the nearby wooded foothills and were soon skirmishing with small groups of Germans roving the hillside. The Americans held back from chasing after them.[50] Their orders were to maintain an "aggressive defense" of the roadblocks southeast of Gardanne, not to go looking for trouble. 2nd Battalion moved on the town of Gardanne in the mid afternoon. Up until that point, save for a sticky grenade thrown at a jeep, 2nd Battalion's march from the northeast had been uneventful.[51] As the men of the 2nd closed to within 2,000 yards of town, however, the Germans greeted them with heavy machine gun, mortar, and artillery fire. The fire was bad enough, but the fact that the road was mined compounded the battalion's problems.

To force the Germans back, some M8 self-propelled howitzers from Cannon Company and the four TDs from 2nd Platoon of B Company of the 601st Tank Destroyer Battalion, moved forward to respond. At 3:50 P.M., the TDs opened fire with their earsplitting three-inch guns, pumping fifteen quick rounds of high explosive into the brush and buildings where the doughs had spied telltale gun smoke or muzzle flashes. The heavy fire silenced several machine gun nests.[52] Some of the German defenders gave up when confronted with the sharp counter-fire and submitted to preliminary interrogation. They were members of 305th Regiment, 198th Division. Some reported that more than 400 of their comrades were holding Gardanne. They also claimed many more Germans were circulating in the highlands northwest of town.[53] Staffers with 2nd Battalion figured they were in for another very long evening.

At 6:55 P.M., G Company tried advancing closer to Gardanne but was forced to hold up 500 yards short after drawing another flurry of German mortar and small arms fire. The TDs and M8s were called forward a second time, but the Germans stubbornly held Gardanne through nightfall. With no daylight left, 2nd Battalion suspended the fight well short of its objective.[54]

Just when things seemed to have finally settled down, a slow low-flying German plane buzzed 2nd Battalion command post at 9:40 P.M. and dropped several flares. The men guessed it was an artillery observation plane painting the area for an attack, and although many anxious minutes followed, nothing came of it.[55]

Farther southeast of both 2nd and 3rd Battalion areas, 1st Battalion also ran into some resistance the same day after departing late from the Rougiers roadblock. A French unit was supposed to relieve the battalion, but never showed up.[56] French tardiness, like English "tea times" held in the middle of battle, was a custom the Americans never got used to. The battalion advanced on Auriol at 9:00 A.M., and discovered freshly placed anti-tank mines in the road along the way. Thankfully, they were not well concealed and easily avoided.

By 11:20 A.M., 1st Battalion was still east of Auriol tangling with a full company of Germans and several anti-tank guns. The fight lasted all afternoon. Finally, at 8:00 P.M., the battalion overran the town and captured twenty-five soldiers from 934th Regiment / 244th Division, four anti-tank guns, demolition equipment, and a truck full of medical supplies.[57]

Captain Redle, 1st Sgt. Nusz and the remainder of the command and service sections of B Company, struggled to keep up with the rapidly moving infantry battalions. After re-servicing 1st and 2nd Platoon tanks the night before, they set out in the late morning of August 20 along Route 7 from Tourves to Pourcieux with a convoy of other divisional command and service units.[58] Several bottlenecks developed as a result of the same destroyed German vehicles passed earlier by the infantry.

Captain Redle and his jeep driver, Pfc. Gene Palumbo stopped to help clear debris at one of the traffic jams.[59] The overpowering stench of death hung in the air. The dead Germans strewn about had already been turned black by the sun and were covered with flies. Redle had seen all manner of death during his fighting throughout Italy. He couldn't say he was used to it, but he had learned to live with it. This time was different. For the first time he actually touched death by helping pull German corpses from their battered vehicles. It was a disgusting job he would never forget.[60]

Once Redle's new CP was established at Trets, Orient's tanks were recalled from Auriol and a roadblock near Belcodène.[61] The infantry's rapid advance made it impossible to service Orient's tanks until the sixth evening of the invasion. The M4 Sherman required constant tinkering. Tread links wore out quickly on the rough pavement, and overtaxed engine parts required replacement before they failed on the battlefield.

The break was good for the crews as well. The men received time away from the skirmish line, and S/Sgt. Oliver finally exchanged his shredded DD-tank for his regular M4 from the Italian Campaign.[62]

At first light on August 21, 2nd Battalion rattled Gardanne with an artillery barrage. Before the dust could settle, G Company poured into town only to discover that most of the German defenders had left under cover of darkness. Aside from clearing out a few snipers and putting up with a few rounds of harassing mortar fire, the town was theirs.[63]

With Gardanne now under regimental control, 3rd Battalion loaded onto trucks and moved northwest beyond Gardanne, setting up roadblocks late in the afternoon near Luynes and Les Milles.[64]

1st Platoon of L Company was manning one of those roadblocks along with some 3rd Infantry Division engineers when Pfc. Arco Ciancanelli crossed the hot blacktop road. The angry buzz of a fast-approaching motorcycle reached his ears. When he turned to look, the first thing he spotted was a German soldier hunched over the three-wheeler's handlebars with his girlfriend riding in the sidecar. The German was drunk, singing at the top of his lungs and seemingly oblivious to his surroundings. One of the engineers down road began yelling for the motorcyclist to "halt!" To show he was serious, the GI ran to the middle of the road waving a Molotov cocktail. The cyclist couple was either high, crazy, or wanting to exit life in a blaze of glory. The engineer ignited the cocktail and was nearly clipped as the motorcycle blew past him. Just as he jumped aside he flung his jar of gasoline, hitting the German soldier squarely in the chest. Both riders burst into a brilliant comet of flames. The motorcycle shook violently for a few seconds before swerving off the road and slamming into a ditch. The flames burned brightly for a few minutes before dying down. Ciancanelli and a few of the others walked over to inspect the wreckage. They hoped to find some clue as to why the couple refused to stop, but found nothing of military value among the wreckage or the two broken bodies.

The man's clothes had burned off and he was lying splayed out immodestly on the ground. The intense heat had swelled the man's genitals into a ghastly simulation of sexual arousal. One of the doughs, hardened by war, joked that at least the German died with a "hard-on." Everyone laughed, but each in his own way felt a little guilty about it. The death of the man and his girlfriend was tragic and senseless. Ciancanelli and the others had to find something about the incident they could put into a neat box. Gallows humor was often the only way to cope with the absurdities of war.[65]

At 8:00 P.M., not far from Ciancanelli's roadblock near the town of Les Milles, members of 2nd Battalion discovered a hospital filled with sick and wounded Germans.[66] 3rd Battalion sent troops from Battle Patrol to help guard the prisoners that included over 350 German patients, a staff of fifty, and a German Navy Admiral.[67] A U.S. Air Force technical sergeant shot down over Toulon and recovering from fractures was discovered among the patients and repatriated.[68]

While 15th Infantry Regiment manned roadblocks and processed captured German patients, the remainder of the division expanded its holdings. 30th Infantry Regiment spent the day taking Aix-en-Provence section by section through a series of firefights. The process went well, but for the first time in southern France the men of 3rd Division were running up against panzers.[69] Fortunately, the German street defenses were not well established and they withdrew with their tanks before the fighting became too intense. By 10:00 P.M., Aix had completely succumbed to 30th Infantry Regiment.[70] Once it was apparent the city would fall, 7th Infantry Regiment bypassed Aix and began moving northwest to Saint-Cannat.[71]

The fall of both Gardanne and Aix opened up numerous opportunities for the division to aggressively patrol northwest, west, and southwest.[72] Before the day closed, recon units probed as far out as ten miles, reaching the shore of the large inland salt lake "Etang de Berre."[73] Here and there they encountered periodic light opposition, but nothing resembling a hard defensive line.

The news from other Allied units fighting in southern France was also encouraging. More than three-quarters of Toulon had fallen to the French. Other French units pushing along the coastline had battled to within three miles of Marseille. In the northeast, 45th Infantry Division pressed through the towns of Barjols and Rians, crossed the Durance River, and began fanning out along the northern bank.[74] Though low on supplies and challenged by rough terrain, Task Force Butler raced 100 miles north and was cutting westward toward Montélimar on the Rhône River.[75]

That evening, all battalion staff and liaison officers met at 15th Infantry Regiment Headquarters to review the regimental plan for blocking Marseille while French forces moved on the city center. They

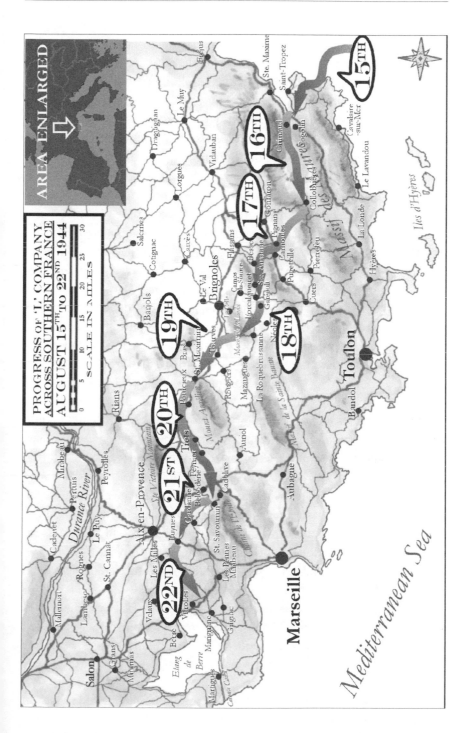

discussed the possibility of the German garrison in Marseille attempting escape through the isthmus northwest of the city. As a deterrent, 3rd Battalion was ordered to move along the isthmus and set up another series of roadblocks. However, the new primary concern was that the German Nineteenth Army might show in force and try mounting a counterattack to rescue the Marseille garrison. Panzer sightings were no longer the unconfirmed rumors of civilians and irregulars. 30th Infantry Regiment had run into a several enemy tanks while taking Aix, and American recon units were spotting them in numbers. Twelve Mark V "Panthers" were seen moving northwest of Aix along Route 7,[76] and another patrol counted four heavy and five light tanks outside of Aix.[77] It was now clear 11th Panzer Division had arrived in the region. General O'Daniel took the threat very seriously and ordered every 3rd Division unit to prepare for a vigorous German counterattack.[78]

O'Daniel was also concerned about overconfidence among his troops. As a hands-on commander, O'Daniel constantly circulated among his rank and file to judge firsthand their mood and battle readiness. The grizzled old general saw men distracted by all the civilian attention and lulled by the lack of intense combat. Little things he observed in their habits and appearance gave him reason to be concerned. The men were dressing down and not shaving daily. Infantry in the field were not wearing their helmets or maintaining their weapons at all times. Shipment numbers on new vehicles were not being replaced with the appropriate tactical markings. Instead of looking for Germans, the boys were talking of going to town and looking for fun. To put a stop to all the sloppiness, O'Daniel issued a general order that henceforth, every button was to be buttoned, every face would be clean-shaven, and all equipment maintained at inspection readiness. No one was allowed into a town unless billeted there, and to conserve fuel, all motor movement was to be kept to an absolute minimum.[79]

Southern France thus far had been a mixed bag of modest challenges to 3rd Infantry Division. Though the overall progress far exceeded expectations, a few units experienced tough, if relatively brief, combat. 7th Infantry Regiment overcame very determined pockets of resistance on the beach at Cavalaire and during the drive toward Toulon. 30th Infantry Regiment found its troubles at Brignoles and Aix. 2nd Battalion of 15th Infantry Regiment had two rough spells at Hill 551 and Gardanne, and 1st Battalion saw action at Ramatuelle and Auriol. In the grand craps shoot of combat encounters, 3rd Battalion seemed to be enjoying a string of lucky rolls, and the tanks from Lt. Orient's 3rd Platoon were plodding right along with Boye's men as if on a summer road trip.

During the six full days of marching and fighting from Saint-Tropez to Marseille, no solder from L Company was lost. Other than the three men who stepped on land mines the first day, and Sgt. Rovas' near-miss while on patrol, no one else in the company was wounded. Aside from a few brief firefights, everything had been easy—too easy.

Coles, Burks, and all the other L Company veterans knew their good luck wouldn't last forever.

Chapter 7
Roadblock

Aside from the unremitting distant rumble of Allied naval guns firing on Marseille,[1] the morning of August 22 remained relatively quiet for the three battalions of 15th Infantry Regiment. 1st Battalion headquarters near Gardanne sustained a few harassing rounds of artillery at 6:45 A.M.,[2] but other than that, the Germans were conspicuously silent. The expected German breakout from Marseille had yet to take place. Either the German garrison was too preoccupied with French forces moving along the coastline, or too exhausted to attempt an escape. The weather remained unmercifully hot.

2nd Battalion continued manning roadblocks north of Gardanne until 6:00 P.M., at which time it moved out northwest with 30th Infantry Regiment.[3] The march was intended to fool the Germans into believing 3rd Division was beginning a new offensive on Avignon. In reality, 2nd Battalion had orders to take up defensive positions northwest of Marseille between the towns of Grans and Miramas on the very north edge of Etang de Berre. As the regimental backside, the battalion would watch for 11th Panzer Division and any hint of an enemy counterattack. 15th Infantry Regiment had orders to hold "at all costs" a thin defensive line nearly twenty-two miles long.[4]

A few hours before 2nd Battalion's departure, most of the units making up 3rd Battalion set out from Les Milles and Luynes for positions much closer to Marseille—inside the isthmus northwest of the city. Two platoons from 601st Tank Destroyers Recon Company led the move. By 2:45 P.M., the 601st Recon team radioed its arrival in Luxembourg, a small cluster of farm buildings southeast of Vitrolles. The enemy remained eerily silent and out of harm's way.[5]

I, K, and L Companies, meanwhile, together with Lt. Finley's tank destroyers and Lt. Orient's M4 tanks followed the fifteen miles of asphalt road between Les Milles and Luxembourg before fanning out in different southeasterly directions. K Company moved toward Septèmes[6] while I Company proceeded to Gignac.[7] L Company and two tanks arrived at Luxembourg in the late afternoon and set up a command post and tents. At 5:45 P.M., L Company's 1st platoon accompanied one of 601st Tank Destroyers Recon platoons to Martigues, a key canal town fifteen miles away on the far western edge of the isthmus.[8] Their instructions were to seize the main bridge in town and secure the canal between the lake and the sea. No one was sure what to expect, but word through the FFI was that the Germans had left and that French partisans were holding Martigues.

With midnight approaching, 1st Platoon and 601st Recon arrived at Martigues along with one tank and a tank destroyer. No resistance or difficulties were encountered anywhere along the advance.[9] A little after midnight, the men secured the damaged bridge that was their objective. Local partisans and civilians were already hard at work repairing the structure. Most of the Germans had evacuated, just as the rumors indicated. A few lingering groups attempted a dramatic dead-of-the-night escape on barges along the Caronte canal, but were detected and mercilessly "blasted like ducks in a barrel" by the American TD and tank. None got through.[10] By 10:00 A.M., sixty German stragglers were rounded up from around town and taken as prisoners of war.[11]

The evening before, while 1st Platoon set out for Martigues, L Company's 3rd Platoon moved four miles west of Luxembourg to reconnoiter Marignane and establish perimeter roadblocks.[12] The men also investigated the airport north of town on the lake's edge.[13] By 9:15 P.M., an advance patrol from 3rd Platoon radioed that it had arrived at Marignane and was beginning a survey of town.[14]

At 8:00 A.M. the next morning, August 23, a 3rd Platoon patrol moved out to the airport. Leading the way was Pfc. Earl Potter, walking point with his Tommy gun. As a scout, Potter carried only the bare essentials in case he needed to hightail his way out of trouble. The small, thin teenager probed ahead of the others through field and shrub until he could make out the shattered buildings of the airport and the twisted remains of German aircraft lining the tarmac. Instead of finding German defenders, the Americans stumbled upon French partisans busily filling in the bomb craters dotting the runway and marking buried land mines with small flags. Other than the craters, the runway was free of any obstacles and appeared ready for use by Allied aircraft.[15] The patrol radioed in its findings and returned to Marignane, relieved over the lack of enemy encounters.

The remainder of L Company—2nd Platoon, Weapons Platoon, and the company HQ and service sections—established camp by a long stone wall in a field northeast of Luxembourg.[16] For the first time in a week, the kitchen was set up and hot food served. The men were also able to pitch sleeping tents.

2nd Platoon and some Weapons Platoon machine gunners deployed in fields south of the road connecting Luxembourg to the crossroads hamlet of "Le Griffon," roughly 300 yards to the west. Orders were to dig in and keep their guns facing south. All eyes warily scanned the muskmelon fields,[17] farms, and thick brush line in the distance. Roughly a mile beyond was a forested hill chain screening Marseille and the Mediterranean—and the German garrison. The L Company men had orders to expect the Germans to cross that hill chain and break through the brush line at any minute, with numbers that could reach into the thousands. The unremitting rumble of naval guns in the distance only underscored the potential for peril. The L Company doughs decided terrific fighting was taking place in the city, and their turn would arrive sooner rather than later.

From his vantage point along a dry creek approximately 100 yards south of the road, 2nd Platoon rifleman Pfc. Floyd Owsley kept close watch on that distant brush line, fully expecting to see grey uniforms pouring out of it at any moment. He tried to remain as calm as possible, but couldn't dispel the thought that his little section of L Company was nothing but a "speed bump," a pitiful foil for the thousands of German soldiers they had been told to expect. Other than a few machinegun positions and a handful of riflemen stationed on point past the dry creek, there was nothing to stop a determined enemy attack.[18] Owsley tried to think of something more pleasant to pass the time.

Although Owsley and others in L Company felt alone and exposed that day, in fact they had more support nearby. At Le Griffon, Lt. Orient masterfully deployed his tanks. His own took up a position behind the protective corner of a small hotel building so the main gun could fire with ease down the south and the west roads. He stationed another tank from his platoon between Le Griffon and Luxembourg, well concealed along the tree-lined roadway and ready to counter a threat from any direction at a moment's notice.[19] Artillery and heavy mortars settled into positions behind and east of L Company. Batteries A, C, and the headquarters of 3rd Division's 39th Field Artillery Battalion unpacked in the western fields of "Montvallon," a 17th century chateau[20] a quarter of a mile north of Luxembourg,[21] which served as the estate's mill and work- shops.[22] The terrain was ideal for the emplacement of the 39th Field Artillery's towed 105mm and 155mm howitzers. Montvallon was situated at the southeastern edge of the Chaîne de Vitrolles highlands. A steep 100-foot tall plateau wrapped around the northern and western edges of the Montvallon estate in horseshoe fashion, providing protection and observation points at the rear and on the sides.

The castle itself was a four-story yellow stone building with turrets on both sides and service wings extending south on either side of the courtyard. The castle also had a large basement.[23] The Army customarily asked the homeowner's permission before taking over a property, but as a practical matter no one could really refuse. Most French considered the request as an honor. Montvallon belonged to the Olive family, and its members welcomed the Americans with open arms and an almost giddy enthusiasm.[24] Because Montvallon was a vast and thriving vegetable farm, the family—particularly the children—entertained all sorts of requests from the GIs to swap chocolate and chewing gum for fresh tomatoes and cucumbers. For the most part, the Olive's happily gave their produce away and the Americans presented them all sorts of treasures in return, including a Rudy York model baseball bat.[25]

During the evening of the 22nd and early morning of the 23rd, Montvallon transformed from a pastoral estate into a bustling army camp. The field artillery appropriated the chateau cellar as a communications headquarters, stringing wire across the courtyard and installing antennae on the red-tiled roof. Truck engines droned and snarled everywhere as artillery pieces were situated and ammunition canisters unloaded. A medical detachment arrived with jeeps and ambulances and set up an evacuation center in one of the courtyard buildings.[26]

Half a mile east of Montvallon, 1st Platoon from B Company, 3rd Chemical Mortar Battalion, positioned its fearsome 4.2-inch mortars around the fields of the Coulon farmstead and sent up Piper Cub spotter planes to watch for German mortar or artillery smoke to the south.[27]

Approximately three miles southwest of Montvallon and Luxembourg, I Company established roadblocks at Gignac. K Company was six miles east near Cabriès.[28] Lt. Finley's TDs and the remaining tanks of Lt. Orient's platoon were split between both positions.[29] The Americans might not be able to stop a determined effort by the German garrison to break out of Marseille through the L Company's roadblock, but at least Pfc. Owsley's "speed bump" would not be trampled unnoticed.

Another L Company rifleman on point was Pfc. Lloyd M. Rowe. Like his comrades, he too wondered how his company could survive if the Germans tried a breakout. He and a squad mate were positioned south of Le Griffon on a dry creek bank near a simple road bridge. With hands dripping from constant sweat, Rowe fiddled with a pair of binoculars and lifted them to his stinging eyes. As he had been doing for hours, Rowe scanned the brush line and distant highlands for any sign of German activity. The thought crossed his mind that somewhere in those hills, a man dressed in grey and every bit as nervous as he was, was staring back through his own binoculars. About 5:30 P.M.[30] Rowe realized he was losing his struggle against the late afternoon glare. The detail and color of the trees, the hill features, and even the rooftops of the distant town of Les Pennes Mirabeau were smearing together in one haze of long shadows. Everything was beginning to dissolve ominously into . . . grey.

Without warning, the rustic calm was shattered by a series of explosions directly overhead. Pfc. Rowe and his friend instinctively hugged the ground as sharp hot shrapnel rained down around them, slicing through the brush and thudding into the ground. Rowe was no green recruit. He had been a member of the Massachusetts National Guard since 1937,[31] and joined L Company as a replacement prior to the Anzio breakout.[32] He knew immediately their position was being plastered with German "air-burst" artillery. Seconds later, another series of shells exploded overhead. Their position had been zeroed in. Someone in grey saw them first. The dry creek bed offered little if any protection against this kind of attack. They needed head cover—fast. Rowe and his buddy bolted for the bridge a dozen yards away on their left. As they scrambled along the creek bed, more shells exploded above. Rowe felt something hit his thigh, but the adrenaline kept him running. They reached the bridge and took refuge beneath it along with two elderly French farmers who had already beaten them there. Rowe reached down to check his aching leg. To his dismay, he discovered a hunk of shrapnel sticking out of his left thigh. The blood oozing from around the wound produced a spreading dark red stain in his ODs. As blasts split the sky overhead, Rowe reclined against the bridge footing while his friend administered first aid. The two French farmers looked on, unable to help and frightened by the artillery barrage. There was nothing more any of them could do but wait out the attack.[33]

The sudden artillery attack blanketed a wider area than just the bridge south of Le Griffon. Along the same creek bed but closer to Luxembourg, Pfc. Owsley and his squad mates were subjected to the same battering. The instant the bursts began exploding overhead, Owsley fell down and embraced the ground next to his useless rifle, waiting and praying as dirt kicked up around him and spinning bits of metal whistled just above his head. Owsley was also a veteran of Anzio. He had been through this many times before and knew that the worst thing to do was panic. After weathering the first few volleys, Owsley felt something strike the back of his right arm. He assumed he was hit by a stone or divot of soil kicked up by the blasts. The pain wasn't bad and he could do nothing about it anyway, so he remained still and continued praying as the onslaught continued.[34]

Meanwhile, airburst fragments at Montvallon ricocheted against the stone of the stately front façade and rattled across the courtyard grounds, leaving puffs of black smoke wafting against the blue sky overhead.[35] The medical team scrambled for the cover near their building, but shrapnel struck one of the doctors in the arm while he climbed out of his jeep.[36] The euphoria of liberation quickly left the faces of the Olive daughters as they raced in terror from the courtyard to find sanctuary between a retaining wall and a farm building.[37]

The men manning the 105s and 155s in the fields adjacent to Montvallon also scrambled for cover. A direct hit demolished one of the parked trucks, but no one near it was hurt.[38] At the Coulon farm, a shell struck an ancient tree near the farmhouse, splintering the trunk and toppling it over with a giant crash. Everyone, family and doughs alike, dove for cover as additional rounds rained down around the home.[39]

It did not take long for the Chemical Mortar Platoon crews south of the Coulon farm to determine that the German artillery attack originated from Les Pennes Mirabeau.[40] The crews aligned their mortars and let fly a counter response. The long distance tit-for-tat shelling by both sides continued for about two hours. At 6:30 P.M., roughly 100 Germans were spotted trying to escape out of Les Pennes Mirabeau,[41] but the 4.2-inch mortar fire dispersed them. A few minutes later, the German artillery attack fell silent.

Colonel Thomas ordered A Company, a heavy machine gun platoon, and a platoon of M8 assault guns to shift down from Gardanne[42] and reinforce L Company's positions between Luxembourg and Le Griffon.[43] The move commenced immediately.

Once the German aerial assault dissipated, Pfc. Owsley's squad sergeant noticed that the thin young rifleman was bleeding from the back of his arm. During the excitement, Owsley had completely forgotten about the bump on the arm and was simply relieved to have survived the barrage. The sergeant held Owsley's limb steady as he yanked out a chunk of shrapnel about two inches long and placed it in Owsley's hand. The private had a hard time believing he had been walking around with a piece of metal that large sticking out of his arm, and didn't know it. Fortunately, the fragment was nearly spent before it hit him; otherwise, the metal would have sliced off his arm. Still, the wound ran deep into the triceps muscle. The sergeant advised Owsley to seek proper medical attention. Disgusted, the private tossed the shrapnel away and walked to a nearby medic. Owsley argued that he could tough out the wound and remain at his post, but the medic thought otherwise. Owsley climbed into an ambulance for a ride to the nearest field hospital.[44]

As Owsley sought medical help, Pfc. Rowe and his buddy emerged from beneath the bridge. While waiting out the attack, Rowe realized he had been badly wounded in the right thigh as well as the left, but there were no bandages to dress the second wound. With his friend supporting him, Rowe began limping north toward Le Griffon. Up ahead, a jeep emerged from the tiny town and sped toward them. 1st Sgt. Works was at the wheel. The jeep screeched to a halt, and Works bounded out to assist him. Once Rowe was securely aboard, Works whipped the jeep around and hightailed back through Le Griffon and on to Montvallon. The medical team took over and rushed Rowe into their makeshift surgery room to attend to his wounds.[45] Once his bleeding was stabilized, medics stuck Rowe alone on a second ambulance and moved him to a field hospital.[46]

As dusk began to settle over the area, the M8s and the quartermaster trucks carrying A Company and the heavy machine gun platoon arrived.[47] The reinforcements barely took up their new positions when a second series of deafening blasts split the air. The Germans were not yet finished. This new artillery attack originated from beyond Gignac to the southwest.[48]

Pvt. Bernard Greive was an L Company replacement, and had only been with the company since the end of May. Just as his squad relocated near the scene of Pfc. Rowe's wounding, the men were ordered to a take up a position on a small hill a few hundred yards south of Le Griffon. "Dig in," was the terse order.[49]

As if cued by some malicious director, artillery shells suddenly began exploding in the sky around them. Greive gazed up in disbelief as the first few puffs of black smoke emerged from thin air—momentarily detached of the mortal danger. He hadn't even removed his backpack yet. When he snapped to his senses, the private hit the dirt like everyone else. He huddled alongside Pfc. Winsome Enzor, his best army buddy since their basic training days together in the States.

One shell exploded directly above them with a concussive jolt that whipped the ground and knocked Greive's helmet from his head. A sharp, searing pain coursed through his left arm. Not wanting to look, but unable to resist, he lifted his head to examine the damage. A big piece of shrapnel had ripped open the inside of his arm, leaving about twelve inches of flesh dangling from the bone. Blood was pouring freely from his severed muscles and arteries with compounding and excruciating pain. Greive succumbed to sheer panic. Jumping to his feet, he screamed repeatedly for a medic. In desperation, he began running toward his platoon's rear positions closer to Le Griffon. Unfortunately, the artillery bombardment had not yet stopped.

Greive's squad mates, including Enzor, who was wounded in the elbow by a small piece of shrapnel, hollered for him to get down, to no avail.[50] Greive passed his platoon leader, 2nd Lt. Fred Hodgdon, who was also prone and yelling between the unremitting explosions for the wounded private to hit the deck. As the shells ripped the sky above him, Greive located "Doc" Lefevre, who promised to help but only if the private laid down. The assurance was enough to get Greive to come to his senses. Once flat, Lefevre rolled over to apply a tourniquet and give him a morphine shot.

The painkiller took effect almost immediately, allowing Greive to relax and take inventory of his surroundings. The bursts were still ongoing, and everyone was still hugging the ground except a little French girl no more than three or four years old. She was frightened and crying and running directly toward Greive and Lefevre. Greive suddenly forgot about his mangled arm. Both he and Lefevre called and motioned for her to run to them, but before they could grab and protect her, another round exploded directly overhead. Greive felt his left leg slam hard against the ground. The sudden shock jarred him so hard that it knocked him out of his own senses. A bizarre feeling overwhelmed Greive. He was keenly aware of his surroundings, but from a disembodied perspective. He could not rouse his limbs or move his mouth to talk or yell. However, he could plainly see the condition of his leg. A large piece of shrapnel had ripped into his thigh and snapped the femur completely in two. Lefevre was stirring nearby, bleeding heavily from a cut above his eye, but otherwise okay. Standing between them was the little girl. By some miracle she was unharmed, but crying loudly.

While Greive was enduring his horrific ordeal, Lt. Orient and his crew at Le Griffon were "buttoning up" their tank hatches as the German barrage ripped the air above them. Throughout the intersection, riflemen from L and A Companies ducked for cover into doorways and behind walls. Others dove underneath Orient's tank to avoid the indiscriminate shrapnel pinging off the road and rooftops. Orient was pulling shut the door halves to his turret hatch when an airburst showered his M4 with hot metal. One piece slipped through the open hatch and struck Orient in the side of the head. He slumped forward unconscious, bleeding profusely from the wound.[51]

The 105s and 155s near Montvallon responded, laying down a relentless barrage into the hills beyond Gignac.[52] As this thundering aerial duel persisted, and despite the personal danger, 1st Sgt. Works, Lefevre, and a few others helped move the critically wounded Greive onto a stretcher and shuttle him toward a waiting ambulance. Another casualty had already been loaded ahead of Greive and placed on the overhead litter. He was motionless, his head twisted on his neck at an unnatural angle.[53] Despite the dressings, the soldier was bleeding heavily

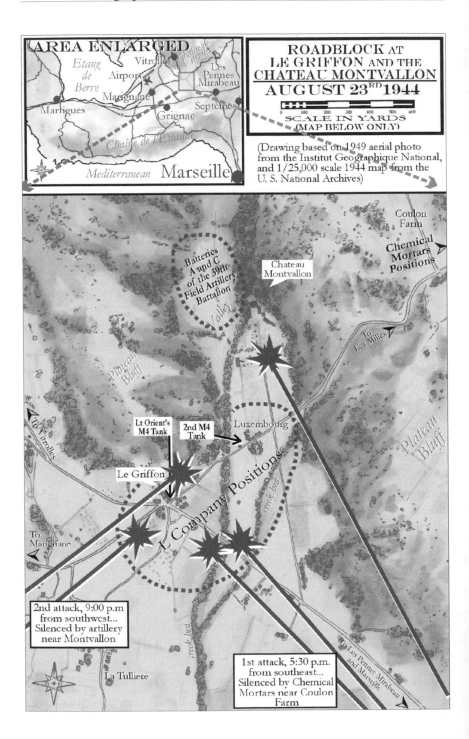

AREA ENLARGED

Etang de Berre

Vitrolles   *Chaine de Vitrolles*

Les Pennes Mirabeau

Airport

Marignane

Martigues

Grignac

Septèmes

Chaine de l'Estaque

Mediterranean   Marseille

ROADBLOCK AT
LE GRIFFON AND THE
CHATEAU MONTVALLON
AUGUST 23RD1944

0 100 200 300 400 500 600
SCALE IN YARDS
(MAP BELOW ONLY)

(Drawing based on 1949 aerial photo
from the Institut Geographique National,
and 1/25,000 scale 1944 map from the
U. S. National Archives)

Coulon Farm

Chemical Mortars Positions

Batteries A and C of the 39th Field Artillery Battalion

Chateau Montvallon

Valley

Plateau Bluff

To Les Milles

Lt Orient's M4 Tank   2nd M4 Tank

Luxembourg

Plateau Bluff

To Vitrolles

Le Griffon

L Company Positions

creek bed

To Marignane

2nd attack, 9:00 p.m
from southwest...
Silenced by artillery
near Montvallon

creek bed

La Tulliere

1st attack, 5:30 p.m.
from southeast...
Silenced by Chemical
Mortars near Coulon
Farm

To Les Pennes Mirabeau and Marseille

from a severe skull fracture.[54] Greive heard someone remark that the wounded officer was hauled out of a nearby tank. His name was Orient.

Enzor climbed aboard with bandaged elbow and reclined on the litter opposite of Greive.[55] Lefevre also joined so that he could attend to the three casualties during the trip. Just as the back doors were about to close, Sgt. Works popped in to check on Greive one last time.

"You have a nice long rest in the hospital now." Works said in earnest before the doors squeaked and slammed shut.

Grieve drifted in and out of consciousness during the ambulance ride that night. Above him, Orient lay limp and in shock in his OD coveralls, moving only when the ambulance shimmied back and forth over a rough stretch of road. The tanker continued to bleed from his horrific head wound. His long shot chance at survival was slowing draining away, trickling drop by drop onto Greive below, and there was nothing anybody could do about it, including Lefevre.

When the ambulance finally arrived at the 10th Field Hospital[56] and the three wounded men were unloaded, so much of Orient's blood covered Greive that the doctors had to cut all the rifleman's clothing off in order to locate and treat his wounds. Greive tried to inquire about the tanker's condition, but passed out.

The two German airburst attacks wounded six soldiers from L Company. In addition to Greive, Enzor, Rowe, and Owsley, the injured included S/Sgt. Lewis K. Marsh and Pfc. John R. Clifford. Clifford's wounds were not as serious, and he remained on duty with the company.[57] The aerial bombardment also inflicted additional casualties in other area units. In total, the local aid station evacuated seventeen victims.[58]

The 9:00 P.M. German artillery attack from the southwest was not as long as the first attack from Les Pennes Mirabeau—perhaps only fifteen minutes in duration.[59] The rapid response from the 39th Field Artillery at Montvallon silenced the German guns before any more damage could be done. In all, Allied guns fired 223 rounds into the coastal hills beyond Gignac, with 140 dispatched from C Battery alone.[60]

Perhaps discouraged by the counter-response of the American mortars and artillery, the German Garrison never did break out of Marseille in force. Whatever the reason, many enemy soldiers decided to surrender to the French. Others continued with the street-by-street fighting. The Americans quickly collected and disarmed those few who escaped from Marseille's city limits. L Company took nine of them prisoner during the same day and evening of the artillery attack.[61]

The situation in Marseille became desperate for those Germans who chose to fight on. Toulon had completely fallen as of August 23. Because of Hitler's withdrawal orders and the evolving strategic situation swirling around the Nineteenth German Army, the Marseille garrison had no hope of rescue. The sudden appearance of Task Force Butler closing in on Montélimar far to the north triggered immense concern and preoccupied General Wiese, whose soul concern was now how to get his army out of southern France. To prevent the entrapment of his army, Wiese rushed the bulk of 11th Panzer Division north to preserve a viable escape route along the Rhône River.[62] The German armor arrived in time to cut their way through Task Force Butler tanks and TDs and keep the way clear. To bolster his rearguard, Wiese prudently retained approximately ten Mark V Panthers. The tanks moved behind his Army as a foil to 3rd Division during the long exodus out of southern France.[63]

Across nearly the whole of France, Germany's once seemingly invincible military machine was waging a fighting retreat. Paris was liberated to ecstatic throngs as Allied forces confidently pressed ahead. Opposition seemed to be collapsing everywhere. For the first time, German prisoners of war exhibited resigned and even fatalistic attitudes toward the war effort. Perhaps more telling was that Hitler's orders were being ignored or refused. Despite orders to the contrary, the German commander at Paris refused to reduce the city to ashes, and the garrisons at Marseille and Toulon did not fight to the death of "the last man." Was the war moving swiftly toward a conclusion? Although a few men dared hope as much, the bitter reality of the fighting prowess of the German army quickly shredded the idea. Fighting on the defensive, with German soil behind them, the German soldiers were determined to find a way to hold back the Allied advance.

For two men, however, the war was indeed over. Pvt. Bernard Greive awoke the following morning after successful surgery on his arm and leg. He breathed a heavy sigh of relief when he realized he was still alive, and that nothing had been amputated. One of the first people he saw was medic Lefevre. Greive asked about the bleeding tanker, but Lefevre shook his head sadly. He didn't make it.[64]

News of Lt. Orient's death raced through 756th Tank Battalion's B Company early the next morning. Orient's men knew their beloved platoon leader's wounds were mortal. No one could have survived such a horrendous injury, and no one expected a miracle. Still, the official declaration was difficult to accept, and Orient's platoon fell into a state of shock.[65] Their lieutenant was admired for his combat leadership, fairness, and kind personality. He was an officer who always put the needs of his men first, and everyone would miss him.

The provisional cemeteries of Europe were filling fast with thousands of other similarly gifted young leaders, but the war was not about to stop with the death of any of them. The call went out from 756th Tank Battalion to find a replacement officer.

Chapter 8
Pursuit North

1st Lt. Edgar R. Danby was experiencing a month of extremes. Two weeks earlier, he was on top of the world celebrating a long overdue promotion to first lieutenant with his friends. But on August 23, he found himself stuck in replacement depot limbo with the whole war seemingly passing him by. Danby had spent the prior ten months as an instructor with the Fifth Army Invasion Training Center (FAITC) in Oran, Algeria and the Invasion Training Center (ITC) in Naples. When he volunteered for the Army, he did not expect to become a teacher.

Danby enlisted in the infantry in July 1942. He was thirty-two years old and married with two young boys and a very busy life. But the attack on Pearl Harbor deeply gnawed at his conscience and compelled him, as it did so many others, to volunteer. He discussed these feelings with his wife and she accepted his calling—but with understandable reluctance. Danby's decision not only meant a long absence from his family, but the suspension of a very promising career as a musician. His abilities as an organist and choir director with the Episcopalian Church in Detroit earned him a reputation as one of the nation's finest.

Danby finished basic training at Camp Custer and qualified for officer candidate school. Fascinated with tanks, he decided to specialize in the newly formed armor branch with training at Fort Knox, Kentucky. In order to keep up the musical skills, he played organ on the side at both Catholic and Protestant services on base. He turned down an offer to play on a full time basis. "I did not sign up for the Army to play the organ!" he explained.

Once he received his commission and pinned on his gold second lieutenant's bars, Danby was sent to Camp Campbell as a tank platoon leader in the newly forming 12th Armored Division. His tanks consisted of the new M4 "Shermans," widely considered at the time to be cutting edge technology and America's answer to Germany's legendary panzers. The physically demanding training was held in cold, wet, and uncomfortable conditions. For Danby, who was something of an outdoorsman anyway, the entire experience was simply part of the adventure. The bottom line was that he was leading modern tanks in a motivated unit preparing for combat. In terms of Army life, he couldn't be happier.

In June 1943, Danby received surprise orders to leave the 12th Armored Division and ship out immediately to North Africa. The Army desperately needed French-speaking American officers in the Mediterranean Theater. Born in Montreal, Canada, Danby spent the better part of his boyhood reading, writing, and conversing in both French and English with equal proficiency.

Initially, his new orders presented an exciting change. The ship's voyage across the Atlantic, the exotic atmosphere of Casablanca, and the knowledge that epic battles were being fought just beyond the nearby desert made Danby feel as if he was part of history-in-the-making. But after sitting for weeks on end in a hot dusty replacement depot, the lanky officer wondered whether history was passing him by. Danby was experiencing what many others had come to understand was the Army's "hurry up and wait" policy. His experience was typical. To pass the time until his new orders were cut, he played cards with officers stuck in the same administrative cul-de-sac, smoked cigarettes, and wrote letters home to anyone he could remember.

In September 1943, Danby's new orders finally arrived. He packed his few belongings and boarded a train bound for Oran, Algeria. After an uncomfortable 300-mile journey, he reported as a new instructor with the amphibious training section of the FAITC. His assignment had little to do with armor, but it was certainly better than the insufferable tedium of the replacement depot. Danby's new duties included schooling soldiers in a gamut of skills, from waterproofing vehicles to assaulting pillboxes on the beach. The job presented many challenges and rewards, and was certainly never boring. Because of his fluency in French, much of his day was devoted exclusively to training Free French and French Colonial units.

Danby knew his work directly helped the war effort, and his responsibilities were above his pay grade, which gave Danby great hope for an early promotion. Every OCS second lieutenant dreamed of one day pinning on the double bars of a captain. Danby counted many friends among the other American instructors and the French officers who passed through his classes. That camaraderie helped alleviate much of the homesickness that set in at the replacement depot. FAITC training was often dangerous and included live fire drills, from which Danby received light shrapnel wounds from time to time. Each day he practiced scenarios as close to combat as a man could experience without actually being in combat.

But it was not combat. That gnawing guilt he experienced after Pearl Harbor was back with a vengeance. When he first volunteered, he did so expecting combat and its entire bitter spectrum of hardships and horrors. He wanted nothing less. Determined to see the front firsthand, he put in transfer requests for a combat unit. Danby had no illusions about the hell he was asking for, nor did he entertain delusions of glory. He had good friends from OCS, the replacement depot, and the FAITC who went up to the front and did not come back—or did not come back whole. What Danby wanted most was to return to a postwar life where he could look any other combat veteran in the eye as an equal. To his dismay, the Army turned down each request.

Danby took every "no" in his stride with his customary unflappable low-key demeanor, and then immediately put in for another transfer request. Each time, the Army replied that he was more useful where he was. He remained an instructor until every planned Allied amphibious operation in Europe was complete, and the ITC disbanded. Danby's last assignment was in Naples during the summer of 1944, helping the Seventh Army train for the French Riviera.

On August 8, 1944, as the invasion fleet assembled and loaded in Naples harbor, the thirty or so officers of the ITC threw a huge farewell bash to celebrate their accomplishments and the dismantling of their unit. Everyone dressed in his best for the evening festivities. When Danby arrived, ITC commander General Wolfe pulled him aside and informed him that he was not wearing the appropriate rank insignia. Puzzled, Danby checked his collar. His gold second lieutenant bar was polished and properly placed. When he looked up, the smiling general was holding a shiny set of silver first lieutenant bars. Despite a months-long freeze on Army promotions for non-combat personnel, Wolfe had lobbied hard for Danby. The gesture was a tremendous compliment and an unexpected parting gift.

A few drinks and many guffaws later, the junior officers gathered in a circle outdoors for a friendly shoving match. After a several rounds the game broke apart, but one particular second lieutenant who had an egotistic reputation, brimmed with jealousy over Danby's new silver bars. He shoved the tall and slender Danby to the ground. The newly minted first lieutenant jumped back up and landed a haymaker with as much force as he could muster. The shove and follow-up punch quickly evolved into a mini-melee. Danby's best friend and roommate, 2nd Lt. Raymond Zussman, was knocked out cold. Once "Little Zuss," a happy-go-lucky popular Jewish guy from Detroit, went down hard, everyone seemed to realize things had gotten out of hand and sobered up enough to stop brawling. Except for a sorry looking bunch of junior officers, the crazy evening triggered little fallout the next morning. And so the proud history of the ITC came to a fitful end.

Once the Seventh Army invasion fleet was underway, the Army assigned Danby and the other officers of the ITC to new units or sent them directly to a replacement depot. To their dismay, Danby and Zussman ended up in the 24th Replacement Depot near Naples. The Army had a unique way of building up a guy and knocking him down. One minute a man was prized, promoted, and kept out of combat because of his value, and the next minute he found himself stuck in tent-city limbo to slow roast under a hot Italian sun.

The world beyond the 24th Replacement Depot was spinning rapidly. Virtually all of the war news that reached Danby and his comrades was positive. On every front, the once seemingly invincible German war machine was being turned back. The Russians were closing in from the east, while the Brits, Americans, French, and other allies were cutting across the north of France. The Southern France landings went off without a hitch, which surprised nearly everyone. Hints in the newspapers and the speculation around camp were that the war would be over soon, certainly by Christmas. With things going so well, a French-speaking instructor with ten months experience organizing mock beach assaults was not going to be in high demand. Danby resigned himself to the fact that he would never see combat. He convinced himself that he served his part and surrendered to the expectation of a long and boring autumn in the "Reple Deple." At least Zussman, always full of humor and good cheer, would be entertaining company.

About a week later, Danby was given an unexpected dose of hope. One of the three independent tank battalions fighting in southern France needed a company commander to lead a medium tank company. As a first lieutenant with an armor commission and plenty of training with M4 medium tanks, Danby certainly qualified. Suddenly, a chance at combat and a shot at that prized captaincy beckoned.

The interview for the position went extremely well, and Danby walked out believing he nailed the position. Reality set in quickly enough when news reached him that the battalion preferred a candidate with combat experience. The opportunity melted away as quickly as it had materialized. Danby had often requested combat, only to be turned down each time. Now, when a chance to get to the front offered itself, he was turned down for not having combat experience. The rebuff steamed the lieutenant. The months of rising frustration finally overwhelmed his unassuming personality. Anyone connected with the interview received an earful, and when he had no one left to complain to, Danby vented his remaining anger in a letter home to his wife. "Now that gripes me plenty because these men, once they get out of combat don't want to go back in, while we who have never been in combat are just waiting and itching to get in and do our share," he complained. "Ever since I've been in the army I've asked for combat and today I thought I was going to get it. I know what I can do, and I know I'd make as good a combat soldier as anyone else."

He continued:

> I want a crack at those Germans before it's all over. I'm sick and tired of this everlasting teaching and instructing—it gets on your nerves so you feel like going crazy sometimes. I want to get out and do something for a change instead of running some rifle range or some such silly thing. France is the country for tank warfare, it is open, rolling county—look what our tanks are doing there now. It is ideal for the employment of tactics on a grand scale.
>
> The armored force has finally come into its own—that is still my branch of service, you know. I was trained in the armored force and I would give anything to be back in it now. But the Army seems to have a penchant for getting and keeping men in some place where

they don't belong. I raised somewhat of a racket over the whole thing, and the only consolation (if you can call it that) was that special notice was taken of my fluency in the use of the French language. That knowledge may take me to Southern France in the near future—I hope so, anyway, because I believe I can do more good there than here. So, I'm mad at everybody today and am not fit to live with.[1]

The letter wasn't going change his circumstances, but writing helped put the frustrating experience behind him. Danby was now ready to go back to his tent, swat flies, sweat nonstop, and wait for the headlines of *Stars & Stripes* to proclaim "WAR ENDS!" —And when that happened, Zussman wouldn't have to listen to his bitching anymore, either.

The next morning, August 24, Danby was floored by the news he received: report to the 756th Tank Battalion in southern France. He nearly fell out of his folding chair when he read the order. He didn't land a company commander position, but the opportunity to make that step was once again on the table. Danby was to assume command of an M4 tank platoon in Captain Redle's B Company as Lt. Andrew Orient's replacement. Technically, a first lieutenant was "overqualified" for the assignment. Tank platoon leaders were generally second lieutenants. A first lieutenant in a medium tank company was either the executive officer or a newly appointed CO. It seems Danby griped loud and long enough, and the Army responded with, "Okay, let's see what you can do." After a two-year wait, Danby was finally about to head into combat.

Danby said some quick goodbyes to Little Zuss and the others and hastily gathered his belongings. Before closing up, he took a few moments to attend to one last detail. He pulled a razor from his personal hygiene kit and shaved off his trademark dark brown moustache.[2] 3rd Infantry Division was General O'Daniel's outfit, and O'Daniel had been the CO of the FAITC prior to Danby's arrival. Danby knew the tough-as-nails general frowned upon officers sporting moustaches. If he was going to join an O'Daniel-led outfit, he had better look the part. Perhaps the change might even bring good luck. Once finished, the new-look Danby headed to the airfield outside of Naples with orders he had long yearned to hold, gripped tightly in his hand.

At the airfield, Danby climbed inside a C-47 parked on the tarmac while soldiers stuffed it with blood plasma. He stowed his gear in a vacant spot between the boxes of plasma. A solitary passenger dressed in tanker field attire with armor insignia and the silver bars of a first lieutenant was already aboard. Danby sat next to the man and struck up a conversation. The officer's name was 1st Lt. Arthur Abrahamson, and the two had something in common: both were replacements bound for the 756th Tank Battalion.

Once packed with supplies, the C-47's twin engines rumbled to life and the plane taxied down the runway. Just as the wings began to pull skyward, a tire exploded with a jarring bang, forcing the pilot to loop around and a make a rough return landing. The plane skidded safely to a halt—much to the relief of everyone aboard. The two jostled officers hoped the episode was not an indication of things to come.

Everything aboard the aircraft was transferred to another waiting C-47, and before too long they were airborne again without incident, cruising high over the sunny Mediterranean toward southern France. With the steady drone of the engines providing the background noise, Danby and Abrahamson continued with their lively conversation.

Abrahamson was twenty-six years old, a native of Chicago with eighteen months of combat experience with 1st Armored Division. His tank outfit, Company I of the 13th Armored Regiment, landed at Oran in November 1942 and fought through some bloody battles, including Kasserine Pass and Salerno. While fighting through Artena during the relentless drive toward Rome, German panzers and anti-tank guns ripped Abrahamson's tank battalion to pieces. Only two of seventeen tanks in Abrahamson's company survived. The losses were so severe that the entire battalion was deactivated and its survivors dispersed. The Army dumped Abrahamson in the 24th Replacement Depot, where he waited three months for this next assignment. His new orders were for him to join Company A of the 756th Tank Battalion.

After several hours soaring over sunny flat seas, the men finally made out the coastline of southern France. Jutting out from the hazy horizon was their destination: the Saint-Tropez peninsula. Allied ships of every shape and size were cutting through the shimmering waters below, sailing to and from harbor. The C-47 banked and descended toward a temporary beach airstrip constructed out of Sommerfeld steel matting by the Army engineers.

Nine days after 3rd Division landings, the field was still in heavy use. Planes, vehicles, and stockpiles of war materials lined the makeshift tarmac. Men, jeeps, and vehicles were buzzing about in all directions.

When the C-47 touched down and taxied to a stop, Danby and Abrahamson disembarked while Air Force grunts clambered aboard to unload the precious blood plasma with the precision of a pit stop crew. Before the two officers had a chance to absorb their new surroundings, a jeep came by and picked them up for the long overland journey to their new assignment.[3] The 756th Tank Battalion headquarters was nearly 100 miles away at Aix, moving with 3rd Division as it drove northward in pursuit of the retreating Germans.[4] The two replacements prepared themselves for a long and bumpy ride.

Danby and Abrahamson joined 3rd Division on a remarkable day. The division drove rapidly through miles of enemy territory without any real fighting for the entire twenty-four hour period. August 24 was probably the division's quietest day of "combat" in the entire war.[5] The only enemy contact consisted of rounding up a few stragglers. Rumors of larger German troop concentrations within 3rd Division's operational area were aggressively investigated, but no enemy was located.[6] The divisional Recon Troop probed as far northwest as the city of Arles on the Rhône River, but partisans had already cleared and secured the town.[7] The absence of resistance was a strong indication that the German Nineteenth Army had shifted into full retreat.

The day began with a slow start for most of 3rd Division. 15th Infantry Regiment, in particular, could not join the northward pursuit until French units arrived to relieve it at the roadblock positions outside Marseille. The French relief was supposed to arrive at dawn, but the French did not arrive on time.[8]

L Company spent most of the morning camped in the Luxembourg and Marignane areas awaiting relief from the French. The L Company platoon and recon unit also waited at Martigues for the same.[9] After weathering the airburst attacks the prior evening, L Company was eager to move on. Captain Coles was certainly not one for sitting still. The morning was another warm one, but welcome clouds brought some respite from the blistering sun.[10]

1st Battalion at Gardanne was the first to begin moving north. Since the battalion was in regimental reserve, it could roll without having to wait for the French relief units to arrive. Around 8:30 A.M., 1st Battalion loaded up on 3rd Quartermaster trucks and departed for the regiment's designated assembly area at Saint-Cannat, northwest of Aix.[11]

Lt. Col. Frederic Boye's 3rd Battalion endured a longer and more frustrating wait. Although word came down at 10:30 A.M. that the French 1st Armored Division and units of Moroccan "Goums" would arrive by the early afternoon,[12] the hours came and went without their appearance. At 4:20 P.M., General O'Daniel decided he could wait no longer and ordered 3rd Battalion to begin boarding trucks bound for the Saint-Cannat assembly area so it could join with the waiting 1st Battalion.[13] Just as L Company was ready to leave at 6:00 p.m, the French Goums finally arrived wearing their strange mix of Arabic clothing and long knives, accessorized with modern web gear and weapons.[14] Their impressive physical presentation was a good fit for their fierce reputation.

3rd Battalion finally arrived at 10:30 P.M. in Saint-Cannat and assembled on a school grounds.[15] The new location was only twenty miles due north of Luxembourg, but the journey was slow and arduous because streams of newly liberated French civilians, on foot and in vehicles, clogged the roads.[16] For the first time the French were more of a hindrance than a help. To make up for lost time, General O'Daniel considered trucking 3rd Battalion directly to Apt, the next planned assembly point farther to the north, but scrapped the idea in part because of the jammed road conditions.[17] 2nd Battalion was still waiting in Grans and other towns north of the lake for transport to Saint-Cannat. Later that evening, available quartermaster trucks moved out to retrieve them.[18]

Shortly after midnight on August 25, 1st and 3rd Battalions boarded a long convoy of tanks, TDs, M8s, kitchen trucks, jeeps with trailers, and seventy-five quartermaster trucks.[19] Any motorized vehicle that could carry the drowsy doughboys through the calm cool darkness was put to good use.

The convoy rolled over unforgiving hilly territory toward the distant city of Apt. To avoid detection by any German aircraft or artillery forces still lingering in the area, every headlamp in the column was switched off, a reasonable decision, but one that made the journey more treacherous. For the next few hours, a chorus of belabored motors and whining transmissions serenaded the riders. Though the men could see little more then the subdued red taillights ahead, only the most blessedly serene individuals dared close their eyes. Every tight turn and dramatic shift in grade along the invisible snaking road shook them. Sleep was impossible.

The Durance River presented a major obstacle. Since most of its bridges had been blown, the convoy was forced to detour twenty miles east and cross at Mirabeau on a recently erected pontoon bridge. Once across, the convoy backtracked west for fifteen miles before heading north once again. Just after daybreak, the column finally rolled into Apt. The entire journey from Saint-Cannat to Apt covered sixty miles and passed through the towns of Lambesc, Rognes, Le Puy, Peyrolles, Mirabeau, Pertuis, and Cadenet.[20] Only one vehicle was lost during the all-nighter. At 4:00 A.M. in Pertuis, one of the M8s from Cannon Company slid off the road and overturned into a deep ditch, seriously injuring two crewmembers.[21]

Four hours after 1st and 3rd Battalions set out for Apt, 2nd Battalion, traveling by truck, had only reached Saint-Cannat. The battalion would continue lagging behind in the hours and days to follow. The rapid advance since the moment the Americans landed in southern France, was straining transportation capabilities to the breaking point. The constant demand for trucks, tanks, and other vehicles pushed the machines and their crews beyond their maintenance limits. The deep advance also created logistical difficulties. The farther 15th Infantry Regiment advanced into France, the longer and more tenuous the supply line, which stretched all the way back to the landing beaches. Orders for gasoline became more difficult to meet with each passing hour. The problem would only worsen with every mile, until 3rd Infantry Division faced the stark choice of either slowing down considerably or continuing the pace while compromising its fighting effectiveness. During the morning hours of August 25, the division decided slowing down was the wiser course.

By late morning, Colonel Thomas established 15th Infantry Regiment CP at Apt. Thomas and his men spent that afternoon preparing for General O'Daniel's next order to resume the northward push.[22] As the headquarters and supply personnel from organic and support elements of the division arrived and reorganized within a wickedly compressed time schedule, the surroundings of Apt took on the air of organized chaos. The command and maintenance sections to various artillery, quartermaster, and armor units resumed field operations as soon as they arrived. Among them was Captain Ambrose Salfen's B Company headquarters for the tank destroyers. By noon, Captain Redle's headquarters had also arrived and unpacked after traveling nonstop for sixty-five miles from Velaux.[23] Even before the scorching sun could fully dissipate the exhaust fumes,

O'Daniel finalized plans for them to move again. After five o'clock that afternoon, Colonel Thomas received orders to push his regiment forward to Carpentras.[24]

756th Tank Battalion HQ rolled in from Aix by the middle of the afternoon to add to the bustle in Apt.[25] After a long exhausting jeep ride, Lts. Danby and Abrahamson finally caught up with the 756th and reported for duty. Before being released to their companies, however, the two new officers had to undergo a brief orientation session with the battalion operations officer (S-3) Maj. Oscar Long.

The two replacements met Lt. Col. Rogers and were appraised of the tactical situation. They discussed every practical issue imaginable, including how to maintain and supply their tank platoons during battle. After the briefings, the two were taken around and introduced to a few of the other staff officers around camp before visiting battalion supply to be issued any equipment required for their new responsibilities. The entire process lasted a few hours. Early in the war, new officer orientation consumed several days, but increasing combat pressures forced the adoption of abbreviated programs. Fast track to integration notwithstanding, by the time the briefing concluded, the officers' respective companies had already rolled out of the area. Until new transportation arrived for Danby and Abrahamson, there was nothing to do but linger with the battalion's supply and maintenance areas for the remainder of the day.[26]

Throughout the day, 3rd Division recon patrols probed the northern countryside in an effort to locate the German main line of resistance. Despite aggressive efforts to trigger a fight, enemy contact remained surprisingly light. The strategic cities of Avignon, Cavaillon, and Orange fell without a challenge, demonstrating once again that Nineteenth Army had little interest in laying down a defensive line or mounting a counterattack on the advancing 3rd Infantry Division. Given the difficult strategic situation they faced, the Germans were far more focused on the situation evolving thirty miles farther north.

For the last four days, lead elements of 36th Division, rushed north of Montélimar to reinforce Task Force Butler, threatened to sever Nineteenth Army's only escape route through the Rhône River valley. The FFI's successful destruction of a key bridge at Livron over the Drôme River made the German escape more problematic by forcing a slow ford of the river through shallow areas.[27] VI Corps commander,

General Lucian Truscott, had gambled that he could get enough of 36th Division in place to block the Germans at the ford while 3rd Division came up from the south. Truscott hoped that thus trapped, Nineteenth Army would face the stark choice of wholesale surrender or annihilation.

Truscott's plan did not develop as he had envisioned. On August 21, General Wiese rushed most of 11th Panzer Division north of Montélimar.[28] For four days, 11th Panzer, along with supporting grenadiers, fought tenaciously to keep open the escape along Route 7. 36th Division and Task Force Butler, hampered by the area's mountainous terrain and beset with logistical challenges far worse than those of 3rd Division, could not close the trap. They slowed down and bloodied the Germans with harassing artillery from a distance, but were unable to stop the retreat.

Although 3rd Division was still well southeast of Montélimar, pressure from Truscott fell squarely on General O'Daniel to push his troops with all haste up from the south, and attack the bulk of the German Nineteenth Army still south of Montélimar. 3rd Division's operational plan called for 30th Infantry Regiment to push through the highland hills on the right flank while 15th Infantry Regiment pressed along National Route 7 and the Rhône on the left. First, however, the men of 15th had to move northwest and achieve a new assembly point at Carpentras.

15th Infantry Regiment began moving as soon as O'Daniel's late-afternoon orders reached Colonel Thomas. A convoy comprised of every available mode of transportation departed from Apt, moving west along the Coulon River and then north through L'Isle and Pernes before arriving unopposed at Carpentras. 3rd Battalion, with tanks and TDs, led the column, followed by 1st Battalion and the regimental headquarters.[29] By 10:30 P.M. that same evening the town was secured and the regimental CP established.[30] As a final order of business, sixteen trucks with low fuel gauges rumbled south to retrieve the lagging 2nd Battalion.[31] The scarcity of fuel, however, kept both the trucks and 2nd Battalion stranded in Apt until well into the next morning.[32]

Nevertheless, the early evening move put two-thirds of 15th Infantry Regiment within striking distance of the retreating Germans. Fresh reconnaissance reports and observations from the locals indicated that the Germans were in force only fifteen miles north of Carpentras.[33] The rush to attain Carpentras, however, added twenty more miles of transport distance to the thinly stretched supply lines. A round trip to the beach depots required a 200-mile journey. The shortage of gasoline strained the movement of the entire division, particularly those units spearheading the drive.

Spare parts were also difficult to obtain. As a result, tank maintenance suffered terribly. Of the fifty-four medium tanks assigned to 756th Tank Battalion, seven broke down during the August 24-25 overland push, and eight more succumbed mechanically the next day (August 25-26). In just two days, the battalion lost roughly one-third of its strength without a single German shell fired in its direction.[34]

One of the tanks that sputtered to a halt was Sgt. Anderson's old M4 mainstay. To keep 3rd Platoon stocked with four operational tanks in anticipation of Lt. Danby's arrival, Anderson swapped his broken down "B-14" for a working model from A Company. His replacement was a maintenance tank, an older M4A1 with a rounded cast hull and an "A-16" designation sprayed on the back deck.[35] A tank was just a tank to any outsider, but to a tanker it was both home and a 33-ton talisman. Anderson was hardly the superstitious type, but he hated to let go of his old "dog" tank. It had been a loyal friend since Cassino.[36]

Late-night rumors swirled around Carpentras that large groups of German soldiers, trucks, and tanks were pulling out of towns immediately to the northwest. Unbeknown to the Americans, the Germans had established a defensive boundary of sorts beyond Carpentras running southwest to northeast dubbed the "Lindequist Line."[37] "Line" was an overgenerous description. The defense was more akin to a flexible, semi-permeable series of outposts intended to alert the German command of enemy incursion and retard, but not repel any 3rd Division attacks.

The responsibility for protecting the retreat's rear flank was entrusted to the remaining German troops of 757th and 933rd Regiments of 338th Division, the same outfits badly mauled at Brignoles. Assisting them were 669th Pioneer Battalion (Engineers) and several tanks and anti-tank guns from 11th Panzer Division reserved by General Wiese for rearguard purposes. These defenders erected ad hock roadblocks at key intersections in such towns as Vaison and Nyons. They reported directly to LXXXV Armeekorps HQ situated in the small town of Allan three miles southeast of Montélimar. As a defensive scheme, the network hardly compared to those masterfully employed in Italy, but the Germans in southern France were as short on materials as they were on time and

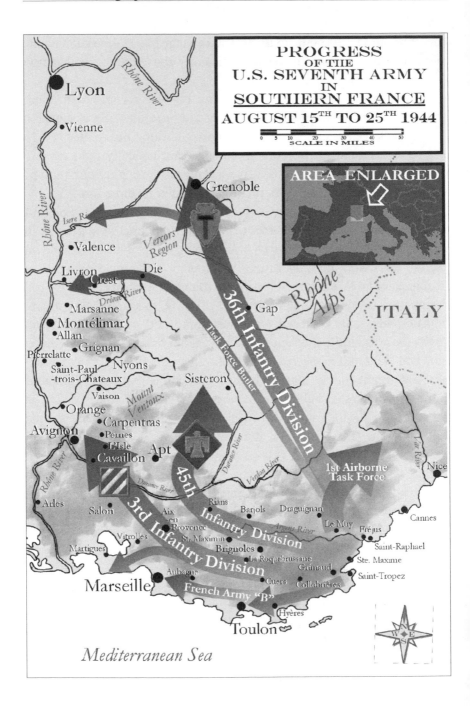

comparable defensible terrain. The "Lindquist Line" would have to suffice.

The retreat through the Rhône Valley was a confusing, chaotic, logistical nightmare requiring the coordination of troops numbering into the tens of thousands, all their equipment and horses, and thousands more organic and commandeered vehicles, carts, and trailers. Planning an effective rearguard against 3rd Division represented one more giant layer of complication. To avoid wider confrontation altogether, the key was to remain at least one day ahead of the Americans. The staff of LXXXV Armeekorps believed this possible as long as viable roadblocks were maintained in the south as the korps' eyes and ears on 3rd Division's progress.

By 5:00 A.M. on August 26, enough gasoline had arrived for two of the three 15th Infantry Regiment battalions to begin moving again.[38] Even so, not all of the jeeps, trucks, and tanks could set out with the troops. Those still in need of fuel or spare parts would have to catch up later. As for the doughs, the day's gains would have to be won on feet still sore and blistered from the miles of marching the week before.

Acting as the regimental left flank, 1st Battalion set out at dawn, moving west-northwest from Carpentras toward Orange by way of Sarrians and Jonquières. As it moved, contact patrols fanned out along the south to coordinate with 7th Infantry Regiment's western movements. At the same early hour, 3rd Battalion jumped off in a more north-northwesterly direction acting as the regimental right flank, working toward Violès and Cairanne.[39] 2nd Battalion remained stalled near Apt until more gasoline could arrive from the beachhead.

The advance for both battalions was slow. The fuel situation hampered the ready movement of vehicles, and the arrival of another oppressively hot morning slowed the boots on the ground. The terrain added further complications. The Ouvèze and Aigues rivers and tributary streams crisscrossed the area. Unfortunately for the advancing soldiers, the destruction of many local bridges (which had been blown by either FFI operatives, Allied aircraft, or the Germans) slowed the movement significantly, as did the destruction of a key link across the Ouvèze near Jonquières. Precious time was lost seeking alternative bridges or shallow fords for crossing.

Fuel and maintenance problems meant that both 1st and 3rd Battalions had to depart Carpentras without Sherman tanks, other vital armor pieces, and mechanized weapons teams. As a result, the infantrymen advanced more slowly and with greater caution. 1st Battalion moved without any armor support whatsoever, and neither 1st nor 3rd Battalion had any heavy mortars.[40] 3rd Battalion was more fortunate. Moving with it were Lt. Finley's four TDs and two M8s from Cannon Company.[41] However, tank destroyers and M8 assault guns were not designed to provide the kind of close infantry support that a Sherman could, and their crews would understandably balk at accepting a tactical challenge routinely faced and tackled by a Sherman crew.

In order to reach Jonquières, 1st Battalion had to ford the Ouvèze River roughly a mile south of the broken bridge.[42] Once on the western bank, the battalion marched northwest of Orange and established roadblocks later in the afternoon at Piolenc and on the road south of Bollène. Throughout the day, 1st Battalion CO called upon the regiment to send tank destroyers, but he had to wait until 5:00 P.M. before three of them arrived.[43] The refueled Shermans did not reach the 1st Battalion roadblocks until after nightfall.[44] Aside from two burned out and abandoned self-propelled anti-tank guns passed while moving through Piolenc, 1st Battalion saw little sign of the Germans during its daylight advance.[45]

2nd Battalion finally departed Apt on trucks at 8:00 A.M. and arrived at Jonquières by midday.[46] Soon after, Colonel Thomas moved his regimental CP from Carpentras to join with 2nd Battalion at Jonquières.[47] Once settled, 2nd Battalion ranged out to the northwest of town and discovered a small airfield with an abandoned German JU88 bomber and a night fighter. The retreating Germans left them rather then risk losing them and their pilots to Allied planes patrolling the skies. Near the landing strip, the GIs also found several abandoned anti-tank guns with unused ammunition. With the exception of these items, the entire place had been thoroughly looted.[48]

That same morning, 3rd Battalion marched seven miles from Carpentras to Violès. A predawn patrol indicated the way was clear of danger.[49] L Company led the foot march at the onset, followed by I Company; but by mid-morning K Company rode through on the decks of the TDs and the M8s to assume the vanguard.[50] With the approach of noon, the battalion established contact with 30th Infantry Regiment patrols near Violès and sweeping northward on the battalion's right.[51] Just to the north of Violès, the bridge over the Ouvèze was blown, so 3rd

Battalion sought a ford across the river.[52] Though precious minutes were consumed hunting for a crossing, the men didn't mind wading through the cool refreshing water.[53]

After traversing the Ouvèze, 3rd Battalion pressed northward toward Cairanne, trying to make up for lost time. During the five-mile march, a message came through from the regiment advising of FFI reports of as many as 2,000 enemy soldiers with tanks and artillery holding the high ground beyond Cairanne.[54] After eleven days running through southern France, the long pursuit seemed to be nearly over. The race was now against nightfall.

After being delayed all day at Carpentras for lack of fuel, a platoon of 4.2-inch chemical mortars moved up and joined the battalion march about 4:30 P.M.[55] With K Company and armor still at the head of the column, the battalion rolled into Cairanne by 6:00 P.M. Through a stroke of good luck, the bridge over the Aigues River west of town was still intact. Lt. Col. Boye wired Colonel Thomas with the good news, and reported that he was immediately dispatching an armored patrol two miles to the northwest of the bridge to the town of Sainte-Cécile.[56] Boye intended to flank the suspected German positions in the immediate north.

At that same hour, however, the gasoline problem again caught up with 3rd Battalion. Throughout the column, jeeps, trucks, and armor pieces began sputtering to a halt. The situation was beyond frustrating. Known for his trademark cool in every situation, Lt. Col. Boye's legendary patience finally failed him. "Cannot move vehicles again. No gas!" Boye radioed Colonel Thomas.[57] His battalion was far short of where O'Daniel wanted them for the day, and Boye knew the tough old general would not be pleased. Montélimar was still a good twenty miles distant. If given the order, Boye would have taken his battalion all the way to Paris, but he couldn't do a thing until the division gave him gasoline. The lieutenant colonel underscored his frustration by repeating the obvious to Colonel Thomas via radio: "Future moves necessitate vehicles."

General O'Daniel was tough, but he was not insufferable. He fully understood the logistical situation and accepted the reasons for the day's disappointing progress. However, at 8:50 P.M. he informed Colonel Thomas that he wanted 15th Infantry Regiment ready to roll by 4:00 A.M. Despite the fuel shortages, 15th Infantry Regiment had to find a way to reach Montélimar by noon the next day—even if it called for a couple more hours of predawn marching.[58]

Before sunset, 3rd Battalion scrounged together enough fuel to send the two M8s and a K Company patrol on a reconnoitering mission northwest to Sainte-Cécile. The remainder of K Company followed behind on foot. L Company also followed on foot, passing through K Company's positions at Sainte-Cécile, before proceeding another 2½ miles west to the town of Rochegude. There, Coles' men arrived before nightfall to the cheering throngs of happy townspeople. Four German stragglers were captured while establishing outposts north and east of town.[59] The remainder of the battalion and the four diesel-starved TDs, held up at Cairanne until they could be re-supplied during the night.[60]

In the twilight, K Company worked another patrol four miles northwest of Sainte-Cécile to the outskirts of Suze-la-Rousse. The retreating Germans had just mined the main road leading into town, but brave townsfolk were already removing the deadly devices by lamplight ahead of the arrival of the Americans.[61] The same villagers cautioned the liberators against heading north out of town because of a large German tank—possibly a Panther—positioned in ambush beyond a bridge. Because of the warning and the darkness, the men of K Company decided to stay put until morning. However, the two M8s moved forward from Sainte-Cécile and assumed defensive positions at the southern entrance of Suze-la-Rousse. Any Germans lingering north of town could not fail to take notice of the rumbling sounds of American armor moving into the area. Silence reigned for a few hours until in the middle of the night, the German panzer engine snarled to life. A few moments later, the sound of its engine faded away as the tank and its crew rolled northward.[62]

To the south at Sainte-Cécile, other K Company patrols fanned out into the vineyards and fields surrounding town, where they exchanged a few shots with German stragglers and took eight prisoners in the process.[63]

As 3rd Battalion took up its positions for the evening, Colonel Thomas completed a six-mile move of his regimental HQ from Jonquières to Sérignan in the northwest.[64] After a full and tiring day of travel, Captain Redle and most of the tanks and crews of Company B also settled in near Sérignan. All three platoons were positioned a short distance from the CP with their tanks in various states of readiness. The maintenance crew buzzed about them, replacing worn parts and tinkering in the back engine compartments. While the mechanics worked, crewmen double checked ammunition supplies and stocked up on whatever was needed. The gunners and loaders carefully inspected each round for shipping damage and calibrated the delay fuses for the high explosive shells. Once set, they found a home for each shell inside the turret and the ammunition compartments of the hull.[65] Whenever a fresh shipment of gasoline arrived, every five-gallon "Jerry Can" was emptied into the gas-guzzling M4s the moment they were handed down off the supply trucks.[66]

That same evening, Lt. Danby hitched a jeep ride from 756th Tank Battalion CP at Carpentras to the B Company camp at Sérignan[67] and met Captain Redle for the first time. With the camp commotion and a red setting sun as a backdrop, the two sat down for forty-five minutes of conversation. Redle never relied upon a set introductory speech or followed any formal orientation schedule for his new officers. Instead, he preferred to hold an informal chit-chat to gain a sense of a man's character, put him at ease, and answer any of his questions. Redle wished he could spend more time easing a new man into his platoon command, but life on the front line did not allow such luxuries. A new officer had to learn to sink or swim on his own. This sad reality not only applied to replacement officers, but also to everyone brought in to fill out the enlisted ranks. Although the discussion was short, Redle was impressed with Danby's past service as an ITC instructor, his fluency in French, and his enthusiastic attitude. The only quality the new officer seemed to lack was combat experience. Redle was enough of a veteran to know everyone had to start somewhere. By all indications, after the next twenty-four hours, Danby would no longer lack that quality.

Capt. Redle briefed the willowy officer on the tactical situation he expected his platoon would face the following day. He described some of the personalities and expectations of the infantry officers with whom Danby would be assigned, and how his platoon would be resupplied while in the field. After all the basics were covered, the captain walked Danby over to meet S/Sgt. Oliver and the other three sergeants of his tank platoon. Once the introductions were at an end, Redle returned to his CP. 3rd Platoon had its new leader. [68]

At 9:00 P.M., the tanks of 1st Platoon rumbled out of the bivouac area to join with 1st Battalion in the northwest.[69] After calling for them all day, the infantry was finally getting their armor. 1st Battalion would act as the regiment's left flank during the morning attack against the retreating Germans. Tanks would be essential to that drive because everyone expected the Germans massed south of Montélimar would put up heavy resistance, throwing everything they had at the Americans, from machine guns and mortars to anti-tank guns and panzers.

Lt. Col. Boye and 3rd Battalion, however, would have to wait until dawn for their tanks. Danby's crews needed a few hours rest, and it was wise to avoid nighttime travel whenever possible. In the dark, nobody could tell if a rumbling tank engine was an approaching friend or foe. Once joined in the morning by Danby's platoon, 3rd Battalion would move on Montélimar and act as the regimental right flank.

So long as gasoline arrived in a timely fashion, 2nd Battalion and the tanks from 2nd Platoon would follow the advance in reserve.

During the late evening hours, once all the dizzying introductions and platoon preparations were finished, an elated but exhausted Lt. Danby found a shaded light source and scribbled a letter home:

> Dearest –
>
> Well, darling, it finally came – I am now in actual combat with the Seventh Army in southern France. I am back to my first love – I'm leading a platoon of medium tanks. Action came fast after that last letter I wrote you from the replacement depot. I flew over here the next day. Within eighteen hours after leaving the R.D. I was up with my unit in the front lines.
>
> Now dear, I don't want you to worry about me because it won't do any good, and anyway I'm not worrying. I will be as careful as I can and I'm old enough to know how to take care of myself. Just have faith in me and trust in God to look after me, just as I trust in Him to look after you and the boys until I get back. Just say a little prayer for me every day, and that will help me to keep going, I know. You are a remarkable woman, my dear wife, you are strong mentally and spiritually, and I know that you won't give way to any weakness such as anxiety or worry. I'll be back, never fear – I wasn't made to die yet.
>
> We are moving fast – the Germans are retreating so fast that we are having a hard time catching up to them. We are moving up just where I told you in my last letter that I had visions of going, so watch our progress.
>
> I'll write whenever I can but I can't say how often that will be. However, you know that I will be thinking of you every day, as I make this my greatest sacrifice for freedom and liberty.

God bless you, dearest one, and keep you. This won't last long now and I'll be seeing you before long.
All my love to you as ever,

Your loving,

Edgar[70]

Alone with his thoughts, a multitude of questions poured into the young lieutenant's mind; Was he ready for this? How would he do? Would the men accept him? He had no time to absorb his new surroundings, no time to befriend anyone. He had no time to tap into that wealth of combat experience amassed by Redle, Oliver, or any of the others. No time to pick their sharp minds for those gems of practical wisdom that couldn't possibly be taught at OCS or Armor School . . . the tiny often overlooked details that saved lives and assured successful missions.

Few men truly desire combat. Deep down, what they're really after is a chance to prove themselves under life's harshest trials and gain the acceptance of other men who have survived the same ordeals. This is a bond of brotherhood that runs deeper than blood.

Danby would have to rely on his training and strength of character to earn his way into that brotherhood. He had nothing more to do but to say some quiet prayers and try to catch a few hours of sleep.

Tomorrow would be his trial by fire—the day he thought would never arrive.

Chapter 9

Armor Column

A t 4:00 A.M. on August 27, Lt. Col. Boye's 3rd Battalion began moving forward.[1] A short time earlier, the men of K Company, positioned around Sainte-Cécile, stirred and cussed after their officers woke them after a short night of sleep. Some splashed canteen water on their faces to wake up; others groaned as they slipped their blistered feet back into boots still wet and stinking of sweat. Within a few moments, they were stumbling through the predawn darkness along the road from Sainte-Cécile to Suze-la-Rousse. They had four miles to cover before dawn, on joints still stiff from sleeping on the hard ground. The lucky few scrambled for places atop Lt. Finley's tank destroyers as the four 33-ton beasts moved in from Cairanne and rumbled to the head of the battalion column.[2] After their noses adapted to the acrid smell of the diesel exhaust, they rested their legs and tried to squeeze out a few more minutes of precious semi-sleep.

Meanwhile, to the west at Rochegude, the men of L Company also arose, packed, and began a three-mile trek north to rendezvous with the head of the battalion column at Suze.[3] Many of the guys had a difficult time walking because of painful blisters on their feet.[4] At the same early hour, I Company pulled out of Cairanne southeast of Sainte-Cécile to bring up the rear of the march.

The battalion's first vehicles pulled into Suze thirty minutes later, met up with the two M8s, and collected the K Company platoon stationed south of town. The mines south of town had been cleared, but the north bridge over the Lez River was still booby-trapped.[5] The Americans were fortunate that the bridge was still there. The departing Germans either did not have the time or the means to demolish it. The battalion's Ammo and Pioneer (A & P) Platoon was called forward to remove the threats.

Despite the early hour, a good number of civilians and FFI members were intermingling with the Americans, offering food and information. Unfortunately, the town was completely dry of gasoline, and had been for some time. The citizens had also been without electricity, radio, and newspapers, and were starving for war news. They told the Americans that there were so many retreating Germans that they took five full days to pass through town. The enemy, they continued, were desperate for any means of transport available. The townsfolk had to hide their carts and bicycles from them. Once the end of the enormous column cleared town the prior afternoon, the local FFI took parting shots from the fields.[6] The shots were answered, of course, with rifles and machine guns, but the Germans weren't about to go chasing after anyone.

As the rear of the 3rd Battalion column arrived at Sainte-Cécile, Danby's tankers in Sérignan fired up their engines and set out to join it.[7] With dawn breaking, the four Shermans thundered northward along the five miles of narrow highway stretching between the two towns, passing row after row of magnificently maintained vineyards along the way. On their right, the men could see the hazy outlines of Mount Ventoux and the Rhône Alps ascending—and at the same time—receding into an infinity broken only by the rising sun. Idyllic orange-tiled homes and stone farms dotted the timeless countryside. Here and there, a French farmer was already tending his fields, passed down through countless generations. The history of this land receded into that same infinity. The telegraph poles and the asphalt road surface were circa 1944, but closed eyes and a vivid imagination was all anyone needed to hear a Roman legion marching along the same route—and feel a strange kinship with them. The rhythmic clanking of tank tread links against the road echoed the rattle of their ancient armor. It was a good day to be alive. A soldier never knew if a morning like this would be his last.

Danby's tanks caught up with the rear of 3rd Battalion[8] at 6:14 A.M., rolling past I Company marchers along the tree-lined streets of Sainte-Cécile.[9] More happy townspeople emerged from their homes to greet and congratulate the passing tanks and infantrymen. The morning only seemed to be getting better with each passing hour.

Because Lt. Col. Boye needed the tanks up at the front of the column, the crowded road opened before them like the parting of the Red Sea as jeeps and trucks turned aside and sergeants pulled theirs squads onto the road shoulder. By 6:43 A.M., Danby's tanks were rolling past the magnificent ochre-colored hilltop castle dominating the center of Suze-la-Rousse. Moments later, they arrived at the head of the column and integrated with L Company and the TDs.

As L Company and the armor moved out of Suze, I Company, M Company, and the battalion HQ Company followed behind on over-loaded jeeps and trucks. K Company brought up the rear on foot. The battalion snaked its way north across the Lez Bridge while local farmers waved them on and pushed fresh melons into passing hands.[10] The day's first objective was only eight winding miles to the northwest: the large town of Saint-Paul-trois-Chateaux.

Lt. Burks and approximately eighteen men from L Company's headquarters section were riding behind the tanks and TDs in a captured German truck. The truck was a recently adopted "unofficial" company HQ vehicle, and repainted with U.S. insignia. If Uncle Sam couldn't give them all the wheels needed to move, resourceful GIs found their own. So long as the battalion CO didn't mind—and Boye didn't in the case of captured trucks—the vehicle remained. L Company wanted to keep a German motorcycle found around the same time they appropriated the truck, and Captain Coles liked the idea, but the battalion ordered him to give it up.[11]

When Burks' HQ truck began to sputter and cough, its driver pulled out of the column and parked on the road shoulder just as the motor gave out. He tried in vain to restart the truck. The battalion, meanwhile, pressed past and L Company soon disappeared beyond a bend in the twisting road. Unfortunately, captured German trucks did not carry a convenient assortment of parts and were not easily repairable. Burks and his men had little choice but to sit idly by along the roadside until someone from maintenance arrived to help them.[12]

Burks and the L Company HQ were not the only ones prematurely sidelined from the march. The Chemical Mortar Platoon ran out of gasoline again and dropped out of the column.[13] The mortar men had only rejoined the battalion during the late afternoon on the previous day. Their devastating and indispensable 4.2-inch mortars helped silence the first German airburst attack at Luxembourg four days earlier. If the battalion ran into similar trouble, Boye could not call upon them until they were resupplied with fuel and caught up with everyone else.

Midway through the advance on Saint-Paul, K and I Companies swapped column positions to give the men of K a chance to ride for a while and rest their feet. I Company brought up the rear on foot. It would remain there as the reserve company for the balance of the day.

By 8:55 A.M., L and K Companies entered Saint-Paul, with Lt. Col. Boye's Headquarters Company arriving shortly thereafter. Once the men dismounted, a convoy of the battalion trucks and jeeps sped back to help I Company close the gap. The bridges and roadways throughout town were inspected for mines and obstacles. One of the Saint-Paul bridges was out, but the loss presented little delay to battalion plans.[14] Despite the eight-mile move, the enemy was nowhere in sight, but local reports of their proximity increased and were delivered with more emphatic language. With the morning's first objective met so quickly, planning for the day's next move was set in motion. Lt. Col. Boye gathered his key officers together and the men enjoyed a quick breather and a cigarette. The adulation of the local populace was an added benefit.

While waiting with his squad, T/5 Herman Cogdell felt someone tugging on the back of his trouser leg. He turned around to find a little French boy pointing toward the window of a nearby building and whispering secretively "Les Boches," a derogatory French nickname for Germans. Cogdell gathered some of his squad mates together to investigate. A dozen German Mauser rifles were found, neatly stacked in the corner of the basement. Seated nearby was a small group of German soldiers, frightened and eager to surrender—particularly to Americans.[15]

Sgt. Edmund Rovas hadn't felt right all morning. Though his forehead was still bandaged and healing from his near miss nine days earlier, Rovas was certain the symptoms had nothing to do with it. Trusting the strange sensations would soon pass, he tried to keep moving. He was wrong. Without warning, his left side went numb like a cascading power failure. His tongue grew thick and he had difficulty putting words together. After a few more seconds, he collapsed to the ground in a heap, unable to move. The stricken squad leader's nearby comrades jumped to his assistance, hollering for a medic. Rovas had suffered a severe case of heat exhaustion and was immediately evacuated to the battalion aid station. Sgt. Roy Sanders was now in charge of the squad.[16]

Though the battalion had achieved Saint-Paul by mid-morning, Boye could already see that reaching Montélimar by noon was out of the question—at least for his battalion. The German column creeping along

Route 7 was still a good ten or fifteen miles to the north-northwest, and Montélimar lay another five or six miles beyond that. The infantry, exhausted and footsore, simply couldn't march any faster. The weather was hot, and nearly everyone had blistered feet. Moving the battalion forward piecemeal, shuttling vehicles back and forth was also not a viable option because there was not enough fuel to do so. Boye had already lost the Chemical Mortars to the fuel shortage, and couldn't afford to lose anything else. The cool and stately lieutenant colonel concluded that his only option was to divide his command, sending some of his battalion far ahead to strike hard into the German column. He had an idea of who might want to lead that mission. Boye called over Captain Coles and asked him if Company L was up for the challenge. Coles responded that his men were willing, but many were having a difficult time walking.[17] Boye assured him he would have sufficient wheels and tracks for his men to ride, and that marching would be kept to a bare minimum. With that understanding, the two tall officers began fleshing out a practical plan.

Lt. Danby's tanks were waiting along the roadside for their orders. For some reason, Danby's SCR-528 radio mounted in the back of the tank turret began cutting in and out, leaving him unable to communicate properly with his platoon or Captain Redle's command post, which was now moving up from Sérignan. Danby couldn't determine if the radio had a mechanical malfunction or if the hilly terrain was causing signal interference. The tank's FM radios were notoriously fickle around hills and buildings. Danby had to find a solution, and he needed one fast. Boye was staging the next move and was sure to send a runner back for him.[18]

Danby ordered driver T/5 Jesse Rickerson[19] to pull up alongside Sgt. Roy Anderson's tank. The new lieutenant called over to ask Anderson if his radio was working. Despite the M4A1's aged appearance, everything aboard Anderson's borrowed tank was working fine—including the radio. That meant in all likelihood, Danby's radio problem was mechanical. He asked Anderson to swap tanks. As the two hurriedly dismounted and assumed posts inside their new turrets, Danby told Anderson to hang back with the battalion until the radio was fixed. When Anderson nodded his acknowledgement, Danby drove off in a cloud of exhaust. Along with him went Anderson's tank and crew.[20]

Moments later, L Company was clambering aboard an idling armor column. At the forefront were the two tanks commanded by Danby and

S/Sgt. Oliver. Finley's four tank destroyers and a 2½-ton truck followed them. Bringing up the rear were two M8s from 1st Lt. Lloyd Cotter's 2nd Platoon of Cannon Company. Normally, Cotter's platoon consisted of three assault guns, but the M8 that overturned near Pertuis during the night march of August 25 was from his platoon.[21] Because of unrepaired damage, he was still short that gun. During most of the action in southern France, Cotter's platoon worked with the regimental Battle Patrol and had only recently shifted over to help out 3rd Battalion.[22]

An M8, like the M10 tank destroyer, was a bit of a bastard vehicle. In some respects it was a Frankenstein-like creation that only a junkyard engineer or a team of young men trying to survive a war could love. In order to give each infantry regiment some indigenous mobile artillery, the Army took an outdated M5 light tank chassis and topped it with an open turret and a short-barreled 75mm howitzer gun. An M8 was small and thinly armored, which was great for fuel economy but not so good for crew protection from anything larger than .50 caliber bullets. The purpose of the open turret was to allow for the quick dissipation of cannon smoke, but like the M10 tank destroyer, the crew was vulnerable to airbursts.[23] The howitzer lacked the muzzle velocity of the gun of a Sherman or an M-10, but retained one redeeming quality; since a howitzer was an artillery piece, the rounds could be fired in arcs over buildings, trees, and hills, whereas a tank or TD could only fire on a flat "line of sight" trajectory.[24] The M8's special niche was its ability to "lay one in on a target" as far as 9,500 yards—far beyond the range of mortars alone.[25] This particular attribute made the M8 a perfect weapon for harassing a mass of retreating Germans from a distance. Though the M8 was not designed for close infantry support, a .50 caliber machine gun was mounted on the back of the turret, just in case.

1st Lt. Lloyd Cotter was a soft-spoken and serious officer, very protective of his men and his vehicles.[26] Though he was only twenty-two years old, he was already married and had six years of military experience.[27] He had enlisted at sixteen into the California National Guard by misrepresenting his age. Cotter stood six feet two inches tall with a lanky build, sky blue eyes and short brown hair.[28] He and George Burks had been OCS classmates and barracks mates at Fort Benning, where the two men became casual friends. Cotter was motivated, intelligent, and prepared himself for anything. While at the OCS barracks, he did pull-ups in the rafters to improve his upper body strength.[29] When the Army discovered that he excelled at trigonometry, Cotter was zipped into artillery studies. He did so well that Fort Benning retained him for a time as a lecturer. In early 1943, the shortage of officers in the Mediterranean Theater forced Cotter overseas, where he joined 15th Infantry Regiment's Cannon Company on the Anzio beachhead. Within days of his arrival, the young officer was shot in the leg during combat operations. Recovery took three long months, but he recuperated in time for the landings in southern France.[30]

Lt. Cotter's platoon sergeant was Technical Sergeant (T/Sgt.) George Polich, a short, tanned fellow of Croatian descent with jet-black hair and a big toothy smile. Polich came from a large Iowa farming family and fostered a similar sense of kinship within the platoon.[31] He was twenty-three years old and had been a member of 15th Infantry Regiment since July 1940, when he began his service as a cook in M Company.[32] Polich's natural leadership abilities were quickly recognized, and he served stints as a mess sergeant and a drill instructor before voluntarily forfeiting his stripes for a shot at combat. He joined Cannon Company as a private in September 1942 when the unit was shipping out for Casablanca. By the time 3rd Infantry Division reached Italy twelve months later, Polich had advanced five grades and was the technical sergeant in charge of 2nd Platoon after Cotter.[33]

Cotter's duties as platoon leader often took him away from the M8s and crews. In times of battle, the lieutenant usually positioned up with the infantry along with his radio, jeep, and driver. There, he could coordinate with the infantry commander and call artillery coordinates back to Polich. Despite Cotter's protective instincts, he had absolute confidence in Polich to manage the guns in his absence. Together, the two men formed a formidable leadership team.

Once L Company was packed atop the eight armor pieces, truck, and two jeeps of the column, the small task force set out from Saint-Paul for Montélimar.[34] Its orders were to flank with all haste and then rain havoc upon the German exodus.[35] The column lurched forward in segments, with about 100 yards separating each piece of armor. Within moments, every vehicle was rolling north at a steady 10 mph clip. Ironically, Lt. Danby led the affair. His was an extraordinary transformation of circumstances. Only seventy-two hours earlier, Danby was a discarded ITC officer sweating it out in a Naples Reple Deple. Now he was sweating it out inside a tank heading for battle. His was not just any tank, but the lead tank for the entire 3rd Division's spear thrust up the Rhône river valley.

Riding in his jeep and trailer combination nearby was Captain Coles, hulked alongside the driver, with his red freckled face and arms glinting in the morning sun. The all-important battalion radio was at his side, and Coles was his usual animated and alert self, impelling the men and tanks forward with his confidence and determination. His men always responded well to him when they were bound for battle. Lt. Danby was in good hands.

The American column thundered for several miles down a blacktop roadway that was unusual because it was perfectly straight. The Romans built the original road 2,000 years earlier.[36] Here it was 1944, and it was still moving armies. A flat landscape of fields and vineyards lay on either side, peppered here and there with stone farms. Several hundred yards to the right was a long descending ridge and series of hills, holding countless ideal places for German observation or artillery ambush. As the column passed, nearly every eye studied the hills, focusing particularly on the distant buildings of La Garde-Adhémar, a picturesque walled village on the ridge.

The hillside town passed without incident, but moments later at 9:40 A.M., two rounds of artillery exploded in front of the advancing column. The bursts were followed by all manner of small arms.[37] The men of L Company dismounted the tanks "like fleas jumping off a dog," remembered one eyewitness, and took cover among the roadside ditches.[38] Ahead and to the right, nestled within a thicket of trees near the estate of Chartroussas, the Germans had established a defensive position. At first blush, it appeared to be a simple roadblock consisting of one or two anti-tank guns, a machine gun position, and several riflemen.[39]

Captain Coles radioed the battalion to inform Boye of the situation while Danby and Oliver moved their tanks forward and blasted away one anti-tank gun and a machine gun nest. Their aggressive response dispersed the other German defenders. L Company troops maneuvered forward and stormed the position, capturing the second anti-tank gun and three trucks.[40] The remaining Germans, numbering as many as thirty, withdrew into the woods leaving three dead comrades behind.[41]

The German roadblock was comprised of members of 2nd Company / 669th Pioneer Battalion (engineers).[42] Most of the defenders were between the ages of thirty and forty, and were previously wounded on the

Russian front. The 669th, under the command of the German 338th Infantry Division of the LXXXV Armeekorps, was entrusted with the responsibility of blowing bridges and establishing roadblocks ahead of the advancing Americans.[43] Other 669th Pioneer Battalion roadblocks were organized along a fifteen-mile chain from Donzère in the west to Valaurie, Grignan, and Taulignan in the east.[44] L Company had unknowingly broken the soft link between Donzère and Valaurie and was about to slip through. Nothing stood between them and the German traffic jam south of Montélimar except for one unknown and rather surprising obstacle: the LXXXV Armeekorps headquarters at Allan.

The German roadblock team was simply overmatched. In all likelihood, its members did not expect their first clash to involve a line of American armor. Almost certainly their hopes were to knock out a few leading jeeps or trucks and scatter the first American troops for several hours. They were at Chartroussas to make some noise and buy their retreating comrades a little time, and nothing more. A set of stationary AT guns, however, had little chance against eight mobile cannons. An AT gun could not effectively track moving targets and offered little crew protection save for a thin frontal plate only useful for deflecting small arms fire. The instant the two German AT guns fired, the element of surprise was lost and the cannon smoke compromised their positions. The Shermans maneuvered out of their line of fire and blasted high explosive shells in counter response. No direct hit was necessary. The concussion alone was enough to take out the gun crew. With the first AT gun gone, the Germans at the second one didn't wait to be reduced to body parts draped in nearby trees. Their small arms support didn't linger, either. A rifle or machine gun was only useful for chipping paint off a Sherman's hull.

Though the engagement was short and ineffective, the Germans bought just enough time to alert the LXXXV Armeekorps HQ and Nineteenth Army of the American intrusion, and that it was advancing with armor.[45]

After the area was thoroughly checked and declared clear of additional threats, Captain Coles reorganized his men and ordered them back on top the sun-baked decks of the tanks. By 10:30 A.M. the column was again rolling toward Montélimar. It passed unopposed through the crossroads hamlet of Le Logis de Berre and into the small forest of "Bois de Mattes."[46]

3rd Battalion, meanwhile, set out from Saint-Paul in L Company's wake. K Company and the battalion HQ departed first, with I Company bringing up the rear.[47] A short time later, Lt. Col. Boye established a temporary command post near the blasted Chartroussas roadblock and waited for his men marching on foot to catch up.

Captain Redle had monitored the entire roadblock episode while moving his command post from Sérignan to Saint-Paul.[48] Inside a captured German trailer used by B Company as a mobile command center, 1st Sgt. Alvin Nusz was listening to the radio traffic on both tank and infantry bands and apprising Redle of key developments.[49]

Redle felt some degree of relief. The German AT fire had missed his B Company tankers, and Lt. Danby passed his initial combat test with flying colors. Redle could never be certain how a new platoon leader would act under fire. The lieutenant himself wasn't even sure. Redle had witnessed a gamut of behavioral extremes in officers faced with their first combat test, from one who became giddy and took irrational chances, to another who withdrew inside his tank like a tortoise in a shell and refused to answer the radio.[50]

Danby's test was a small but important one. More challenges, more difficult and more decisive, promised to follow. A bitter and maddening principle of war was that a lesson learned in one fight did not necessarily apply to the next one. Redle knew this well. Danby suspected as much.

 Chapter 10

Allan

F ive miles north of the advancing L Company column was a small farming town named Allan. And the place was buzzing with enemy activity.

One week earlier, the German LXXXV Armeekorps had moved in and set up operations. The korps staff had to juggle many concerns—not the least of which included the Americans. The korps' primary responsibility was to get as many of its own out of southern France to fight another day. Coordinating the chaotic retreat traffic through the Montélimar bottleneck was an all-consuming operation. On top of managing that nightmare, the korps staff had to prepare a plausible rearguard against the American forces closing in from the south, and remain alert for FFI and partisan guerrilla-style attacks that often came at anytime and any place.

German intelligence believed the American 3rd Division was far enough south and sufficiently hampered by supply shortages, that the korps could squeeze out one more full day of work in and around Allan before it had to leave. However, the early and shocking loss of the XXII Armeekorps headquarters at Draguignan to Allied paratroopers alerted the LXXXV staff to the danger from the skies and the cost of being unprepared. Immediate preparations ensued to defend the town with armor.

The Germans knew how to prepare for the arrival of American infantry. Daily intelligence reports allowed them to locate the Americans on a map and extrapolate the times and places the enemy infantry would appear. The FFI and FTP were far more problematic and exasperating. French Resistance fighters blended in easily among the general populace and were notorious for striking without warning and without concern for Geneva Convention rules. The psychological effect on the Germans was evident. The occupiers called French Resistance fighters "terrorists," not so much out of disdain for their tactics, for the Germans were just as brutal, but because they were genuinely terrified of them.

For the most part, the French public was sympathetic to the FFI and FTP, but deeply concerned about the ramifications of supporting their efforts. Certain regions and towns were more deeply connected with the Resistance movement than others—even at the risk of German reprisals. Allan was one of those towns. Twice during the prior six months, the Germans threatened to randomly select citizens of Allan and execute them. With the influx of so many Germans into the village after the Riviera landings, the levels of discomfort and mistrust on both sides rose rapidly and threatened to explode out of control.

Allan was a valley village of roughly 400 citizens situated three miles southeast of Montélimar. The town consisted of several dozen buildings constructed of the region's usual fieldstone with terra cotta roofs. A Catholic Church and bell tower rose above the village center at the northeast corner of the town's angled crossroads. Mature, stately platane trees lined the main street and the village square in the town's southeastern quarter invited travelers to stop and enjoy the cool shade and a sip of licorice liquor. But the LXXXV Korps erected its headquarters in Allan during the week of the German retreat not for its beauty, but because of its strategic location.

A third of a mile east of Allan was a large hill with the ruins of a walled medieval village clinging to the slope. Its thick crumbling walls and parapet foundations dated back 800 years—the remnants of "Old Allan," the ancestral home to many of the farming families still living in the newer town of the same name. When advances in warfare made walled cities obsolete by the eighteenth and nineteenth centuries, the old village was abandoned and rebuilt at the crossroads below, closer to the fields and the vineyards. Many of the "new" buildings of Allan were constructed from stone cannibalized from the old village. On the morning of August 27, 1944, German officers in town warned the townspeople of a brewing battle with the approaching Americans; many civilians sought refuge and safety among those ancient ruins. This time, they were hoping "Old Allan" would save them from modern war.[1]

Modern wars had already extracted a high price from the town. Many local sons, fathers, and husbands marched off to fight in the "Great War" of 1914-1918 and never returned. In the cemetery north of town, a monument to the First World War was erected with the inscription "Morts Pour la Patrie" (Died for the Homeland). Below this simple chiseled phrase were the names of twenty-one Allan men.[2] Everyone in town lost someone to that war—a family member, a neighbor, or a friend.

In 1940, when Germany invaded France for the second time in a generation, fifty men from Allan left their fields and shops to defend the homeland yet again. Seventeen were captured and ended up in prisoner of war camps in Germany. The welfare of these men was of constant concern to their families and neighbors. Despite times of material scarcity, the town sent weekly Red Cross packages to their POWs filled with whatever comforts they could spare.

After the sudden and shocking capitulation of the French government, Allan became part of Vichy territory. The people of town tried to carry on with their lives with some degree of normalcy, but experienced constant reminders of France's great national disgrace. When the Allies landed in North Africa in November of 1942, the Axis responded by moving forces into Vichy France. This included the deployment of an Italian alpine artillery unit at Allan.

The citizens initially regarded their Latin interlopers with great suspicion. Patrolling Italian soldiers appeared unexpectedly in unusual places—like in the middle of the fields when the farmers were trying to work. In time, the French realized the reason; the poor fellows were hungry and foraging for any vegetables left behind by the farmers. Although armed with rifles, the Italians never displayed hostility toward anyone. In fact, they became something of a joke to the locals. Even their oversized capes and feathered hats presented an image more comical than threatening. The bizarre occupation lasted but a few weeks, and then one day the Italians were gone. The whole episode could have served as an amusing vignette in the middle of an opera were it not for the war.

Many French towns helped conceal young French men avoiding compulsory military service or work assignments. Under these German instituted programs, business leaders, farmers, and essential farm workers were exempt from mandatory service. However, French authorities sympathetic to the Resistance discovered that these exemptions were quite easy to manufacture. The local civil magistrate and the mayor of Allan falsified certificates for fourteen young men so they could pass as essential farm workers and work the local fields. Some of these men were members of the French Resistance and were specifically placed in the area with the assent of the town fathers. Though most were not native to the region, the people of Allan adopted them as sons and watched out for them.

By early 1944, the FFI had become quite active in the Montélimar area. The Resistance throughout the Rhône Valley was well-organized and integrated into a network of more than 100 separate Resistance groups spread throughout southern France. Through the organizational efforts of steely-nerved undercover agents, such as British SOE officer Major Francis Cammaerts and FFI leaders like Raymond Daujat and Pierre J. L. Raynaud, the groups coordinated activities and received supplies via clandestine Allied parachute drops.[3] The increased FFI activity around Montélimar did not go unnoticed by the German authorities.

An FFI cell was established on a farm near Allan, and many of the townspeople were aware of them and their activities. The group operated under the tactical name "103rd FFI Group," and consisted of around a dozen young men. Most were former students and tradesmen from the Lyon area. They operated from the "Aubagne Farm," an abandoned stone homestead, in the hills to the southeast of Allan. The group was led by Lieutenants Marcel Delaby and Daniel Quinaud. For some time, the cell carried out their network orders in relative anonymity. One day, however, a routine assignment went terribly wrong.

Late in March 1944, in the town of Châteauneuf a few miles to the east of Allan, a German tanker truck filled with precious gasoline pulled up and parked outside a repair garage. The tractor section was separated from the trailer, evidently for repairs. For eight days, the fully laden tanker trailer sat in the driveway, like a big ripe plum ready for the picking. Word of this spread quickly throughout the FFI network. The Resistance leadership considered the target too good to pass up, so the 103rd FFI Group was instructed to steal some of the fuel. During the early hours of March 30, 1944, Lts. Delaby and Quinaud and several of their comrades set out from Aubagne Farm. Each man carried with him an empty container.

When the men arrived at the repair garage before dawn, the tanker trailer was still there, unguarded and full of gasoline. Once they determined the way was clear, they broke open the spigot lock and began filling cans. After loading up with all they could carry, they agreed to split into two groups and take separate routes back to the Aubagne Farm. The first group left promptly in one direction, while Lts. Delaby, Quinaud, and two others in the second group set off in another. After walking a short distance, a German truck filled with soldiers appeared out of nowhere. Before the second group could dip into the brush, the large truck pulled alongside them and screeched to a halt. Grey uniformed figures poured from the back with guns raised and stern voices barking, "Halt!" "Hände hoch!" ("Stop!" "Hands up!")

The four Frenchmen realized they were about to be arrested by the dreaded Waffen SS. The unguarded tanker was a setup. The French Resistance men dropped their canisters and sought out ways to escape, but there were no good options available. One thing was certain, however: they would not to go willingly with the SS.

The SS troopers fanned out and moved quickly toward their stunned prey. Some focused on Delaby and Quinaud, while others closed in on the other two FFI men standing farther away. Without warning and in absolute desperation, all four FFI men pulled out hand grenades, tossed them toward the truck, and ran for their lives. The grenades exploded, but did little damage. The angry soldiers answered with a concerted burst of submachine gun fire. The first bullets tore into the back of Lt. Delaby. He mustered a few more steps before crumpling to the ground. The same burst blew open Lt. Quinaud's knee and he also collapsed into a helpless heap. Both officers were quickly surrounded and unceremoniously stripped of any additional weapons. A third man from the group was also captured, but the last man managed to disappear into the shadowy woods, an escape purchased at a very high price.

The three captives were tossed on the SS truck and taken across the Rhône to the nearby town of Viviers for medical attention and interrogation.[4] Delaby died of his wounds before they arrived. For him, death would prove a blessing. The Germans were notorious interrogators, particularly of "terrorists."

The first band of FFI men who departed in another direction, meanwhile, heard the nearby explosions and shots in the early dawn air. They knew turning back to help their comrades would be suicide. Instead, they scrambled over the tracks of a nearby railroad for the safety of the wooded hills. Though the Germans did not see them, they knew they had escaped into the neighboring countryside. Agitated that the sting operation was not yet a complete success, the troopers spent the next hour searching high and low for the nearby gasoline thieves, shooting up any suspicious-looking tree, bush, or thicket. The Germans called off the hunt at 6:30 A.M. They had not given up. Instead, they changed their plans for the fate of the FFI group.

The survivors of the debacle hustled on foot across several miles of forests, fields, and ravines in an effort to warn their friends at the Aubagne Farm. As they struggled through the terrain, the SS troopers boarded another truck and set off toward Allan. Early rising farmers attending the southern fields of town watched with curiosity as a German officers' car and a large gray truck approached from Malataverne. Everything about the passing vehicles held an ominous aura, from the growling motors to the stern faces of the officers and their dark helmeted cohorts. Both vehicles slowed upon entering town before downshifting as they approached the crossroads. The drivers turned their wheels hard right without stopping and exited southeast of the village, leaving behind rude puffs of exhaust smoke. The passing of such heavily armed Germans was not an everyday occurrence in Allan. Those watching feared the worst, for the SS troopers seemed to be heading directly toward the secret FFI farmhouse. As the exhaust smoke dissipated and the two vehicles disappeared beyond the trees and farms of Aiguebelle road, the witnesses realized how powerless they truly were to stop what was about to take place.

At 9:30 A.M., the two German vehicles stopped on the road a short distance away from the Aubagne farm. The troopers filed off the truck, fanned out, and began maneuvering up the southern foot of the wooded hill and toward the secluded stone building. The move caught the FFI fighters completely off guard. Their comrades who escaped Châteauneuf had not arrived in time to warn them. The Waffen SS nearly had the house surrounded before they could even consider fleeing. A few opening shots quickly escalated into a major small arms battle.

One member of the Aubagne group was returning from Montélimar on his bicycle by way of Aiguebelle road. As he labored up the long winding road, shots echoing through the hills reached his ears. He continued peddling nonetheless. As soon as he rounded the curve at Col des Ormes, two SS troopers with Schmeissers intercepted him and motioned for him to stop. Both men spoke in perfect French with the accents of southerners—Frenchmen who had joined the Waffen SS. With an arrogant tone typical of their uniforms, the two collaborators demanded the cyclist's identity papers and quizzed him suspiciously about his travel. When they discovered that the man's papers were not properly credentialed, they ordered him to leave his bike and accompany them up the hill.

The three walked toward the gray truck parked farther up the road. Along the way, the two French SS enlistees openly discussed the ramifications of their arrest. Before reaching the truck, they concluded that apprehending the cyclist due to a document with a small technical violation risked merciless ridicule from their peers and their German NCO. In a surprising about-face, they told the cyclist he was free to go.

The thoroughly relieved young man didn't wait for them to reconsider. He sprinted back to his bicycle, hopped on the seat and started off in the direction he came from, all the while clutching the jacket he left on the bicycle seat before his arrest. Inside the coat pockets were incriminating papers and banned books. The two French SS members never bothered to search the garment. As if to underscore their amateurishness, the two French SS men fired a burst of machine pistol slugs in the cyclist's general direction—not to hit him, but only to scare him for a cheap laugh. Once safely away, the cyclist reflected on what had transpired and realized that he had been extremely fortunate.

The sounds of rifle and automatic fire at the Aubagne farm alerted additional members of the 103rd FFI group at a second farmhouse about one mile away. Out of concern for their friends they decided to investigate. Surreptitiously approaching the Aubagne farm, they observed Germans with machine guns blocking the road leading to the homestead. Attacking such heavily armed positions was out of the question. After returning to their farm, they packed their weapons and a few belongings and disappeared deeper into the highland woods.

By the time the Aubagne gunfight seeped into its third hour, everyone inside the house knew the situation was beyond desperate. Two young FFI men were dead outside the stone home. Another, a Hungarian student before joining the FFI, took a bullet in the foot and had hobbled off into the woods. Events would prove how fortunate his wound was. He eventually reached the safety of the Aiguebelle convent several miles distant.

The remaining six irregulars were fighting from behind the protective walls of the farmhouse. With the Germans squeezing in from all directions, they stubbornly continued to fire away, their dwindling supply of ammunition eventually exhausted. Once the Germans moved close enough to toss potato masher grenades through the windows, the six finally surrendered.

Back at Allan, some of the citizens had gathered and nervously listened to the distant commotion. When the gunfire ceased, many began to fear a reprisal on their village. At four that afternoon, the two German vehicles returned via Aiguebelle and parked before the town hall. Several officers emerged from the car, grinding their tall black boots into the ground as they rose and spun around to face the truck. They stood impatiently as six bound prisoners were shoved out of the cargo bed by unsympathetic guards. Once everyone was out, the driver muscled the transmission into gear and drove off in the direction of Châteauneuf.

The SS commander stormed into the town hall and demanded to see the mayor. The civil magistrate rose to inform him that Mayor Georges Almoric was out attending his farm. The magistrate was escorted to the car, told to join the other officers inside, and ordered to guide the SS to the mayor's farm. A few minutes later, the car reached the Almoric homestead. Summoned from the fields, the young mayor was ordered into the car. During the return ride to the village, the SS commander told Almoric that he was going to witness the execution of six "terrorists" near the town hall in one hour. He was also ordered to gather all the townspeople as witnesses.

Mayor Almoric had no desire to cooperate with the hated SS, but neither did he wish to provoke the agitated German officer into doing something even worse than executing six men. All he could think to do was to stall for time. He protested that an hour was not adequate enough to summon all the citizens of Allan. Many were working farmers scattered about the countryside. The commandant acknowledged Almoric's protest, but refused to alter his time schedule. Instead, he reduced his witness requirements to that of Almoric's staff and the other civilian officials of the town. Once the car returned at the village square, Almoric reluctantly sent for the others.

Over the next hour, shaken town leaders gathered near the eastern wall of the town hall. Among them was Maurice Martel, a civil engineer who rushed over to determine the identities of the captured young men.[5]

Martel's nineteen-year old son Lucien was hiding from mandatory work service and lived on a nearby farm under an alias. Both Martel and his son had provided supplies, safe haven, and information to FFI members.[6] To his relief, Lucien was not among the six bound and battered prisoners. Martel was visibly troubled, however, by the fact that a Catholic priest was not present. When he offered his services to Almoric, the mayor agreed and Martel ran to the church rectory. The town priest was absent, but the priest from the nearby town of Espeluche was visiting. Martel informed him of the situation while the two raced back to the grim scene. Mayor Almoric introduced the priest to the SS officer and pleaded for the condemned to be given access to the holy sacraments. The German agreed, but with the stipulation that the process be done quickly.

As the six young men were paraded before the distraught gathering, the priest implored the SS man to spare their lives. He refused. The priest selflessly offered to die in their place, but the commandant remained unmoved. SS soldiers prodded the condemned toward the eastern wall of the town hall while the priest suggested every plausible alternative he could come up with, but to no avail. The SS officer finally waved him off. He had heard enough.

At precisely 5:00 P.M., the scheduled time of execution, the German officer divided the condemned into two sets of three. The first set was lined up with their faces toward the wall—a position of disgrace. The priest met with each man for a few moments of final prayer and absolution. When his work was complete and nothing further could be done, he stepped back with great reluctance.

Mayor Almoric read a brief statement and moved aside. The words were obviously not his own. The SS commander cleared his throat and addressed the gathering. In his speech, he referred to the six men as "traitors" and expressed regrets for having to shoot them in the back. He presented his version of events and stressed how the six FFI fighters shot and wounded some of his men, and then fired on a medic trying to render medical assistance to them. His excuses played to an unsympathetic crowd.

Once he finished, the French witnesses shuffled behind the firing squad so they would have to face the horrific scene. Without further delay, the SS officer gave the command: "Feuer!" Deafening bursts from submachine guns ripped into the first three prisoners, splattering their blood and chipping the stone and mortar from the wall behind them. They slumped to the ground together like discarded rag dolls. Save for the involuntary gasps and sobs of the witnesses—and the faraway chirping of birds oblivious to the drama and disputes of mankind—an eerie calm followed.

The second set of prisoners was brought forward to stand before their fallen comrades. The three men faced the wall and waited with the same quiet defiance as the first group. Just before the "fire" order was given, one of the condemned turned to lambaste the Germans for not shooting all six of them at the same time. His protest ended in mid-sentence with gunfire. His riddled body, with those of his two friends, buckled and collapsed atop the others already sprawled on the ground. In a stroke of finality, one of the German soldiers strolled forward and casually put a bullet into the head of each corpse, just to make sure. Another uneasy stillness settled upon the village.

The SS commander allowed the horrific scene to sink into the psyches of the witnesses for a few moments, before strutting forward to address them again. This time his comments were angry and accusatory, his body language vigorous and provocative. He directed his tirade primarily toward Mayor Almoric, whom he accused of having knowledge of the nearby "terrorist" camp and doing nothing about it. He closed with a threat to the mayor and the other town leaders that any future incident of a similar nature would lead not only to the deaths of those directly responsible, but of them as well. He made certain that particular point was perfectly clear.

As soon as the speech ended, Mayor Almoric boldly asked for permission to remove the bodies for proper burial preparation. Visibly irritated by the request, the SS officer not only refused, but also forbade their removal until noon the following day. No one could even touch them until that deadline had passed. His decree made certain that the corpses remain in their tangled, macabre positions as a brutal warning to those who dared cross their German occupiers.

The SS officer and his partners in this war crime disappeared inside his car. When the vehicle sped away toward Châteauneuf, the mayor and his assistants gazed in shock and sadness at the execution wall. The blood from the lifeless bodies had spread across the ground and pooled against the wall. It was at that point when the emotional dam broke. Tears flowed freely as the mayor and townsfolk comforted one another. They had no way of knowing that their nightmare was not yet at an end.

Ninety minutes after the men had been executed the S.S. truck reappeared in the village. The vehicle rumbled to a stop near the execution wall. The limp corpse of Lt. Delaby was pulled from the deck and dumped along the wall with the other bodies. The SS men hauled Lt. Quinaud off the truck. He was in terrible pain, weak, and unable to stand because of his mangled knee. The SS commander summoned Mayor Almoric a second time that fateful day, and allowed him to call for the priest. By this time, however, the priest from Espeluche had left the village to locate Allan's priest, and neither had yet returned. Unwilling to delay the inevitable, the commander ordered Quinaud dragged to the execution wall, where the guards released him and stepped away. The lieutenant's wounded leg buckled and he fell to the ground. While he was struggling to lift his torso in the hopes of a brave and dignified death, the submachine guns blazed a third time. As a final insult, the executioners ripped open the clothing of the dead victims so the bullet wounds would be more visible to passers-by. And then they left.

A short time later, the two priests arrived. When they realized what had transpired in their absence—that they were too late to comfort Lt. Quinaud in his final agonizing moments—the distress on their faces were clear for everyone to see. In direct contradiction of the SS officer's orders, the pair of priests covered the remains with blankets to protect them from the sun, insects, and scavenging animals. Throughout the night, townspeople took turns watching over the bodies. Fortunately for the citizens of Allan, the Germans and their vengeful officer never returned to check on whether the orders were obeyed.

The next morning, the local civil police brought to Allan the bodies of the two FFI fighters killed in the shootout at the Aubagne farm. In total, ten victims waited to be identified and buried. Even though the SS officer's noon deadline had not yet arrived, the civil police began searching the bodies for any clues to their identification. They found nothing. The Germans had removed most personal effects prior to execution. Early that afternoon, the victims were relocated into the town hall for the Montélimar coroner to examine and to take notes and photographs. Only then were they prepared for burial.

A funeral was held in the Catholic Church the following afternoon. Virtually everyone from Allan and the neighboring communities attended. When it ended, ten coffins were transported to the cemetery north of Allan and laid to rest side by side in the ground next to the Great War monument.

While Allan mourned, the Germans hunted. The SS soldiers fanned out across the countryside searching vigorously for any accomplices. The Gestapo returned to the Aubagne farm and scoured the place for clues. Like the unfurling tentacles of an octopus, they spread out among the nearby farmhouses to interrogate their occupants. When it suited them, they used physical intimidation, but no one interviewed admitted to knowing anything. When nothing else produced results, the Gestapo agents focused their suspicions on the convent at Aiguebelle.

For many months, the Catholic sisters at Aiguebelle had been operating a clandestine safe house for Jews, Resistance members, and many others hiding from the Gestapo. However, the wounded Hungarian student's unexpected visit two days earlier sent the sisters into a hasty flutter to relocate their refugees and purge the compound of any incriminating evidence. When the Gestapo arrived, they searched high and low with little regard for sanctity. After several hours of fruitless rummaging, they finally gave up. But before leaving, they threatened the Mother Superior with violence and the destruction of the convent.

For the next few days, anyone in the area appearing suspicious to the Gestapo was stopped, questioned, and searched—particularly young men. Some were imprisoned for days and threatened unless they talked. No one did. In the weeks that followed, the Gestapo moved on to other matters. Allan and its surrounding communities were left to mourn alone.

*   *   *

Two months after the execution, Allan's citizens rejoiced over the news of the successful Normandy landings. Several times that the summer, the Allies parachuted supplies for the FFI in the foothills southeast of Allan. Six young townsmen with a thorough knowledge of the footpaths served the FFI as drop zone guides. With liberation seeming more likely with each passing day, Resistance activity in the area took on a new life.

Normandy excited the people of Allan and others in southern France, but news of the Riviera landings on August 15 produced an overwhelming sense of euphoria throughout the region. Nearly everyone wanted to help in some way, or at least express their hopes in some concrete fashion. The people of Allan convened for prayers of thanks and protection and vowed to erect a memorial to the Virgin Mary at the end of hostilities. On the same day, they watched in awe as waves of Allied planes bombed the distant hangers at Montélimar-Aucône airport. Liberation truly seemed close at hand.

That initial euphoria melted temporarily into a sense of horror when news of nearby tragedy swept the village. Bourg-Saint-Andéol was a small Rhône River town adjacent to a key bridge about nine miles southwest. The Allied bombers trying to knock out that bridge missed and leveled the town instead. Some 160 villagers perished.[7]

By August 20, any remaining joy gave way to apprehension when long columns of retreating Germans appeared in the area. Initially, the snaking row of troops and vehicles was restricted to National Route 7, but the two-lane highway was not adequate for the numbers. The Germans began spilling over onto secondary routes. One of these routes passed directly through Allan, two miles east of National Route 7.

During the evening of August 21, an unmarked truck appeared in Allan. It remained only long enough to drop off a band of FTP partisans before driving away. The FTP posted sentinels around the village and established a base of operations at the Mège homestead in the hills just beyond the old village ruins. No one was quite sure if the strangers were shadowing the Germans as part of larger Allied plans or freelancing on their own.

The next morning, a second unmarked truck rumbled in from the south and halted at the market square near the town hall. A German warrant officer and other soldiers stepped out. They made a cursory examination of their surroundings, waving arms and discussing observations no one but they could hear. The FTP partisans prudently chose not to confront them. Instead, they slipped like shadows among the buildings, alleys, and walled gardens where they could observe without appearing suspicious.

No one wanted anything to do with the Germans. The townsfolk who had been outside attending to their morning activities withdrew inside and shuttered their doors and windows. Within moments of the truck's arrival, the vibrant village took on the appearance of a ghost town. Unconcerned, the German warrant officer walked up the deserted main street and stopped at the crossroads to continue his assessment. As he strolled, the other soldiers remounted the truck and drove up to meet him.

With a look of decided satisfaction, the officer rejoined his countrymen. The truck turned around and lumbered south toward Malataverne. In its wake lingered an ominous sense that they had not seen the last of the Germans. As a precaution, the FTP repositioned their sentries farther out of the village.

In the early afternoon, a lone German car approached Allan, also from the direction of Malataverne in the south. This time the FTP decided to act. About one mile south of Allan, the partisans set up a gun position in the thick brush along a creek. As the car drew near a small bridge, the partisans riddled the vehicle and its occupants with bullets. Two Germans inside were killed instantly and a third seriously wounded.

The loss of the car and men compelled the Germans to send a heavily armed force to investigate. Later that same afternoon a second gunfight erupted at the creek bridge. This time the outnumbered and outgunned FTP partisans fell back eastward into the wooded hills without losing anyone. The Germans knew better than to pursue them into the unfamiliar terrain. These Germans, however, were not interested in revenge. They wanted the road and the town of Allan.

With the route cleared, the Germans arrived *en masse* with their trucks, horses, and tanks. Six hundred yards south of Allan, the general staff of the German LXXXV Armeekorps and 338th Division set up temporary headquarters in Eugene Rozel's farmhouse. The Germans were polite and respectful, but appropriated every room but one for their use. All manner of telephone lines, maps, and equipment were spread about the place. With little living space, Rozel's wife, mother-in-law, and two young sons moved out to live with other refugees camped in the eastern hills. The Germans allowed Eugene to remain in the unused room and tend to his farm.[8]

With the headquarters and communication center established at the Rozel farm, the first German units diverted from Route 7 arrived. In varied and broken groups they moved northward along the road from Malataverne and on through Allan. But as the evening descended, their departure swelled into an incessant cacophony of motors, horse hooves, and boot steps. Most villagers stayed inside to avoid the din, peering occasionally from behind curtains or half-shuttered windows, wondering when the last German soldiers would file past. The column was filled with of all manner of vehicles. Many were stolen from the French and included cars, buses, bicycles, and even street vendor carts. The passing soldiers looked haggard and resigned. They were allowed little respite, save for the few who stopped briefly to water their horses at the town's crossroads fountain.

The noisy, relentless stream continued unabated throughout the night and into the afternoon of Wednesday, August 23. At 5:00 P.M., however, the FTP partisans observing the mass evacuation from the ruins of Old Allan could no longer contain their aggressive impulses—even at the expense of common sense. Some moved down among the brush and trees at the base of the hill, and brazenly began taking random shots at the passing column. The Germans on the receiving end, who had been wearily filing along the road between the town and the north cemetery, took immediate cover. The ill-planned ambush brought the trucks behind the attack point screeching to a halt. Within mere moments, more than 300 vehicles in the town itself had skidded to a complete standstill. With a domino effect, the entire column extending south to Malataverne soon fell idle.

The Germans were in no mood for interruptions. Adept officers and NCOs beckoned several tanks forward and positioned them along the road between the village and the cemetery. With similar efficiency, machine gun crews unpacked and dispersed along the same line, while a large caliber artillery piece rolled next to Pont Neuf, a small concrete bridge spanning a dry ravine 100 yards north of town.

Once in place, German guns large and small ripped into the hillside with unbridled fury. For the next half hour, explosions split trees, tossed soil, and rattled the ancient ramparts of Old Allan. However, the fierce barrage failed to dislodge the FTP riflemen, who continued taunting the Germans with sporadic return shots.

The aggravated Germans worked two large patrols along the dry ravine toward the hillside while other soldiers moved to seize crucial observation points in town. They rattled the locked large wooden doors at the entrance of the Catholic Church. The soldiers didn't bother to wait for an answer. They smashed open the old handles with axes and rushed inside to the top of the bell tower. Other grey uniforms stormed the alleyway behind the church, seeking access to a long row of shops and homes overlooking the eastern hill. More doors were forced open, and terrified citizens were shoved aside as soldiers trampled up into the higher floors and attics of their homes.

The priest rushed from the nearby rectory to protest the intrusion into the church and the homes of his parishioners. He was loud and emphatic, but none of the Germans understood French and mistook the Father's animated scolding for belligerence. A sea of soldiers surrounded him and shoved rifle barrels against his chest and into the small of his back.

Tensions in the village, already high, were near the breaking point and in danger of spinning out of control. The Germans were passing through an unfamiliar town and had grown increasingly frustrated over their inability to distinguish a partisan from a civilian. The FFI and FTP had harassed them throughout their humiliating retreat from southern France, picking off longtime friends and associates along the way. The German officers were keenly aware of the American forces trying to cut them off and annihilate them to the north of Montélimar. On top of it all, everyone had to watch constantly for Allied air attacks. The Germans were exhausted, slightly terrified, and simply wanted out of the area. Patience in dealing with delays was a non-existent virtue that day.

The priest and the citizens of town wanted the Germans out as well. They were sick of the occupation, sick of the executions, and sick of living under the constant fear of the Gestapo. Though loyal to the Resistance, the townsfolk could not fathom why a few FTP zealots with rifles chose that particular moment to take pot shots at an entire army on the way out of France. The partisans had placed the town in grave danger for little if any gain. No one had enjoyed a good night's sleep in days, and few on either side could bridge the language barrier.

The priest continued his vigorous objections until a German soldier struck him with the butt end of a hatchet. The soldiers manhandled the priest toward a group of officers congregated at the crossroads, some of whom spoke French. Escorted with the priest were five other citizens, restrained for making similar objections. A sixth was thrown in after taking an untimely stroll down the main street. Between the muzzle blasts of a nearby panzer, the bilingual German officers interrogated the priest and the others while watching the tank's high explosive shells pummel the hillside. Their aggressive questioning did little to mitigate the toxic mistrust between sides.

For a full hour the column of vehicles and troops remained bottlenecked at Allan, as the one-sided firefight raged east of town. When the German patrols finally threatened to flank the FTP's hillside positions, the partisans evaporated into the woods. The Germans did not attempt to mount a pursuit, but remained stationed along the hill in case the partisans returned. With the nuisance gone, the German column resumed its retreat. The priest and the others were released, but only after being threatened with personal harm and reprisals upon the town as a whole.

The next morning, the Germans interviewed a number of the townspeople. They were anxious to learn anything about the partisans in the hills. Since the FTP had only recently arrived, the people knew little about them. Even so, they weren't about to betray them. The Germans received only vague and contradictory responses.

The priest, still upset over the previous night's events and fearful the Germans would not spare the village if attacked again, slipped off alone into the eastern hills. There, he met up with two guides who agreed to show him to the FTP hideout. Warmly greeted upon his arrival, the partisan leaders were anxious for any details of the German reaction to their attacks. When the priest described just how tense and precarious the situation had become in town the previous evening, the young men's jaws dropped. They were completely shocked, for none of them had thought through the consequences of their acts. The commander thanked the priest, apologized, and promised to refrain from causing any more disturbances in the area. He kept his word.

For two more days and nights the relentless procession of soldiers and vehicles continued to thunder through the village. With each passing hour, the marchers' steps became more hurried and their faces more furrowed with concern. Many were not seasoned combat soldiers but administrators and other uniformed service personnel. By the evening of August 25, Allan's unwelcome grey stream finally ran dry. Nevertheless, the Germans maintained a substantial military presence in and around town. The LXXXV Armeekorps HQ and associated units remained, working tirelessly to coordinate and protect the retreat through other areas. The "Lindquist Line" was established in the south and anti-aircraft artillery was brought in to guard against the increasing number of Allied air patrols. Despite their best efforts, the traffic west on National Route 7 remained heavy and slow.

In a move of consolidation—and perhaps out of continued concern over the FTP lurking in the area—the korps moved its communications and command center from the Rozel farm into the relative safety of

Allan. Once the Germans left, Rozel's family rejoined him at the farmhouse.[9]

In town, the German officers, clerks, wiremen, and radio operators appropriated homes along the village's main north-south route, and returned to managing the business of war. A colonel acted as liaison between the korps and town officials, but the relationship was clearly not intended to be among equals. One of the colonel's first proclamations was for every village door to remain unlocked at all times. He also expected the villagers to prepare their homes for "guests" and welcome anyone wanting to stay inside.

For the most part, the German visitors exhibited pleasant, even gentlemanly behavior, and some were surprisingly candid company. A big tall officer politely asked Maurice Martel to accompany him on a walking tour of the village. The officer was impeccably dressed, highly educated, and quite deferential to his host. His French was also exceptional, though spoken with a heavy German accent. During their walk, the officer never once let slip his professional demeanor. However, after the tour when the two men arrived inside Martel's home near the crossroads, the officer collapsed in a chair and buried his head in his hands. After a few seconds, he looked up at his host with a dejected gaze and raised his hand to his throat in a leveling motion.

"The war," he muttered, waving the hand for emphasis, "up to here."

Martel was speechless.

"I am university educated, Catholic, and an enemy of Hitler," he continued. He stopped himself, checked his watch, and shifted thoughts in midstream. "Today, at eleven o'clock we attack at La Coucourde. If we do not pass, tomorrow the Americans will make us prisoners."

Martel was completely unsure about how to respond to the officer's sudden openness. And then the big German dropped a bombshell: "Do you have any civilian clothes?"

The officer told the Frenchman about a family in Bordeaux who might be willing to help him because he had once showed leniency to a prisoner who was related to them. The desperate officer's ill-developed plan had many glaring problems. For starters, the German was nearly twice the size of Martel. This obvious flaw prompted Martel to speak up. He pointed out that the big man would look more like a circus clown than a civilian in his undersized clothing. He also reminded him that Bordeaux

The attack transport U.S.S. *Henrico* (APA-45), one of 800 ships involved in Operation Dragoon and home to the 3rd Battalion, 15th Infantry Regiment from Naples to Saint-Tropez, France. *National Archives 80-G-202879*

Pre-invasion aerial view of Pampelonne Beach looking SSW. The 3rd Battalion was to land near the "513123" coordinates, but ended up south about 600 yards (near the "Y" in "yellow.") The DD-tank commanded by Sgt. Roy Anderson had to carefully negotiate the pole obstacles in the lower section of the photo. *National Archives – Record Group 38, Action Reports, Box 299*

L Company Commander Capt. James "Red" Coles (kneeling, left). Next to him is Pfc. Rheinhold Bonnet. The two other men were not with L Company for the Southern France landings. They are (left to right) S/Sgt. Donald Marcum and Pfc. Henry Patchin. Photo taken near Naples, Italy in mid-June, 1944. *Arnold Mackowsky family*

Top: As H-hour (8:00 A.M. local time) approaches, the first wave of LCVPs approach a smoky Yellow Beach while waves of rockets scream overhead. The "PA-26" on the bow indicates this boat is from U.S.S. *Samuel Chase* (APA-26). *Chase* carried members of the 1st Battalion. Beyond are likely 3rd Battalion LCVPs. *National Archives 80-G-258084*

Bottom: Beachhead just to the north of 3rd Battalion landing area. Smoke obscures beach activities from German artillery spotters. Sgt. Anderson's stalled DD-tank can be seen on the right. (See enlarged inset). *National Archives 80-G-258109*

DD-tank and infantry on the beach at Pampelonne. The tank appears unattended and may be the one that threw a track. The soldier in foreground is a rifle grenadier. *National Archives SC-246270*

Captured and Relieved. German prisoners march down a beach road constructed by U.S. Army engineers while a DD-tank and crew looks on. Only two DD-tanks made it inland, so this tank belongs to either Lt. Orient or Sgt. Stout. *National Archives SC-212358*

1st Lt. George S. Burks, L Company Executive Officer, in Naples Italy in June 1944. This is the only overseas photo of 1st Lt. Burks in uniform. The photo is creased and worn because Burks carried it throughout his stay with L Company. *George Burks*

Pfc. William McNamara (kneeling with the BAR) and Pfc. Arco Ciancanelli (to his left with 3rd Division patch on shoulder.) The others are unidentified, but are probably members of the "unruly" 1st Squad/1st Platoon, L Company. The photo was taken mid-June 1944 near Naples, Italy. Pfc. Joseph Leithner is not in the photo. He was in the hospital still recovering from wounds received during the Anzio breakout. *William McNamara family*

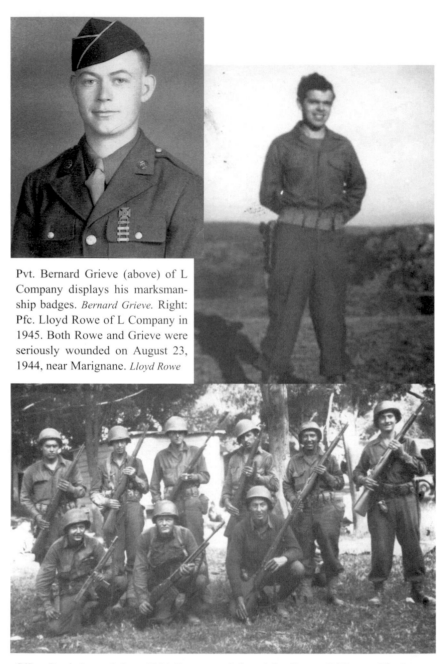

Pvt. Bernard Grieve (above) of L Company displays his marksmanship badges. *Bernard Grieve.* Right: Pfc. Lloyd Rowe of L Company in 1945. Both Rowe and Grieve were seriously wounded on August 23, 1944, near Marignane. *Lloyd Rowe*

S/Sgt. Rovas' squad, June 1944. Front row, left to right: Rovas, BAR man Pfc. James Morrow, and Sgt. Roy Sanders. Standing behind Rovas is Pfc. Harvey Legault. Standing on the far right with the big smile is Pfc. James Lovascio. The others are unidentified. Harvey was wounded at Allan, Lovascio was killed, and Sanders was captured. Rovas missed the battle due to severe dehydration. *Edmund Rovas*

Capt. David Redle, the commanding
officer of Company B/756th Tank
Battalion. *David Redle*

1st Sgt. Alvin Nusz, B Company/756th
Tank Battalion. *Randall Nusz*

2nd Lt. Andrew Orient at OCS school.
Diane Ryglewicz

Sgt. Roy Anderson and S/Sgt. Haskell
Oliver in Italy, 1944. *Roy Anderson*

No fuel in Carpentras. Photo caption reads: "Soldiers sleep alongside their jeep in the 3rd Division gasoline dump. Due to the serious gasoline shortage, they are unable to travel in their vehicles." The shortage was at its worst on August 26, 1944. Troops waiting on the trucks may be from 2nd Bn./15th Inf. Regiment. *National Archives RG407, Entry 427, Box 2572*

German Panther tank from the 11th Panzer Division rolls through the village of Suze-la-Rousse on August 25, 1944. The following evening, 3rd Battalion/15th Infantry Regiment arrived. It is possible this same Panther was involved in the subsequent fight at Allan. *Felix Roux*

1st Lt. Edgar R. Danby, replacement officer and platoon commander of 3rd Platoon/B Co./756th Tank Bn. *Author*

Cpl. Steve "Pista" Vargo, tank gunner, 3rd Platoon/B Co./756th Tank Bn. *John Forro, unidentified 1940s newspaper)*

Pvt. Dual F. Dishner, just before enlisting. Loader, 3rd Platoon/B Co./756th Tank Bn. *Sidney Dishner*

T/5 Emil Tikkanen, Tank Driver, 3rd Platoon/B Co./756th Tank Bn. *Carol Westcomb*

Pfc. Donald R. Sigrist, 3rd Platoon, L Company, awarded a Bronze Star for his actions at Allan, France. *Altoona Mirror*

Pfc. (later Sgt.) Rudolph Jantz, radioman in L Company at Allan, France. *Rudy Jantz*

Pfc. Joseph W Leithner, Jr. of the 1st Platoon, L Company, was awarded a Silver Star for his actions at Allan, France. *Donna Nussbaum*

2nd Lt. Arnold Mackowsky led the reconnoitering platoon into Allan on August 27, 1944. His serious appearance is misleading. "Mack" had a great sense of humor and was well liked by the men he led. *Arnold Mackowsky family*

Pfc. Earl V. Potter and Pfc. Luther Prentiss, 3rd Platoon/L Company pose near Rome, Italy, in June 1944. A good scout, Potter knew how to get away in a hurry. *Earl V. Potter*

Cpl. Dominick Delmonico, assistant squad leader, 3rd Platoon, L Company, at Allan, France. Alone, he eliminated two German machine gun nests along the dry creek bed north of town. *Delmonico Family*

Some of the men of Weapons Platoon, L Company, in June 1944: (1) Pvt. Carl Sutton; (2) Sgt. Fred Gant; (3) S/Sgt. Ed Rider; (4) Pfc. Richard Guimond; (5) Pfc. Kenneth Lynch; (6) Pfc. John Krok; (7) Pfc. Fred Scarpa; (8) Pvt. John Downing. Others are unidentified. *Arnold Mackowsky family*

Left: 1st Lt. Lloyd Cotter, commanding officer of 2nd Platoon/Cannon Company/15th Infantry Regiment. *Lloyd Cotter family.* Right: T/Sgt. George Polich of Cannon Company. Polich's M8s protected the rear flank at Allan during the late afternoon and evening hours of August 27, 1944. *George Polich*

On the morning of August 28th, T/Sgt. George Polich (driving) and his men inspect one of two German cars they shot up the prior afternoon. The other captured car is in the background. The American flag flies from the car's radio antenna to protect against friendly fire. The photo was taken by a camera found in one of the cars. *George Polich*

Ruins from different eras. The stone ruins of the ancient medieval village of Allan overlook a burned German Marder III destroyed near the new village. By the 1800s, the old walled town was abandoned in favor of a new one below. When war came in 1944, however, it was the ruins of the old town where the villagers fled for safety. *Lucien Martel*

Allan in 1948. This view of the village is from the eastern hill with the ancient ruins. On the left side are the south creek, Protestant Church, and small woods near the town hall. On the right side, the Catholic Church towers above the crossroads area. The trees in the foreground are wounded survivors of a German artillery barrage during the evening of August 27, 1944. *Lucien Martel*

Left: Damage to the Martel home just south of the crossroads. Building position and entry angle suggest the damage was caused by a ricochet shot from the direction of the cemetery. Above the broken stone, Maurice Martel (top right), an eyewitness to the combat of August 27, 1944, and author of the book *Allan: Mon Village*, proudly displays the French tricolors. *Lucien Martel*

Above: Eugene Rozel in 1942. As the Americans approached Allan, Rozel risked his life by running to Lt. Danby with information on the nearby Germans—and to give him a bottle of wine in appreciation. *Rozel Family*

Right: The severely damaged Mourier home on the south edge of town. View is north toward the town's main crossroads. *Lucien Martel*

Three-year old Jean Pic poses behind Lt. Danby's burned out tank several months after the battle. The north bridge is just beyond the white rectangular sign on the right, and beyond that is the cemetery, small woods, and bend in the road where the German Panther was hidden. The "A-16" painted on the hull indicates this was originally the "A" Company maintenance tank. It had been swapped with "B" Company, but was destroyed in battle before a new "B" Company designation could be painted on it. *Jean Pic*

A 25-ton Flakpanzer IV möbelwagen was one of several pieces of equipment abandoned by the Germans near the Dessalles and Borne farms on the northern outskirts of Allan. The child in the photo is Jean Dessalles. The man holding the 37mm anti-aircraft clip is a refugee from southern France. *Photo: Robert Borne / Description: Pascal Delaire*

August 28, 1944. Vehicles burn in the destroyed German column south of Montélimar, France. The village of Allan is about one mile to the right of this location. *National Archives SC-193410*

South of Montélimar, France, August 28, 1944. T/Sgt. Polich's M8s depart Allan and travel up Route 7. In the distance on the right is Montchamp hill. T/5 Cecil Stinson is driving the M8. Seated in the turret is Sgt. Donald C. Wittwer, and standing behind him without the helmet is Cpl. Joseph J. Ranke. The other two men are unidentified. T/Sgt. Polich's M8 follows in the distance. *National Archives SC-193797*

was on the other side of the country. How would he get there? How well did he really know that family?

The officer snapped out of his despondency like a phonograph needle skipping to an entirely different song. He stood up at once and regained his composure. Beckoning Martel to continue the tour, the two men returned to the street. The officer never mentioned the plan again, but Martel could never look at another German officer in quite the same way again.

Martel and the officer walked a short distance outside of town along the road to Montélimar. Positioned among the nearby brush and trees were several German anti-aircraft guns with their long barrels trained skyward. Without any warning whatsoever, the AAA guns erupted with earsplitting frenzy in a desperate attempt to claw down several emerging Allied airplanes high in the hazy blue heavens. The blinding, disorienting muzzle flashes and the incessant noise, made Martel recoil involuntarily from the overloading assault upon his senses. His German companion, however, reacted with cool indifference. He never so much as flinched or stole a skyward glance toward those same Americans he feared might soon capture him. Something else, though, attracted his notice and cracked his stoic exterior. One hundred yards away, a young French cyclist who had also been startled by the barrage dove for the cover of a roadside ditch.

After the barrage fell silent, the officer pointed in the direction of the frightened cyclist and glanced over to Martel. "Terrorist?" he asked, with unmistakable panic in his voice.

For a second time, Martel was speechless.

By August 26, the Germans at Allan bustled with the urgency of an armed camp preparing for battle. During the previous day, the LXXXV Korps brought in armor—and plenty of it. Seven self-propelled antitank guns and two larger sturmgeschütz assault guns from 11th Panzer Division's 61st PAK (Anti-Tank) Battalion, rolled in to help defend the korps.[10] Most PAK guns were of the Marder III variety. These were small, thinly-armored tracked vehicles topped with a long and deadly accurate 76.2 mm gun. A crew of four manned the Marder III, but only the driver and assistant driver were fully protected inside. A two-man gun crew sat behind the gun breech, protected only by a frontal shield.

The vulnerability of the Marder crews was symbolic of the LXXXV Korps' strategic situation—vulnerable at the top, rear, and the flanks.

The dangers from above were particularly alarming. Allied air attacks on the retreating Germans became increasingly effective. Twelfth Air Force squadrons were repositioning from distant Corsica to new airfields along the French coast, enabling more Allied pilots to conduct "seek and destroy" missions along the Rhône River. The attacks were so numerous that during daylight hours the Germans had to hide their armor or risk losing it.

LXXXV Korps parked many of its trucks and anti-tank guns among a cluster of farms north of Allan. The Borne home, in particular, had many large mature trees that formed an ideal canopy beneath which the Germans hid their vehicles from marauding Allied pilots.[11]

On the morning of August 27, a huge 45-ton Panther tank rumbled in from Montélimar via the northwestern road, shaking the foundations of Allan as it passed. The crew was in a hurry and didn't bother to slow as they executed a sharp left turn at the crossroads. The thick armor skirt plates of the beast scraped a corner wall, breaking loose mortar and large stones that were instantly vaporized beneath the Panther's wide chattering treads. Before the dust settled, the huge armor piece disappeared north beyond the cemetery road bend. Its grumbling motor did not quiet until it also found refuge beneath the trees of the Borne farm.[12]

After the arrival of the Panther, the German colonel warned Mayor Almoric that the town was no longer safe and that all remaining residents should evacuate. American ground forces were expected at any time, and the town would likely become a battleground. The colonel couldn't be more specific, but had just received the alarming dispatch on the intrusion of the American armor column six miles south at Chartroussas. As the colonel returned to a staff thrown into near pandemonium, Almoric spread the warning throughout the town. Many of the remaining townspeople fled immediately for the safety of Old Allan or to neighboring farms and hamlets, but some could not be convinced to leave.

At 10:00 A.M., several German vehicles emerged by way of Aiguebelle road and halted near the crossroads. A group of Wehrmacht officers popped out from their cars with concerned looks on their faces. They stood, fidgeted, and conferred for a few moments, glancing and pointing at times to the roadway stretching south toward Malataverne. This was the likely direction from which the American column at

Chartroussas might arrive. As the officers clambered back into their cars and drove away, other German soldiers rushed to water their horses at the crossroad fountain. Some animals were led to the Mourier blacksmith shop, where the Germans impressed the proprietor and his father to do last-minute farrier work.

Not everyone seemed concerned. The French proprietors of a food truck couldn't hide their elation over the prospect of liberation. They parked their vehicle next to the church, and brazenly offered free food and wine to the small number of fearless citizens who chose to remain in town and attend Sunday Mass. The Germans were too preoccupied with their own preparations to suppress the impromptu celebration—or to even care.

While a few outside laughed and prematurely toasted to a Free France, others inside knelt down quietly among the cool musty pews to pray that Allan and her people would be spared from the coming destruction.

⬤ Chapter 11
Reconnaissance

A t 10:30 A.M. on August 27, a silver American P-47 Thunderbolt flew low and fast over the village of Allan. The low pitched drone of its radial engine shook the ground as it swooped by.[1] Something on the outskirts of town caught the attention of the pilot. Perhaps it was a poorly camouflaged AAA flak wagon, or maybe grey uniforms scrambling for cover in the woods. The pilot banked his plane around, wings shimmering in the morning sun, and returned with all eight machine guns blazing. Much to the dismay of those on the receiving end of his fire, the attacking pilot was not alone. Moments later, several companion P-47s flew fast and low, strafing the same woods. The attack lasted only a few minutes before the team buzzed off in search of easier targets. National Route 7 was lined with hundreds of them, and the pilots had to make the most of their fuel in order to make the long flight back to their coastal bases.

The monstrous German Panther tank and its Marder III attendants hidden near the Borne farm, were spared the aerial assault. They dared not venture into the open until the skies were clear again. Earlier that summer, the Luftwaffe had all but abandoned southern France in a vain effort to roll back the Normandy invasion. The German planes never returned. Now the skies over the Rhône River valley belonged solely to the Allies, and an entire German Army lay at their mercy below.

Meanwhile, two miles south of Allan, the American L Company armored column approached the hills of Montchamp and Roucoule. A two-lane asphalt ribbon beckoned them up a long gentle rise that crested as a saddled gap between the two hills. Montchamp was the large conical hill to the west, covered with trees and crowned with a tiny white stone chapel rising a good 500 feet above the plain. Roucoule was equal in height but more scarred and craggy, extending eastward as a ridge before dissolving into the wooded highlands and foothills of Aiguebelle.

Once L Company reached the apex of the saddle, its members enjoyed a spectacular vista as the entire northern valley spread out below them. With noon approaching, the sun had burned off the morning haze, affording the Americans a clear view of Montélimar five miles north. From the small city sprawled in the distance, National Route 7 trailed down on the left and disappeared behind the west side of Montchamp. Its entire length was clogged with slow moving trucks, buses, bicycles, troops, and horse drawn carts. In some sections, however, the massive column was broken and reduced to chaos. Thick black smoke rose, only to be gently dispersed in the blue sky.

Through his binoculars, T/Sgt. Polich watched as the smoke columns were fed by the flaming wrecks of trucks and buses. Around each attack point were vehicles scattered haphazardly into the surrounding fields. Others detoured through adjacent farm lanes in an effort to keep the column moving north. The Air Force had recently hit the column hard, but the attacks had not stopped the German exodus.[2]

Polich was astonished at how desperate the Germans were to get out. They were no longer waiting for the cover of darkness to flee. With steady hands, he focused his binoculars up and down the line of moving vehicles. Many were heavily camouflaged with branches and foliage and had the ridiculous appearance of moving scenery on some epic Hollywood set. The effect was quite the opposite of what the Germans intended—telegraphing to everybody that the lumbering vehicles were filled with escaping Germans. Southern France was filled with natural wonders, but moving shrubbery was not one of them. The Germans vehicles could have been dressed as giant yellow ducks and been no worse off. The valley already looked like a shooting gallery, and the Americans in the L Company column were anxious to take their turn at them.

They did not have to wait long. A half-mile down the road from the American armor column was a speeding convoy of approximately fifteen German vehicles. L Company quickly dismounted as the small column veered left at a "Y" intersection and raced along the base of Montchamp toward the town of Malataverne. The American tanks, TDs and M8s, hastily pulled onto the road shoulder and opened fire on the smaller

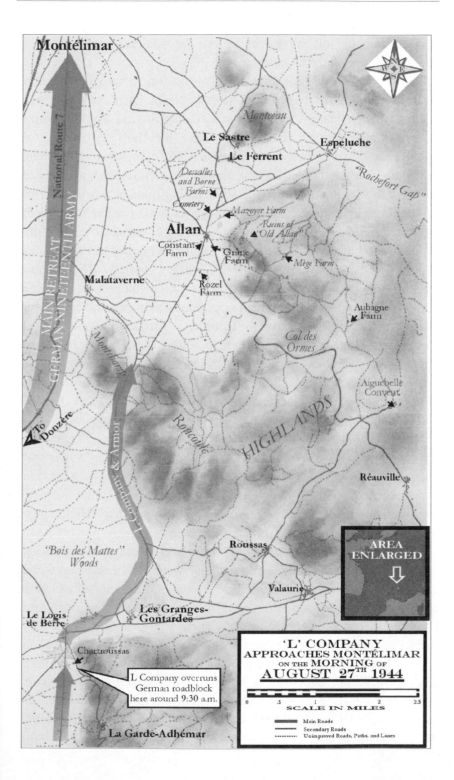

Montélimar

National Route 7

MAIN RETREAT
GERMAN NINETEENTH ARMY

To
Donzère

Monteau

Le Sastre

Le Ferrent

Espeluche

"Rochefort Gap"

Dessalles
and Borne
Farms

Cemetery

Mazoyer Farm

Allan

Ruins of
"Old Allan"

Constant
Farm

Grâne
Farm

Mège Farm

Malataverne

Rozel
Farm

Aubagne
Farm

Montchamp

Col des
Ormes

Aiguebelle
Convent

Roncolle

HIGHLANDS

L Company & Armor

Réauville

"Bois des Mattes"
Woods

Roussas

AREA
ENLARGED
⇩

Valaurie

Le Logis
de Berre

Les Granges-
Gontardes

Chartroussas

L Company overruns
German roadblock
here around 9:30 a.m.

'L' COMPANY
APPROACHES MONTÉLIMAR
ON THE MORNING OF
AUGUST 27TH 1944

0   .5   1   2   2.5
SCALE IN MILES

Main Roads
Secondary Roads
Unimproved Roads, Paths, and Lanes

La Garde-Adhémar

convoy,[3] picking off six trucks before the vehicles could disappear completely around the hillside.[4]

Some L Company squads fanned out to form a moving perimeter while the remainder climbed back atop the tanks. Each lurched forward in turn. Rather than pursue the small convoy around to Malataverne, Captain Coles directed his force to take the right jog at the "Y" intersection downhill and move toward Allan. According to his maps, this route would not only outflank much of the congestion south of the city, but also take them directly to ideal high ground between Allan and Montélimar. From there, the TDs, tanks, and M8s could lay into the German column crawling in the distance along National Route 7. With a little luck and maneuvering, the havoc wrought might sever the column and lead to the capture of thousands of enemy soldiers.[5] The potential prize was enormous. Truscott's ambitious goal could be met, at least in part, and L Company had a golden opportunity to avenge a hundred-fold the losses they suffered at Anzio. In order to succeed, however, Coles' men had to move while they still held some element of surprise. The gamble was that Allan was not heavily defended.

The small American column ventured steadily down the road toward Allan, passing a line of pine trees and a few isolated farms through terrain that alternated from cultivated fields to unkempt brush lines and patches of woods. Vigilant scouts patrolled along the roadside, visually scouring the countryside for any sign of German defenses. Lt. Danby's tank once again led the charge. The first indication of trouble was a gut-wrenching stench carried on the hot breeze. Near a small field pond were the sprawled and bloated bodies of two dead German soldiers. By the looks of them, they had been there for days.[6]

The tanks and doughs passed over the same creek and small bridge where the FTP attacked the German car the week before, then negotiated a slight road jog. Several hundred yards ahead Danby spotted a German motorcycle with a sidecar idling on the asphalt in front of the Rozel farm. Once the surprised driver realized the approaching engines belonged to American tanks and not German panzers, he swung his cycle around and kicked open the throttle to alert the korps back in Allan. Danby's gunner, Cpl. Steve Vargo, zeroed in on him through the main gun's telescopic sights and let fly a high explosive round. A split second later, the motorcycle and driver tumbled together in flaming wreck. The machine's mangled chassis came to an awkward rest in the middle of the road while twisted metal remnants rained down on the pavement and bounced haphazardly into nearby vineyards. The broken body of the unlucky driver ended up on a hawthorn hedge near the Rozel farm.[7] His message died with him.

Danby's tank rumbled forward without delay. To avoid the burning wreck, the driver T/4 Emil Tikkanen swerved the tank treads off the left side of the road and clipped several rows of grapevines before regaining the pavement. The vehicles behind him followed suit.

Eugene Rozel and his family witnessed the motorcycle's destruction and the arrival of the Americans from their farmhouse. In the 1920s, Rozel served with an elite French Army mountain unit. Ironically, his résumé included a service rotation in the post-WWI occupation of the German Ruhr region.[8] Despite the dangers, the French veteran felt compelled to tell the Americans of his military observations and to warn them of the German presence in the area—especially in the woods west of town. He also wanted to express the tremendous gratitude he felt, so before bolting out of the front door he grabbed a bottle of his finest wine to share with France's liberators.

Lt. Danby saw the thin sun-tanned farmer waving as he raced toward the tank. He radioed Tikkanen to halt and gestured Rozel to the side of his turret. Over the noise of the idling engine, the two men conversed briefly in French. Rozel reached up and handed Danby his bottle of wine, wished him well, and departed from the tank's rounded hull. As he raced back to the safety of his home and family, Danby leaned down inside the turret and secured the wine gift inside an empty ammo ring along the back. A space meant for a cylinder of destruction now held one intended for celebration. Perhaps later that evening, Danby and his crew could share that wine—as combat equals. He had earned that privilege. However, an unfinished mission and a tough day's fight still awaited them.

Danby signaled Tikkanen to move out and the tank lurched in the direction of town. One by one, the remaining pieces of American armor rumbled past the Rozel home with infantry flanking on foot. Rozel, his wife, and sons watched the astounding sight from their dining room with a combination of fear, joy, and the dreamlike realization that they had just sampled freedom.[9]

Once the column cleared Rozel's farm, the tanks, TDs and M8s pulled off the road about 500 yards shy of Allan and spread out across a field path connecting Malataverne and Aiguebelle roads.[10] Both men and machines waited while the officers cautiously surveyed the town with binoculars and planned their next move. Danby relayed Rozel's information on to Captain Coles so that particular attention would be paid to the nearby woods.[11]

The town itself remained obscured by a small grove of trees immediately to the south, making it impossible to fully examine all the buildings and homes. Even so, several potential locations ideal for German observation or mischief were identified—including the church tower and two farmhouses bracketing the southern outskirts like wide bookends. A small concrete bridge near the left farmhouse held the potential for mines. An approach in that direction demanded extreme caution. 1st Lt. Cotter had concerns about the two-story homes lining the narrow main street beyond the bridge. Every upper floor window was an ideal place for an enemy soldier to drop a grenade into the open turret of one of his assault guns.[12] The crews of the tank destroyers had the same concerns.

There was no obvious German activity in Allan. Still, Coles was enough of a soldier to know he could not risk moving his column through the potentially fatal trap without first sending a patrol to reconnoiter the town. The job called for about forty men. Their first objective would be to secure that farmhouse near the bridge as a base of operation. Coles called upon 2nd Lt. Arnold Mackowsky to ready his platoon for the assignment.

Arnold Mackowsky— his men of 1st Platoon called him "Lt. Mack" for short—was a young man of average height with brown hair and piercing blue eyes.[13] He joined the company in early June 1944, as one of the many replacements brought in after the Anzio breakout.[14] Initially he approached his command like a man on fire, talking tough and acting like nothing could bring him down. But after becoming extremely seasick on several occasions during the summer's amphibious training, the fit and thin lieutenant mellowed.[15] Pfc. McNamara jokingly addressed Mackowsky as "The Whip" (as in "crack the whip") for storming into the platoon like a lion.[16] The men also kidded him constantly on how his "tough guy" persona contrasted with his weak sea legs, but Mack always countered with sharp-witted responses to put them in their places. This humor quickly endeared him to every man in his platoon. Mackowsky wasn't married or engaged. He had a brother, but their parents died when they were teenagers.[17] Lt. Mack joined the Army not only out of patriotism, but because he didn't have anyone at home.[18] His platoon was his family.

Coles instructed Mackowsky to lead 1st Platoon into Allan, set up a command post at the southwest farm, and report back with his findings.[19] Though they were only a quarter-mile shy of town, Coles wanted to make sure they maintained direct contact. The handheld SCR-536 "walkie-talkie" radios used for platoon communication could cover distances up to a mile over flat ground,[20] but because of the potential for interference from the buildings and trees, Coles didn't want to rely on them. He told Pfc. Rudy Jantz to take his more powerful SCR-300 radio and stick by Mackowsky. Coles would remain back and monitor them over the company's remaining SCR-300 at rear of his jeep. As an extra precaution, Coles also sent along the company runner, Pfc. William R. Shook.

When everything was ready, 1st Platoon set out for town. Some of the men cut through the fields on foot, but in order to quickly move most of them, Mackowsky, Jantz, and about twenty-five others packed aboard the 2-½ ton battalion truck. The driver transported them up the blacktop road and stopped south of the small bridge and long rectangular stone house, known locally as the "Constant farm." As soon as they arrived, small arms fire from the woods beyond sent the Americans vaulting over the fenced cargo bed, exchanging shots as they dropped and scrambled for cover. As soon as the last man piled off, the driver spun his six wheels around, gunned the gas, and shot back down the road.

The tanks and TDs at the support line 500 yards south took notice of the German positions along the wood line and began blasting at them with high explosives. Their suppressive fire enabled Mackowsky's men to cover the ground between the road and the farm. Jantz and Mackowsky were among the first to reach the gray field stone building. They checked the place for occupants, but it was deserted. Mackowsky directed the other arrivals toward the stable half of the building and told them to begin setting up a command post.

Jantz removed the heavy radio from his back and tried without success to hail Captain Coles. He didn't have the time to recheck the codes or settings. Mackowsky was already calling for him, Shook, and a few others to follow him into town so they could determine the size and strength of the German presence. Coles needed to know as soon as possible whether he was dealing with another weak roadblock or something more substantial. The faster L Company could gather that information, the greater the tactical advantage, and with tanks and TDs as companions, the infantry had a special obligation to locate any hidden anti-tank guns before they could strike.

Mackowsky's small patrol set out north from the Constant farm, scurrying about the garden walls and alleyways until they reached the main crossroads. At first glance the streets of the town appeared completely deserted. Not a soul—German or French—was anywhere in sight. Mackowsky eyed the tall church tower just to the east of the intersection. The structure was an ideal observation post or sniper nest. He sent Shook on the mission and watched the young, almost childlike soldier dash across the empty street past the fountain and into the church without incident.[21]

While Shook made his way into the tower, Mackowsky probed farther among the alleyways, leaving Jantz behind to fiddle with the SCR-300 radio. Again, he had no luck raising Coles. Jantz tried screwing together segments of the 15-foot antenna and attaching it to the set in the hope that the longer mast would solve the transmission problem. He tried calling over the handset again, but still failed to make a connection. This sort of thing had happened before. The radio had notorious temperamental spells, but in this instance the timing could not have been worse. Jantz tried not to let his concerns dissolve into frustration. He remained calm and started testing the equipment from square one: Was the battery low? Connections bad? Wrong code? Wrong channel? Jantz checked and rechecked.

Mackowsky was the first to realize that L Company may have bitten off more than it bargained for. To his surprise, northwest of town were Germans swarming in sizeable numbers, perhaps a battalion strong, with all kinds of vehicles massing along the western road.[22] Other troops were moving swiftly into the areas west and north of Allan, obviously in response to the American intrusion. Several self-propelled Marder III anti-tank guns were bouncing and weaving as they gained the edge of the village. A pit formed in Mackowsky's stomach; his small patrol was just mere moments away from being cut off from the rest of the platoon at the Constant farm.

The young lieutenant hastily retraced his steps back to the crossroads and found Jantz still trying to work the SCR-300. When he told the busy radioman that they had walked into the middle of a hornet's nest of

Germans and were about to be surrounded and captured, Jantz looked up in disbelief. Young, "invincible," with an untempered instinct to fight, Jantz suggested shooting their way out of the situation. Mackowsky bluntly dismissed the idea as suicidal. To emphasize the point, he had Jantz peek around the corner and observe a German tank accompanied by a considerable complement of infantry closing in along the road. Grounded in reality, Jantz had little stomach for the thought of becoming a prisoner of war. Fighting, he agreed, was futile. Surrender was preferable to death. Unfortunately, they had no way to inform Coles about their situation or of the mobilizing Germans.

Realizing it was his task to destroy the radio and dispose of the codebook, he became alarmed at the thought that he might not have time to do so. Mackowsky told him to get right to the job, and that he was going to try to stall for time and arrange a peaceful surrender for them. With that, the thin lieutenant disappeared in another direction.

Working with all haste, Jantz pulled open the codebook, tore it into tiny bits and buried it in a nearby manure pile. He disassembled the radio, smashed the handset and interior components, and buried them as well. As he was tearing it down, he realized he would never know why the damn thing didn't function properly. Finally, Jantz unfastened his .45-cal sidearm from its holster, popped the clip and flung the ammo away. With trembling fingers, he disassembled the pistol, breaking what parts he could and scattered them around the same manure pile. He didn't want to destroy the weapon, but he didn't want to see the Germans take it as a trophy, either. No sooner had he finished his tasks when a group of Germans surrounded him.[23] Mackowsky was right. They wouldn't have survived a fight.

While Jantz was doing his duty, Mackowsky ventured out and ended up trapped alone in a back alley with the Germans closing in. Before he could place his hands in the air, one of them shot him in the right knee.[24] Mackowsky slumped in pain to the ground and was quickly surrounded, disarmed, and taken out of town. When Shook realized what was happening, he remained hidden in the church tower, hoping somehow to slip back out of town to alert Captain Coles of the trap.[25] The other 1st Platoon men from the ill-fated patrol managed to return to the Constant farm because they hadn't scouted as far into the village.[26]

Meanwhile, at the Constant farm, 1st Platoon was enduring a renewed hail of gunfire. The men responded in kind, unaware of the fates of Mackowsky, Jantz, and Shook.[27] Pfcs. Robert V. Tyler, Pat Cardelli, and Rheinhold Bonnett were investigating one of the nearby vineyards when they suddenly found themselves completely surrounded by enemy infantry.[28] Tyler's first thought was that they had unwittingly walked into a trap. The three riflemen tried to dive for cover and hide among the grapevines, but were easily discovered and disarmed. After a brisk and intimidating shakedown, the three anxious and bewildered GIs were escorted northwest of the village and reunited with Mackowsky and Jantz.

The Germans were unsure what to do with their five American prisoners.[29] Their camp was in a state of chaos. Some soldiers were flowing toward town while others were piling aboard overloaded vehicles bound for Montélimar. After several minutes of nervous waiting, the Americans were finally directed by another German soldier to march up the road toward Montélimar. They helped Mackowsky along as they walked, passing more German infantry and a panzer of some sort sitting off in the field.[30] The Germans were completely preoccupied, some moving away from Allan, and others moving back toward it. No one even looked twice at the Americans striding in their midst. The only German who seemed to have any concern about them was their guard, but only because he was following orders.[31] The guard finally showed the American POWs to a busy German field army hospital tent, where Mackowsky had his knee examined. The remaining four Americans were pulled aside and searched more methodically by a new group of German soldiers.

A hauptfeldwebel (first sergeant) searched Jantz and relieved him of his Swiss Army knife, cartridge belt, and canteen. While rifling through his shirt pockets, the German NCO came across Jantz's tin covered New Testament Bible. He pulled it out and looked it over suspiciously.

He held it up to Jantz and asked, "Was ist das?"

"A Bible," answered Jantz. The NCO understood instantly. The word was pronounced virtually the same in both English and German.

"Ist gut," he commented approvingly before placing it back into Jantz's pocket. He turned to fellow soldier and remarked, "Sehr jung!" ("So young!")[32]

Another German searching Tyler discovered the private's little camera, which he examined with great interest. Tyler hated to lose it. Cameras weren't easy to come by, and he had taken some very good photos of his buddies in Italy during the prior months. All those prized photos remained undeveloped on the roll. The German asked Tyler what types of photos were inside the camera. Tyler had two years of high school German, and fully understood the man's question.

Unsure how to frame his response, Tyler opted for a creative answer: "Mama und Papa."

Surprisingly, the German handed the camera back to Tyler and told him to keep it.[33]

After the second search was over, the four Americans were left unguarded in a corner of the medical tent. Even so, escape was impossible. With Germans constantly streaming past them, they couldn't take a step without drawing instant attention. For some time, they stood alone in quiet resignation and watched the doctors attend to a large group of wounded brought in after the latest round of Allied air force attacks. Jantz was somewhat shocked to see that that one of the physicians had a Walther pistol strapped to his belt. Under the Geneva Convention, doctors were not allowed to carry a weapon of any kind. Every American doctor Jantz had ever seen was always unarmed.[34] This particular German doctor probably began carrying a sidearm while serving on the Russian Front, where rules of warfare were rarely observed.[35]

Another uniformed German turned from one of the operating tables after bandaging a comrade. When he saw Jantz and the others standing off to the side in their U.S. Army ODs, he became very agitated. He yelled and gestured toward them angrily—perhaps blaming them for what happened to his friend. Suddenly, everyone in the tent took notice of the four Americans. The situation was awkward and not a little distressing. A German NCO and a second soldier rushed over to the four and motioned with his rifle for them to move away. They were taken outside, separated into pairs, and loaded onto a waiting bus.[36]

Across from Jantz's bus seat was a tall German guard with his rifle positioned stock down between his knees. An intent stoical look never left his face. Looking for some way to connect with his alien surroundings, Jantz tried engaging the big man in a bit of small talk. The guard responded with a glare and a slap of the rifle stock with his big hand. Jantz got the point and shut up. After the bus was fully packed with grey uniforms, the doors closed and the wheels rolled. It soon joined a convoy of vehicles heading toward Montélimar, which in turn merged in with the massive northward exodus creeping along National Route 7.[37]

Jantz, Tyler, Cardelli, and Bonnett were now trapped in that same vulnerable column they had observed earlier from the hillside with such astonishment—a column that they were supposed to be attacking. The trucks, buses, cars, and horse drawn carts all around them were the survivors of the morning air raid . . . and the targets of the next one about to strike.

Whether one was a soldier, a beast of burden, or a prisoner of war in the German Nineteenth Army made little difference. Everyone shared a common interest at that particular place in time. Everyone was trying to survive.

Chapter 12

The Crossroads

Captain Coles' L Company, reconnoitering Allan, was far ahead of the balance of 15th Infantry Regiment, which was spread out over many miles. The remainder of 3rd Battalion was still five miles south and plodding through the Bois des Mattes.[1] Captain Redle's command post caught up with them after leaving Sérignan and passing through Saint-Paul.[2] 2nd Battalion, following in reserve and still hampered by the low fuel supplies, had only reached Saint-Paul.[3] Lead elements of 1st Battalion were eight miles southeast of Allan, advancing from Pierrelatte toward Donzère slowly after encountering panzer and mortar fire.[4] For all practical purposes, Coles' L Company was alone.

Captain Coles' looked at his wristwatch. It was 1:30 P.M. He had been waiting impatiently at his jeep for forty-five minutes for news from Lt. Mackowsky.[5] His remaining SCR-300 radio droned only empty static on Jantz's frequency, and the runner, Pfc. Shook, was nowhere to be seen. What he saw and heard from across the vineyards and tobacco fields south of town during those minutes, was anything but encouraging. Despite the suppressing fire delivered earlier by the armor to cover 1st Platoon's advance, a firefight again flared at the Constant farm. This time, however, the popping rifles and chattering submachine guns joined with the more ominous sound of heavy motors resonating from the buildings within town. The Germans were establishing a defensive position, and it was imperative to disrupt them before they could finish.[6] Though Coles had no clear idea what he was up against, he knew he had to act swiftly to avoid the annihilation of 1st Platoon.

Coles split his force into two sections, keeping two TDs, the M8s, and some infantry in reserve while 2nd and 3rd Platoons from his company rolled forward with Danby's tanks and the remaining two TDs.[7] Coles was not about to sit out this fight. He wanted another crack at the Germans since the Anzio breakout, and was tired of chasing after them across the Riviera. As the line of men and machines closed fast upon the town, Coles buzzed back and forth in his jeep and trailer combo signaling commands with the passion of a symphony conductor.

The advancing Americans took over the Constant farm swiftly. Coles directed 2nd Platoon to relieve 1st Platoon positions. The Germans harassing the farm were forced to withdraw into the gardens west of the village. The nearby road and small bridge were found free of mines, so Danby and Oliver's tanks crossed into town without delay, turrets traversing to and fro as the infantry sprinted and fanned out alongside of them. The TDs halted south of the bridge with diesels idling and 3-inch guns at the ready. Until the upper floors of the homes along the main street could be declared free of enemy, the gun crews held back, scanning the town for trouble from the tops of their turrets.

Amid the sporadic shots of unseen German rifles, the two tanks and escorting infantry probed along the tree lined main street. Danby was in the lead, with Oliver following fifty yards behind. Their fast charge, however, quickly slowed to a crawl. Every yard gained brought a new series of potential ambush traps and shooting angles in need of scrutiny. Out of symbiotic necessity, many GIs bunched along the two slow moving tanks for protection from the rebounding bullets, all the while watching for anti-tank guns or panzerfausts that might instantly snatch that same protection away.

Someone spotted the first serious threat only 100 yards away. To the right and through the cluster of trees south of the town hall, a Marder III was maneuvering back and forth next to the small Protestant church on Aiguebelle Road. The Marder had a long deadly gun but an extremely limited independent traverse capability. In order to properly sight the gun, the entire unwieldy vehicle had to pivot, making it a poor match against close moving targets. Trying to deal with this handicap, the Marder's driver was struggling to zero his gun in on one of the nearby American tanks. Before he could lock his target, Danby and Oliver easily swung their guns around on him. One of the tanks fired in haste, sending an AP round hurtling toward the Marder at 1,700 feet per second.[8] The shot missed by mere inches, slamming cleanly through the wall of the small church and showering the Marder's gray metal deck with stone fragments and dust. The stunned German driver threw both tracks into reverse and disappeared with a burst of engine noise and a belch of smoke behind the shops of Aiguebelle Road.

The crew of a second Marder lurking in the shadows of the town hall thought better of challenging the two Shermans and withdrew deeper into the town's interior. A third Marder made an audacious dash through the crossroads in full view of the two American tanks before disappearing up the road toward Montélimar. Before Danby and Oliver's crews could react, the second Marder followed in the wake of the daredevil driver and succeeded in making the same daring escape.

Coles' instincts were correct. The Germans were attempting to establish a defensive line with tank traps across the center of town. His decision to press into the town caught the enemy off guard. The sudden arrival of American tanks and troops in the town's south quarter forced the withdrawal of much of that nascent German line. The only question now was how far back the Germans would fall before trying to establish another one.

During the Italian Campaign, the German defenses set up like curing concrete; the more time they had to prepare, the harder they were later to crack. On the other hand, an infantry commander had to be wary of stumbling into an ambush or wasting time and energy by committing men against empty or "ghost" enemy formations. The Germans excelled at such deceptions. Any commander could easily miscalculate by attacking too soon with too little, or by not attacking all. Unfortunately, during fluid combat situations, the information needed to make these life and death decisions was generally scant. The only comfort was in knowing that the officers making the same decisions on the other side of the field were operating under the same fog. This is where personality especially came into play. Consistent with their general nature, some officers erred on the side of caution. Others, however, naturally moved aggressively without much if any hesitation. The choice boiled down to the basic personality and battlefield experience of the individual commander. As a general rule, Captain Coles preferred to attack and keep his opponents unbalanced. This instinct, coupled with the battalion's explicit orders to reach Montélimar and attack the long German convoy, compelled him to push ahead. As a result, he ordered L Company to secure the town with all haste.

The reserve TDs, M8s, and remaining infantry in the fields south of Allan repositioned closer to the village. 1st and 3rd Platoons divided up and spread out in three directions to take the town itself. Some of the men headed west to engage the Germans holding the western gardens, while others swung east, where the first Marder originally operated. The remaining men and the two Sherman tanks continued pushing along the main street toward the crossroads. Their objective was to seal off the escape of any remaining German armor prowling about the east side of town.

At first, the operation unfolded like the typical reduction of a German strongpoint. Coles and his men had no idea they were attacking the perimeter elements of a German armeekorps headquarters. Beyond their view in the fields and farms north and northwest of town, their intrusion had stirred a hornet's nest, the korps HQ thrown into a state of near panic.[9] The sudden appearance of the Americans at Allan—particularly Americans with tanks—shocked the Germans, who feared more enemy armor was only a short distance away. A mad scramble ensued to organize a second line of defense to cover the evacuation of the korps staff and other units caught in the immediate area. Trucks, buses, and cars were jammed full of equipment while soldiers dashed in all directions. This was the bewildering chaos that Jantz, Tyler, and the others had witnessed shortly after their capture.

Beneath the wooded canopy of the Borne farm north of the cemetery, the Panther crewmen cranked their monstrous panzer to life, sending twin plumes of oily exhaust raging through the dancing leaves above. A nearby Marder crew also started up its machine.[10] Once both engines had sufficiently warmed and the crews settled into their positions, the two guns thundered forward past the Borne home and into the scorching sunlight heading south into the Dessalles vineyards, where the drivers kicked their transmissions into high gear. The machines crushed row after row of perfectly aligned vines until attaining the cover of a small woods along the cemetery's north wall. After the tank and Marder vanished among the shadows, their crews trained their barrels on the town 400 yards away and shut down their engines. They waited in steely silence hidden among the brush, trees, and the tombs of the dead.

Meanwhile, back in town, Lt. Danby's tank crept forward along the narrow main street, negotiating through the tricky sunlight patterns filtering through the gently rustling leaves of the platane trees overhead.

Every ghostly flicker off a stone wall or glint behind a half shuttered window mocked mortal danger. Danby's tank idled frequently in order to not outpace the doughs jockeying in fits and starts among the nearby buildings, and the M4A1's motor growled as if annoyed and uncomfortable over the delays. From the turret hatch, Danby watched and listened for any other Marders attempting escape through the crossroads. Inside, Cpl. Vargo kept the main gun ready with his hands resting on the traverse controls and his foot hovering near the fire switch. Pvt. Dishner sat cramped and sweating on the opposite side of the main gun, ready to recharge the barrel with a new round of AP or HE.

The tank and infantry team progressed without incident past the Mourier blacksmith shop, the post office and Martel's home. As they drew near the crossroads, however, a bitter chorus of German small arms fire crackled with sudden vitality, the bullets hissing and popping through the hot air. Some shots pinged off the tank hull while others screamed as they ricocheted in wild directions off the stone and asphalt. The Germans were not going to relinquish the crossroads without a fight.

Concerned about being hit by a panzerfaust, Danby ordered Tikkanen to halt the tank until the infantry could clear the immediate area. While sergeants barked orders and encouragement, the men shot forward, leapfrogging along the walls and doorways and returning fire with their M-1 Garands and BARs. The advance fell far short of dislodging the determined German defenders, and a static firefight ensued. Amid the shots and shouts, several men on both sides fell wounded or dead. Two Germans positioned behind a tree in front of Mayor Almoric's house were gunned down in a hail of American fire. Their rifles clattered to the ground as they buckled and fell against the tree trunk. Both men quickly expired, their blood flowing freely and pooling over the hard dirt.

Sensing that Coles' men were gaining the upper hand, Danby ordered Tikkanen to roll forward to root out the remaining Germans from the recessed positions among the buildings. Tikkanen eased the tank past the fountain and into the intersection parallel with the church façade. From there, they could see past the road jog. To the American tankers, the road appeared clear all the way to the cemetery. What they could not see was that a Panther and Marder were waiting for them, concealed in the woods beyond. The German tank crews spotted the Sherman's high profile as it emerged entering the intersection. Both German guns fired at once, sending two AP rounds rocketing down the road toward town at speeds exceeding 3,000 feet per second.[11] The rounds arrived ahead of their own sound waves.

One of the shells grazed the left side of Danby's tank turret, carving out a gouge of shiny steel before ricocheting into the doorway of Martel's home.[12] Stones and mortar sprayed and tumbled on the road, and the door was completely blown off the hinges. For a few stunned seconds the crew in Danby's tank wondered if the deafening clang was the knock of death, but no telltale smoke flooded the interior and no one was injured. With the hull still ringing from the near miss, Tikkanen threw the gearshift into reverse and jerked the tank out of the line of fire. Several more volleys of German anti-tank fire zipped through the intersection, slamming against walls or tearing through the trees farther down the street. Even though the Sherman succeeded in backing safely out of the shooting trap, the blind volleys from the cemetery continued on for several more moments before ending as abruptly as they began.

Danby parked his tank a few yards south of the fountain. Its retreat from the intersection triggered a new round of infantry fighting, which redoubled in intensity. At the same time, another firefight erupted in the western gardens, where elements of 1st and 3rd Platoons were systematically expelling the German defenders. The area was difficult to defend because it was low and flat with few trees or cover. The fighting there was brief, with the Germans taking a number of casualties. Some of the wounded were dragged with them as they fell back beyond the raised roadbed to the northwest.[13]

Pfc. Albert Whisnant was a longtime rifleman in 3rd Platoon, and had befriended Pfc. McNamara of 1st Platoon during their patrols together in Italy. While Whisnant and his squad maneuvered and fired their way along the western edge of town, he came across McNamara laying prone behind his BAR, studying the northwestern road out of Allan intently. Two German cars and a small van were approaching the village. The van was in the middle of the formation and appeared to be a commandeered French vehicle. McNamara suspected the van was delivering ammunition. When one of the vehicles crossed within shooting range, McNamara drew back and released the charging handle of his BAR and let loose several short violent bursts, ripping holes like a sewing machine into the side of the van. When Whisnant joined in with his Garand, the van skidded wildly off the road and careened into the ditch. As the driver threw open the door and ran for his life, the two accompanying cars spun 180 degrees and sped back the way they had come.

Once the two men determined the way was clear, they slipped over to inspect the abandoned van. When they determined the cabin was empty, they moved around to the back and unlatched the cargo door. The inside was crammed with tank ammunition stacked to the ceiling. Some of the shells had spilled about the deck and daylight was streaming in through the fresh bullet holes perforating the sheet metal. Both men were surprised the whole thing didn't explode on impact.[14] They decided to leave the scene a little faster than they had arrived.

Farther up the road, a German column of approximately fifteen vehicles—including the two Marders that escaped town earlier—sped away in the direction of Montélimar.[15] They were gone before McNamara, Whisnant, or anyone else could stop them. The TD crews posted south of town listened to the escalating sounds of battle among the buildings and trees ahead, expecting to be called forward at any minute. They were unsure, however, if the infantry had cleared out the top floors of the homes along the main street. One building troubled them in particular: the Mourier house. The second floor windows provided ideal observation points for everything happening south of the village. Some of the anti-tank rounds from the cemetery passed directly overhead, and the TD crews didn't know if the shots were intended for them or not. They decided, however, that the Mourier upstairs was too suspicious to leave unaddressed any longer. With a thunderous boom, a charge of HE was sent directly into the upstairs, blasting out the windows and shutters and sending a small avalanche of fieldstone cascading into the courtyard below.[16]

Unbeknownst to the Americans, Mourier and his wife had taken refuge in their kitchen on the ground floor. Because he was the town's skilled blacksmith, the Germans forced Mourier to work for them. This, in turn, meant he and his wife were unable to escape into the hills with their fellow villagers. The explosion sent rubble and debris raining down across their only doorway from the room. Shaken from the concussion but otherwise unhurt, Mourier tried unsuccessfully to free he and his wife from the smoke-filled room. When a second round from the TD crews slammed into the upper story, the entire house shook to its foundations and knocked the Mouriers to the floor. Somehow both remained unhurt.

They scrambled back to their feet and found the blocked exit had miraculously cleared. Coughing and choking on the smoke now rapidly filling their home and billowing from the windows and roof, they emerged into the daylight.

From a neighboring home, two refugees from the southern coast watched the plight of the Mouriers with growing alarm. One of the men was a marine fireman from Toulon. Despite the ricochets of errant bullets, the fireman and his associate raced out into the open to help the couple to safety. Once the Mouriers were safely away from the house, the fireman and his brave companion rushed inside the smoldering structure to rescue whatever personal items they could for the couple. Within a short time, smoke and fire made further salvage impossible.

At 2:00 P.M., the combat in Allan ceased momentarily and an eerie calm prevailed. Rising and falling in pitch was the sound of a solitary engine. One Marder was trapped on the eastern side of town. Its crew dared not to run the crossroads guarded so closely by Danby's tank. Instead, the Germans turned their version of a tank destroyer up the narrow alleyway behind the Catholic Church and pivoted east onto a dirt lane north of the village. Once it was fifty yards east of town and concealed behind a small row of trees, the driver spun the left track around until the long gun pointed squarely south and cut the engine.

Prior to the Marder's move, German snipers posted along the row of buildings behind the church stalled the advance of the L Company men sent earlier to secure the east side of town.[17] The Americans remained pinned down in the ditches and fields, unable to do anything except exchange shots with their well-concealed German tormenters. From among those ditches, Pfc. Joseph W. Leithner watched the distant Marder III emerge from the church alley and reposition itself in ambush along the lane. He understood that the big gun presented not only a threat to him and his friends trying to maneuver through the sniper fire, but to the entire right flank of the company. Without hesitation, the twenty-one year old leaped from the ditch and dashed across seventy-five yards of open field, varying his speed and direction with leaps and bounds. He provided his own covering fire by resting the stock of his Garand against his hip and firing randomly as he ran. The effect gained him the cover of a nearby building corner, where he surprised and shot three Germans before they could respond.

Leithner took a few seconds to acclimate himself to his new surroundings before methodically inching his way along the backside of the rowed shops and homes overlooking the eastern fields. Within a few minutes he was within fifty yards of the Marder III.[18] Leithner waited a few moments to make sure his incursion went undetected, popped a fresh clip into his M-1, and raised it slowly, drawing a bead on the head of one of the crew. He gently squeezed the trigger. The man dropped dead like a sliding sack of flour. Two nearby Germans, shocked by the proximity and accuracy of the unseen American rifleman, froze in place and raised their hands to surrender.[19] Leithner's buddies, following in to assist him, beckoned the prisoners to approach. Word passed back to the TD and M8 crews south of town on the precise location of the Marder III. The small tank remained a threat because nearby German riflemen protected it and two of its crewmen remained inside.[20] A few moments later, about 2:30 P.M., a gust of American shells from the south set the Marder ablaze. Unable to escape, the driver and assistant driver died in the inferno.

While L Company was fighting to clear out Allan, Lt. Col. Boye and 3rd Battalion established a command post on the southeastern side of Montchamp hill within a wooded area off the main road leading up to the saddle. The position gave Boye an excellent view of Donzère and National Route 7 to the west, and placed him to within three miles of L Company. From Coles' frequent radio updates, he was well aware that L Company was meeting stiff resistance. If Coles made a special request for reinforcements, Boye was in a good position to send help.

Across the road on the Roucoule hillside, Captain Redle established his B Company CP. The higher elevation enabled him to better monitor the radio communications of the three tank platoons under his command. 1st Sgt. Nusz opened up the captured German box trailer that B Company used as a small mobile office, adjusted the radios and his papers, and then sat down to work. Redle hovered nearby and listened in to the crackling voices crisscrossing over several different radio frequencies. Some voices were infantry traffic to and from 3rd Battalion; others were from 756th Tank Battalion headquarters, mundane instructions for coordinating movement and re-supply. However, every now and then Redle's tankers would break in, and when they did the young captain strained to catch every word. The messages were usually brief and sounded meaningless to non-tankers, but Redle understood a host of details by what was and was not said. Sometimes his tankers called for him specifically, but normally the dialogue was restricted to the tactical operations of the platoon.

Through the infrequent chatter, Redle tracked 1st Platoon moving slowly with 1st Battalion against resistance approaching Donzère. 2nd Platoon was quietly in reserve and traveling with 2nd Battalion through Saint-Paul to the south. The progress of 3rd Platoon, however, had Redle's special interest. Based on the content of the strong AM transmissions of 3rd Battalion and the weaker FM signals between Danby and Oliver, Redle had a good idea of L Company's general circumstances in Allan.

The situation was not to Redle's liking. He believed that Boye's decision to divide Danby's platoon into sections was a mistake, because only two tanks were operating in town, which meant each was able to lend little if any support to the other through the street fighting. Every infantry battalion commander split the tank platoons up, and they had the authority and their reasons for doing so. Redle, however, never liked the practice. On the other hand, Redle had great confidence in the experience and judgment of Captain Coles and S/Sgt. Oliver. Danby was operating with a veteran team during his first day of combat, but since he was also seeing the heaviest action, Redle stayed glued to the radio, processing every new detail of the drama unfolding up the road. He looked at his watch. The local time was 3:00 P.M.

Back in Allan, meanwhile, the ebb and flow of afternoon's battle had decidedly broken in favor of the Americans; L Company was poised to take the town. The GIs had spent the last hour systematically expelling the German defenders from the western and eastern quarters. The crossroads firefight had waned to a few occasional stray shots. The unseen big guns that nearly knocked out Danby's tank earlier had been completely silent since 2:00 P.M. The German defensive front seemed to be evaporating, much like the resistance had during the morning encounter at Chartroussas.

Coles could not afford to ease up on the pressure. The resistance at Allan put the company a couple hours behind schedule for its planned attack against the Route 7 column. However, plenty of daylight remained to accomplish the mission if the town fell quickly. The experience gleaned in the fighting thus far, forced one tactical change. Rather than take the western exit out of Allan, Coles decided to outflank the enemy by sending L Company north beyond the cemetery to the small hamlet of

Le Ferrent, where it would swing westward. Orders for the move passed down through the scattered line of tanks, TDs, and M8s, for them to reform a column and prepare to move. As the armor gathered, the infantry would clear out any stragglers at the crossroads and check the road leading to the cemetery for hidden dangers. The armor column could not pass beyond the crossroads without sufficient evidence that the German anti-tank guns ahead had fled.[21]

Fifteen soldiers moved out to comply with Coles' order. In a bold and brave small-unit thrust, they charged *en masse* from the town square up the main street. Their sudden appearance in the crossroads surprised a few remaining Germans still holding positions near the church rectory. A shower of bullets cut down the defenders, who had little chance to respond. Those who did not fall to the pavement riddled with small arms fire, withdrew in haste.

The fifteen continued trotting boldly up the road toward the cemetery. The regular cadence of their boot steps broke into a multitude of rhythms as the formation slowed and spread out along the road. Leading the group were two scouts, Pfc. Earl Potter and Pfc. Rick Evans. The eighteen- and twenty-year old, respectively, charged past the dirt lane leading east up to the old ruins on the hill. Out of the right corner of his eye, Potter noticed something burning about 150 yards away.[22] He turned briefly to see thick black smoke billowing out of the Marder III that was earlier destroyed by Leithner's actions. Other than the flaming armor spectacle, the lane appeared deserted.

The two scouts and their comrades proceeded up the main road to the small concrete bridge 100 yards north of town. Potter, Evans, and a few others crossed it while everyone else either dropped down along the dry creek bed or fanned out among the fields and brush in search of Germans. As the advance group dispersed, other L Company men worked in from the west along the dry creek bed toward the north bridge.[23] Strangely, no one opposed them. The entire area was unexpectedly silent.

Potter and Evans advanced together up the road well ahead of the bridge and everyone else. They slowed up as they closed in on the cemetery 300 yards away, cautiously covering each step with their Tommy guns trained forward and their eyes sweeping from side to side. The entire walk was intense, but eerily calm. Though unbearably hot, the countryside was lovely and inviting with its bright green fields and distant shimmering sunlit hills. If he wasn't drenched in sweat and wearing the same uncomfortable smelly woolen ODs since the landings, while toting a submachine gun in the middle of a war, thought Potter, he would have sworn he was taking a stroll in the park back home with his gal. Potter looked over at Evans, who looked just as wretched as he did. He wasn't much of a date, Potter concluded.

Coles' jeep emerged from town with trailer in tow. The big captain was sitting next to his driver with the radio and a machine gunner positioned in the back seat. In the small trailer, several alert riflemen sat with their legs dangling over the sides, ready to leap out and deploy at the first sign of trouble. The jeep traced the same path, pausing at times for Coles to survey the situation or bark out additional instructions to the advance party. The vehicle combination crossed the small bridge, and crept toward Potter and Evans as they neared the road bend.

Thick brush obscured most of the cemetery. The thicket of trees beyond the far wall also presented a contrasting visual challenge, their low leafy branches shimmering with bright green brilliance against dark formless trunks and murky shadows. In a few places, the men glimpsed faraway green fields through small openings. To their surprise, not a single German was anywhere to be seen. Everything was silent and exceedingly ordinary. The enemy, Potter concluded, had conceded the whole area to the Americans.[24]

Back in Allan, the armor column assembled along the main street and prepared to move forward. Danby's tank waited in front just south of crossroads while men from the Weapons Platoon lined up nearby in loose formations. Several riflemen climbed onto the back deck of the old M4A1, hoping to save a few steps and rest their aching feet once things got moving. One of the young men was Pfc. Arthur Schrader, the rifle grenadier of 1st Platoon. Earlier in the morning, Schrader had been upset when 2nd Lt. Mackowsky chewed him out for spraining his ankle in a jump from a tank. Though his ankle was still sore, Schrader felt guilty about the incident. No one had seen Mackowsky since 1:00 P.M., and the nineteen-year old from Buffalo, New York, was growing concerned over what may have befallen his platoon leader.[25]

While Schrader thought of Mackowsky, Lt. Danby wondered if the column's advance was overdue. Nearly thirty minutes had passed since the L Company patrol took the crossroads and disappeared into the northern fields. Coles' jeep had also ventured far beyond the bridge without incident. Aside from the brief encounter with the straggling

Germans near the rectory, nothing else was happening. Nobody wanted to keep the gruff but charismatic captain waiting, and Danby was determined not to become the cause of another delay. He radioed instructions to Oliver, whose tank was idling roughly fifty yards behind his own, to follow his lead out of town and to relay the message down the column.[26]

Oliver didn't like Danby's idea at all. As far as he was concerned, the entire situation felt like a trap. He had seen this before many times in Italy. Unlike Danby, Oliver knew the Germans were patient opponents who liked to allow the small stuff to pass to lure more lucrative prizes into the killing zone. With the caution born from experience, Oliver wanted to wait until they were absolutely certain the route was clear.

He cleared his throat and flicked on the microphone. "Lieutenant," warned the platoon sergeant, "I wouldn't go out of town like that."

The remark irritated Danby because Coles, who had already driven up the road without incident, had prearranged the move. The combat green lieutenant wasn't about to second-guess the accomplished captain or risk losing Coles' confidence by appearing timid. The decision seemed no more of a gamble then the earlier smashing of the Chartroussas roadblock, or the more recent attack on Allan when they had forced the Marders out of the village.

"Sergeant," replied Danby with terse finality, "I'm the leader of this platoon and we'll move as I say."[27]

With the decision made, Danby switched his microphone and headsets from radio to intercom settings so he could communicate with his tank crew, and settled into a relatively comfortable position on the tiny fold down seat latched to the interior wall of the turret. With his head and shoulders riding high out the hatch, he checked to make sure the infantry was clear of either track and signaled Tikkanen it was time to roll.

Danby's tank rocked forward with all tread links clattering. With a walking escort of infantry spread out in front and along either side, the old M4A1 rolled slowly past the church entrance and into the road jog where it had nearly been knocked out two hours earlier. A few anxious moments passed but no new shells came zipping down from the cemetery. Nothing could be heard but the loud radial engine laboring to pull the 33-ton vehicle.

Danby's tank passed the lane with the burning Marder, but still nothing happened. Oliver's M4 also emerged from the crossroads of town and followed unmolested. Deeper in the village, the chain of TDs began rolling ahead in intervals. The entire column was again moving forward.

As Danby's tank approached the small bridge, he observed GIs patrolling along the dry creek and across the nearby fields. Farther up the road was Coles' stationary jeep and trailer, and beyond them the distant figures of Potter and Evans at the road bend. Everything appeared routine.

Walking ten yards ahead of Danby's tank was Pfc. Fred Scarpa and his machine gun squad from Weapons Platoon. Scarpa had been in L Company since February.[28] Prior to joining, he served as a tanker in 752nd Tank Battalion (light) before its reorganization. Since he knew a lot about machine guns, the infantry snatched him out of a Replacement Depot.[29] A short fellow with a wide smile, Scarpa quickly became popular with his mates. On this particular afternoon, however, Scarpa wasn't sure whether he was better off inside or in front of a moving tank. In order to make certain he was maintaining a safe and proper distance, he turned his head back to locate Danby's tank.

At that very instant the entire chassis shuddered with an earsplitting thump. A four-inch hole opened on the left side of the gun mantlet, perforated cleanly as if by a giant invisible paper punch. A millisecond after slicing through the two-inch armor, the deadly filler cap in the German AP round exploded with a deafening roar. Pvt. Dual Dishner received the full force of the blast, which simply vaporized him.[30] The sudden violent overpressure and spray of molten shrapnel ripped apart both Danby, in the tank hatch, and Vargo, seated on the opposite side of the gun breech. All three men died instantly without ever realizing what had transpired. The force of the explosion jettisoned smoke, debris, and human remains out the turret hatch, including the lifeless head and shoulders of Lt. Danby, which tumbled onto the asphalt below.[31]

Miraculously, the two remaining men in the tank survived the blast. Tikkanen, who was shielded somewhat in the driver compartment below, was jammed forward into the steering controls. Keeping his wits about him even as a searing pain shot across his back, Tikkanen pulled hard on the controls and skidded the tank to a halt. He tore off his leather football-style helmet and headset and released the overhead hatch spring.

Though six-feet tall and broad shouldered, he snaked through the narrow opening like a contortionist and slid down from the rounded hull.[32] The bow gunner seated across the transmission housing from Tikkanen didn't bother with the overhead hatch. Instead, he kicked out the wider floor plate below his seat, spilled onto the road, and scrambled out from under the smoking tank.[33]

Neither Pfc. Schrader nor any of the other doughs seated on the back deck of the tank, was killed or injured by the direct hit. Each man jumped clear of the doomed machine and dashed for cover along the roadside.[34] Only a handful of yards away were Scarpa and his squad mates, who had already taken up protected positions while straining to locate the source that had delivered the sudden death blow.[35]

Shorts in the electric wiring inside the turret ignited the leaking fuel vapors, which triggered an eruption of flame inside the interior of the tank with the fury of a blast furnace.[36] Flames roared out the commanders' hatch with a blowtorch effect, and everything inside was instantly consumed, including the mangled bodies, the treasured photographs, and personal effects of home. With them went Mr. Rozel's shattered bottle of wine, from which none of them would ever sip.

Soldiers hunkering down along the dry creek twenty-five yards away on the left side of the road helped a stunned Tikkanen to safety. The infantry knew the tall driver from their previous days traveling together and appreciated him for his quiet, friendly disposition. They had nicknamed him "Whitey," on account of his blonde hair.[37] The happy-go-lucky personality was gone. "Whitey" was both irate at the enemy and deranged with grief over the deaths of his friends.

"Give me a rifle! Give me a rifle!" he screamed.

Pfc. Patrick "Joe" Rodger and the others grabbed him before he could seize a weapon and attempt his insane plans of solitary vengeance.[38] They continued holding him back until he regained his senses.

Three hundred yards north of where Danby and his tankers met their end, Potter and Evans heard the thud as the round pierced Danby's tank. The two scouts turned, thinking the Sherman must have seen trouble and fired its main gun. Instead, they saw pandemonium near the bridge. The tank was grinding to a halt while smoke poured from its turret. American troopers were scattering in all directions. Even from that distance, Potter could make out the blonde-haired driver struggling through the top hatch and dropping to the ground.[39]

The scene puzzled Potter, who speculated to himself that a German grenadier hidden near the bridge must have nailed the tank with a panzerfaust. Before he could fully process the thought however, he heard a deep-pitched engine awaken from behind the cemetery. Both he and Evans spun back around in time to see an enormous German Panther pulling out from the shadows.[40] At the same time, the woods, bushes, and ditches before them erupted in a wave of grey uniforms. With the exception of a prisoner of war pen, Potter had never seen so many Germans in one place so close. Unlike POWs, however, these were armed men shooting their weapons in his direction. Sgt. Oliver's instincts had been right after all; The Americans had stumbled into a well planned ambush.

As bullets whizzed and snapped around their heads, Potter and Evans dove for cover in the roadside ditch. Occasionally, they raised their Tommy guns and fired short bursts for effect, but with enemy small arms fire spraying over them from three directions, they had no chance to aim at anything or anyone in particular. Their situation was nearly hopeless. Within a short time their ammunition was expended and both men knew they would be overrun and killed within a handful of seconds.

"What do we do?" Evans yelled in Potter's direction.

"Well, I don't think I want to die," Potter shot back.[41]

The men pulled out white hankies and waved them skyward. The nearest German was walking only a few yards from them. When he spotted the universal signal of surrender, he yelled out, "Herausgekommen!" ("Come out!"), waving the barrel of his Mauser for emphasis.

Potter and Evans tossed aside their useless Tommy guns and slowly rose to their feet, at the same time unclipping and discarding their empty ammo belts. Despite personal fear and the unnerving battle raging around them, the two scouts did their best to make sure each move appeared nonthreatening.

A second German rifleman ran over to assist. He looked to be about forty-five years old. Potter and Evans recognized him as one who had been firing at them only seconds earlier. To their surprise, he spoke perfect English. With an odd combination of affability and caution, he promptly escorted the two prisoners off the immediate battlefield into enemy-controlled territory. Once there, the krauts searched them thoroughly for weapons, papers, or other useful information. Satisfied they were clear, the middle-aged soldier stepped back and studied them with a quizzical look.

Again, in perfect English he observed, "Things must be bad in the U.S. to be drafting kids so young." He was completely serious. He followed up his remark by asking the scouts a number of questions about how things "really" were back in the States. He seemed to have some preconceived notion or hope that Americans were just as exhausted over the war as his German comrades.

Potter and Evans assumed this was their interrogation and tried to respond as little as possible. Their captor didn't press them much for answers. Instead, he recounted with great excitement his upbringing in Milwaukee, and spoke of his wife and two sons minding the family tavern back home. He explained that when he traveled to Germany in 1938 to visit his parents, the state drafted him into the German Army before he could return. He had not been "home" in six years. Potter and Evans listened quietly as the Wisconsin man continued with his life story awhile longer, unsure how to process this new twist of unreality that had suddenly raised its head in the middle of a war zone. "Wasn't this supposed to be their interrogation?" Potter wondered. And this man who had been shooting at them only a few minutes earlier was an American?[42]

The German guided the men to what they figured was a temporary German command center in a French farmhouse. Two other captured men from L Company were moved over to join them. The men all knew one another. The new prisoners were Pfc. Frank Mangina and Pfc. James D. Engel, both picked up early in the same counterattack.[43]

The Germans made the four Americans sit in a circle on the courtyard ground and told them that they would be questioned one at a time.[44] Potter was first. He was marched into a room in the house where another English-speaking German began asking him questions. Several other Germans stood quietly nearby. At first, Potter was asked for basic information such as his name and rank, but then the Germans wanted to know about troop strength, airplanes, and so forth. The questions were well above Potter's pay grade, but he figured he could fabricate a good story. He said that he heard of five or six divisions moving in right behind 3rd Infantry Division. He told of thousands and thousands of planes and tanks on the move. The Germans listened intently. Potter did not know if they bought all his bullshit or not, but he felt proud of himself for trying.

Once released, he returned to the courtyard and sat down with the other three prisoners. Concerned that his tales may have been a little too tall, Potter whispered a general description to the others of what he had told the enemy so they could repeat a similar story.[45]

The guard became suspicious. "Nicht sprechen!" ("Do not speak!") he growled, abruptly ending the conspiracy.[46]

One by one the remaining three were interrogated. The Germans seemed content enough with their stories and dropped the matter. Why they were so interested in what four lowly privates had to say was unclear. If there was one principle true for every army, it was that a private was never told a damn thing, and beyond his line of vision, he usually had no idea what was transpiring.

Immediately after Danby's tank took its fatal hit, Pfc. Arthur Schrader jumped clear and ran for the cover of the dry creek. The burst of adrenaline pumping through his limbs made him forget all about his tender ankle. Schrader arrived on the bank of the creek with a few of his comrades and dove flat to the ground. Across the fields before him were dozens of Germans spread from left to right, advancing and shooting with control and confidence. They had good reason to feel confident. Behind them was an enormous Panther tank creaking its way from behind the cemetery, trailing after the German infantry like a mother grizzly watching over her cubs.

The Americans scattered along the creek and fields near town, returned fire with as much nervous ferocity as they could muster. The sudden shift in initiative had taken everyone by surprise. As the Germans closed in, their bullets began to zing and slice through the foliage near the creek. Schrader waited to line up a clear shot. He spotted a German corporal walking in the distance holding a submachine gun while gesturing for his men to keep moving forward. Schrader took a deep breath to relax. He repositioned his Springfield by resting the stock on the ground and pivoting it until the German corporal was in his sights. Just as he was about the squeeze the trigger, the gun jerked and the entire barrel disappeared—ripped off cleanly by a sudden burst of close-range machine gun fire from the right.

The shock over losing his weapon coupled with the unrelenting sounds of a battle closing in broke Schrader's nerves. His mind seized upon the thought of returning to the safety of town. As he jumped up and began running, another part of his mind screamed that his decision was rash and suicidal. The Germans always employed a sharpshooter with the specific job of picking off guys like him. Schrader remembered this from Anzio, and expected at any instant to feel a bullet slam into his back. His legs, however, only pumped faster. Divots of dirt and grass began churning and flying apart around feet. A machine gun was trying to cut him down, but Schrader kept going. He dashed past S/Sgt. Oliver's tank as it was backing up and firing parting shots while retreating into the village. To Schrader's astonishment and relief, he arrived inside the village alive. Inside Allan, the armor column was completely disorganized, with the TDs scattered haphazardly off the narrow street, maneuvering to find additional protection behind buildings and walls.

Amid the disarray of diesel exhaust and soldiers running in nearly every direction, Schrader paused to catch his breath and reflect upon his narrow escape. He wondered if these Germans were as well trained as those at Anzio, or if Fate had somehow intervened on his behalf. Maybe he was plain lucky. Perhaps he had a few more minutes to live and none of these thoughts would matter anyway. Perhaps a certain German corporal up the road had similar questions flashing through his mind.[47]

As Schrader contemplated his existence, Oliver's tank pulled back behind the protection of the crossroads.[48] His Sherman was no match for the Panther roused from its ambush den. The big German tank had a cannon with twice the muzzle velocity of Oliver's 75mm "pea shooter," and frontal armor nearly twice as thick. A Sherman's three-inch bow plate offered little protection against the Panther's gun at any range, whereas Oliver could spend the entire afternoon bouncing AP off the Panther's front at point blank range and never break through.[49] Oliver's only chance was to outflank the Panther and nail it from the side or the rear, where its armor was much thinner. Under the prevailing circumstances, however, that option was unrealistic. With their options narrowing, Oliver realized that the sudden German attack had trapped his Sherman and the TDs along the narrow streets of town with no room left to maneuver. The legendary gunnery team of Bert Bulen and Ed Sadowski was effectively benched.

At his CP south at Roucoule, meanwhile, Captain Redle had been monitoring communications when he heard Danby's radio fall silent. He hailed Oliver to find out what was happening.[50] The troubled veteran's voice crackled over the speaker in reply: "Danby's tank has been knocked out . . . the new lieutenant and two others are dead . . . and the remaining two crew members escaped with light wounds." An ashen-faced 1st Sgt. Nusz listened in and jotted down the particulars to relay on the battalion HQ channel once Redle finished.[51]

As if to punctuate the report Oliver was relaying to Redle, Danby's tank hissed and sputtered in raging inferno of flame and black smoke. Ammunition rounds exploded sporadically inside, sending shrapnel out the hatches and into the branches of nearby oak trees.[52] Some of the men trapped in the creek took cover beneath the concrete arch under the bridge to escape the flying debris.[53] Along the nearby creek bank, Scarpa and his men exchanged shots with the advancing Germans. One of Scarpa's men shot a German as he tried to cross the road, but too many others closed in from unseen angles. The brisk enemy attack forced Scarpa's men to pull back behind a stone building.[54]

Along the western creek bed, Whisnant, Rodger, and others held their ground, laying down a heavy field of fire.[55] T/5 Herman Cogdell burned out the barrel of his BAR in the exchange.[56]

The eastern side of the road was another matter entirely. As soon as the counterattack began, Captain Coles, his driver, and the other riders of the jeep/trailer combination took cover along the ditch near their vehicle. Coles managed to hail the battalion CP on Montchamp with his remaining radio. He had barely enough time to tell Boye that his company had stumbled into heavy resistance leaving the village, and that the tanks had run back into town.[57] A string of German mortar rounds burst in succession around the jeep, killing or wounding several of Coles' men and scattered the survivors deeper into the fields. Coles took a small piece of shrapnel to the backside and abandoned the radio and jeep for cover. [58] The wound was painful, but a minor nuisance for the combat veteran.

Sensing that the situation was rapidly spinning out of control and that his company was descending into chaos, Coles crouched to his feet and dashed 200 yards toward town in leaps and bounds. His daring run drew a rain of German bullets, but none found their mark and he limped into town having survived the easy part of his trial.[59] Though an experienced battlefield leader, the timing and potency of the counterattack had caught Coles off guard.[60] He had to set aside his offensive instincts and rally a makeshift defense against a battalion-sized wave of enemy soldiers sick of being chased and humiliated for the last twelve days.[61] This was not

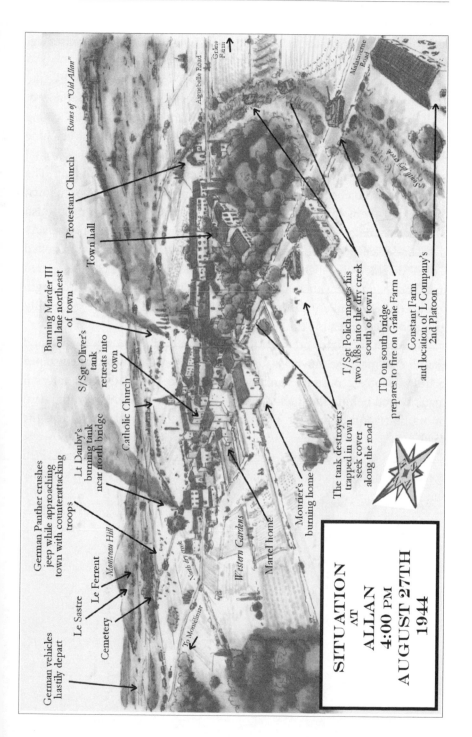

German vehicles
hastily depart

Le Sastre

Cemetery

German Panther crushes
jeep while approaching
town with counterattacking
troops

Le Ferrent

Montreau Hill

North dry creek

To Montelimar

Western Gardens

Martel home

Lt Danby's
burning tank
near north bridge

Catholic Church

Mourier's
burning home

SITUATION
AT
ALLAN
4:00 PM
AUGUST 27TH
1944

The tank destroyers
trapped in town
seek cover
along the road

Burning Marder III
on lane northeast
of town

S/Sgt Oliver's
tank
retreats into
town

Town hall

Protestant Church

T/Sgt Polich moves his
two M8s into the dry creek
south of town

TD on south bridge
prepares to fire on Gräne Farm

Constant Farm
and location of L Company's
2nd Platoon

Ruins of "Old Allan"

Aiguebelle Road

Gräne
Farm

Malataverne
Road

South dry creek

just some brief encounter. L Company was fighting for its very existence, and Captain Coles was well aware of the stakes.

The Germans advanced on Allan with the Panther tank acting like the sole queen on a chessboard.[62] Its crew was obviously experienced, perhaps battle-hardened survivors of the 11th Panzer Division's long deployment on the Russian Front. They skillfully wielded their machine with complete confidence in the superiority of their gun and frontal armor. The time and place of Danby's demise was no accident. The burning Sherman not only pinned the remaining American armor in town and sealed them from the only exit and bridge to the north, but also provided a smoke screen behind which the Germans could maneuver. As if to underscore the triumph of the moment, the Panther approached Coles' disabled and abandoned vehicle on the roadside. The tank veered just far enough to lay one of its two-foot wide tracks over the entire length of the combination, crushing the jeep, the radio, and the trailer as readily as a boot crushing a pie tin.[63]

As men in field grey uniforms secured the eastern fields and established machine gun nests, the Panther settled a comfortable distance behind Danby's burning tank and fired into town. Occasionally, it maneuvered behind the thick black veil of smoke and fired again, intent on nailing another tank or TD masked among the buildings down the road.

Once he knew Danby's tank was gone, Captain Redle maintained constant radio contact with Oliver. At 4:00 P.M., Oliver's radio abruptly fell silent.[64]

Chapter 13

Trouble in the Rear

S outh of Allan, T/Sgt. George Polich was preparing his M8s to settle into the rear of the column when all hell broke loose. Three of the four TDs moving ahead of him scattered when Danby's tank was destroyed, eliminating the armor column's cohesion and adding to the confusion. The remaining TD halted on the south bridge near the Constant Farm with a crew unsure what, exactly, to do next. Its crew kept the machine on the road, its long gun pointed north. Polich and the others caught south of town could hear the oscillating clamor of the renewed battle reverberating from beyond the church. Every now and then, a large thundering gun joined the muffled fray.[1]

With Lt. Cotter trapped somewhere in town with his jeep and driver, the immediate responsibility for the platoon fell onto Polich's shoulders. His first concern was to find cover for both M8s. He ordered the crews to seek the best protection along the nearby dry creek. To further conceal their location, Polich ordered both drivers to turn off their engines after they found a good spot.[2] All four tank destroyers, including the one on the bridge, went silent with the same reason in mind.

As the battle raged beyond their view, Polich took a few moments to examine the situation. Surveying the terrain from the top of his M8, he scanned the front looking for alternate positions, while considering his options should the forward lines collapse. To his left, a TD held the small bridge. Some infantry were at the Constant farm, but the Germans certainly prowled the woodland beyond. Above the trees before him stretched Allan's church spire and rising plumes of smoke. Beyond that, Polich had no idea what was transpiring. On the right stood the big hill topped with the old ruins. To his dismay, Polich discovered little room to flank or maneuver in any direction. It was an unsettling prospect, and remaining stalled only heightened his concerns. Nevertheless, he decided to keep his M8s quiet and still until he more clearly understood the situation.[3]

When Cotter radioed to let Polich know he was safe in town and to check on the status of the platoon, Polich told him of the move into the dry creek. Cotter advised him to sit tight.[4] Although the conversation was brief, Polich inferred that his platoon leader was gravely concerned about the way events were unfolding.

Cotter was not only pondering the immediate deteriorating tactical situation facing his platoon. Also on his mind was how the entire campaign had unfolded thus far. On the whole, resistance in southern France had been exceedingly light. Cotter's men had grown accustomed to rolling mile after mile with little more than an occasional sniper or anti-tank gun to slow them. The thin, thoughtful lieutenant knew those days had abruptly ended at the crossroads in Allan. Here, finally, the Germans drew a line and said "no more."[5]

Only minutes after Polich put down his radio mike, he heard the droning motor of a solitary vehicle approaching town from the south. The time was 3:45 P.M. All eyes stationed along the rear flank strained to locate and identify the source of the surging engine somewhere out among the trees and farms. Finally, a German car appeared on Aiguebelle road, approaching Allan at a leisurely pace. The driver and passengers were completely oblivious to the dangers ahead. In all likelihood, they were messengers bringing LXXXV Korps staff an update on the advancing 3rd Division, not realizing that 3rd Division was already in Allan.

As the car neared the Grâne farm just southeast of the village, GIs stationed at the Constant Farm 200 yards to the west opened fire with machine guns and rifles. The car swerved before accelerating until it disappeared behind the buildings of the Grâne Farm. The driver hit the brakes and skidded to a halt behind the main L-shaped building of the compound.

For a few quiet moments, the Germans sat in their car and considered their poor range of choices. At the same time, the Americans prepared to deprive them of at least one choice. The crew of the tank destroyer on the south bridge cranked up their motor and slowly traversed their open turret.[6] Centering their 3-inch gun squarely on the Grâne Farm, the crew fired their notoriously loud gun. In the same split-second, an AP round smashed through both near and far walls at the center of the main building. As the M-10 carriage rocked from the recoil, the loader hunched amid the rapidly dissipating cordite smoke and slammed another AP round into the gun breech. The gunner fired a second time. The Grâne Farm building shuddered again as a new wound opened on its ancient exterior, showering stone and mortar in all directions and revealing daylight on the other side. The TD crew repeated the sequence several times, with every new impact revealing more and more of the courtyard through the shattered building center. One of the rounds penetrated four walls of the same L-shaped building.

With some of the TD rounds passing too close for comfort, the five Germans in the car realized they could no longer remain in the courtyard. They decided their best option was to abandon the car and escape on foot in an effort to reach headquarters. The group split into two groups and dashed for town. Two made a direct run through the tobacco fields between the Grâne Farm and town. Despite drawing intense rifle and machine gun fire from the Constant Farm, the Germans reached the village. Their luck, however, would prove fleeting. Once they entered the town they were promptly captured.

The other three men bounded straight for the eastern hill with the intention of tracing north along the base until they reached their lines. At first their daring flight seemed to go as planned, and they were able to dash beyond the effective range of the American rifles and automatic weapons. However, once the TD began firing high explosive rounds at their heels, they panicked and dove for cover in a ditch beneath a tree. This was the worst possible choice they could make. Clustered and stationary in the middle of an open field, they were sitting ducks waiting for the hunter to reload. The next TD shell burst directly on their position, killing two of the hapless Germans instantly. The third man jumped to his feet and ran frantically until disappearing out of view into the eastern fields of town. Whether mortally wounded and acting out his final moments, or just unbelievably lucky, was impossible to know.

No sooner did that incident end, when two more German cars appeared from the south, this time approaching rapidly from Malataverne. As with the first car, these drivers also behaved as if they had no idea of the American presence in Allan. T/Sgt. Polich swung around the .50-caliber machine gun mounted on the back of his M8 turret and began firing short bursts. The nearby infantry joined in with their rifles and BARs, but Polich's shots were the first to spray across both targets. Both cars screeched to a halt haphazardly aligned on the road. The occupants of the far car were unhurt. When they promptly raised their arms to surrender, the Americans beckoned them forward and searched them thoroughly. Polich's bursts killed the driver of the closest car. The sergeant could clearly see that one of his .50-caliber bullets had ripped him open. His passenger was also motionless, but no one was about to check him until it was clear no more enemy vehicles were approaching from that direction.[7]

The sound of combat south of Allan, particularly the noise of the TD's booming gun and diesel engine, attracted the notice of the Panther tank operating north of village. The big grey machine shifted from the road beyond Danby's smoldering tank to a new location in the field. Though the Panther crew was still unable to see anything beyond the church crossroads, it did not mean they could not fire their big gun. The TD crew at the south bridge was turning their machine around to react more quickly to any new German threats at the rear. Halfway through the maneuver, the Panther began firing blindly through the trees overhead. With branches tumbling and platane leaves fluttering to the street, the TD driver spun his treads until the turn was to complete and then cut the engine.

The latest developments convinced Polich to reposition his M8s facing south. Just the few seconds of noise from restarting their engines and swinging around was enough to cause the Panther to shift focus and begin firing through the treetops over the heads of the M8 crews.[8] Polich's crews completed the pivot and cut the engines, but endured several nervous minutes as AP rounds zipped overhead. Just as abruptly as the firing began, the Panther fell silent.

The situation along the rear flank seemed stable enough for one of the infantry sergeants to ask Polich if he wanted to inspect the two shot-up cars. Polich agreed, but did not think his .45-cal pistol was adequate protection, so he borrowed a rifle and set off with the sergeant.[9] The passenger in the first car had been faking death, but he showed no threat or resistance when the GIs approached. The only body was that of the dead driver. No articles or papers of any military importance were found in either car. However, Polich did find a pair of binoculars and a camera that he considered worthy of "liberation."[10]

The two men walked with the prisoner back to their posts while the sporadic sounds of battle filtered down through town. With little news trickling down from the north, and no idea of what further surprises might drive in from the south, they settled in along the dry creek bed and fought back a creeping sense of isolation.[11] From time to time the unseen Panther sent another harassing round hurtling over their heads. No one along the rear flank could do anything about the situation except sit and wait.

* * *

Captain Coles spent the first half hour of his return bustling around the village on his bad leg, reassuring his men and reorganizing his company's forward defenses. He was gravely concerned the Germans would try reentering the town to sever his thinly spread company. For the moment, however, the Germans stopped along the north creek bed—unwilling, unsure, or unable to retake the town. The L Company men stubbornly defending the creek may have given the Germans pause. Perhaps they balked after hearing the TDs and M8s maneuvering in the south. Maybe the counterattack was only a stopgap to buy others time to retreat—a true rearguard action and nothing more. Whatever the reason, Coles welcomed the delay, which gave him time to clear his head and plan his reaction.

With the front line holding, Coles dashed back to the Constant Farm to gather reinforcements. A fresh group moved up the main street of town with a TD trailing behind.[12] In order to sound ten times their size to the Germans listening in the north, they fired off their automatic weapons in a rolling fashion. Unimpressed with the display, the Panther tank crew responded by firing in their direction with more blind shots. The threat was enough to force the TD to hold up. The infantry continued forward and fanned out through the village to embark on a house-to-house search. No Germans were discovered, but a few citizens remaining in their homes had to be reassured the town was not under attack again. With Allan under tenuous American control, Pfc. William R. Shook, the missing runner who evaded capture earlier, finally emerged with relief from the church tower.[13]

Back at 3rd Battalion Command Post on the southeast side of Montchamp, Lt. Col. Boye was torn between assisting L Company, which was almost certainly in trouble in Allan, and dealing with a large concentration of Germans moving 1,000 yards west and northwest of his CP. From the hillside, Boye's observers counted more than 100 German vehicles, including another Panther tank and several anti-tank guns, moving into the area. Hundreds of German soldiers accompanied them, and not all were heading north. A few of the vehicles were backtracking south, apparently to counter 1st Battalion's advance on Donzère.[14] Many others were spilling over into the fields north of Montchamp. These represented a direct threat to the rear flank of L Company. In order to help L Company in the north and simultaneously aid 1st Battalion to the west, Boye ordered the battalion's mortars and anti-tank guns to shell any Germans moving in those directions.

The Germans responded with their own artillery. Though unobserved and sporadic, some of the explosions fell close enough that Boye called regimental for reinforcements.[15] When one of the rounds devastated a parked jeep belonging to the regiment,[16] Boye was promised that three more tanks would be sent his way.[17] To further shore up L Company's rear flank and also protect his HQ, Boye ordered K Company to move up the road between Montchamp and Roucoule and assume defensive positions beyond the saddle. I Company was directed to establish roadblocks at the battalion's rear.

Across the road on Roucoule, Capt. Redle contemplated the meaning of the sudden loss of communication with S/Sgt. Oliver. He feared the worst. The battalion's AM radio connection with L Company had also been silent from the moment Capt. Coles reported meeting heavy resistance. Unable to sit through another hour of radio silence, Redle decided to leave his CP and investigate for himself. He tossed on his oversized helmet and slung his Tommy gun over his shoulder. Earlier in the war, Redle removed the gun's stock to create a makeshift machine pistol. Born and raised a Wyoming westerner, Redle could claim a strong shot on rifle but knew he was weak on pistol. A rifle or carbine, however, was too cumbersome in close combat situations. If Redle was going to stumble into a sudden unpleasant encounter with the enemy, he wanted the quick compact burst of a fully automatic pistol to help him get out alive. The U.S. Army didn't have such a weapon, so Redle made one. Luck alone hadn't gotten him this far in the war.

Redle informed Nusz of his plans and climbed aboard his jeep with driver, Pfc. Gene Palumbo.[18] Once the two men began motoring down the long narrow stretch of road leading to Allan, Redle began to have misgivings about the noisy way he was approaching a combat zone. As they passed blindly through the stretch of road lined with evergreens, Redle was convinced his method was foolhardy. He ordered Palumbo to stop the jeep, drop him off, and return to the CP. The young private was more than happy to oblige.

Redle continued forward on cautious feet as the laboring whine of the jeep engine faded in the distance. He passed through the "Y" in the road and continued walking a another 800 yards. Above the distant trees, Redle made out the church tower at Allan. More important, he could now hear the muffled sounds of combat.

Something only a few hundred yards away in the foreground caught his eye. Amongst the trees were soldiers milling about an indistinct shape that looked like a tank. "Why had L Company fallen back so far from town?" wondered Redle. When the late afternoon sun gleamed off the backpacks of the distant soldiers, he realized his mistake. The reflections were from aluminum mess kits issued by the German Army. Fearing discovery, Redle leaped off the road for the cover of a nearby ditch. Just seconds later, the shadowy tank's gun barrel flashed and an ear-splitting explosion shook the road precisely where he had been standing. The concussion blew Redle deeper into the brush and sent his helmet spinning away. In spite of the violent tumble, Redle scrambled from the area with only minor scratches. His helmet had protected him through other close calls at Cassino and during the march on Rome and he hated to leave it behind, but some things weren't worth risking one's life over. Neither was a continued walk toward Allan. Redle decided to head back for Roucoule by avoiding the road altogether. The journey was slow and circuitous through field, brush, and woods. He left his CP expecting a surprise and he got one—just not the sort his stockless Tommy gun could handle. As he walked it struck him that some trivial detail he picked up in the past about German field gear saved his life. Though he had plenty of time alone with his thoughts, the captain didn't dwell long on his latest near-miss. His concerns were that Oliver and crew had met the same fate as Danby.[19]

* * *

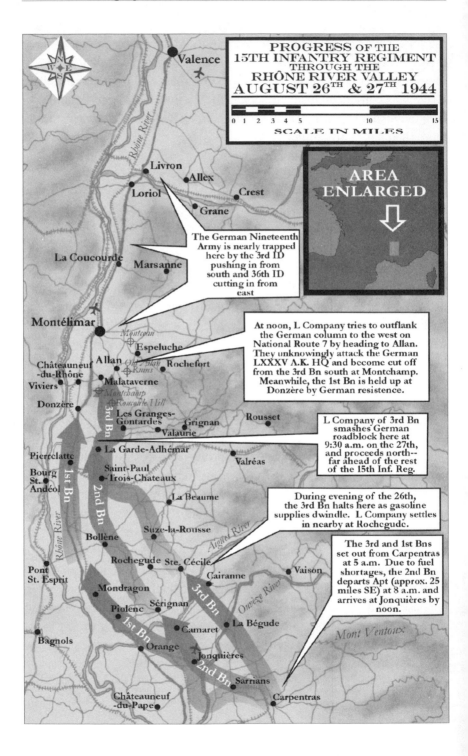

PROGRESS OF THE
15TH INFANTRY REGIMENT
THROUGH THE
RHÔNE RIVER VALLEY
AUGUST 26TH & 27TH 1944

0 1 2 3 4 5   10   15
SCALE IN MILES

AREA
ENLARGED

The German Nineteenth
Army is nearly trapped
here by the 3rd ID
pushing in from
south and 36th ID
cutting in from
east

At noon, L Company tries to outflank
the German column to the west on
National Route 7 by heading to Allan.
They unknowingly attack the German
LXXXV A.K. HQ and become cut off
from the 3rd Bn south at Montchamp.
Meanwhile, the 1st Bn is held up at
Donzère by German resistence.

L Company of 3rd Bn
smashes German
roadblock here at
9:30 a.m. on the 27th,
and proceeds north--
far ahead of the rest
of the 15th Inf. Reg.

During evening of the 26th,
the 3rd Bn halts here as gasoline
supplies dwindle. L Company settles
in nearby at Rochegude.

The 3rd and 1st Bns
set out from Carpentras
at 5 a.m. Due to fuel
shortages, the 2nd Bn
departs Apt (approx. 25
miles SE) at 8 a.m. and
arrives at Jonquières by
noon.

Late that afternoon, 1st Lt. George Burks and L Company's headquarters section sputtered into 3rd Battalion CP aboard their old German truck. After the early morning mechanical breakdown, Burks' guys were finally able to get the temperamental engine turning again, only to crawl and pick their way through miles of frustratingly slow traffic comprised of 3rd Division reserve and support vehicles and personnel. The large brown garden snails that appeared with every sunset throughout the area, would have made better time.

Starved for information, Burks jumped down from the truck to locate the communication section amid the bustling camp. Lt. Col. Boye promptly informed him that L Company was fighting in Allan, but physically cut off from the battalion and out of radio contact. Boye asked Burks if he had an extra SCR-300 radio, but the lieutenant did not. It was then that he thought of Coles' prophetic Anzio advice about always keeping a spare handy. The events of the intervening months blurred with so many distractions, demands, and preparations that Burks had forgotten to follow through. Spare radios weren't easy to find, and yet almost anything could be obtained under the table, especially through 1st Sgt. Works' informal supply connections. Burks mentally kicked himself for the oversight.

In his next breath, Boye asked Burks to go up the road, find out what was happening with L Company, and report back to him. Burks was eager to go, but asked his twenty-eight year old battalion commander for some practical means to get to and from Allan in one piece. For a variety of reasons, their undependable German truck was a poor choice, and walking the route was out of the question. Boye suggested Burks take one of the battalion jeeps mounted with an M2 .50-calibur machine gun. It was exactly what Burks was hoping for; something small with speed and heavy firepower.

Burks and the jeep driver climbed aboard the quarter-ton truck and headed out of camp. They crested the hill saddle, passed through K Company positions, and coasted down the long narrow road toward the "Y" crossing. Hot air swirled past Burks' helmet and the sleeves of his ODs flapped an unremitting rhythm as the driver skillfully balanced speed with control of the vehicle. Jeeps were notoriously bouncy no matter who was driving, and Burks did his best to keep his butt to the seat while watching for hidden dangers.

The driver braked slightly and downshifted gears to snake efficiently through the road "Y" before the final two-mile sprint to the village. As they passed a gentle "S" in the road beyond the intersection, Burks sensed they had entered "no man's land." A few shots cracked out of the thick trees and brush, but Burks couldn't see the shooters. As the jeep engine strained to regain RPMs lost in maneuvering, more mocking shots, heavier in intensity, rang out from unseen assailants. Moments later, mortar rounds began to explode along the route they were traversing. The driver tossed aside all caution, flooring the gas pedal while dodging through the mortar bursts until the small woodland gave way to open fields. Once beyond the roadside foliage, the attacks abruptly ended. Burks breathed a heavy sigh of relief. The Germans had limited their roadblock to a fire zone instead of physically blocking the road. Even so, he wondered how much longer the route would remain passable. If they reached Allan and found L Company still intact, Burks knew he had little time to gather basic details and race back to Boye—if the way back remained open.

The jeep swung past the mangled German motorcycle and the Rozel farm, closing fast on the village. Ahead, Burks could see the church tower rising above the trees and soldiers in prone defensive positions along the roadside ditches near the south bridge. Burks motioned for the driver to slow down and cut back on the engine noise. The jeep eased to a stop near the rearmost soldiers and Burks slipped out as quickly as possible. Before leaving, he told the driver to keep the engine idling, and then ducked down among his men to find out what was happening and where he could find Capt. Coles.

The first men he queried could only tell him that the company was taking heavy fire north of town. After Burks jumped from position to position and asked the same question, he determined Coles was in town and that a big German tank was holding everything up. The men were frustrated over their inability to move anti-tank fire forward and the lack of artillery support. They needed help from the battalion.

Before dashing back to the idling jeep, Burks told the men to pass word on to Coles of his visit, and that he was returning to Boye with a request for immediate assistance. To avoid alerting nearby Germans with unnecessary engine noise, he enlisted several big GIs to help rotate the small jeep around. After a few pushes and pulls in neutral, the jeep was realigned south and Burks hopped on back behind the .50-caliber machine gun. He did a quick check of the ammo box and ribbon and pulled back the bolt to seat the first round. The M2 was a powerful gun intended primarily as a defense against strafing airplanes. However, its .50-caliber spray was equally effective at chewing up anything from ground troops to light armor. Whatever dangers lie ahead, just being behind the long black barrel and receiver brought Burks some degree of confidence.

Under the circumstances, a stealthy return was impractical, so the driver gunned the gas. As the jeep lurched forward and gathered momentum, he tore through the gears and they blew past the Rozel farm at top speed. As they approached the wooded curves, they encountered the same small arms and mortar resistance, though with much more intensity. Just like the first time around, Burks couldn't see a single enemy soldier. Nevertheless, he swiveled the M2 and began firing short bursts into places he suspected the Germans were hiding, hoping his counter fire would silence the fire or kill a few enemy troops. The crouching driver plowed though the shell bursts and snapping bullets while Burks stood and fired using his legs as shock absorbers over every jolt and buffet. After the jeep snaked past the "Y" intersection, the tormenting fire finally stopped. Burks loosened up his cramping hands and fell back against the rear railing. While the jeep labored up the long hill, he drew a deep breath. It felt safe—almost miraculous—just to breathe again.

When they pulled into the CP, Burks leaped from the back of the jeep and ran over to Boye. In what can only have been a breathless report, Burks told him everything he learned of L Company's predicament.

"Yeah," Boye nodded with a matter-of-fact expression. "We just heard from Lieutenant Cotter of Cannon Company. He's off in the fields to the right of town and knows that you guys are blocked, so he's trying to get fire for them."

Burks felt a wave of immediate relief at the news. Some form of communications was reestablished with the company, and help was sure to follow. It was only then that the irony of situation hit him. While he nearly lost his butt trying to obtain information, Cotter independently called in with the same details over one of the M8 radios!

The irony struck Boye, too. "Oh," added the battalion commander. "Great job, great job!" Boye cast his eyes over the jeep parked beyond Burks. "You guys are pretty lucky, aren't you?" he smiled dryly.

Burks wasn't sure what he meant. "What do you mean, 'lucky?'"

Boye lifted a hand and pointed toward the jeep. Burks followed his gaze. "Did you see the jeep?" Boye asked.

Burks' mouth dropped open. The jeep was riddled with shrapnel holes from front to back. The chaos of running the German roadblock twice and the surge of adrenaline both times left Burks and the driver too distracted to notice how effective the enemy fire had actually been. Why neither man's body mirrored the sorry condition of the jeep was a mystery neither could explain. It was also a minor miracle.

Burks knew he could not return to Allan. The jeep's mangled frame was a sobering testament of that fact. The conscientious lieutenant felt tremendous guilt for not fighting with his company.[20] To pass the time, he paced camp and tried to stay out of the way of those hurrying about their business. The battalion radio remained maddeningly silent. Knowing Coles' aggressive approach and how utterly unconcerned the big sunburned man was for his own safety brought little comfort to Burks. For all he knew, his captain was dead and L Company was in need of a new leader. The two men had an unspoken understanding that such a moment could arrive at any time. Every executive officer of an infantry company at war had to be prepared to carry on after the loss of the captain.

That moment could have already come and gone for Burks, and yet he was absolutely powerless to do anything for his men because he was not with them.

As long as Lt. Cotter's radios maintained their silence, Burks had no way of knowing if his concerns were born of worry or intuition.

Chapter 14
The Gauntlet

At 5:30 P.M., Lt. Col. Boye dispatched a brief report to the regiment reporting on L Company's precarious situation. The message reflected Boye's straightforward and succinct style: "L Company is in Allan, 947473. Company is disorganized. Lost contact with two platoons. Request reserve platoon of tanks and TDs."[1]

Based on what his battalion observers and scouts were seeing, and what Burks experienced, Boye grew increasingly concerned about the Germans spilling in behind L Company. The battalion's intermittent mortar attacks were not dispersing them. Coles and his men were in real danger of being completely cut off and annihilated. Boye ordered the K Company riflemen and M Company with its heavy machine guns and 81mm mortars to push forward toward the road "Y" and concentrate fire on the Germans moving eastward from Malataverne.[2] He also called forward an I Company bazooka team with the hope it might penetrate into Allan once the way was clear.[3]

Around the same time, Capt. Redle arrived upon the road between Montchamp and Roucoule after his slow and winding trek through the countryside. Before returning to his own CP, Redle decided to visit 3rd Battalion and learn if any further information had come in from Allan. He located Boye and was surprised to learn that, aside from Cotter's M8s to the rear of town, the company remained incommunicado and isolated. The lieutenant colonel knew very little about the situation in or north of town—including the fate of Oliver and his crew. This was not the good news Redle was hoping to hear. After filling Boye in about his tank encounter, Redle decided to remain with the battalion command staff and listen for updates.

Back at Allan, meanwhile, the Panther tank no longer posed an imminent threat to the village. Like a restless and distracted predator, the mighty panzer backed farther into the northwestern fields of town where its crew could better observe the territory south of the village. Even with this repositioning, the furious gun battle raging along the north creek did not lessen in intensity. The Germans had established a small network of machine gun positions that pinned down the men of L Company in the fields, and kept American reinforcements frozen in the village. Two of Coles' men, however, decided independently to take drastic personal measures to break the impasse.

Cpl. Dominick Delmonico, a strong and husky twenty-nine year old from Cincinnati and an assistant squad leader in 3rd Platoon, crawled out alone from the safety of a nearby house toward chattering German machine gun positions 100 yards away.[4] Delmonico had a reputation as a talkative guy, but on this afternoon he was all action. An avid amateur basketball player before volunteering, Delmonico brazenly decided to rely on some of his court footwork for survival.[5] With bullets whizzing overhead, he maneuvered to within twenty-five yards of the nearest machine gun and tossed two grenades in quick succession. Both landed and exploded directly in the nest, killing the two-man crew instantly and seriously wounding two supporting riflemen.

The audacious attack drew unwelcome attention in Delmonico's direction, especially from a second machine gun nest 100 yards to his left. A heavy shower of automatic and rifle fire kicked up the soil around his prone body. Rather than lie and wait for the bullets to eventually find him, Delmonico scampered for cover along the banks of the dry creek. Once there, he discovered to his dismay that he was still exposed to enemy fire. The unrelenting rain of bullets continued snapping past his face and peppering the ground around him. When he realized that waiting for his squad mates to catch up with him and silence his tormentors was a poor choice, he took matters into his own hands a second time. Using the north bank of the dry creek as cover, Delmonico crouched and crept toward the second machine gun nest. At times along his perilous journey he was fully exposed and forced to scramble ahead of the German bullets trailing his every move. By sheer luck or the grace of God, he made it within thirty yards of the nest. Though better protected, he had nowhere to go but forward.

Delmonico was just beyond the range of an accurate grenade toss, but he figured he could still use one as a distraction. He pulled the pin and hurled the bomb toward the second nest. After waiting a couple seconds, he leapt to his feet and charged the position with his raised M-1. Locking his gaze on the nest, he spotted the distracted machine gunner in his sights and shot him dead just as the grenade exploded. Three other Germans at the position, stunned by the grenade blast and Delmonico's looming figure, raised their hands in surrender. Shortly afterward, Delmonico's squad and other L Company men moved in to secure the territory the native Ohioan had single-handedly cleared.[6]

Another 3rd Platoon man, Pfc. Donald Sigrist, a nineteen-year old kid from Altoona Pennsylvania,[7] also decided to take matters into his own hands. A German machine gun nest positioned no more than seventy-five yards away, not only kept he and his squad mates pinned down with frustrating efficiency, but maintained a clear field of fire across most of the north side of Allan that prevented the arrival of reinforcements. The enemy gunners knew it, too, and flaunted their superior position with zeal.

The chaos of battle often makes the coordination of effort impossible. Men drilled ceaselessly to act as a team, think like a team, and automatically follow the commands of a team leader, often abruptly reduce to mere individuals once the shooting begins in earnest. A man hugs the ground, lifts his rifle from time to time, and attempts to return fire on an enemy he usually cannot see. His action adds little more than a whisper into an already hellish cacophony—a din that he ceaselessly prays will just go away. He sees a squad mate a dozen yards away in the same situation—embracing the ground and struggling with shaking hands to pop a fresh ammo clip into his rifle. He wonders if his own eyes carry that kid's same petrified and bewildered stare. Often he doesn't even know his battlefield companion's name, only that he's a replacement from West Virginia. He no longer tries to learn names for fear of losing another friend. He listens for, but never hears the voice of his sergeant. He wonder's if his sergeant is even alive. This is often the isolated and terrifying world of a combat rifleman.

During such times, an individual has nothing to draw upon but his training and an inner strength that lies dormant in every man, but untested in most. He must squarely confront those fears that have been his constant companions. Usually he tries to alleviate the fear by telling jokes, horsing around, or drinking alcohol.

Captain Coles had long since realized that the true enemy in battle lurked in one's own mind. A dark, elusive demon peddles incessant anxieties and doubts about pain, maiming, death, and failure—anything to ensnare and paralyze an imagination and lead a man to ultimate ruin. To some, Coles' mastery of battlefield fear seemed superhuman, other-worldly, and frustratingly unattainable. To others who saw him daily for the flawed and mortal man he was, they grasped his simple secret of success. It was the sliver of light in a pitch-black maelstrom. In order to have a chance of surviving the day, winning the war, and making it home alive, a man had to surrender everything for the chance to win it back again.

Pfc. Sigrist suddenly saw that light. He no longer feared a bullet ripping through his head or his chest. He no longer thought of his parents or his three sisters at home.[8] He had no future or past. His whole focus became the eternal present dominated by a single reality; an intolerable machine gun nest seventy-five yards away had to be eliminated, and the nine-pound rifle in his hands was the instrument of deliverance. Sigrist stood up in clear view of everyone and locked his M-1 on the two men manning the gun and feeding the ammo ribbon. He emptied an eight-round clip into the two before they had any chance to react, then popped in another clip and emptied that for good measure. Courage was all that was needed to silence the gun, and Sigrist's bravery left the seemingly invincible two-man crew sprawled out dead next to their machine gun. Before Sigrist could slip in a third clip, two remaining German riflemen supporting the position scrambled away into the brush.[9] Either man could have easily shot Sigrist as he stood to fire, but their fears got the better of them. They were still overly worried about what he was not.

That afternoon at Allan, L Company bent and twisted under pressure, but did not break. The company's first real battle since the bloody Anzio breakout escalated into another surprising test of survival. Despite a swarming counterattack, a stubborn string of machine gun nests, and a marauding panzer with a veteran crew, the men of L Company not only held their line but also fought back with grit and spirit; a summer filled with endless training, the stability the veterans as mentors provided for the replacements, the "follow me" example and bare-knuckled discipline of Captain Coles—all were factors that helped avert disaster. Above all, individuals like Sigrist, Delmonico, Leithner, and others overcame their personal fears and risked their lives to regain the initiative. Their unselfish actions saved the company and helped break the German stranglehold north of Allan. The fight for Allan, however, was not yet at an end.

By this time, the Panther tank had withdrawn deeper into the northwestern fields to better focus its efforts on disrupting the arrival of reinforcements at L Company's rear. Its long gun hurled round after round of high explosives into the distant sides of Montchamp and Roucoule and others thundering along the ribbon of road leading down from those two hills. The effort was too scattershot and remote to have any practical effect, but was an ominous development nonetheless. K Company held positions in those areas, and was in the process of moving forward. By all appearances, the Germans to the north and south of Allan were trying to coordinate operations.

K Company's leading edge was chafing against pockets of German resistance in the fields southeast of Malataverne. Some were well equipped and organized. One group included some thirty soldiers and a Mark IV tank, a piece of armor equivalent in size to a Sherman but with a lower profile. The tank may have been the same one Redle encountered earlier, and the soldiers were among those who had nearly destroyed Burks' passing jeep.

Hoping perhaps to make amends for those earlier near misses, the Mark IV and supporting infantry advanced brazenly against K Company. Pfc. Sedric Porter stepped out from the pale twilight shadows and fired his M-1 into the approaching force. For the next ten minutes, Porter expended four clips of ammunition while stubbornly defending his company—despite the deadly distraction of machine gun fire raking the ground around him. When the enemy attacked failed, the German soldiers broke rank and scattered, leaving behind four wounded men. Unsupported, the Mark IV also withdrew. The brisk engagement cost K Company one man wounded.[10]

With 8:30 P.M. approaching and daylight dwindling, the odds of either side launching a successful offensive operation diminished. The American focus shifted to settling in and shoring up defenses. For the Germans, the coming night offered the chance to retreat in relative peace—free from artillery observation or the harassment of Allied planes.

Back in Allan, the Panther and its supporting infantry withdrew north and northwest beyond the cemetery. They had accomplished all they could for the day. From their perspective, the rearguard action at Allan allowed the armeekorps staff to safely withdraw fifteen miles north to Les Petit Robins near Livron.[11] The fighting stopped the advance of L Company at Allan—and indeed the entire right flank of the 15th Infantry Regiment—and gained precious time for more troops, trucks, and weapons to withdraw and fight another day.

At the southern base of Montceau hill approximately one mile north of Allan, some of the Germans jumped onto trucks containing American prisoners. Others had to walk. What equipment the Germans couldn't take they either destroyed or set aflame, including several pieces of armor. Fortunately, these fires did not spread into the dry brush and fields nearby.[12] However, not everyone fled the area. The Panther and her crew, together with a strong contingent of foot soldiers remained behind as the last of the rearguard.

Captain Coles used the last minutes of daylight to solidify his company's positions in and around town, establishing roadblocks and dispatching patrols to neighboring farms. Despite the uneasy combat lull, everyone operated with extreme vigilance because they knew the village was still surrounded by Germans.

The price for taking Allan was high. A Sherman tank was destroyed, along with three of her crew. Among them was 1st. Lt. Danby, killed in his first battle, and Cpl. Steve Vargo, who had fought in every action waged by 756th Tank Battalion. Captain Redle did not yet know it, but S/Sgt. Oliver's tank had also been incapacitated, with Oliver and three of his crew wounded. Although none of the injuries were life-threatening, all four required varying degrees of hospitalization and were sidelined from duty for up to three weeks.

In addition to losing about one-fifth (20%) of its effective fighting strength in the Allan combat, L Company lost a jeep and trailer, both battalion radios, and the codes to the radio that Coles abandoned with the jeep were captured.[13] Coles descended on Allan with about 130 men early that afternoon.[14] After several hours of battle, five men were killed, thirteen captured, and seven seriously wounded and awaiting evacuation, a total of twenty-five.[15] A few others, Coles included, received light wounds but remained on duty.

The fighting cost the company dearly in terms of experience and leadership. One platoon leader, 2nd Lt. Mackowsky, was captured. Two platoon sergeants were lost; T/Sgt. Wallace Lawrence was captured, and T/Sgt. Donald Bowman was killed when a shell fragment split open his left side. Bowman was married and twenty-seven years old. He signed on for Army service in August 1940, long before the national mobilization began. When Japan attacked, Bowman had "Remember Pearl Harbor" tattooed on his right forearm.[16] Other NCOs lost that afternoon included S/Sgt. James Pierce and Sgt. Melvin Singer, both wounded, Sgt. Roy Sanders, captured, and Cpl. William Leaman, dead. Two of the other three killed, Pfc. Louis Polonsky and Pfc. James Lovascio, were veterans of Anzio. The remaining dead soldier, Pfc. Norval Monroe, arrived after Anzio as a replacement.[17]

One of the wounded, Pfc. James Doolin, was fighting for life after a bullet pierced his right chest.[18] His wound required far more medical expertise than "Doc" Lefevre or any field medic could provide. Coles saw the pale twenty-year old sprawled out and barely moving, his breathing belabored and heavy, as if each deep breath would be his last. Coles decided to risk running Doolin back to the battalion surgeon at Montchamp. With the company unified, a defensive perimeter established, and most of the fighting abated, Coles was confident his men could handle his absence. What he needed most was a jeep. Though he no longer had one, he knew of someone who did.

Coles and a few others lifted the wounded soldier and carried him southeast of town, where the captain found Lt. Cotter near his repositioned M8s. Coles pointed out the wounded GI. Although the medic had dressed the chest wound, it was obvious that unless the soldier received proper medical attention, he was not going to make it.

Starved for information, Cotter asked Coles to fill him in on the situation north of town. Coles briefly explained the counterattack, the Panther, and that his company had taken significant casualties. "I need to get back to the battalion CP to replace the jeep and radio we lost this afternoon," he explained. "And maybe we can save this guy's life if we get him back."[19] He continued by asking if he could borrow Cotter's jeep.

"Sure," Cotter replied, "but I'm going with you." Coles had no problem with the condition.

Cotter wasn't seeking death-defying thrills by accompanying Coles. He had served in the Army long enough to know that "borrowed" jeeps had a way of disappearing, and they were extremely difficult to replace unless "borrowed" from someone else. Although Cotter had no reason to be suspicious of Coles, he had no idea who else in the battalion might take a sudden liking to his four-wheeled buddy. A jeep was a man's horse in the modern U.S. Army. Wherever there were horses, there were horse thieves.

The two officers gently placed the wounded man across the front hood of Cotter's jeep. To make the most out of the trip, one of the German prisoners was ordered to climb in for the ride to battalion S-2 for interrogation. Because of the earlier actions involving the German cars, Cotter suspected trouble during the journey back. He had an idea that didn't quite square with the Geneva Convention, but might save their lives. He suggested they sit the German prisoner atop the radiator at the front of the jeep with an empty rifle. If they encountered more Germans along the way, they might fool them into believing it was their own men passing by on a captured American jeep. The illusion was far from perfect, but any hesitation it would create might be enough to keep them alive and get them down the road. Coles agreed, and the prisoner was placed atop the radiator grill with an unloaded rifle.

The big captain climbed in back, and Cotter settled into the side seat next to his driver, Pfc. Gerald Pier. They rolled a short distance to T/Sgt. Polich's M8. Cotter explained where they were going, and told Polich to watch over the platoon during his absence. The news relieved the technical sergeant. The entire southern flank of town was still thinly protected, and someone was finally going for reinforcements. Still, he wasn't expecting much sleep that night.

Pier eased the jeep and its unusual cargo forward while Cotter struggled to get a firm hold on the wounded man draped across the hood. Once he found a secure grip, Pier punched up the speed down the road toward Montchamp. Cotter split his attention between holding down the wounded GI, watching the German prisoner on the hood, and sweeping the countryside for hidden dangers. He was also prepared to grab the wheel if Pier was shot, and kept shifting his knees in order to keep his rifle balanced across his lap and ready for use.

The jeep rolled for several hundred yards through the grey dusk, passing trees and fields without incident. Suddenly, Cotter, Coles, and

Pier spotted several shadowy figures moving ahead along the edge of a small roadside forest. As the jeep approached, the figures turned, raised their rifles in their direction, and fired several shots. Coles hollered for Pier to stop while Cotter grabbed his rifle. Both officers vaulted out of the jeep with Coles leading the two-man charge, shouting wildly and firing off his M-1 in the direction of the mysterious assailants. Cotter did his best to follow alongside—yelling and firing as well. For a guy wounded in the backside, the big captain moved fast. Before the figures melted into the woods, Cotter got a clear glimpse of their clothing and hollered for Coles to stop shooting. They were French. The plan to sit a uniformed prisoner on the hood had backfired when the local partisans mistook them for Germans.

Cotter signaled for Pier to pull the jeep forward so the two officers could hop back aboard. When the jeep lurched to a halt, the German prisoner was quickly moved next to Coles in the back seat. Cotter took the prisoner's empty rifle and wedged it alongside his hip on the outside edge of the seat before settling in and resuming his hold of the wounded man. The jeep heaved forward with a groan and they were underway again.

A short distance beyond the woods, more shots splintered the air, joined quickly by an angry chorus of various weapons. Bullets bounded and whistled past their heads as they sped past the point of eruption. Whether these new attackers were French or German was impossible to know because it was too dark to see clearly, and they weren't about to stop and find out.

Cotter held fast to the wounded man, keeping his head down as they barreled through the gauntlet. The rough ride couldn't be doing the poor fellow any good. Pier hunched over the wheel, holding the accelerator to the floor while he whipped them through the S curve. When figures walking along the road suddenly appeared, Pier continued at speed, forcing them to jump off the road to avoid being hit. They were unmistakably German, and some of them opened fire. Once past the turns, the shooting abruptly stopped and the jeep was in the clear.

As they began the long slow ascent toward the battalion CP, Cotter began to notice some pressure on his right hip. He reached down to alleviate the discomfort, but felt something wet between him and the empty rifle along the seat. Cotter brought his hand up in the dim light and saw blood on his finger. One of the bullets had struck him in the right buttock, and he did not even realize it. He checked the unloaded rifle and found a bullet hole clear through the receiver. Had the rifle not been there, the bullet would have surely passed through both of his hips and possibly into Pier.[20] The placement of the gun probably saved his life. Thankfully, the wound did not hurt or bleed all that much.

The jeep was approaching the battalion CP just as Captain Redle crossed the road heading toward Roucoule hill. After waiting in vain for several hours for news from Allan, he decided to return to his own CP to check 1st Platoon's progress in Donzère. The unmistakable whine of the approaching jeep stopped Redle in his tracks. When he recognized Coles sitting in the back, he flagged down the driver.

"Where's the battalion CP?" asked Coles.

Redle pointed toward a patch of woods. "About fifty yards that way."

Coles staggered down from the back with his apprehensive prisoner while Cotter eased out of his seat holding his hip. Although both were wounded, and looked like hell, they lifted Doolin off the jeep hood and walked toward the CP.

"Do you have any news about Oliver and his crew?" asked Redle.

To his relief, Coles replied that they had received minor wounds but were otherwise fine.[21] "The tank's radio antenna was shot off during the first half hour of the counterattack," he added, which explained why Redle had lost communications with the tankers.

Once at the CP, Coles reported to a grateful Lt. Col. Boye, who was deep in discussion with 2nd Battalion's Lt. Col. Thomas Davis.[22] Davis's men were assembled near Chartroussas, five miles to the rear of 3rd Battalion CP, and the two commanders were coordinating plans for the next morning.[23] Coles reported that Allan was secure, but that he had one tank and four tank destroyers still in town in dire need of fuel and all forms of ammunition.[24] The Germans, he continued, were withdrawing north and abandoning equipment. Others, however, were filtering through the area—especially along the road between the battalion CP and town. Coles also let them know the road back to Allan was dangerous, as evidenced by the two Germans they nearly ran over during the wild jeep ride to the CP.[25]

"What are your plans, Captain?" inquired Davis.

Coles answered without missing a beat, "I need a radio, and I'm going back."[26]

While Coles talked with Boye, Davis, and Redle, Cotter walked over to the battalion aid station, where he watched Doolin disappear inside a surgical tent. A doctor appeared and told Cotter to lie down so he could examine his wound. With a sterile finger, he probed the gash at the side of his buttock and announced with some surprise that he could feel the bullet. Using pair of forceps, he extracted the slug with minimal effort. With a hint of dramatic flair, he told Cotter to hold out his hand, and dropped the misshapen bullet into the lieutenant's dirty palm.

"Well, that's an easy Purple Heart for you, isn't it son?" the doctor declared wryly.

The doctor irrigated, stitched, and bandaged Cotter's wound, and within a few minutes the tall slender officer was walking out of the aid station to look for both his jeep and Captain Coles.[27]

He found the captain with Boye and the other officers discussing the feasibility of a return trip to Allan. Boye was skeptical that reinforcements could be pulled together within the next few hours. 3rd Battalion was having a hectic evening. During the afternoon, it provided mortar and artillery cover during 1st Battalion's push on Donzère. It also harassed some 1,000 Germans overflowing the fields beyond Malataverne. The attention came with a price: German ire. As recently as 9:00 P.M., the enemy pounded the stone chapel atop Montchamp with artillery fire. If Boye's observers were stationed anywhere, that was the best place for them to be.[28] Though that particular attack was over, the situation in the immediate area remained precarious. The news did not trouble Coles, who insisted on returning immediately.

A spare radio, Boye explained, would be difficult to locate. If he had had one, he continued, he would have given it to Burks earlier in the day. All functioning battalion jeeps and other vehicles were in use or needed elsewhere. Cotter's damaged jeep had developed a loud muffler. The Germans would hear it coming a mile away, so using it to get back to Allan was out of the question. Boye's spare jeep, shot up during Burks' journey, was inoperable. The earliest he could get Coles a free jeep, he admitted, was about two hours.[29] Coles was not one to take "no" for an answer. Although he was out of ideas, he was bound and determined to return to his company—one way or another.

Redle listened intently as the infantry officers discussed the situation. When they reached the impasse he spoke up, suggesting that if Coles was going to return to town, he should take a vehicle more substantial than a jeep. The Germans would be expecting another jeep and were long overdue for blowing one off the road. Coles needed more protection. Redle's company maintenance tank was sitting idle with a crew at Redle's CP across the road. It was a fully armed Sherman equipped with extra tools and spare parts. Redle suggested that Coles could displace the bow gunner for the journey and use the tank's two-way FM radio for communication once he got into town. Redle's CP could then relay his messages over to the battalion via an AM frequency.

Everything about the plan was solid except that the maintenance tank was more than a little noisy. It was an old M4A1 with a Continental radial engine, meaning it sounded like an airplane. The recent supply squeeze left 756th Tank Battalion without the fifty-weight oil the Continental engine required. Instead, its crew burned lighter thirty-weight oil, which belched a steady plume of blue smoke out of the tank's exhaust system.[30] The smoke wasn't so much of a factor in darkness, but the noise sure was. The Germans would hear the Sherman approaching from a long way off and have plenty of time to prepare for its arrival. On the other hand, one could not shoot what could not be seen. As long as the tank steamrolled forward with the headlamps off, the Germans probably couldn't do much to stop it.

Everyone thought the plan was worth the risk. Despite his earlier jeep concerns, Cotter also wanted to return to his platoon and volunteered to ride on the back deck. Boye ordered a handful of I Company men to ride along as a support contingent. Cotter welcomed the armed guard on the back with him.

At 11:30 P.M., the officers and the small group of riflemen crossed the dark road to Redle's CP and gathered around the maintenance tank. The engine was cranked slowly to avoid blowing a cylinder. Once started, the driver revved the RPMs above a brisk 1600 to avoid a stall while the engine warmed. Amid the noise and thick acrid smoke hanging heavily in the night air, a crewman secured the front headlamps into their fender sockets. The driver briefly flashed them on and off to make certain they worked.

Coles pulled himself up onto the front deck, which was still warm after absorbing a long day of hot sunshine. Still sore, he slipped his big body into the bow gunner's hatch. At first, his broad shoulders presented a challenge, but by allowing one side to dip and the other to follow, he squeezed past the narrow oval opening. Cotter and the riflemen from I

Company, climbed atop the back engine compartment and huddled behind the turret for protection.

After a few last minute preparations, the tank commander signaled from his turret hatch that they were ready to go. Over the roaring idle noise, the young sergeant shouted into his intercom microphone for his driver to roll. The tank heaved forward, popping stones and fallen branches along the path leading toward the road. After a few dozen yards, the treads clawed the asphalt. The driver pivoted onto the roadway and shifted gears to maintain optimal engine speed.[31] The old tank growled into the night, rolling past the faint outlines of trees and telegraph poles and gathering steady speed down the gentle slope toward Allan. Cotter and the topside doughs held on tightly as the driver swerved into the "Y" crossing at top speed. He barreled through the "S" curve without braking, but could no longer see well enough to judge the road edges. The driver threw on the headlamps, illuminating grey uniformed figures scrambling across the road just a handful of yards ahead of the tank. Coles fired several short bursts from the .30-caliber bow gun to help them along and clear out any other Germans lurking beyond the edge of the light.

Just as it looked as if the danger had passed, the unmistakable features of a medium German tank appeared dead ahead straddling the road and shoulder. The M4A1 driver swerved but could not avoid grazing the panzer. The sides of the two enemy machines met for a brief instant in a violent shriek of grinding metal and a bursting spray of yellow sparks. Beyond the spectacle, more grey uniforms dove for the safety of the roadside. Some managed to mount a parting protest with rifle and submachine gun fire, but the old Sherman was already receding into the distant night. With the roadblock smashed and the American tank triumphantly rumbling toward Allan, the Germans decided against waiting around for any more surprises. They started their tank and withdrew westward immediately.[32]

Coles' had been gone from Allan for about two hours. During that time, his troops suffered under a long harassing mortar attack that frayed nerves and increased tension. The anxiety began almost immediately after Polich and the men at the rear flank watched Cotter's jeep set out for the battalion CP and disappear beyond a line of trees. Seconds later, they heard the rifle shots and feared for the worst.[33] As darkness enveloped the town, the Germans to the north peppered the fields between the village and the hillside ruins with mortar shells. A high velocity gun just beyond the road curve to the north, joined in, firing directly over the heads of L Company men posted at a farmhouse in the northeastern fields.[34] For a full hour, the Americans rode out the assault, never sure where the next blast would fall. Fortunately, the spotting was off and most of the rounds exploded harmlessly in the fields east of town. No one was hurt during the attack, and the only structural casualty was an isolated farmhouse vacated that morning by a family seeking the safety of the wooded uplands.[35]

The Americans had just begun to find some comfort in the relative calm when the muffled sound of an approaching engine was heard cutting through the heavy night air. The sound droned like a distant slow moving airplane. As it rumbled closer, everyone could hear the unmistakable clanking of treads. Polich and the nearby GIs wondered whether a night attack was underway. Was a German tank about to roll into their ranks?[36] BAR men and riflemen clambered into position and readied their guns with a chorus of clicks. The diesel engine of the TD posted at the south bridge awakened with a loud snarl before settling into a grumbling purr. Inside, the turret crew huddled around the main gun, already armed and aimed squarely down the darkened road. Everyone was tense, waiting for the tank to emerge from the darkness.

Suddenly, headlights flickered and flared from beyond a brush line in the distance before blinding the Americans with a brilliant light. A prisoner taken earlier from one of the bullet-riddled cars began yelling something in German, which only increased everyone's stress levels. When the unidentified machine moved squarely in the TD's sights, the gunner hesitated, his foot hovering over the main gun trigger. All he needed to unleash death was the slightest provocation or a quick signal from his sergeant.

One of the nearby infantrymen yelled out, "Who's there?"

"Don't shoot! Don't shoot! American tank!" It was Coles and Cotter, yelling together in reply above the din of the clattering engine. Cotter jumped down and ran alongside the tank, emphatically waving his arms.[37]

The tank slowed upon approach, and all the men along the southern flank drew big sighs of relief. Once the machine halted near the creek bed, Coles popped out of the bow gunner hatch and bolted into town to check on his men. Cotter limped over to Polich, who was watching the handful of I Company riflemen sliding off the back deck.

"This is it for the reinforcements?" Polich thought to himself.[38]

Fortunately, no additional reinforcements would be needed. Aside from an occasional rifle shot ringing out from the direction of L Company outposts lining the perimeter, the balance of the evening and early morning remained remarkably quiet in and around Allan. Under the cloak of darkness, the Germans took their mortars and anti-tank guns and withdrew north and northwest. With combat waning, several FFI men came down from the eastern hill to join and congratulate the Americans in town.[39]

The remainder of 3rd Battalion settled in along the road between Montchamp and Roucoule. K Company held the fields between the road "Y" and Malataverne adjacent to the northeastern base of Montchamp, driving out any Germans still wandering over from National Route 7. I Company held the battalion rear, but not without incident. After midnight, a German AAA unit smashed through an I Company roadblock, but the lead truck was brought to a halt with a concentration of small arms fire. A flak wagon and towed anti-tank gun were captured along with several prisoners.[40] The incident was a stark reminder that well-armed Germans were everywhere, and some were quite desperate to rejoin their comrades retreating northward.

Before August 27, 1944, L Company already had a reputation within the division for discipline and resilience. The dire challenges its men faced down in Allan only added to their "Can Do" reputation in a regiment known for its "Can Do" spirit. Although Coles' men never did manage to claw into the long German column crawling along Route 7, they routed and nearly captured a German armeekorps headquarters instead. Events rarely if ever unfold in war as planned. The best commanders at every level accept this and adapt to whatever the battlefield throws at them. The inadvertent attack on Allan sent panic and confusion rippling throughout the entire rear half of the German retreat. Other units of 15th Infantry Regiment would fully exploit that disarray in the hours and days to come.

Allan was another victory of sorts. While a whirlwind of destruction raged across all of Europe, leveling entire cities and snuffing out the lives of millions of people, L Company saved one tiny French town from German defenders who were prepared to sacrifice it down to its foundations. Miraculously, not a single citizen of Allan was lost. Nine Americans perished; German losses, although indeterminate, were much higher. The fighting forced the Germans to relinquish territory long under the heavy grasp of the Waffen SS and the Gestapo. Although an American victory, no parades, celebrations, or memorial services would be held to honor L Company. Coles' men rested and reorganized the next day while others fought on ahead of them.

But that was all right with them. It was celebration enough to witness another sunrise.

Chapter 15

A Small Revenge

During the early morning hours of August 28, 2nd Battalion passed through 3rd Battalion positions at Montchamp and advanced as far as the Rozel farm, where it established a temporary bivouac along the road and among the fields.[1] To the rear at the same creek where the FTP attacked the German car a week earlier, a battery of towed 105mm howitzers unpacked and prepared what promised to be a full day of shelling.[2] While some of the enlisted men snatched one or two hours of sleep, officers reviewed orders calling for the battalion to assume the regimental left flank on the sustained drive toward Montélimar.

At 5:30 A.M., Mr. Rozel and his family played happy hosts to one of 2nd Battalion infantry companies resting around the yard outside their farmhouse. Rozel welcomed the American captain and his associates into their home, where Madame Rozel brewed coffee and fussed with concern over their comfort. One of the soldiers had terrible blisters on his feet. He took a seat at the kitchen table and removed his boots to seek relief. While Madame Rozel prepared a foot soak for the exhausted man, her youngest son Gerald climbed onto the young soldier's lap to enjoy the attention of the room and the quintessential American gifts of chewing gum and chocolate.

As the captain enjoyed his cup of coffee, he unfurled several maps across the kitchen table and studied them with care. Rozel raised his eyebrows in shock. The Americans had an astonishing arsenal of state-of-the-art rifles, tanks, and weapons of every sort, and were well supplied with food and ammunition. Yet, their young officers were using corner-store Michelin road maps to find their way across the French countryside![3]

As the new day broke an hour later, Rozel's guests packed and moved out. The French family watched the entire 2nd Battalion file past their stone farmhouse in the direction of Allan. Tanks, jeeps, and trucks accompanied the marching troops. The scene was reminiscent of the first Americans arriving the afternoon before—but on a much larger scale. The Rozels were sad to see them go, and sadder still to not know the names of any of them. They watched them leave with heavy hearts, knowing that many of those young faces, fighting to liberate their country, would die in the days and weeks ahead. On the other hand, Polich, Cotter, and all the weary men posted south of Allan were glad to see them coming. Reinforcements had finally arrived in large numbers.[4]

2nd Battalion clattered through town past Danby's smoldering tank, the small bridge, and Coles' flattened jeep. The GIs passed through L Company positions in the northern fields and assumed the flank lead. The men spread out and advanced methodically through the cemetery and small woods toward the Dessalles and Borne farms. Most of the Germans had evacuated the area during the night, but they left behind equipment of every sort and size, including tracked vehicles and tanks.[5] A small firefight erupted at a farmhouse across the road from the Borne farm, but it died down almost as quickly as it began. The small German contingent wisely chose to surrender once they realized the overwhelming odds they faced.[6]

By 8:25 A.M., G Company was on Montceau hill ("Hill 280") roughly one mile north of Allan. Distant columns of German trucks, tanks, and horse drawn carts were spotted moving northwest toward Montélimar.[7] A rush ensued to secure the rest of the hill. At 9:40 A.M., 2nd Battalion established its headquarters at the southwestern base of Montceau in a two-story house within the hamlet of Le Sastre.[8] 1st Platoon's TDs moved forward and established a firebase on the northwestern face of the hill.[9] Mortar crews from heavy weapons H Company also moved in. Within minutes, their tubes opened a deadly barrage into the slow-moving distant German column.[10] The mortar fire, described by one witness as a "turkey shoot," would continue until sundown.[11] Two or three miles to the southwest, meanwhile, 1st Battalion pushed up from Donzère along National Route 7, attacking into the long column and capturing Germans in droves.

To help fill the gap between the advancing flanks of 1st and 2nd Battalions, 3rd Battalion's I Company moved forward. Joining it were three M4 tanks from B Company's 2nd Platoon. Just after the noon hour, I Company and the tanks set out along the northwestern road from Allan toward Montélimar.[12] The march had scarcely begun when the scouts spotted several men dressed in civilian clothing approaching from the north. They were moving covertly through the fields—actions that naturally aroused suspicion. The scouts dove to the ground, which triggered a domino effect as everyone behind them followed suit. When the young men waved handkerchiefs, the scouts slowly stood and approached them with care. The civilians turned out to be young Frenchmen from the area who had been hiding from the Germans. They were returning to check on the welfare of their families and neighbors. One was Mr. Martel's nineteen-year old son Lucien.[13] The teens passed through and I Company continued its advance.

The GIs gradually worked their way toward a gentle road curve, covering several hundred yards of roadway without incident.[14] Riding inside the lead jeep,[15] Captain Warren Stuart caught a glimpse of a large gun barrel projecting from a brush line along a second road bend roughly 400 yards distant.[16] He ordered his column to halt just shy of the first curve and summoned his 3rd Platoon leader, Lt. John Tominac to the front, where the commander and gunner of the lead tank joined them.[17] Satisfied the German gun crew was not yet aware of their presence, the four Americans climbed into the attic of a nearby farmhouse, where they studied the situation and discussed a solution to the problem. Through sheer luck, Captain Stuart had pulled aside Cpl. Leonard Froneberger, perhaps the best gunner in B Company. His reputation for shooting accuracy was rivaled only by Bert Bulen of Oliver's tank crew.[18] After surveying the gun position and the surrounding terrain from the attic window, Froneberger voiced confidently that he could take on the enemy gun.

The young corporal and his tank commander returned to their M4 and chambered an AP round into the breech. The loader neatly arranged several others on the nearby floor. Froneberger rough-set the barrel for a 400-yard trajectory and steadied his hands on both the turret traverse and gun elevation wheels. He signaled to the commander that he was ready. The driver nudged the tank forward to the road curve and held up. The crew did one final readiness check before the go-ahead. Froneberger peered into his gun sight eyepiece, as the driver punched the tank around the bend and skidded to a halt, with the bow squarely facing the threat. Froneberger adeptly fine-tuned the gun traverse and elevation and pressed the floor trigger switch. The entire tank shuddered with a deafening roar as the 75mm gun recoiled, ejecting a hot smoky casing to the floor with a metallic clatter. The loader slammed another AP round into the breech.

The first AP round sliced squarely through the center of the enemy barrel, bending the front half skyward at an odd angle and rendering the gun useless. For good measure, Froneberger hit the foot switch again. The second AP round severed the barrel and sent the front half tumbling to the ground with a dead thud.[19] With the smoke still lingering in the air, I Company riflemen and BAR gunners maneuvered into position and overwhelmed the Germans, as the three M4 tanks followed behind them. To everyone's surprise, the long barrel was once attached to a well-concealed Panther tank—the same one that had killed Lt. Danby and wreaked such havoc for L Company the prior afternoon in Allan. One by one, five haggard but self-assured crewmen emerged from the hatches with their hands up.[20]

The veteran German crew could smile or glare all they wanted, but they had finally met their match.

Epilogue

At 1:00 P.M. on August 28, Capt. Redle, 1st Sgt. Nusz, and the other personnel of B Company's CP packed up and moved from Roucoule to Donzère roughly three miles to the west.[1] Since Allan was no longer as dangerous as it had been the previous evening, the maintenance tank rejoined Redle's CP. 2nd Battalion and I Company mopped up enemy stragglers along the regimental right flank. The operation involved a few short firefights and the gathering and processing of small groups of prisoners. Redle usually closely monitored their progress, especially since it involved 2nd Platoon tanks, but events of even greater significance were unfolding to the west along National Route 7.

1st Battalion, still operating as the regimental left flank, drove north out of Donzère that morning and took a bite out of the tail of the German column still trapped south of Montélimar. Tanks from S/Sgt. James Haspel's 1st Platoon and TDs from 601st Tank Destroyer's 2nd Platoon, B Company, anchored the assault. The rapidly firing gun crews knocked out vehicles left and right, forcing the Germans to abandon hundreds more along the road and flee for their lives on foot. The stunning assault destroyed, trapped, and captured everything from draft horses to 88mm AAA guns.[2] Prisoners by the hundreds raised their hands in surrender.[3] Haspel's gunners and 1st Battalion accomplished what L Company's armor column had set out to do the day before—and likely would have done had it not been delayed by the battle in Allan.

Determined to remain close enough to keep Haspel's crews properly supplied, Capt. Redle relocated his CP closer to the National Route 7. Before departing, however, Redle briefly returned to the spot where the

German tank nearly killed him the afternoon before. The captain hoped to find his helmet. Search as he might, it was no where to be found. In all likelihood, one of the German soldiers who looked for him after the encounter nabbed it as a souvenir.[4] Redle let go of his disappointment when he climbed back into his jeep. He knew he was lucky just be alive. Losing that helmet was infinitely better than losing his head.

Back in Allan, Polich and his men took a break from M8 maintenance and resupply to inspect the two cars they captured the prior afternoon. Polich handed his captured camera to a platoon mate and posed for a few snaps behind the wheel. One of the cars was in fine working order and some of the fellows wanted to burn a little rubber off the tires. To avoid a friendly fire incident, they fixed a large American flag to the antenna. The M8 crews took turns testing the car's limits, knowing the odds were they would soon be ordered to abandon it. Lt. Cotter found out and feared that some overzealous GI might overlook the flag and blast the thing off the road. Nevertheless, he allowed Polich to keep the car temporarily. A few days later, however, the axle cracked after a wild bunch took it for a spin.[5] With that, both the car and Cotter's worries were gone.

L Company spent the day in the fields north of Allan resting, reorganizing, and resupplying. Burks, Works, and the headquarters section reunited with the company and immersed themselves in the task of rebuilding the unit's battle readiness.

Captain Coles' heroic efforts to save Pfc. James Doolin by running the German roadblock were not successful. The young man expired at the battalion aid station during the evening, his system too shocked and his wounds too extensive for the doctor to stabilize and repair.[6]

2nd Battalion continued gathering German stragglers on and around Montceau hill. Afterward, it pushed northwest into the outskirts of Montélimar. It made contact with lead elements of 30th Infantry Regiment near Espeluche, but not without a little drama. The 30th was operating as 3rd Division's right flank. When faint engine sounds began reverberating through the hills east of Allan,[7] the men of 2nd Battalion were not sure who was coming. For several anxious moments, they thought the Germans had found their way into their rear. Within seconds, a column of vehicles emerged three miles away, rolling down through the Rochefort Gap toward Espeluche. To the relief of every man in 2nd Battalion, they were painted with big white star markings.

By the end of the busy day, 2nd Battalion had gathered approximately 200 prisoners. Most were processed and passed on to division, but seventy were still being held in the attic of the battalion CP at Le Sastre for lack of transport.[8] Inundated with prisoner pick-up requests, the divisional S-2 section was doing its best to keep up by running trucks all over the countryside. 3rd Battalion had also gathered its share of prisoners—almost without trying. Though technically in reserve, Boye's five companies rounded up ninety-five prisoners by evening's end.[9]

By August 29, the city of Montélimar had fallen to all three regiments of 3rd Infantry Division. 1st Battalion of 15th Infantry Regiment was credited with single-handedly capturing or destroying 500 vehicles and taking more than 800 prisoners, mostly along National Route 7 south of Montélimar. This amazing accomplishment earned 1st Battalion the Distinguished Unit Citation by President Roosevelt.[10]

The damage to the German Nineteenth Army was even greater north of Montélimar. There, the Germans had been clashing intermittently with 36th Infantry Division since August 21, and was later ravaged by American artillery and Allied aircraft. Along a ten-mile corridor, an estimated 2,000 vehicles lay stranded or destroyed, many parked in double and triple rows. Some were still burning or smoldering days after they were hit. Most were cargo trucks, buses, or requisitioned French civilian sedans and carts. However, scattered throughout the wreckage were deadly AT guns, AAA guns, and artillery pieces thankfully removed forever from the war. Several huge rail guns of the "Anzio Express" variety were also captured.

Interspersed within the doomed column were more than 1,000 killed or trapped horses.[11] Many were beautiful Belgian draft horses, suffering as innocent victims to mankind's folly. A few fortunate survivors, unscathed by the hard hand of war, wandered away from the road and were taken in by nearby farmers. Others had to be freed by GIs scouting ahead of the bulldozers. Many of the unfortunates, however, suffered terribly—writhing on shattered legs or walking aimlessly about dragging their own entrails behind them.[12] Even men hardened by months of battle had a difficult time staying composed as they put the poor beasts down with a pistol shot to the head. These same men forever remembered—and wondered—how they could feel guilty about shedding tears over broken horses, but no longer even looked askance at broken people.

Like some ghastly museum from Hell, the long abandoned column showcased the twisted remains of hundreds of men, and in some cases, the women who loved and followed them.[13] Their burned, mangled, and dismembered bodies clung to the wreckage or littered the roads and nearby fields. A retching and ubiquitous stench of death hung everywhere. Some corpses were frozen in gruesome poses. A truck driver burned beyond recognition was still clenching a warped steering wheel while staring out of a jagged windshield with empty eye sockets. Other remains were no longer identifiably human. To reduce the horrible stench and inhibit the spread of disease, the GIs covered anything dead in lime until Graves Registration arrived.[14]

The battle at Montélimar was especially costly for the German Nineteenth Army. In addition to the estimated 600 killed and 1,500 wounded, 5,800 soldiers fell into Allied hands between August 21 and 31, 1944. According to Allied estimates, the German 338th Infantry Division was operating at only 20% effectiveness, and 198th Infantry Division was also badly degraded, operating at 60% effectiveness.[15] The loss of materials, particularly artillery pieces, was a huge blow to the Germans. By comparison, Allied losses were surprisingly light: 187 killed, 1,023 wounded, and 200 to 300 captured.[16] The supplies and men pouring in from the Mediterranean quickly replaced what little the Allies lost in terms of materials or fighting effectiveness.

Nevertheless, the Allied victory fell far short of what might have been. 11th Panzer Division's rearguard stand kept the escape route open along the Rhône River. Despite the difficult conditions it faced, the division managed to withdraw 75% of its tanks and artillery pieces and most of it personnel.[17] Behind the panzer shield, most of the German Nineteenth Army slipped away to fight on another battlefield. The retreat allowed the Germans to claim a victory of sorts, evading what could easily have been total annihilation. The American thrust inland had come within one sustained roadblock of trapping the bulk of the enemy army. "In my opinion," wrote Major Georg Grossjohann, a battalion commander with the German 198th Infantry Division, "all that the Americans would have had to do was to climb down from their secure heights above the Rhône north of Montélimar into the valley and to fight. They could have bagged us all."[18]

Trapping and destroying the German Nineteenth Army was exactly what General Truscott intended and expected. The reality of logistics, terrain, time, and a stubborn capable enemy, however, interfered with his plans. In the event, he was unable to move enough men and material up to Montélimar in time to fight the battle of annihilation every general dreams of waging.

The units opposing Major Grossjohann's battalion belonged to 141st Infantry Regiment, 36th Infantry Division. The 141st was thinly stretched along a six-mile front. The rough terrain and the long supply line back to the coast made timely reinforcement impossible and resupply a supreme challenge. On the early evening of August 25, two companies from 141st Infantry Regiment's 2nd Battalion, augmented with four tanks and seven TDs, moved down near La Coucourde and actually blocked National Route 7 for several hours. Though the position proved untenable and the regimental commander wanted them withdrawn, Truscott ordered that they remain as long as possible. By 1:00 A.M., the German panzers smashed them, routing out the infantry and reducing three of the tanks and six of the TDs to flaming hulks.[19] Even a commander as aggressive and gifted as Captain Coles would not have been able to hold out for very long without supplies or reinforcements.

A ghost from Anzio returned to spoil Truscott's opportunity. His VI Corps might have trapped the German Nineteenth Army at Montélimar if only more fuel had been loaded aboard ships at Naples. Worried about another bloody and protracted breakout, the invasion planners underestimated the gasoline supplies. The objective of Operation Dragoon, however, was to expel the Germans and seize Marseille and Toulon—which fell much sooner than anyone dreamed possible—and not to surround and capture the Germans in southern France. The capture of these two ports established a vital supply route into France. Through this route poured an almost limitless stream of soldiers, tanks, and planes for the final drive on Germany. The "tall tale" answers Pfc. Potter offered his captors during his interrogation at Allan were, after all was said and done, understatements.

* * *

3rd Infantry Division continued its drive north, passing through the miles of wreckage littering the landscape beyond Montélimar. Many wondered how anyone could have survived such carnage. And yet many did, including several American prisoners from L Company. Pfcs. Jantz,

Tyler, Cardelli, and Bonnet were trapped in that moving column during the retreat. Much of the dangerous journey was subjected to waves of horrifying air and artillery attacks. They experienced firsthand how the other side lived—and died.

After the four Americans were captured early in the afternoon of August 27, they were split into two groups and packed uncomfortably aboard waiting buses. The journey was initially slow and chaotic. The roads and intersections were jammed with traffic of every description. The regard for organization and logistics ranged from poor to non-existent. Horse-drawn artillery, in particular, seemed to be slowing everyone down.

Tyler tried to make some conversation with the soldiers guarding him. He had two years of German in high school and the lessons were fairly fresh in his memory. To his surprise, the guards were Polish, pleasant, and willing to converse.

"Why are you fighting for Germany?" asked a curious Tyler.

"Germans," explained one of the guards, "populate a large section of Poland. We are from that area."

The answer wasn't quite what Tyler was getting at, so he rephrased it. "Why are you fighting for Hitler?"

A light of understanding crossed the guard's face. "Hitler is good!" he replied with childlike enthusiasm.

The answer shocked Tyler, who glanced out the window at the mass of defeated soldiers trying like hell to get out of southern France with their lives. The expressions etched across many of the faces evinced misery, exhaustion, and despair. He didn't see much to get enthusiastic about—nor could he think of any reason to continue the conversation.

The guards treated the American prisoners well. Bathroom breaks were offered each time the bus stopped. Since delays were frequent, they had their pick of when they could leave the bus to stretch their legs and take care of their personal business. During one long stop, a German soldier boarded the bus with a delivery of canned Argentine corned beef. The guards opened the cans and passed them around with spoons. The simple heavy serving filled their empty stomachs and satisfied their hunger pangs.

At nightfall, travel improved somewhat and the delays were less frequent. Nevertheless, the bus barely moved faster than an idling crawl. The steady drone of the motor often lulled the four Americans to sleep.

The slow progress continued through dawn, by which time the Germans seemed to be gaining better control of the traffic flow.

However, the breaking daylight also signaled a return of the terror from the skies. When the Germans spotted a silver pack of Allied planes approaching from the south, the drivers slammed their brakes, stopping their vehicles indiscriminately along the roadside. Doors flew open and grey-uniformed men ran for the safety of the ditches and fields. The bombs tumbling from the sky only added to the pandemonium, consuming trucks and buses with horrific explosions and sending twisted metal and body parts in every direction. As thick black smoke billowed from the wreckage, the planes banked around to strafe remaining vehicles with .50-caliber slugs, weaving through what little ack-ack and small arms fire the Germans managed in response. Once the planes finished, they flew away, shrinking into tiny dots before disappearing altogether into the hazy southern skies. The Germans knew the lull was only temporary. The Americans would land at distant bases, reload, and attack again as soon as possible. Amid the secondary explosions of half-filled fuel tanks and crates of ordnance and the wretched groans and cries of the wounded, the Germans gathered what was still worth salvaging and pressed one.

The deadly cycle repeated itself every passing hour. The American prisoners often joined their German captors as wretched equals, huddling together in the roadside ditches and riding out each attack in quiet desperation. The only "advantage" about being attacked by planes was that they could be seen and heard before they struck. Artillery was an altogether different matter. 105mm or 155mm shells fell from the skies with devastating impact. Artillery attacks never began or ended with any clear pattern. Whether it was planes or unseen howitzers attacking the German column, the result was always the same: more dead, more wounded, more burning vehicles, and more frayed nerves. On several occasions, damage forced the guards to move their American prisoners to different buses or trucks.

During one particularly chaotic exchange, Jantz was separated from his friends and paired with a different American prisoner from another unit.[20] The next morning, airplane engines and automatic machine gun fire shook Jantz and the other American awake. The German soldiers cramped inside the same bus strained to find the source of the noise. Some stuck their anxious faces out the windows for a better look and pulled back inside with urgent shouts. The scene unfolded like a nightmarish déja vu. The convoy slammed to a halt, soldiers jostled for the aisle, and Jantz's guard pointed emphatically for the two Americans to leave their seats.

"Schnell! Schnell!" he yelled.

For the umpteenth time they clambered for the exit behind their terrified guard. When they emerged from the door, the guard yelled something as he ran away from the bus—probably a demand that they follow him. The whole routine was getting old. Jantz and his partner looked at each other with the same thought on their minds: escape. The guard's back was turned and everyone else was preoccupied with saving their own butts. Although there was a risk of being shot, remaining with the column seemed like certain death. With the split-second non-verbal decision made, the two Americans bolted together in the opposite direction. As Jantz sprinted for his life, he stole a glance skyward just in time to see two British Spitfires approaching in tandem low and fast along either side of the road. Jantz recognized the large circle insignias as those of Allied planes, but the terror that pumped through his body was no different than if they had been painted with German crosses. The pilots could not distinguish individual soldiers. The machine guns opened up, chewing neat rows of bullet trails straight down the spine of the column. To Jantz's dismay, the trails were heading straight for them.

The two Americans dove into a roadside cafe as the bullets and planes roared past. Dashing past the chairs and tables, they made their way through the kitchen, bolted out the back door, and emerged in a vineyard. A few hundred yards away was a railroad bed running parallel with the road. Jantz and his companion continued running deep into the vineyard, vaulting row after row of wired vines until they believed they were a safe distance from both the road and the tracks. Out of breath, they fell to the ground among the vines, peering out from the large sunlit leaves to watch as six British Spitfires continued raking the column.

The men were trying to figure out what to do when the sounds of approaching footsteps reached them. Terrified, they lay still and waited. Jantz breathed a heavy sigh of relief when he caught sight of Tyler, Cardelli, and Bonnet scampering toward their prone bodies. He raised himself to a crouch and quietly beckoned them to duck among the thick branches. The three Americans had also decided to take advantage of the chaos and try an escape. The five men quietly discussed their options. By consensus, they agreed to stay put until after dark.

For the rest of the day, the five Americans remained hidden in the vineyard, listening to several more cycles of aerial destruction. An intermittent breeze carried the smell of burning fuel and human flesh through the nearby leaves. That was one thing they could not escape. The stench clung to their clothing, filled their nostrils, and sickened their stomachs. When they grew thirsty, they picked and squeezed the unripe grapes for what little juice was inside. Before too long they discovered they were not as safe as they hoped. Bands of retreating Germans intermittently walked along the rows, moving away from the road and the column to seek safety elsewhere. Some were walking wounded. Sometimes these Germans were so close that the prone Americans could have reached out and grabbed their legs. Each time the enemy approached, the Americans held their breath and waited quietly as they stumbled or walked past, oblivious to their proximity.

Once dusk arrived, the five escapees decided it was time to move. They were hot and thirsty, and wanted especially to find their way back to American lines. They decided their best hope was to walk toward the silent flashes of artillery illuminating the southern horizon. Several times they were forced to stop and hide when groups of Germans noisily made their presence known.

And then their luck abandoned them. After hiding for a few minutes near a brick railroad bridge, the group emerged too soon. Standing before them was a group of enemy soldiers.

Tyler used his German to try and convince the enemy to let them go. "You don't really want the burden of guarding five American POWs—especially under these circumstances, do you?" he asked. Surprisingly, the German soldiers agreed with him.

As the two groups began to part, however, a German dressed in a black uniform stepped out of the dark and angrily leveled a pistol at the Americans. He looked like an SS trooper with a nasty attitude.

A lively discussion between the irate German and his fellow soldiers ensued. Jantz couldn't understand a word of it, but Tyler picked up enough to be concerned. The man in the black uniform was a tanker whose panzer was destroyed during the battle of Montélimar. Bitter about losing his crew, he wanted to shoot every American he came upon. Thankfully, the other Germans were of a different mind and argued with him for a few minutes to calm him. When the time was right, a guard signaled for the five to move on. No one needed a second invitation. Without looking back, the five Americans ran as fast as they could for fear that the panzer crewman might change his mind. After the brush with death, the five decided to stay as far away from the road as possible, traversing instead through the fields and back paths.

Tired and hungry, later that night the men decided to stop and rest in some abandoned foxholes. Each man took a turn at guard duty. When dawn broke, they heard approaching motors and English-speaking voices. The five lay motionless until they were certain they were not being fooled by wishful thinking or a clever German trick. The voices grew louder and they clearly belonged to Americans.

One of the five men jumped up and began shouting, "American! Don't shoot!" He held up his helmet as further evidence of his nationality. The other four joined him. The approaching American soldiers raised their weapons with suspicion. Jantz noticed light blue arrowheads of the "Texas" 36th Infantry Division on their shoulder patches. The "T-patchers" demanded that each of the five men call out his name and unit, an order each cheerfully followed. Still wary of a ruse, one of the 36th Division men asked the strangers to step forward with raised hands. After a closer inspection and a few more questions, they were satisfied of their authenticity and welcomed the five former prisoners of war back into the U.S. Seventh Army.

The small unit of "T-patchers" had been sent out that morning on an attack mission. When they asked Jantz and the others what to expect in the way of the enemy, the former POWs shared whatever knowledge they had gleaned during their times as prisoners and hair-raising escape. When the men parted, Jantz, Taylor, and company were bounced back to the rear echelon, where they hitched rides to 3rd Infantry Division's operational area. A few hours later, Jantz, Tyler, Cardelli, and Bonnet found themselves happily reunited with L Company. Their arrival was tempered by the fact that many familiar faces were missing. Jantz was especially surprised to learn their attack on Allan was against a German armeekorps headquarters.[21]

American forces also recovered 2nd Lt. Arnold Mackowsky, though he would never return to L Company. After his capture and separation from Jantz and the others, the enemy transferred Mackowsky to a

German field hospital. He was the only American in a roomful of wounded Germans. A surgeon examined him and recommended amputation, but a nearby colleague stepped in and vehemently protested. The dissenting doctor pulled rank and took over Mackowsky's case. He turned out to be an excellent surgeon who not only saved Mackowsky's leg, but also restored much of the knee's function. Though morphine was in short supply, Mackowsky's officer status earned him the painkiller. Ironically, he was extended this courtesy ahead of many German enlisted men with more serious wounds. The chaotic retreat made it impossible for the Germans to transport Mackowsky for postoperative treatment, so they left him behind for the advancing Americans to deal with.[22] Mackowsky's ordeal ended on August 29—when Americans found him two very long and trying days after his capture.[23]

After Potter, Evans, Engel, and Mangina were interrogated at the farmhouse north of Allan, the four young Americans were directed to the road and given heavy packs to carry. Along with their guards and dozens of other German soldiers, they walked first to Montélimar and then northward along National Route 7. Although they avoided most of the strafing and bombing because they were on foot, their mode of transportation did not prevent them from witnessing the aftermath of the Allied destruction: hundreds of dead horses and enemy soldiers, long lines of mangled vehicles, and several huge 380mm rail guns sitting silent, damaged, and useless.

For sustenance, the Germans gave each American prisoner a loaf of stale black German bread and two cans of cold pack beef. They opened the beef with their GI can openers, which the Germans allowed them to keep for that specific reason. After several hours of tough marching, the guards directed the four POWs to sit down and eat. Although hungry, Potter expected little beyond the usual bland dining experience he'd grown accustomed to from his daily U.S. Army K-rations. After a few bites of the German bread and beef, however, he found he couldn't get enough of the stuff. The simple meal tasted absolutely delicious.

Several more days of relentless marching produced terrible blisters on their feet. The pain became so excruciating that the men could no longer walk. Their German guards escorted them to a medical tent, where a doctor brushed a black liquid (probably iodine) onto the soles of their feet and ordered them to lie down on cots for the evening. Later that night, an FFI operative covertly cut a slit in the tent and poked his head through. He whispered excitedly and gestured for the four Americans to come through. Despite their raw feet, they readily followed the Frenchman. The escapees hid in a church basement at Valence until other FFI operatives made contact with American forces on their behalf. When the U.S Seventh Army arrived to liberate the town, the four were repatriated.

Rather than fight their way through the endless waves of American troops and vehicles, Potter and his comrades decided upon a more leisurely approach. After their tough ordeal, they figured they earned a little extra time to "enjoy" the journey back to L Company. While scrounging through a garage, they discovered and "liberated" a 1937 Packard. Now they needed a battery to turn over the engine. As luck would have it, they obtained one from another U.S. soldier. After a day or two of touring, the quartet was ready to head back to their unit when they learned the American advance had already passed them by. L Company was now 200 miles north by northwest of Valence, fighting near the town of Besançon.[24] Fortunately, the entire 3rd Infantry Division was delayed long enough for the four privates to rejoin L Company before Besançon fell.[25] After hearing their story, 1st Sgt. Works cut them a break and officially recorded them as "Missing in Action" for the entire time.

Jantz's group, Potter's group, and Mackowsky accounted for nine of the thirteen men captured at Allan. The remaining four—T/Sgt. Wallace E. Lawrence, Sgt. Roy Sanders, Pfc. George Deal, and Pfc. Richard Kirschner—were taken to prisoner of war camps in Germany. Red Cross letters eventually reported on their status and whereabouts.

During the two weeks after the fighting at Allan and Montélimar, L Company and the 3rd Division swept north rapidly. They fought the Germans at Besançon, and afterward at Vesoul. L Company's battle losses continued to mount, with six more men taken prisoner,[26] and six more falling wounded.[27] One man turned up missing and was later declared dead.[28] On September 14 and 15, L Company received a batch of replacements and several recuperated veterans. Among them was Sgt. Edmund Rovas,[29] who returned to a squad with many unfamiliar faces. Half of his men had been killed, wounded, or captured at Allan.[30] Among those captured was Sgt. Roy Sanders, his friend and assistant squad leader.

On September 15, 1944, the Southern France Campaign officially came to an end. There was no particular significance attached to the date other than symmetry; it closed off one round month from the date of the Riviera landings. In reality, the U.S. Seventh Army was well into northeastern France by that time. Thirty-two days after storming the beaches, the "Southern" France Campaign ended 400 miles from the Mediterranean, well above Switzerland and only sixty miles from the edge of Germany. As casualty lists would aptly demonstrate, those sixty miles would prove to be some of the most treacherous and deadly of the entire war. A harsh winter was approaching, and between Seventh Army and the Rhine River were the Vosges Mountains and hundreds of thousands of German soldiers motivated to defend their homeland. Many of those defenders were the same men who had marched, driven, or been transported along National Route 7, avoiding the trap at Montélimar to live and fight another day. Never in history had any invading army crossed the Vosges against organized resistance.[31]

As the Southern France Campaign gave way to the "Rhineland Campaign," L Company and 3rd Infantry Division pushed into the foothills of the Vosges toward the city of Lure. The next day, September 16, the Germans captured Captain Coles during one of his legendary jeep rides. L Company was assigned an outside captain who turned out to be an unacceptable combat commander.[32] After about one month, 1st Lt. George Burks replaced the new captain. Looking back, Burks compared the advance from the Mediterranean into the Vosges to the compressing of a spring. "It was easy to do at first," he explained, "but the harder you pushed, the harder the resistance."[33]

The fighting in Southern France was nothing compared to what the Americans later faced in central Europe. Just as Cotter had predicted, the engagement at Allan was only a sampling of things to come. On November 9, 1944, Lt. Burks fell seriously wounded while leading L Company near Epinal, France. Anyone hopeful the war would end by Christmas had few illusions as the calendar turned from November to December. They would have to stay alive until May 1945 to witness that happy event. During those intervening months, 3rd Infantry Division fought in some of the most desperate battles of the Western Front. From December 1944 to January 1945, the division slugged slowly through the "Colmar Pocket," an exceptionally difficult and costly campaign for both sides. If bullets and artillery didn't fall a man at Colmar, then trench foot or frostbite would. Misery heeded no rank or nationality.

Captain Redle's B Company, 756th Tank Battalion, suffered heavy battle losses during this period. By the end of January, it could field only three operational tanks—even though it had been restocked several times with new M4s and replacement crews.[34] B Company rebounded after Colmar and fought with 3rd Infantry Division into Nuremberg, Germany. The tankers and infantry of this proud outfit ended the war in Salzburg, Austria, but only with a handful of the men who remembered events before Colmar. Captain Redle was one of those lucky few survivors.

3rd Infantry Division was one of only three American infantry divisions to begin and end the war in Europe. Its two and a half years of combat cost it 4,922 killed in action (plus 636 more who died of their wounds) and 18,766 wounded—a stunning total of 24,324 battle casualties.[35] An infantry division's organizational strength during that time was just over 14,000 men (excluding attached units, such as tanks or tank destroyers). Put another way, these statistics illustrate that 3rd Division's casualty rate was nearly double its divisional strength. The odds of being killed during the war while serving in 3rd Infantry Division were worse than one in three.

The division's non-battle casualties were also high at 46,416.[36] This number represents soldiers pulled from the line for illnesses such as malaria and hepatitis, conditions like trench foot, or emotional breakdown often labeled "battle fatigue." These men accounted for a 330% turnover. Together, battle and non-battle figures combine for 70,740 casualty incidents. In other words, there was an appalling 500% wartime turnover rate for the division. (Note: These figures include recuperated soldiers returning for duty, as well as replacements.)

No American army division paid a higher price in World War II than 3rd Infantry Division.[37]

*   *   *

After its liberation on August 27, 1944, life in Allan gradually returned to something approaching normal. Although dead soldiers and

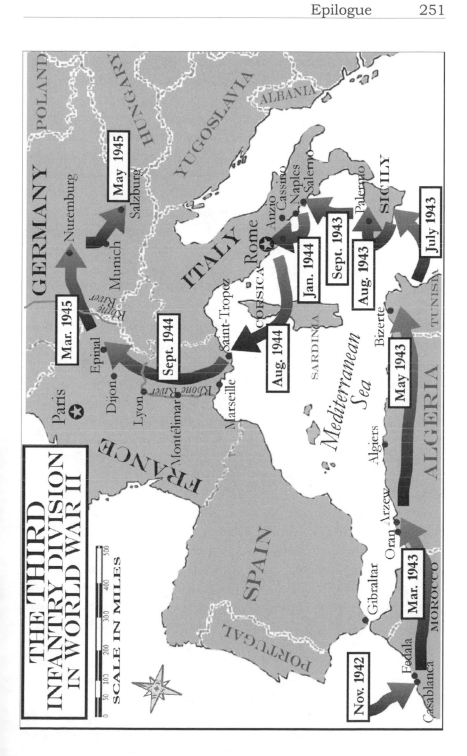

THE THIRD INFANTRY DIVISION IN WORLD WAR II

SCALE IN MILES
0 50 100 200 300 400 500

Nov. 1942
Mar. 1943
May 1943
July 1943
Aug. 1943
Sept. 1943
Jan. 1944
Aug. 1944
Sept. 1944
Mar. 1945
May 1945

GERMANY
POLAND
HUNGARY
YUGOSLAVIA
ALBANIA
ITALY
FRANCE
SPAIN
PORTUGAL
MOROCCO
ALGERIA
TUNISIA
SICILY
SARDINIA
CORSICA

Mediterranean Sea

Nuremburg
Salzburg
Munich
Rhine River
Epinal
Dijon
Lyon
Paris
Montélimar
Rhône River
Marseille
Saint-Tropez
Rome
Anzio
Cassino
Naples
Salerno
Palermo
Bizerte
Algiers
Oran
Arzew
Gibraltar
Fedala
Casablanca

wrecked machines cluttered their streets, abandoned weapons and casings littered their fields, and several of their homes and shops lay in ruins, the townsfolk considered themselves very fortunate. Not a single citizen of Allan perished during the fight, a fact its people considered miraculous and attributed to the special protection of the Virgin Mary. Nevertheless, Allan was forever changed, and the physical damage and reminders of war would take a long time to repair or remove altogether. Some things, such as the ghastly scenes of aftermath, would forever haunt the memories of those who witnessed them.

On the afternoon of August 28, Lucien Martel and his friends approached Allan from the northwest. After spooking I Company scouts on the outskirts of town, they continued into town unsure what they would discover. Lucien walked down the road from the cemetery past several American soldiers loading the body of a dead infantryman onto a jeep trailer. He also passed the smoldering remains of a Sherman tank, still radiating intense heat and wisps of smoke. Mixed among the burned ration crates and personal items blown from the deck and scattered on the road was the charred head and shoulders of a dead crewman.

Lucien walked toward the church. When he saw the damage to the front of his parent's home, he stopped cold in his tracks at the crossroads. He asked a neighbor to check inside for him, and trembled with fear that his parents were dead. His neighbor entered and reported the house unoccupied. Lucien later learned they had taken up refuge at a nearby farm and were unharmed.

He walked the path of Old Allan toward the burned out Marder. A black jacket lay discarded on the nearby ground as if the owner had only stepped away for a cigarette. Inside the charred hulk at the driver and assistant driver's stations were two metal belt buckles with the inscription "Gott Mitt Uns" (God With Us). On the floor below were the remnants of steel-toed boots. A thick layer of ash covered the metal seats and floor of the scorched interior. A sickened Lucien realized he was looking upon the cremated remains of two crewmen.

Something nearby smelled abominable, yet Lucien was drawn to investigate. A few dozen yards away was what had once been a German machine gun nest beneath a large bush. The gun and ammunition were still scattered on the ground. Nearby, the loader was sprawled out dead, though no obvious wounds were visible. Upon closer inspection, Lucien discovered a second German had suffered the full force of an explosion.

Except for a gleaming portion of spinal column above the belt line, only the bottom half of him remained. The bush above and behind the dead man had been blown upwards. Plastering its leaves and branches were bits of flesh and internal organs. The hot sun and flies were doing their work.[38] Lucien had seen enough. No one was accustomed to seeing such horrors in a peaceful farming town like Allan.

Throughout the day, other townsfolk emerged from their places of refuge among the hills, the old medieval walls, and the outlying farms to return to town, assess the damage, and thank their liberators. To the surprise of citizens and soldiers alike, a local fourteen-year old boy named Michel Imbert survived the entire battle hiding in the northern fields. When he heard the first shots the day before, he took refuge in a crevice along the creek bed and remained hidden even as the fight raged all around him. No one had any idea he was there. The next day, he emerged unscathed and relieved with an amazing story to tell.[39]

The next day, August 29, a U.S. Army Graves Registration platoon stopped in Allan and began collecting American and German dead.[40] The team went about its grim work with methodical familiarity. Some of the bodies were taken to military cemeteries, while others ended up temporarily interred near the village.[41] What little remained of Lt. Danby and his turret crew could not be individually identified, so their tank number was recorded on their death reports.[42] That which was collected ended up in a common grave at the cemetery north of town. The Graves Registration men finished collecting bodies and departed later that afternoon. In their wake were Allan's citizens, left to clean up the battle damage and repair their shattered lives.

In time, Mouriers rebuilt their home. The damage to the Grâne farm, the Martel house, and many other places was repaired. Allan residents collected weapons and casings and either sold them as scrap or rendered them inert and kept them as souvenirs. Outside assistance was requested to cart away the destroyed or abandoned vehicles. For several weeks, however, the Marder III remained east of the village. Its long gun barrel stubbornly projected across the lane, blocking the farm traffic to and from the outlying fields. Mourier, the blacksmith, had the means and the expertise to cut the barrel, but didn't dare out of fear that an unexploded round might still be lodged inside the breech. The farmers put up with this inconvenience until the Army finally sent the proper equipment to haul the whole thing away.[43]

Danby's burned-out Sherman tank remained longer, but the townspeople honored it as a sacred fixture. The charred hulk sat rusting for several months near the bridge with its main gun locked silently upon the cemetery, a sentinel of the hereafter guarding the village against the ghosts of a German counterattack.

At noon on November 1, 1944—All Saints Day on the Catholic calendar—people by the hundreds gathered in the village square for a memorial service. Though the sky was overcast and an icy drizzle chilled the crowd, most of the citizens of Allan and the nearby farms and hamlets were in attendance. They huddled together forming a vast sea of umbrellas. School children in neat rows faced the town hall. An FFI honor guard stood at attention with gleaming rifles on the entrance steps. After several American Army officers arrived, the FFI and some wreath bearers started an orderly procession. Slowly, respectfully, everyone joined the peaceful column as it meandered silently past Danby's burned Sherman on the way to the cemetery.

The rain eased, and a large circle formed around the white crosses marking the graves of the ten executed FFI fighters and the unknown American tankers. Beautiful floral wreaths festooned with rainbow colors were placed on each grave. Speeches of thanks and prayer followed. The FFI guard saluted the fallen with a solemn remembrance that all gave their lives for the deliverance of France. The ceremony ended with a bugle call and a drum roll.[44]

One month later, the Army removed the American remains from the cemetery and reburied them at the U.S cemetery in Luynes.[45] The rusting Sherman was also, finally, hauled away.

When the war ended in May of 1945, the seventeen French soldiers of Allan, captured during the German invasion of France in 1940, happily returned home. After five years in German prisoner of war camps, however, some returned in poor health.[46]

By 1947, very few reminders of combat remained except the bloodstained soil near the tree in front of Mayor Almoric's house, where the two German soldiers had been shot.[47]

On August 31, 1947, the people gathered again, this time to fulfill a promise. They massed on the eastern hillside below the ruins of Old Allan before a newly unveiled eighteen-foot statue of the Madonna with Child. Dignitaries on hand for the dedication included the Bishop of Valence, the priests of Allan and Espeluche, Mayor Almoric, and the

August 31, 1947. Three years after the liberation of Allan, its townspeople assemble for "Virgin of the Liberation" memorial dedication near Old Allan. This view shows the northern fields of town where L Company was pinned. The cemetery's white walls are 1/3 from right near the top. In the hazy distance lay Montélimar and the high western plateau along the Rhône River.
Lucien Martel

monument's engineer, Maurice Martel. Inscribed on the pedestal are these words:

Faithful
To their vow
to
MARY
Their Protector
The Grateful Parishioners of Allan
1940-1944

Today, that same figure of Mary continues her hillside vigil over the village that called for her protection sixty-two years earlier. Just behind her, the ruins of the past crumble and succumb to an earth layered with forgotten eras. Spread before her is a sprawling modern valley with an uncertain future looming on the horizon. The execution wall in Allan, the north bridge, fields, and cemetery lay under her tender and unflinching gaze; terrible places, sowed with violence and death, now tranquil. Madonna watches them all, waiting patiently, waiting for an age when all people live forever in freedom and peace, when men aren't compelled to gamble everything for a few footsteps of soil, when the saintly qualities of bravery and self-sacrifice no longer need to be tested against the demons of combat.

When a whirlwind of war ripped apart an entire continent around them, Allan—like many other communities—nurtured hope through the vital bonds of family and fellowship, and by faith, sharing, and simple living. Today, a loud and hectic world closes in on Allan. World War II is a distant memory. National boundaries, increasing commerce, and technological innovation are melting away the old differences between people. A teeming super highway snakes through the Rhône valley and disappears south between the hills of Montchamp and Roucoule. Thousands of colorful cars and shiny trucks zip over the very places where desperate Germans in drab camouflage once, many decades ago, inched their way along a highway of death. A futuristic array of windmill turbines towers over the valley between Donzère and Montchamp, and every few hours a high-speed train thunders through the valley, ferrying people between Lyon and Marseille at ground speeds unimaginable in the 1940s.

Beneath this veneer of scientific progress and material comfort, the human heart remains unchanged. Inside the human spirit lurks the same evil that plunged 1940s Europe into such cruel and horrific depths. Will it one day unravel again, as it has so many times in the past? Nothing can be taken for granted—particularly the sacrifices of those who offered their own lives to win another chance for those who would come after them. How these individuals faced life's harshest trial is a beacon of light from which we all must learn. Coles met the challenge with bravery and determination; Redle was unselfish and attentive; Oliver was practical, shrewd, and humble, while Danby was inspired with idealistic enthusiasm.

Each offers a small example of the countless others who fought with them against tyranny around the world.

Postscript

2nd Lt. Arthur Abrahamson, the replacement officer who accompanied Lt. Danby on the C-47 from Naples to Saint-Tropez, was assigned to A Company of 756th Tank Battalion as a platoon leader. His tanks supported 7th Infantry Regiment during the battle for Montélimar. Word of Lt. Danby's early death traveled quickly through 756th, and no one was more shocked to hear of it than Abrahamson. He finished the war as a company commander in 756th Tank Battalion. Arthur lives with his wife in the Midwest.[1]

Sgt. Roy Anderson last saw Cpl. Steve Vargo and Pvt. Dual Dishner when he swapped tanks with Lt. Danby near Saint-Paul. Before that, Vargo and Dishner spent six months as Anderson's turret crew. Losing them, Anderson remembered, was like losing brothers.[2]

Two weeks after the battle at Allan, Anderson was promoted to staff sergeant to fill the vacancy left by S/Sgt. Hamilton upon Smith's death on August 18, 1944. On December 23, 1944, while fighting near Colmar France, a German 88 round sliced completely through the turret of Anderson's tank. The high velocity slug entered between Anderson and his gunner George Fick before exiting the other side behind the loader. Miraculously, no one was killed, but the flash and concussion left all three men dazed and bleeding. The shell wounded Fick in the eye and ear and left Anderson temporarily blinded. Somehow, everyone escaped the tank. While recovering in a hospital, Anderson discovered that an address book he kept in his coverall chest pocket stopped a piece of shrapnel from entering his heart. Roy recovered his sight, but his wounds prevented him from returning to the tanks.

When the war ended, he settled in Indiana and worked as an auto mechanic. He married, had a son, and became a manager in the auto parts department at a dealership. In 1953, he and his family moved to Texas, where they live today. Roy still has the torn address book that stopped that shrapnel piece.[3]

Lt. Col Frederic W. Boye returned stateside to his wife and son in November 1944. He had served overseas for two straight years and participated in five amphibious landings (Morocco, Sicily, Salerno, Anzio, and Southern France). After the war, Frederic continued an illustrious Army career. Promoted to brigadier general in 1960, he served in Vietnam and became commander of the Fort Knox Armor School. He reached major general in 1966 and commanded 7th Infantry Division in South Korea before finishing his career at the Pentagon.[4] Frederic passed away in October 2004.

1st Lt. George S. Burks became commander of L Company in late October 1944. On November 9, 1944—the first birthday of Burks' son—L Company was hit hard near Saint-Die, France. During the fighting, the antenna to the company radio was shot off and Burks was unable to call for reinforcements from the battalion. Coles' prophetic advice about keeping an extra radio came back to haunt him yet again. A piece of shrapnel struck Burks, tearing through his left hip and out his right side. A portion of his intestines bulged through the wound and his right leg was injured. Burks held his intestines in place by pulling the right side of his shirt tightly under his belt to form a cradle, but the pain was so intense that walking was nearly impossible without assistance. T/Sgt. Francis Sholly, despite a serious wound that rendered his left arm useless, refused to leave Burks.[5] Sholly propped his company commander up with his good arm and the two staggered an entire mile back to the battalion—all the while under fire. During the agonizing trek, Burks was shot through his forearm, but didn't realize it until much later.

A surgeon who had also served in World War I treated Burks at an Army medical hospital. This doctor told him that if he had suffered the same wound in the earlier war, he would have been set aside to die. Twenty years of medical advances was the difference between life and death.

George was hospitalized a full year before returning home. He was promoted to captain when he was discharged. He and his wife moved to New Jersey and had a second son. Burks retired in 1975 after thirty-eight years in sales, and started a second career as a real estate agent. Two years later, his wife suffered a massive stroke and George lovingly cared for her until her passing in 1988. Today, Burks lives close to his oldest son in Texas and continues to find new interests and sources of joy in a life that nearly ended so long ago.[6]

Pfc. Arco Ciancanelli heard from the Baby Ruth Company several weeks after he wrote them looking for free candy bars. To his surprise, a big box arrived for him to share with the company—with a letter asking him not to write again![7]

On September 12, 1944, on the outskirts of Vesoul, Ciancanelli was scouting ahead of his platoon when a German rifleman hiding behind a bush fired at him and missed. Ciancanelli rushed the position and killed him before he could fire again. When he spotted two more Germans in a nearby foxhole, Ciancanelli raised his rifle to fire. When it jammed, he stormed the German foxhole and killed one man with his rifle butt while the other ran off into a nearby house. Ciancanelli grabbed the dead German's rifle and one of his grenades and gave chase. He tossed the grenade inside the house, waited for it to explode, and then stormed inside only to discover twenty dazed Germans. The grenade blast wounded four of them. All twenty surrendered to Ciancanelli, who was later awarded the Distinguished Service Cross for his heroism.[8]

On October 23, 1944, S/Sgt. Ciancanelli was blown off a tank. Stunned, he sat by a tree and contemplated his situation. As far as he was concerned, he had reached his limit. He had given more than his fair share as a front-line infantryman.[9] After more than 300 days on the front lines, Ciancanelli "just quit."[10] During that time, he received the Bronze Star for his actions at Isola Bella, Italy. He also survived the Anzio breakout with a bullet to the leg and was wounded on two other occasions. He'd seen many good men die in horrific ways—including a friend who was blown apart after stepping on a land mine. His friend's severed arm hit Ciancanelli in the face. An Army psychiatrist diagnosed him with "battlefield fatigue" and recommended that he complete his Army service away from the front. He served out the remainder of the war as a cook.

After the war, Arco returned to Chicago and served as a police officer in a neighboring community.[11] He remained a talkative, lively, and fun-loving soul up until his death on May 28, 2005.[12]

T/5 Herman Cogdell transferred out of L Company in early 1945 on combat points. He served out the war with an ordnance outfit in Italy and returned home to South Carolina with an honorable discharge. In 1946, Cogdell married and went to work for six years with a parts supplier, during which time he attended night school to become a draftsman. After graduating, he worked as an engineering draftsman for twenty-eight years and then retired. He remarried in 1970 and has a stepdaughter and two step grandchildren. Herman Cogdell has not milked a cow since the war.[13]

Captain James W. Coles was awarded the Distinguished Service Cross for his actions at Allan. On September 16, 1944, near the town of Lure, Coles and the tank officer replacing Lt. Danby, 2nd Lt. R. C. Sullivan, went on a jeep reconnaissance trip.[14] As their jeep disappeared into a wooded area beyond a railroad overpass, the men from L Company heard automatic fire. The jeep did not return, nor was it or any trace of the riders immediately found.[15] Two weeks later, the Red Cross reported that Coles and Lt. Sullivan had been captured.[16]

Coles and Sullivan remained prisoners of war in Poland until the Russian Army liberated their camp in early 1945.[17] For two weeks, the two men fought with the Russians before making their way to the Black Sea and hopping aboard an American liberty ship bound for Naples, Italy.[18] The ordeal left Sullivan seriously underweight, and he returned to the States. Coles, on the other hand, remained at a healthy body weight and returned to 15th Infantry Regiment. To his everlasting frustration, the Army placed him in 1st Battalion headquarters instead of assigning him to another company command.[19]

Coles visited 3rd Battalion a few times to check on L Company friends. He told stories of his experiences, including details of his two-week run with the Russians.[20] He relayed how Russian trucks wouldn't start in the winter, and how an American Studebaker was used to jumpstart them.[21] He recalled that Russian soldiers were so laden with grenades and explosives that if they were hit they were likely to explode, and that many Russian officers were illiterate.[22] Coles was also appalled over how the Russians accepted horrific casualties, attacked towns "like a mob leaving a factory," and burned everything to the ground when they moved on.[23] Such senseless destruction angered him, and he could not hide his disdain for Red Army tactics. With indignation mixed with a bit of bravado, Coles boasted that he could take on the entire Russian Army if given one hilltop machine gun and an unlimited supply of ammunition.[24]

Coles remained with 15th Infantry Regiment during the Occupation of Germany and was a major when he was honorably discharged in 1947. He moved to Frankfort to work as supervisor at an automobile plant, and then returned home in 1950 to Encinitas, California, with a German second wife. (His first marriage dissolved in late 1945.)[25] Coles ran a gas station and later purchased a bowling alley with a bar & grill. In the 1960s, he sold his business and worked overseas with a shipping concern. He passed away after a sudden illness on October 27, 1968, and is buried at Tangiers, Morocco.[26] Major Coles is survived by three daughters.

1st Lt. Lloyd Cotter recuperated from his gunshot wound to the hip without missing a day from his command of 2nd Platoon of Cannon Company. On November 3, 1944, at the French town of Nompatelize, Cotter was directing M8 cannon fire from a church steeple in what appeared to be a hopeless cause. Only two rifle platoons from F Company stood between his steeple and hundreds of Germans who threatened to overrun their position. "This is the day I'm going to die," he thought as he watched the German multitude attack across the rolling ground. His thought nearly became reality when a German mortar round scored a direct hit on the steeple. The shell blew Cotter out of his observation position and knocked him temporarily unconscious. He awoke to find himself on the ground bleeding, but he shook the cobwebs off and climbed back up into position. By that time, the Germans were so close Cotter used his M-1 rifle and a BAR for protection while calling for M8 artillery volleys to fall directly in front of him. German artillery and mortars tried to knock Cotter out of the steeple again, but failed to score another direct hit. Eventually, the attack stalled and the Germans fell back, leaving 250 comrades dead or wounded on the battlefield. Lt. Cotter was awarded the Distinguished Service Cross.

While fighting at dawn later in the Colmar Pocket, Cotter was hit at point blank range by a burst of German machine gun fire. Bullets tore through his stomach and chest. He lay on the ground waiting to die, knowing from firsthand experience that anyone shot like him lasted a few minutes at most. Consumed about what he would do after the war, Cotter found some unusual solace that those worries, at least, were at an end.

As he began slipping into unconsciousness, Cotter had a remarkable spiritual experience. An authoritative voice declared that "Jesus did not want him dead yet." Moments later, soldiers arrived and placed Cotter on a stretcher. They rushed him to the battalion doctor who placed him in an ambulance for a 300-mile journey to the hospital. As the ambulance drove off, the battalion doctor told Cotter's friends that he was "a goner."

Throughout the journey, Cotter drifted in and out of consciousness but arrived at the hospital still clinging to life. He recalled waking up on an X-ray table to overhear a surgeon remark on how absolutely miraculous he was to have survived the 12-hour drive. Cotter's wounds were extensive: a torn diaphragm, punctured kidneys, three broken ribs, and fractured vertebrae. A third of his liver was "hanging by a thread" and had to be removed. For a full week, Cotter received a constant blood transfusion until his condition stabilized. Many doctors came in to review his case and left astounded at his survival. In time, he transferred to another hospital for additional surgery and eventually returned home. Before his discharge from the Regular Army, Cotter was promoted to captain and continued service in the Army Reserves.

Cotter became a medical doctor of psychiatry under the G.I. Bill. He practiced in California for many years and retired at the age of sixty-five. Despite the hardships and horrors, Cotter considered his war service as "an adventure." He and his wife of sixty-one years passed away within one month of one another in 2004. The Cotters are survived by two children.[27]

Lloyd Cotter was the highest decorated soldier from Cannon Company of 15th Infantry Regiment.[28] His honors include the Distinguished Service Cross, two Silver Stars, the Bronze Star, and the Purple Heart with three Oak Clusters (representing four separate battle wounds.)[29]

Cpl. Dominick Delmonico was awarded the Distinguished Service Cross for his actions at Allan, France. He was later promoted to staff sergeant, survived the war, signed up for occupation duty, and remained in L Company. One year after the liberation of southern France, the people of Besançon invited their liberators to return for a parade and celebration. During the drive back to base, the truck he was riding in broke an axle, slid off the road, and overturned on top of him, killing him instantly.[30] In his last letter home to his wife, Delmonico had written about how excited he was to return to Besançon as an honored guest.[31]

Cpl. Leonard D. Froneberger, Jr. continued adding to the legend of his tank gunner prowess. He had a particular knack for picking off moving targets at impossible distances—including a German soldier on a speeding motorcycle, and knocking the engine block out of the lead truck in a convoy 4,000 yards away.[32] On December 21, 1944, Froneberger was promoted to sergeant and tank commander. Two days later, as 3rd Platoon advanced on Bennwihr, France, Froneberger leaned out of his hatch to talk to his lieutenant and was killed instantly by a mortar blast that landed squarely on the turret.[33] Froneberger was from Oklahoma.[34]

After suffering severe shrapnel wounds to his arm and legs during the August 23rd artillery attack at Le Griffon, Pvt. Bernard Greive was flown to Naples on a C-47. He spent three months recovering in a body cast, and had to learn how to walk all over again. Greive suffered some residual paralysis to the left arm and required additional surgery after the war. He worked for many years at Johnson & Johnson in Chicago and retired only a few years ago. Bernard currently lives in Florida.[35]

Pfc. Rudolph A. Jantz returned to L Company after his capture and short ordeal as a prisoner of war. Promoted to communication sergeant, he fought with L Company until the end of the war. Jantz jokes about being strafed three times during World War II—once by Americans in Italy, again by the British at Montélimar, and finally by German jets later in the war.

Jantz remained in the Army and received a battlefield commission while fighting in Korea with 35th Infantry Regiment. In the 1950s and early 1960s, he rose through the officer ranks up to the grade of major. During that time, he also married and had a family. Before retiring in 1968, he was a battalion executive officer with 2nd Infantry Regiment in Vietnam.

As of the writing of this book, Rudolph is alive and well and happily settled out West. Even after three wars and more than twenty-five years of itinerant Army service, Rudy Jantz considers himself first and foremost a proud veteran of the "Can Do" 15th Infantry Regiment. He credits his military success and survival to the leadership examples of Captain Coles.[36]

His three-day experience as a prisoner of war, however, left him permanently changed in one respect: he still cannot eat corned beef in any form.[37]

Pfc. Joseph Leithner was awarded the Silver Star for his actions at Allan. He remained in L Company until the winter of 1944, when trench foot forced him into the hospital. After the war, he returned to his hometown of St. Marys, Pennsylvania, and worked as a foreman at a carbon factory. He married and had three children. Though he spoke little of the war, he mentioned from time to time the heartbreaking story of a little Italian girl who had lost both her parents to the war and became a street kid. At the time, he wished he could adopt her and bring her home—but such an arrangement was impossible. Joseph passed away in 1983.[38]

S/Sgt. Haskell O. Oliver recovered from his wounds and returned to B Company three weeks after the fight at Allan. At the same time, a fresh batch of replacements arrived in need of training. Oliver was at his best as a teacher. With an easygoing and brotherly manner, he passed along his tips on how to take advantage of every available opportunity, perform the mission, and survive. "There are a lot of heroes in this war," Oliver would say, "and most of them are dead."[39] Those who crewed for Oliver and later moved up the ranks credit their survival to his wisdom and willingness to share it.

On November 5, 1944, near the French town of Biarville,[40] S/Sgt. Oliver was helping to push a towed 3-inch anti-tank gun after it had become stuck on a gravel road. The gun was freed, but rolled forward over a hidden mine.[41] The explosion sprayed Oliver with shrapnel and gravel, ripping open his forearm and temporarily blinding him in both eyes. The doctors saved his eyesight, but gangrene nearly claimed his arm.[42]

In time, Haskell fully recovered and returned to his wife in the U.S. They had two daughters. He eventually took over his father's ranch in

California. From time to time, the ranch served as an unofficial reunion site for B Company veterans.

Haskell passed away in May 1969. His fellow tankers still remember him with great admiration and affection.

Pfc. Floyd T. Owsley recovered from his wounds received during the August 23rd artillery attack, and returned to L Company on September 29, 1944.[43] About one month later, he became ill and transferred out to a hospital. He did not return to combat. Owsley served stateside in the military police until the end of the war.

After his discharge, Floyd married and worked in Detroit for the Ford Motor Company. In the early 1950s, he graduated from the Cincinnati Bible Seminary and ministered for a few years. He went on to sell insurance and manage a newspaper route. Floyd has three children and is a grandparent and great-grandparent. Retired, he continues to live and preach the Gospel. Floyd wishes now that he had kept that 2-inch shrapnel piece pulled from his arm![44]

2nd Lt. Arnold Mackowsky eventually recovered from his gunshot wound to the knee. He did not return to L Company because he could no longer march, and so was reassigned to a quartermaster unit as a salvage repair officer.[45] He returned home after the war, married, and had children. Arnold always looked back upon his time in L Company with great fondness.[46] He passed away in September 1991.[47]

Pfc. William W. McNamara was awarded the Distinguished Service Cross for his BAR assault at Pampelonne Beach on August 15, 1944. He continued serving in L Company and became a staff sergeant. After the war, he transferred to the Air Force, served in Korea, and retired after twenty-two years. During his military service, William married and had four kids. His wife died while the children were young, and he raised them as a loving single father. A voracious reader and avid movie buff, he remained a generous and witty free spirit up until his death at the age of 77 on April 19, 2002. He is buried in Arlington National Cemetery.[48]

1st Sgt. Alvin Nusz remained B Company's top NCO and Redle's right-hand man until the end of the war. He never got used to losing men. Writing their death notices and sending their personal effects back home had a profound effect on him. After the war, Alvin married and studied to become a minister. He was ordained in 1950 and preached in Southern California for fifty years until passing away on August 29, 1999. Over the years, he struggled with debilitating back problems that began in Italy when he was pinned under the overturned tank. He is survived by his wife, two daughters, and a son.[49]

T/Sgt. George Polich finished the war in Cannon Company and returned home. He became an electrician in Washington state, married in 1948, and fathered three children. In the years that followed, Polich built and sold more than twenty homes on the side. He lost his first wife to breast cancer in 1968 and has since remarried. George retired in 1985. In 1990 and 1994, he returned to Morocco, Sicily, Italy, Southern France, and Germany to retrace his battlefield steps. When he returned home, he penned "Cannons Roar," a self-published book chronicling his service in Cannon Company. He remains active today in the Society of the Third Infantry Division.[50]

Pfc. Earl Potter returned to L Company after his short-term capture. Hospitalized briefly for exhaustion in October 1944, he returned to L Company for the duration of the war and remained during the early months of the occupation of Germany. He returned to Michigan in December 1945 after serving thirty-four months of active duty. Earl married, had two sons, and worked for more than thirty years as a machinist and carpenter. After his first wife passed away, he remarried and is now happily retired.[51]

Despite his terrifying capture at Allan and grueling march that followed, he still loves canned corned beef and pumpernickel bread.[52]

Captain David Redle finished the war as commander of B Company, 756th Tank Battalion. Throughout, he was compelled to endure the steady stream of replacement lieutenants who lost their lives under his command. Throughout his tenure, Redle remained a popular and respected officer both inside and outside his company.[53]

On January 26, 1945, near the French town of Colmar, Redle led an armored task force of tanks and tank destroyers into battle. The Germans opened fire with three machine guns, targeting the exposed tank commanders in their turret hatches. Sgt. Frank Shafer was the first to be hit. He died instantly. The next man to fall was 2nd Lt. James Haspel, a newly commissioned platoon leader. His facial wounds left him partially paralyzed. Redle's was the next tank in line, but he wiped out all three hidden machine gun nests with his turret mounted .30 caliber machine gun before they could zero in on him. His quick action not only preserved his own life, but also saved the entire attack from stalling. He was awarded the Silver Star for his bravery.[54] Redle finished his service with 756th in postwar Germany as the assistant battalion operations officer (S-3).[55]

David returned home and married his fiancé of four years. With his chemistry degree earned at Creighton University, he began a long service at the PPG Company in Akron, Ohio. He and his wife had nine children together. Both are retired now but active in 756th Tank Battalion Association. They enjoy the company of their children, grandchildren, and great-grandchildren.[56]

Sgt. Edmund Rovas led his squad of new faces until he was promoted to platoon guide. On October 25, 1944, Rovas' platoon was fighting near Les Rouges Eaux, France.[57] When a raw recruit was afraid to fire a rifle grenade, Rovas ran over to assist him. A short distance away was a German soldier dressed in an American uniform, lying flat on the ground with a raised rifle. The imposter's shot ripped into Rovas' right shoulder below the collarbone, missing his jugular by a mere quarter-inch. The injury turned out to be the "million dollar" wound that sent him home. Unfortunately, he has never again able to raise his arm above his shoulder.[58]

At first, Edmund found the transition to civilian life quite an adjustment. Sometimes, ingrained mental habits developed in combat take a long time to put fully behind you. He still remembers walking down the streets of his hometown, carefully scanning windows and rooftops for snipers.[59] Edmund married and fathered two children. He worked as a licensed electrician all his life.[60] He is retired and lives on the East Coast.

Pfc. Lloyd M. Rowe was taken alone in a separate ambulance to a distant field hospital after his wounding near Le Griffon. Several days later, he was flown out of France to finish recuperating at a Naples hospital.[61] Though his left leg was not fully healed, he was rushed to L

Company about one month later and the wound reopened. Hospitalized again, he fully recovered but finished the war in an anti-aircraft unit.

Lloyd returned to New England to his wife and young son, had three more sons, and worked as a toolmaker until he turned 65. He is retired today and enjoys fishing and being outdoors.[62]

Pfc. Fred Scarpa, the machine gunner who was walking in front of Lt. Danby's tank when it was destroyed at Allan, became a staff sergeant and squad leader in L Company. He survived the war, served for four months in the occupation of Germany, and returned home to his wife and small son. They had two more children, both girls. Fred worked at the California Naval Yard until retiring in 1976.

After WWII, he became a reservist and served in Korea, this time with the Navy. "I had enough of infantry life in World War II!" he explains, a smile beaming from ear to ear. Nevertheless, Fred and his wife continue to be proud and active members of the Society of the Third Infantry Division.[63]

Pfc. Arthur Schrader, the rifle grenadier who had his Springfield shot out of his hands at Allan, later became a staff sergeant in L Company. He survived the war, returned home, and obtained his BA and MA degrees from the University of Buffalo. After college, Arthur married a university professor and taught high school social studies. His passion, however, was music and history. He combined both as a balladeer, performing music particularly from the American Revolutionary era. He passed away on April 4, 2004, preceded by his wife of forty years.[64]

Pfc. Donald R. Sigrist was award the Bronze Star for his actions at Allan. Seriously wounded in October, he returned to L Company and was eventually made a sergeant and a squad leader. Sigrist was wounded again on December 26, 1944, and returned to L Company a second time. On January 12, 1945, the 20-year-old was killed leading a night patrol. Donald left behind his parents and three sisters in Altoona, Pennsylvania. He now rests in Epinal, France.[65]

Sgt. Lloyd Stout continued serving as a dependable, courageous tank commander in B Company until he was severely wounded on December 26, 1944, while his platoon was supporting 3rd Battalion in battle at

Bennwihr in France. During the action, the .30 caliber machine gun mounted at his turret hatch jammed. In order to clear it, Stout had to leave the turret and cling to the side of the hull. He was working on this task when a German rifleman shot him in the head. The bullet pierced the side of his nose near his left eye, ruptured his right eye, and smashed through his skull before exiting near his right ear. Despite his horrific wound, the redoubtable Stout climbed back into the tank to continue fighting but passed out a short time later.

Unconscious for several days, Stout woke up in a hospital in terrible pain, permanently blind in his right eye. X-rays showed the right side of his skull shattered like glass.

After many months of recovery, Lloyd returned home to Cedar Springs, Michigan. Despite his partial blindness and terrible headaches, he opened a local service station. In the years that followed, he underwent more than sixty separate surgeries, most to remove bone fragments lodged in and around his brain. He never married, believing that opportunity was lost to him because of his severe wound and continued symptoms.

In 1962, he began to feel ill while driving. Lloyd pulled to the side of the road and suffered a massive stroke. Some of the scar tissue in his brain had broken loose. After a heroic eighteen-year struggle, Sgt. Lloyd Stout finally succumbed to his war wounds.[66]

T/5 Emil Tikkanen remained distraught for some time over the loss of his tank crewmates at Allan. However, as he went on to drive other tanks in B Company, his bright smile, hearty laugh, and easygoing attitude returned again. Tikkanen survived the war and returned home to his wife and daughter on their Michigan dairy farm. They had two more daughters together.

After the war, Emil remained in contact with some of his B Company friends, and would occasionally tell his family of his war experiences. Whenever he spoke of southern France, he became profoundly saddened about the loss of his friends Steve Vargo and Dual Dishner, and the lieutenant who was with them for only one day. Emil passed away in May of 1981 at the age of 63.[67]

Pfc. Robert V. Tyler returned to L Company after his brief capture and was promoted to staff sergeant by the autumn of 1944.

On December 26, 1944, while fighting at Bennwihr France, Tyler selflessly attended to a wounded man for thirty minutes. He was exposed and completely vulnerable to the intense gunfire spraying the entire time. The next day, Tyler single-handedly charged a four-man machinegun nest while armed with only a rifle. He killed two Germans and forced the others to flee. For these separate actions, he was awarded the Bronze Star and the Silver Star.

During that same winter, Tyler was stricken with a severe case of trench foot. He only learned of his medals while hospitalized when his brother sent him some hometown newspaper clippings quoting the citations.

Robert never returned to combat. He returned to the states and was discharged in 1945. After completing college, he married in 1947 and spent most of his life working for Massachusetts Mutual.[68] Robert is retired and living on the East Coast.

2nd Lt. Raymond Zussman, Lt. Danby's roommate in Naples, transferred to 756th Tank Battalion two days after Danby's death, assigned as a platoon leader in A Company.[69]

While under fire near the French town of Nory-le-Bourg on September 21, 1944, Zussman literally turned into a one-man army. Confronted with a series of enemy strong points, he dismounted and led his tank on foot. Armed with only a carbine and later a Tommy gun, Zussman killed 17 Germans, took another 92 prisoner, and captured two anti-tank guns. His stunning accomplishments earned him a recommendation for the Medal of Honor.[70] One week later while that request was still in transit, a German "tree burst" shell killed him and his driver as they waited in their idle tank. 1st Lt. Arthur Abrahamson was the first to pull Zussman's lifeless body from the turret. In a death eerily similar to that of Lt. Orient, shrapnel raining down through the open hatch had struck "Little Zuss" in the head.[71] His Medal of Honor was awarded posthumously.

L Company members who survived the war include: Pfc. Pat J. Cardelli, Pfc. James D. Engel, Pfc. Winsome Enzor, Pfc. Thurman R. Evans, Pvt. William F. Hawkins, Pfc. Frank Mangina, Pfc. Patrick J. Rodger, Pfc. Robert Seegitz, Pfc. William R. Shook, Pfc. Albert Whisnant, 1st Sgt. Walter Works.[72]

Sgt. Melvin S. Singer was awarded the Silver Star for his actions on August 15, 1944, at Saint-Tropez,[73] and 2nd Lt. Fred Hodgdon became the commanding officer of F Company and an eventual DSC, Silver Star, and Bronze Star recipient.[74] Both men survived the war and returned home.

Pfc. Rheinhold Bonnett was killed in action near Saint-Germaine, France, on September 16, 1944.[75] Pfc. Harold Noble was shot and killed by a sniper in April 1945 at Nuremburg Germany.[76] Pfc. George Deal, Pfc. Richard B. Kirschner, T/Sgt. Wallace E. Lawrence and Sgt. Roy M. Sanders returned home after the war after living many months as prisoners of war.[77]

The status of the medic "Doc" LeFevre is unknown.

I Company members Captain Warren Stuart and 2nd Lt. John Tominac also survived the war. Tominac earned the Medal of Honor for his actions near Vesoul, France, in September 1944.

Cannon Company jeep driver Pfc. Gerald L. Pier received the Bronze Star his for contributions at Allan and survived the war.[78]

1st Lt. William Finley, platoon leader with 601st Tank Destroyers, survived the war but died in an auto accident one year later.[79]

B Company / 756th Tank Battalion members Pvt. (later T/4) Bert Bulen, Pfc. George Davis, and T/5 Ed Sadowski recovered from wounds sustained at Allan and returned to duty. All of them survived the war, but Sadowski was badly wounded and lost a leg on January 23, 1944, in the Colmar Pocket.

Pfc. Gene Palumbo, 2nd Lt. Bert D. Gilden, and S/Sgt. James E. Haspel also survived and returned home. However, Haspel was wounded and partially paralyzed after becoming a second lieutenant.

The identity of the bow gunner who escaped with Tikkanen from Lt. Danby's doomed tank remains a mystery. He was probably one of the last five privates listed on the DD-tank Bronze Star Award recipients roll in the appendix of this book.

T/Sgt. Donald M. Bowman, Pfc. James T. Doolin, Cpl. William F. Leaman, and 2nd Lt. Andrew D. Orient are buried at the Rhône-American Cemetery in Draguignan France.[80]

Pfc. James J. Lovascio, Pfc. Norval A. Monroe, and Pfc. Louis Polonsky were reburied in the United States at the request of their families.[81]

1st Lt. Edgar R. Danby, Cpl. Steve Vargo, and Pvt. Dual F. Dishner share a common grave and final resting place at the Zachary Taylor National Cemetery in Louisville, Kentucky.[82]

I have been unable to find accurate casualty figures for the number of German soldiers killed or wounded at Allan. Anecdotal evidence indicates that the total killed may have been as many as twenty. The U.S. Army removed some of the bodies, and French civilians buried others. Surviving Graves Registration records are incomplete. After the war, the German government tried to recover all the remains of their fallen men still in the area. The local French are satisfied that the mission was successful. However, the current organization (The Volksbund) in charge of searching for missing German soldiers has records for only four casualties specific to Allan. They are identified only as German soldiers of Russian descent. All four men are buried at Montélimar.[83]

Mothers, fathers, wives, and families never learned what became of their sons, husbands, and fathers. Due to the chaos of the time, the stories of their final minutes on earth and the present location of their remains are known only to God.

*   *   *

The Tragic Story of T/Sgt. Edward R. Rider

T/Sgt. Edward R. Rider is not specifically mentioned in the main story of this book, but he fought with L Company in every action.

Rider was from Texas and looked it. His face blended the fine features and high cheekbones of his mixed Native American ancestry with that of a tanned, rugged cowboy. He was also a steady and dependable soldier. At the time of the Southern France Campaign, Rider was a squad leader in Weapons Platoon. His service with L Company extends as far back as the Fort Ord training days in California—long before the invasion of North Africa. Except for one thirty-day rotation stateside, Rider served in L Company from the beginning to the end of the war—an astonishing two-and one-half years of active service. He ended his service as platoon sergeant.

After the war, Edward was discharged in New York. Rather than board a train for Texas, he purchased a car with the money he saved during his service and set out on the highway. He never made it home. Along the way, he crashed the vehicle and was killed.[84]

No man in L Company traveled so far for so long, only to fall so close to home.

"The pain of war cannot exceed the woe of aftermath."
— Robert Plant, "Battle of Evermore"

Appendix A

Rosters and Awards

(See Glossary for explanation of abbreviations)

DD–Tank Bronze Star Medals

The 3rd Division awarded the Bronze Star to each DD–tank crewmember participating in the first assault wave on August 15, 1944 at "Yellow Beach." Listed below are the twenty members of the 3rd Platoon of Company B/756th Tank Battalion who qualified:

2nd Lt. Andrew Orient
S/Sgt. Haskell Oliver
Sgt. Roy Anderson
Sgt. Lloyd Stout
Cpl. Steve Vargo
Cpl. Delmar McIntyre
Cpl. Raymond Colley
T/5 Edward Sadowski
T/5 Emil Tikkanen
T/5 Jesse Rickerson
T/5 Elbert Rainwater
T/5 Frank Ware
Pfc. George Davis
Pvt. Bert Bulen
Pvt. Dual Dishner
Pvt. George Fick
Pvt. Edward Skinner
Pvt. Ruben Fries
Pvt. Frank Mandalski
Pvt. Merton Weatherwax

Other Medals Awarded to L Company Men for Actions at Saint–Tropez, France on August 15, 1944

Citation, Rank & Name (when awarded)
DSC, Pfc. William W. McNamara
Silver Star, S/Sgt. Melvin S. Singer

Medals Awarded for Actions at Allan, France, August 27-28, 1944

Citation, Rank & Name (when awarded), Unit,
DSC, Captain James W. Coles, L / 15th
DSC, S/Sgt. Dominick Delmonico, L / 15th
Silver Star, S/Sgt. Joseph W. Leithner Jr., L / 15th
Silver Star, S/Sgt. Cedric E. Porter, K / 15th,
Bronze Star, 1st Lt. Lloyd H. Cotter, Cannon / 15th,
Bronze Star, Pfc. Gerald L. Pier, Cannon / 15th,
Bronze Star, +Sgt. Donald R. Sigrist, L / 15th,
+ = KIA later in the war.

Casualties at Allan, France, on August 27, 1944

Killed in Action:

Rank & Name, Unit, Notes
T/Sgt. Donald M. Bowman, L / 15th, KIA SFW left side
Cpl. William F. Leaman, L / 15th, KIA SFW left hip
Pfc. James T. Doolin, L / 15th, KIA GSW right chest, died at Aid Station
Pfc. James J. Lovascio, L / 15th, KIA SFW face
Pfc. Norval A. Monroe, L / 15th, KIA SFW head
Pfc. Louis Polonsky, L / 15th, KIA GSW head
1st Lt. Edgar R. Danby, B / 756th, KIA in tank from German AP round
Cpl. Steve Vargo, B / 756th, KIA in tank from German AP round
Pvt. Dual F. Dishner, B / 756th, KIA in tank from German AP round

Wounded in Action:

Captain James W. Coles, L / 15th, LWA SFW (remained on duty)
*2nd Lt. Arnold Mackowsky, L / 15th, WIA GSW leg (did not return)
S/Sgt. James P. Pierce, L / 15th, WIA details unknown (returned 10/11/44)
Sgt. Melvin S. Singer, L / 15th, WIA details unknown (returned 10/17/44)
Pfc. Harvey Legault, L / 15th, WIA details unknown (returned 12/26/44)
Pvt. Angelo Castillo, L / 15th, WIA details unknown (returned 12/22/44)
Pvt. Lloyd B. Jaynes, L / 15th, WIA details unknown (did not return)
Pfc. Scott V. Szurley, K / 15th, WIA details unknown

1st Lt. Lloyd Cotter, Cannon/15th, LWA GSW right hip (remained on duty)
S/Sgt. Haskell O. Oliver, B / 756th, LWA details unknown (returned 9/19/44)
T/5 Edward J. Sadowski, B / 756th, LWA details unknown (returned 9/5/44)
Pfc. George C. Davis, B / 756th, LWA details unknown (returned 9/6/44)
Pvt. Bertie L. Bulen, B / 756th, LWA details unknown (returned 9/6/44)

Missing in Action:

*2nd Lt. Arnold Mackowsky, L / 15th, Captured 2 days, liberated 8/29/44
T/Sgt. Wallace E. Lawrence, L / 15th, PW (unspecified camp)
Sgt. Roy M. Sanders, L / 15th, PW (Stalag 3C, Brandenburg)
Pfc. Rheinhold E. Bonnett, L / 15th, Captured 3 days, escaped & returned
    8/30/44
Pfc. Pat J. Cardelli, L / 15th, Captured 3 days, escaped & returned 8/30/44
Pfc. George Deal, L / 15th, PW (Stalag 4B, Muhlberg)
Pfc. James D. Engel, L / 15th, Captured 6 days, escaped & returned 9/2/44
Pfc. Thurman R. Evans, L / 15th, Captured 6 days, escaped & returned 9/2/44
Pfc. Rudolph A. Jantz, L / 15th, Captured 3 days, escaped & returned 8/30/44
Pfc. Richard B. Kirschner, L / 15th, PW (Stalag 4B, Muhlberg)
Pfc. Frank Mangina, L / 15th, Captured 6 days, escaped & returned 9/2/44
Pfc. Earl V. Potter, L / 15th, Captured 6 days, escaped & returned 9/2/44
Pfc. Robert V. Tyler, L / 15th, Captured 3 days, escaped & returned 8/30/44
*Lt. Mackowsky is listed on both the Wounded in Action and Missing in Action
    lists.

Roster for L Company/15th Infantry Regiment, August 15 to 31, 1944
(Rank Order) (See explanation notes at the end of the chart.)

The following roster was reconstructed by analyzing all L Company
"Morning Report" entries from January 1 to December 31, 1944, obtained from
the National Personnel Records Center in St. Louis. Data was compared to the
15th Infantry Regiment roster in the book: *The History of the Third Infantry
Division in World War II,* and the online registers of WWII casualties, prisoners
of war, and overseas graves at the National Archives and the American
Battlefield Monuments Commission websites. (See bibliography.) Dates listed
are 1944 unless otherwise noted.

Seven officers and 199 enlisted men are listed—accounting for nearly
everyone on the L Company rolls at the time. (A duty count of seven officers and
203 enlisted men was given for the morning of August 15, 1944.)

The first column lists the names of all members present for duty at any point
during the period August 15 through August 31, 1944. These names are
organized first by rank, and then alphabetically by last name. Individuals not on
duty during the Allan fight are indented with a wedge symbol (>). The asterisk
(*) indicates members with less than four months of service in L Company

(joining after April 15, 1944) Roughly one-third of the company were replacements who joined after that date.

The second column lists each individual's army serial number.

The third column provides up to three separate pieces of information. Whenever reported by the Morning Reports, an individual's Military Occupational Specialty (MOS) is noted first. Some MOS numbers were never given or were several months old. Therefore, the reader should not consider them as very reliable.

All duty status changes between August 15 and 31, 1944 are also noted, along with a few other pertinent changes reported during September 1944.

Finally, the end-of-the-war status for each man is also noted. Of the 206 listed names, twenty-five were killed before the war ended. Twelve others were captured and sent to German prisoner of war camps. Of the 169 survivors, only forty-seven remained with L Company as of January 1, 1945—most others were forced out through the grinding attrition of battle, illness, and prolonged exposure to the elements. Four-and-a-half months after landing at Saint-Tropez and leading L Company, none of the original seven officers remained.

The names of 785 different individuals appear on the L Company "Morning Reports" for the 1944 calendar year. 129 of those names are followed with entries of "killed in action" or "died of wounds." A WWII U.S. infantry company at full strength had 193 men. L Company's 1944 turnover was nearly four times that number, with battle deaths alone accounting for two-thirds of a company roster. This was only one year for an infantry company that served two full years in combat.

Rank & Name, Serial #, Notes

Captain James W. Coles (Commanding Officer) (Captured 9/16), Survived
1st Lt. George S. Burks (Executive Officer) Survived
1st Lt. Robert Bernhardt*, Survived
2nd Lt. Charles Adams (Special Duty at 3rd ID HQ) KIA–1/3/45
2nd Lt. Fred Hodgdon*, Survived
2nd Lt. Woods B. Kyle, Survived
2nd Lt. Arnold L. Mackowsky* (WIA & Captured 8/27, recovered (8/29)
      Survived
1st Sgt. Walter M. Works* (585–First Sergeant) Survived
T/Sgt. Donald M. Bowman* KIA 8/27/44
T/Sgt. Reid L. Houghtaling, Survived
T/Sgt. Wallace E. Lawrence (651–Platoon Sgt) (Captured 8/27, PW) Survived
   >S/Sgt. Sam Badalamento* (651–Platoon Sgt) (Sick 8/22 to 8/28) Survived
S/Sgt. Andrew Christensen*, Survived
S/Sgt. Gervase F. Dauby (821–Supply Sgt) Survived
S/Sgt. George Fischer*, KIA–9/28/44
S/Sgt. Jessie O. Hickerson (Promoted from Sgt 8/21) Survived

S/Sgt. Ewald Kramlich (652–Section Leader) (Sick 8/27-9/13) Survived
>S/Sgt. Robert C. Maddox (653–Squad Leader) (WIA 8/15) Survived
>S/Sgt. Lewis K. Marsh* (WIA 8/23-12/22) Survived
S/Sgt. Wilbur V. Mueller (824–Mess Sergeant) Survived
S/Sgt. James P. Pierce (653–Squad Leader) (WIA 8/27-10/11) Survived
>S/Sgt. James Pilgrim (652–Section Leader) (Sick 8/25-10/4) Survived
S/Sgt. Edward R. Rider (653–Squad Leader) Survived
S/Sgt. Francis P. Sholly (653–Squad Leader) Survived
Sgt. Luther Dillie (542–Communications Chief) Survived
Sgt. Fred F. Gant (653–Squad Leader) Survived
>Sgt. Carlis B. Jackson (Sick 8/23-9/13) Survived
Sgt. Edwin B. Nock (405–Clerk/Typist) DOW–5/5/45
Sgt. John W. Osborne (653–Squad Leader) Survived
Sgt. Edmund J. Rovas (LWA–8/18, Sick 8/27-9/13) Survived
Sgt. Roy M. Sanders* (653–Squad Leader) (Captured 8/27, PW) Survived
Sgt. Melvin S. Singer, (745–Rifleman) (WIA 8/27-10/17) Survived
Sgt. Robert E. Sinks, (Promoted from Pvt. 8/23) Survived
Sgt. Bernard R. Snyder*, (Promoted from Pvt. 8/23) Survived
T/4 Leroy L. Birgam, Survived
T/4 Kenneth D. Lewis, (060–Cook) Survived
T/4 Hercule A. Roy, Survived
Cpl. Phillip J. Byerly, (653–Squad Leader) Survived
Cpl. John F. Da Bell, (WIA 5/24, rejoined 8/18) Survived
Cpl. Dominick Delmonico, (653–Squad Leader) Survived
Cpl. William F. Leaman, (653–Squad Leader) KIA–8/27/44
Cpl. Wayne H. Schmuhl, (653–Squad Leader) Survived
Cpl. Henry J. Tillman, Survived
Cpl. Junior M. Wellfare, (653–Squad Leader) Survived
T/5 Herman B. Cogdell, (653–Squad Leader) Survived
T/5 Melvin C. Heaton, (803–Bugler) (Captured 9/5, PW) Survived
T/5 Edward A. Quirk, (055–General Clerk) Survived
T/5 Woodrow K. Wilson, (511–Armorer, Artificer) Survived
Pfc. Francis J. Andrews*, (745–Rifleman) Survived
Pfc. Dorris J. Barton*, Survived
Pfc. Stephen Basca, Survived
Pfc. Jacques J. M. Belanger*, (320–Intepretter) Survived
Pfc. Owen D. Bell, KIA–9/28/44
Pfc. Rheinhold E. Bonnett, (345–jeep driver) KIA–9/16/44
Pfc. Norwood O. Brooks*, KIA–11/5/44
Pfc. Clifford Buchanan, (604–Light Machine Gunner) Survived
Pfc. Dennis G. Buswell, (675–Messenger) Survived
Pfc. Grover G. Cagle, Survived
Pfc. Pat J. Cardelli, Survived
Pfc. Plynn Q. Carpenter*, (WIA since 5/23, rejoined 8/18-8/29) Survived

Pfc. Arco A. Ciancanelli, Survived
Pfc. John R. Clifford, (604–Light Machine Gunner) Survived
Pfc. Mauyer E. Cox, (607–Mortar Gunner) (Sick 8/29-9/13) Survived
Pfc. William P. Curkendall, (745–Rifleman) Survived
Pfc. Neil W. Daughenbaugh, (675–Messenger) Survived
Pfc. George Deal*, (745–Rifleman) (Captured 8/27, PW) Survived
Pfc. John W. Dearmond*, Survived
Pfc. Neill E. Derick, (675–Messenger) Survived
Pfc. Constantine DiFranco*, (Sick 8/17-10/1) Survived
Pfc. John W. Dolan, Survived
Pfc. James T. Doolin, (745–Rifleman) KIA–8/27/44
Pfc. Chester J. Dylewski, (745–Rifleman) Survived
Pfc. James D. Engel*, (745–Rifleman) (Captured 8/27-9/2) Survived
>Pfc. Winsome Enzor*, (745–Rifleman) (WIA 8/23-10/28) Survived
Pfc. Thurman R. Evans*, (745–Rifleman) (Captured 8/27-9/2) Survived
Pfc. Salvatore Fasciana, Survived
Pfc. Sol Feldman*, (745–Rifleman) Survived
Pfc. Joe W. Finley, (746–Automatic Rifleman) Survived
Pfc. Leo E. Fitzpatrick, (607–Mortar Gunner) Survived
Pfc. John Frazer Jr.*, (745–Rifleman) Survived
Pfc. Michael Gobbi, (675–Messenger) Survived
Pfc. Ralph J. Grenier*, (504–Ammo Bearer) Survived
Pfc. Michael Guerra*, (746–Automatic Rifleman) Survived
Pfc. Walter Harman, (Sick 8/20-8/27) Survived
Pfc. James S. Hart, KIA 10/26/44
Pfc. James W. Hatchell*, (745–Rifleman) KIA 9/28/44
Pfc. Herbert J. Hinson*, (745–Rifleman) Survived
Pfc. Thomas E. Horrobin Jr., Survived
Pfc. James F. Hunt, Survived
Pfc. Rudolph A. Jantz, (675–Messenger) (Captured 8/27-8/30) Survived
Pfc. Elihu Jordan*, (761–Scout, observer) Survived
Pfc. Richard B. Kirschner*, (745–Rifleman) (Captured 8/27, PW) Survived
Pfc. Robert E. Knight, Survived
Pfc. John S. Krok, Survived
Pfc. Raymond R. LeClair, (Captured 9/5, PW) Survived
Pfc. Harvey V. Legault*, (745–Rifleman) (WIA 8/27-12/26) Survived
Pfc. Joseph W. Leithner Jr, Survived
Pfc. George T. Loudermilk, (607–Mortar Gunner) Survived
Pfc. James J. Lovascio, KIA–8/27/44
Pfc. Kenneth D. Lynch, (745–Rifleman) (Captured 9/5, PW) Survived
Pfc. Virgil L. Lytle, Survived
Pfc. Victor M. Madrigal, (675–Messenger) Survived
Pfc. Frank Mangina*, (Captured 8/27-9/2) Survived
Pfc. Dale M. Marker, Survived
Pfc. Nicholas Massow*, KIA–9/28/44

>Pfc. Stanley Matuszewski, (Sick 8/20-9/13) Survived
Pfc. Joseph D. McGahan*, (405–Clerk/Typist) Survived
Pfc. James A. McLaughlin, (Captured 9/5, PW) Survived
Pfc. William W. McNamara, Survived
Pfc. Robert E. Merrow, KIA–10/4/44
Pfc. Charles J. Miller, Survived
Pfc. Norval A. Monroe*, (761–Scout/Observer) KIA–8/27/44
Pfc. Wallace R. Moore, Survived
Pfc. James W. Morrow*, (746–Automatic Rifleman) Survived
Pfc. Clarence H. Nagel*, (745–Rifleman) Survived
Pfc. Merle A. Nelson*, (504–Ammo Bearer) Survived
Pfc. Harold J. Noble, (675–Messenger) KIA–1945, near Nuremburg
Pfc. James W. Odom*, (745–Rifleman) Survived
Pfc. Lee H. Ogletree*, (745–Rifleman) Survived
Pfc. Dominick Ortiz, (675–Messenger) Survived
>Pfc Floyd T. Owsley, (745–Rifleman) (WIA 8/23-9/29) Survived
Pfc. Augustus A. Pacine, (745–Rifleman) DOW–10/22/44
Pfc. Carl Pasternack, (745–Rifleman) Survived
Pfc. Louis Polonsky, (745–Rifleman) KIA–8/27/44
Pfc. Earl V. Potter*, (675–Messenger) (Captured 8/27-9/2) Survived
Pfc. Luther S. Prentice, (675–Messenger) Survived
Pfc. William S. Purnell, Survived
Pfc. Patrick J. Rodger, (746–Automatic Rifleman) Survived
Pfc. Donald C. Ross, Survived
Pfc. Leon W. Rowe, (745–Rifleman) KIA–4/17/45
>Pfc. Lloyd M. Rowe, (745–Rifleman) (WIA 8/23-12/7) Survived
Pfc. Orvin C. Rowland, (745–Rifleman) Survived
Pfc. Anthony L. Scaccia, Survived
Pfc. Fred Scarpa, (504–Ammo Bearer) Survived
>Pfc. William B. Schettini, (Sick 8/27-9/13) Survived
>Pfc. Earl O. Schick, (WIA 8/15-) Survived
Pfc. Arthur F. Schrader, Survived
Pfc. Kenneth N. Scott*, (745–Rifleman) Survived
Pfc. Robert Seegitz, (745–Rifleman) Survived
Pfc. Edwin S. Shoff, Survived
Pfc. William R. Shook, (675–Messenger) Survived
Pfc. Donald R. Sigrist, KIA–1/12/45
>Pfc. Vincent Skerl*, (745–Rifleman) (Sick 8/22-9/13) Survived
Pfc. Harold J. Smith, (060–Cook) Survived
Pfc. Albert F. Steinkamp, Survived
Pfc. Roger L. Swanson*, Survived
Pfc. Alfred S. Szatkowski, (745–Rifleman) Survived
Pfc. Joseph A.Tarczon, (745–Rifleman) Survived
Pfc. Dallas P. Taylor*, (745–Rifleman) (Captured 9/5, PW) Survived

Pfc. Joseph W. Thigpen, (607–Mortar Gunner) KIA–9/27/44
Pfc. Charles L. Thomison*, (745–Rifleman) Survived
Pfc. Benjamin F. Tilley*, (746–Automatic Rifleman) Survived
Pfc. Homer R. Toman*, (745–Rifleman) (Captured 9/5, PW) Survived
>Pfc. Michael Torcivia*, (745) (LWA 8/15, Sick 8/17-9/4) Survived
Pfc. Richard N. Totte, (Sick 7/3, rejoined 8/22) Survived
Pfc. Lamar S. Trude, KIA–9/28/44
Pfc. Euzell L. Tucker, (345–Jeep Driver) (Captured 9/16, PW) Survived
Pfc. Benjamin Turoczi*, (745–Rifleman) Survived
Pfc. Robert V. Tyler, (746–Auto Rifle) (Captured 8/27-8/30) Survived
Pfc. Christopher S. Verzyl*, (745–Rifleman) KIA–9/27/44
>Pfc. Emil J. Vojtek*, (745–Rifleman) (Sick 8/25-10/28) Survived
Pfc. Ralph H. Walburn*, (745–Rifleman) Survived
Pfc. Edward L. Walsh, (504–Ammo Bearer) Survived
>Pfc Thomas F. Walsh*, (745–Rifleman) (WIA 8/15-) Survived
Pfc. Earl J. Whipple*, (745–Rifleman) Survived
Pfc. Albert Whisnant*, (745–Rifleman) Survived
Pfc. Walter F. White, (745–Rifleman) Survived
Pfc. Burleigh F. Whitney*, (504–Ammo Bearer) Survived
Pfc. Morris S. Whitt*, (745–Rifleman) Survived
Pfc. Reece O. Wiles*, (745–Rifleman) Survived
Pfc. Wilmer D. Willard*, (745–Rifleman) Survived
Pfc. Roy R. Williams*, (745–Rifleman) Survived
Pfc. William A. Winters Jr., Survived
>Pfc. James D. Woody*, (745–Rifleman) (Sick 8/26-9/13) Survived
>Pvt. David B. Allen, (AWOL/Arraignment camp 8/24-9/7) Survived
Pvt. George E. Browne*, (521–Basic) Survived
Pvt. Richard C. Carter Jr.*, (745–Rifleman) Survived
Pvt. Angelo Castillo*, Survived
>Pvt. Jessie E. Clark, (AWOL from 8/24-8/28) Survived
>Pvt. Manuel O. Cordova, (AWOL/Arraignment camp 8/24-9/7) Survived
Pvt. Chester L. Darrah, Survived
>Pvt. Michael J. Dower, (Sick 8/25-11/28) Survived
Pvt. Lonnie E. Farmer*, (745–Rifleman) (AWOL 8/15-8/21) Survived
Pvt. Andrew L. Garbarini, Survived
>Pvt. Bernard Greive*, (745–Rifleman) (WIA 8/23-) Survived
Pvt. Harry J. Halenda*, Survived
Pvt. William F. Hawkins Jr.*, (745–Rifleman) Survived
Pvt. Lloyd B. Jaynes*, (745–Rifleman) (WIA 8/27-) Survived
Pvt. John C. MacKinnon, Survived
Pvt. Patrick P. McEldowney, Survived
Pvt. Frederick H. Miller, (745–Rifleman; later, 320–Interpretter) Survived
Pvt. Nick J. Pappas, Survived
Pvt. John J. Pelis Jr., (745–Rifleman) Survived
Pvt. Edward Perlson, Survived

Pvt.Clayton V. Post, (675–Messenger) Survived
Pvt. Virgil L. Reed, (745–Rifleman) MIA–9/12/44 with FOD
Pvt. Harold R. Reyell, (675–Messenger) Survived
Pvt. Joe M. Rico, (AWOL 8/21-8/21) Survived
Pvt. Leonard Y. Rosenberg, (745–Rifleman) Survived
Pvt. James E. Ross*, Survived
Pvt. Bennie C. Skaggs*, (745–Rifleman) Survived
Pvt. Riley L. Sproul*, DOW–2/15/45
Pvt. John D. Stoneking*, (745–Rifleman) Survived
>Pvt. Michael Suhow, (653)(Cpl. to Pvt. 7/29)(Sick 8/26-9/13) Survived
Pvt. Carl S. Sutton*, (745–Rifleman) Survived
Pvt. George W. Watkins*, (745–Rifleman) Survived

The Ten FFI Members Killed in or near Allan, France, on March 30, 1944:

Executed

Lt. Daniel Quinaud (wounded first at Châteauneuf-du-Rhône)
René Barrallon
Jean Brisset
Paul Garraud
Georges Lemaire
André Marron
Louis Vincent

Killed in Combat:

Lt. Marcel Delaby (at Châteauneuf-du-Rhône)
Pierre Masson (at the Aubagne Farm)
Louis Bied (at the Aubagne Farm)

Appendix B

Glossary of Terms, Acronyms,
and Abbreviations

AAA: Anti aircraft artillery
Ack-ack: Anti aircraft fire
Adjutant: Assistant to a commanding officer at battalion level and above
AFHQ: Allied Forces Headquarters
Airburst: Artillery round intended to explode above ground
AP: Armor piercing
AT: Anti tank
AWOL: Absent without official leave
BAR: Browning automatic rifle
Bazooka: Nickname for U.S. handheld anti-tank rocket fired from a tube
Bn: Battalion
Burp gun: GI nickname for a German Schmeisser machine pistol
Cal: Short for "Caliber," which describes the diameter of a bullet or shell.
CO: Commanding officer
CP: Command post
DD-Tank: Duplex drive tank
Doughboy: A slang term to describe a U.S. infantryman popularized during WWI
DOW: Died of wounds
DSC: Distinguished Service Cross
DUKW: 2 & 1/2-ton Amphibious truck (also nicknamed "Duck")
FAITC: Fifth Army Invasion Training Center
Feldgrau: German for "field grey," the color of German Army uniforms
FFI: "Forces Françaises de l'Intérieur" (French Forces of the Interior)
Flak: "Flugzeug Abwehr Kanone" (German term for anti aircraft gun.)
FOD: Finding of Death (Determined in cases where no body can be found)
FTP: "Francs-Tireurs et Partisans" (French communist resistance forces)
G-2: Division-level intelligence officer
G-3: Division-level operations officer
Garand: M-1 U.S. semi-automatic rifle nicknamed after designer, John Garand
GI: "Government Issue." Slang term describing a U.S. soldier.

GSW: Gunshot wound
HE: High explosive
Howitzer: Artillery gun which lobs shells on parabolic trajectories onto targets
ID: Infantry Division
IR: Infantry Regiment
ITC: Invasion Training Center
KIA: Killed in action
LCT: Landing Craft Tanks
LCVP: Landing Craft Vehicle/Personnel
LST: Landing Ship Tanks
LWA: Lightly wounded in action
MIA: Missing in action
mm: Millimeter (25.4 mm equals one inch)
MOH: Medal of Honor
Mortar: Small muzzle-loading, low velocity artillery piece used by the infantry
MP: Military Police
NCO: Non commissioned officer (corporal through sergeant ranks)
OCS: Officer candidate school
OD: Olive drab (as in American uniform and vehicle colors)
PAK: "Panzer Abwehr Kanone" (German term for anti-tank gun)
Panther: Nickname for the German PzKpfw V or "Mark V" tank.
Panzer: "Armor" (German short term for a tank)
Panzerfaust: "Tank fist" (German handheld AT rocket similar to U.S. bazooka)
PzKpfw: Translates as "armored battle wagon" (German abbrev. for a tank)
Pillbox: Small concrete structure housing machine gun or AT gun nest
PW: Prisoner of war
R&R: Rest and relaxation
ROTC: Reserve Officer Training Corps
S-2: Battalion-level intelligence officer
S-3: Battalion-level operations officer
SFW: Shell fragment wound
SP gun: Self-propelled gun (Artillery, AT, or AAA gun mounted on a vehicle)
StuG: Short for "Sturmgeschütz," a German self-propelled AT gun.
SWA: Severely wounded in action
TD: Tank destroyer
Tommy gun: Nickname for .50-cal U.S. Thompson M1A1 submachine gun
Waffen SS: Military forces of the German National Socialist Party.
WIA: Wounded in action
XO: Executive Officer

Appendix C

Tables of Organizations and Rank Insignia

U.S. Infantry Battalion Table of Organization - 1944
(35 Officers, 836 Enlisted Men Total)

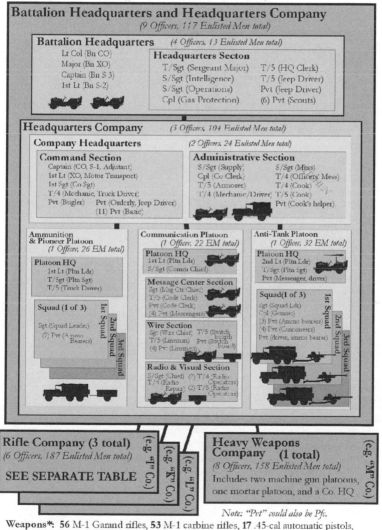

Battalion Headquarters and Headquarters Company
(9 Officers, 117 Enlisted Men total)

Battalion Headquarters *(4 Officers, 13 Enlisted Men total)*

Lt Col (Bn CO)
Major (Bn XO)
Captain (Bn S 3)
1st Lt (Bn S-2)

Headquarters Secton
T/Sgt (Sergeant Major)   T/5 (HQ Clerk)
S/Sgt (Intelligence)   T/5 (Jeep Driver)
S/Sgt (Operations)   Pvt (Jeep Driver)
Cpl (Gas Protection)   (6) Pvt (Scouts)

Headquarters Company *(5 Officers, 104 Enlisted Men total)*

Company Headquarters *(2 Officers, 24 Enlisted Men total)*

Command Section
Captain (CO, S-1, Adjutant)
1st Lt (XO, Motor Transport)
1st Sgt (Co Sgt)
T/4 (Mechanic, Truck Driver)
Pvt (Bugler)   Pvt (Orderly, Jeep Driver)
(11) Pvt (Basic)

Administrative Section
S/Sgt (Supply)   S/Sgt (Mess)
Cpl (Co Clerk)   T/4 (Officers' Mess)
T/5 (Armorer)   T/4 (Cook)
T/4 (Mechanic/Driver)   T/5 (Cook)
Pvt (Cook's helper)

Ammunition & Pioneer Platoon
(1 Officer, 26 EM total)

Platoon HQ
1st Lt (Pltn Ldr)
T/Sgt (Pltn Sgt)
T/5 (Truck Driver)

Squad (1 of 3)
Sgt (Squad Leader)
(7) Pvt (Ammo Bearers)

1st Squad
2nd Squad
3rd Squad

Communication Platoon
(1 Officer, 22 EM total)

Platoon HQ
1st Lt (Pltn Ldr)
S/Sgt (Comm Chief)

Message Center Section
Sgt (Msg Ctr Chief)
T/5 (Code Clerk)
Pvt (Code Clerk)
(4) Pvt (Messengers)

Wire Section
Sgt (Wire Chief)   T/5 (Switchboard)
T/5 (Lineman)   Pvt (Switchboard)
(4) Pvt (Linemen)

Radio & Visual Section
S/Sgt (Chief)   (7) T/4 (Radio Operators)
T/4 (Radio Repair)   (2) T/5 (Radio Operators)

Anti-Tank Platoon
(1 Officer, 32 EM total)

Platoon HQ
2nd Lt (Pltn Ldr)
T/Sgt (Pltn Sgt)
Pvt (Messenger, driver)

Squad (1 of 3)
Sgt (Squad Ldr)
Cpl (Gunner)
(3) Pvt (Ammo bearers)
(4) Pvt (Cannoneers)
Pvt (driver, ammo bearer)

1st Squad
2nd Squad
3rd Squad

Rifle Company (3 total)
(6 Officers, 187 Enlisted Men total)

SEE SEPARATE TABLE

(e.g. "I" Co.)
(e.g. "K" Co.)
(e.g. "L" Co.)

Heavy Weapons Company (1 total)
(8 Officers, 158 Enlisted Men total)
Includes two machine gun platoons, one mortar platoon, and a Co. HQ

(e.g. "M" Co.)

Note: "Pvt" could also be Pfc.

Weapons*: 56 M-1 Garand rifles, 53 M-1 carbine rifles, 17 .45-cal automatic pistols, 8 2.36-inch bazookas, 2 .50-cal heavy barrel machine gun, 3 57mm towed anti-tank guns

Vehicles*: 9 Jeeps, 1 3/4-ton truck, 4 1&1/2-ton trucks, 1 1-ton trailer, 2 1/4-ton trailers

*Totals pertain to Battalion HQ and HQ Companies only, and do not include material assigned to the Heavy Weapons or Rifle Companies

Table based on War Dept Feb 26, 1944 T/O & E 7-16

©2005 Jeff Danby

U.S. Infantry Rifle Company Table of Organization - 1944

(6 Officers, 187 Enlisted Men Total)

Company Headquarters *(2 Officers, 33 Enlisted Total)*

Command Section

Captain (CO)	(3) Pvt (Messengers)
1st Lt (XO)	(17) Pvt (Basic)
1st Sgt (Co Sgt)	
Sgt (Communications)	
Pvt (Bugler)	

Administrative Section

S/Sgt (Supply)	S/Sgt (Mess)
Cpl (Co Clerk)	(2) T/4 (Cooks)
T/5 (Armorer)	(2) T/5 (Cooks)
	(2) Pvt (Cook's Helpers)

Rifle Platoon (1 of 3)

(1 Officer, 40 Enlisted Total)*

Platoon HQ

2nd Lt (Pltn Ldr)	S/Sgt (Pltn Guide)
T/Sgt (Pltn Sgt)	(2) Pvt (Messengers)

1st Squad *(12 EM Total)*
S/Sgt (Squad Ldr)
Sgt (Asst Squad Ldr)
Pvt (BAR)
Pvt (BAR Asst)
Pvt (Ammo Bearer)
(7) Pvt (Riflemen)

2nd Squad *(12 EM Total)*
S/Sgt (Squad Ldr)
Sgt (Asst Squad Ldr)
Pvt (BAR)
Pvt (BAR Asst)
Pvt (Ammo Bearer)
(7) Pvt (Riflemen)

3rd Squad *(12 EM Total)*
S/Sgt (Squad Ldr)
Sgt (Asst Squad Ldr)
Pvt (BAR)
Pvt (BAR Asst)
Pvt (Ammo Bearer)
(7) Pvt (Riflemen)

One of the three rifle Company platoons was led by a 1st Lieutenant.

1st Platoon   *2nd Platoon*   *3rd Platoon*

4th Platoon

Weapons Platoon

(1 Officer, 34 Enlisted Total)

Platoon HQ

1st Lt (Pltn Ldr)	(2) T/5 (Jeep Drivers)
T/Sgt (Pltn Sgt)	(2) Pvt (Messengers)

60mm Mortar Section *(17 EM Total)*

Section HQ
S/Sgt (Section Ldr)   Pvt (Messenger)

1st Squad	Pvt (Assistant)
Sgt (Squad Ldr)	(2) Pvt (Ammo
Pvt (Mortarman)	(Bearers)

2nd Squad	Pvt (Assistant)
Sgt (Squad Ldr)	(2) Pvt (Ammo
Pvt (Mortarman)	(Bearers)

3rd Squad	Pvt (Assistant)
Sgt (Squad Ldr)	(2) Pvt (Ammo
Pvt (Mortarman)	(Bearers)

Light Machine Gun Section *(12 EM Total)*

Section HQ
S/Sgt (Section Ldr)   Pvt (Messenger)

1st Squad	
Sgt (Squad Ldr)	Pvt (MG Assistant)
Pvt (MG)	(2) Pvt (Ammo Bearers)

2nd Squad	
Sgt (Squad ldr)	Pvt (MG Assistant)
Pvt (MG)	(2) Pvt (Ammo Bearers)

Note: "Pvt" could also be Pfc.

Weapons: 143 M-1 Garand rifles, 28 M-1 carbine rifles, 10 .45-cal automatic pistols, 9 BARs, 5 2.36-inch bazookas, 3 60mm mortars, 3 M1903A4 rifles with scopes, 2 .30-cal light machine guns, 1 .50-cal heavy barrel machine gun.

Vehicles: 2 Jeeps with 1/4-ton ammunition trailers.

Table based on War Dept Feb 26, 1944 T/O & E 7-17

©2005 Jeff Danby

U.S. Medium Tank Company Table of Organization - 1944

(5 Officers, 112 Enlisted Men Total)

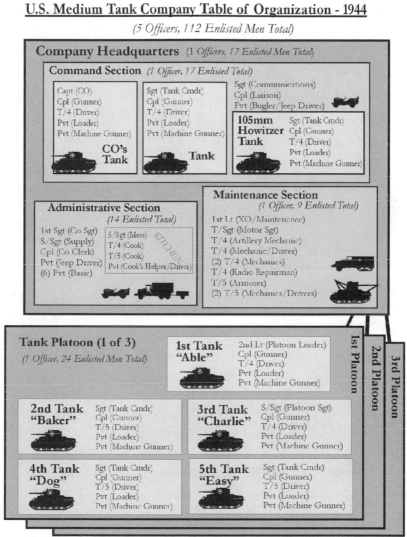

Company Headquarters (1 Officers, 17 Enlisted Men Total)

Command Section (1 Officer, 17 Enlisted Total)

Capt (CO)	Sgt (Tank Cmdr)	Sgt (Communications)
Cpl (Gunner)	Cpl (Gunner)	Cpl (Liaison)
T/4 (Driver)	T/4 (Driver)	Pvt (Bugler/Jeep Driver)
Pvt (Loader)	Pvt (Loader)	**105mm** Sgt (Tank Cmdr)
Pvt (Machine Gunner)	Pvt (Machine Gunner)	**Howitzer** Cpl (Gunner)
CO's Tank	**Tank**	**Tank** T/4 (Driver)
		Pvt (Loader)
		Pvt (Machine Gunner)

Administrative Section
(14 Enlisted Total)

1st Sgt (Co Sgt)
S/Sgt (Supply)
Cpl (Co Clerk)
Pvt (Jeep Driver)
(6) Pvt (Basic)

S/Sgt (Mess)
T/4 (Cook)
T/5 (Cook)
Pvt (Cook's Helper/Driver)

Maintenance Section
(1 Officer, 9 Enlisted Total)

1st Lt (XO/Maintenence)
T/Sgt (Motor Sgt)
T/4 (Artillery Mechanic)
T/4 (Mechanic/Driver)
(2) T/4 (Mechanics)
T/4 (Radio Repairman)
T/5 (Armorer)
(2) T/5 (Mechanics/Drivers)

Tank Platoon (1 of 3)
(1 Officer, 24 Enlisted Men Total)

1st Tank "Able"
2nd Lt (Platoon Leader)
Cpl (Gunner)
T/4 (Driver)
Pvt (Loader)
Pvt (Machine Gunner)

2nd Tank "Baker"
Sgt (Tank Cmdr)
Cpl (Gunner)
T/5 (Driver)
Pvt (Loader)
Pvt (Machine Gunner)

3rd Tank "Charlie"
S/Sgt (Platoon Sgt)
Cpl (Gunner)
T/4 (Driver)
Pvt (Loader)
Pvt (Machine Gunner)

4th Tank "Dog"
Sgt (Tank Cmdr)
Cpl (Gunner)
T/5 (Driver)
Pvt (Loader)
Pvt (Machine Gunner)

5th Tank "Easy"
Sgt (Tank Cmdr)
Cpl (Gunner)
T/5 (Driver)
Pvt (Loader)
Pvt (Machine Gunner)

1st Platoon 2nd Platoon 3rd Platoon

Note: "Pvt" could also be Pfc.

Weapons: 92 .45-cal submachine guns; 25 .30-cal M-1 carbine rifles; 3 2.36-inch bazookas; 1 .50-cal heavy machine gun.

Vehicles: 17 medium tanks with armament, 1 medium tank with 105mm howitzer, 2 jeeps; 1 M3 halftrack, 1 2-1/2 ton cargo truck with 1 1-ton trailer, 1 M32 tank recovery vehicle.

Table based on War Dept Nov 18, 1944 T/O & E 17-27

U.S. Tank Destroyer Company Table of Organization - 1944

(5 Officers, 130 Enlisted Men Total)

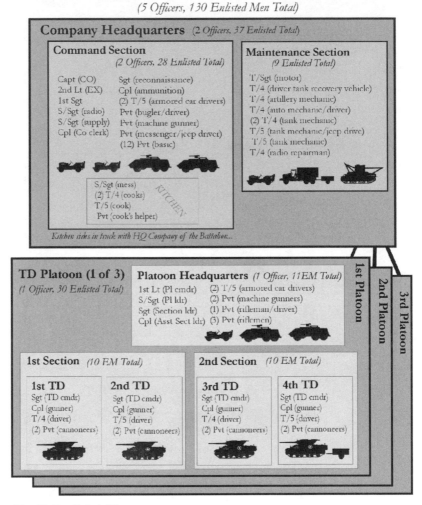

Company Headquarters *(2 Officers, 37 Enlisted Total)*

Command Section
(2 Officers, 28 Enlisted Total)

Capt (CO)	Sgt (reconnaissance)
2nd Lt (EX)	Cpl (ammunition)
1st Sgt	(2) T/5 (armored car drivers)
S/Sgt (radio)	Pvt (bugler/driver)
S/Sgt (supply)	Pvt (machine gunner)
Cpl (Co clerk)	Pvt (messenger/jeep driver)
	(12) Pvt (basic)

S/Sgt (mess)
(2) T/4 (cooks)
T/5 (cook)
Pvt (cook's helper)

KITCHEN

Maintenance Section
(9 Enlisted Total)

T/Sgt (motor)
T/4 (driver tank recovery vehicle)
T/4 (artillery mechanic)
T/4 (auto mechanic/driver)
(2) T/4 (tank mechanic)
T/5 (tank mechanic/jeep driver)
T/5 (tank mechanic)
T/4 (radio repairman)

Kitchen rides in truck with HQ Company of the Battalion...

TD Platoon (1 of 3)
(1 Officer, 30 Enlisted Total)

Platoon Headquarters *(1 Officer, 11 EM Total)*

1st Lt (Pl cmdr)	(2) T/5 (armored car drivers)
S/Sgt (Pl ldr)	(2) Pvt (machine gunners)
Sgt (Section ldr)	(1) Pvt (rifleman/driver)
Cpl (Asst Sect ldr)	(3) Pvt (riflemen)

1st Platoon
2nd Platoon
3rd Platoon

1st Section *(10 EM Total)*

1st TD
Sgt (TD cmdr)
Cpl (gunner)
T/4 (driver)
(2) Pvt (cannoneers)

2nd TD
Sgt (TD cmdr)
Cpl (gunner)
T/5 (driver)
(2) Pvt (cannoneers)

2nd Section *(10 EM Total)*

3rd TD
Sgt (TD cmdr)
Cpl (gunner)
T/4 (driver)
(2) Pvt (cannoneers)

4th TD
Sgt (TD cmdr)
Cpl (gunner)
T/5 (driver)
(2) Pvt (cannoneers)

Note: "Pvt" could also be Pfc.

Weapons: 67 .30-cal Carbine rifles; 55 .30-cal M-1 rifles; 13 .45-cal automatic pistols; 10 .50-cal heavy barrel machine guns; 9 2.36-inch bazookas; 5 .30-cal heavy machine guns; 1 81mm mortar.

Vehicles: 12 M-10 tank destroyers with 76mm guns; 8 armored cars w/o armament; 6 jeeps; 3 M-10 ammunition trailers; 1 2-1/2 ton cargo truck, 1 tank recovery vehicle; 1 1/4 ton trailer.

Table based on War Dept Mar 15, 1944 T/O & E 18-27

© 2005 Jeff Danby

U.S. Army Rank Insignia - WWII

ENLISTED GRADES:

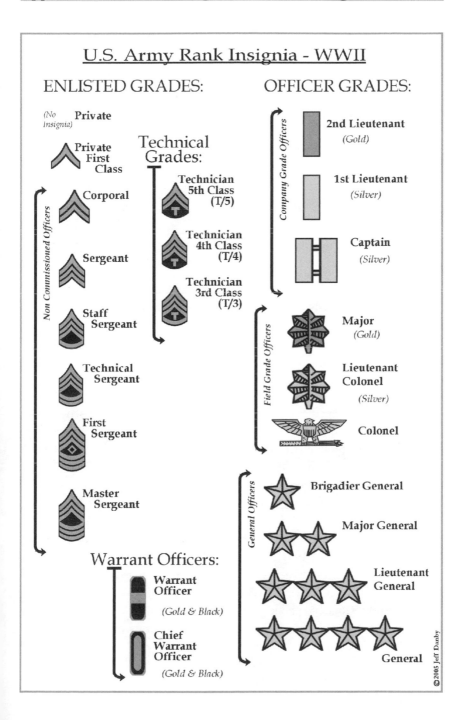

(No Insignia) **Private**

Private First Class

Corporal

Sergeant

Staff Sergeant

Technical Sergeant

First Sergeant

Master Sergeant

Non Commissioned Officers

Technical Grades:

Technician 5th Class (T/5)

Technician 4th Class (T/4)

Technician 3rd Class (T/3)

Warrant Officers:

Warrant Officer
(Gold & Black)

Chief Warrant Officer
(Gold & Black)

OFFICER GRADES:

2nd Lieutenant *(Gold)*

1st Lieutenant *(Silver)*

Captain *(Silver)*

Company Grade Officers

Major *(Gold)*

Lieutenant Colonel *(Silver)*

Colonel

Field Grade Officers

Brigadier General

Major General

Lieutenant General

General

General Officers

©2005 Jeff Danby

Notes

Introduction: The Third Infantry Division and Operation Anvil

1. These five divisions were the 1st and 2nd Armored Divisions, and the 1st, 3rd and 34th Infantry Divisions. Not all elements of each division landed on the first day.

2. General description from "Battle Record of the Third Infantry Division" brochure, USAMHI.

3. Carlo D'Este, *Fatal Decision: Anzio and the Battle for* Rome (New York, New York: HarperPerennial, 1992), 123.

4. "Darby's Rangers" was a provisional Ranger outfit comprised of three Ranger battalions commanded by Col William O. Darby. They fought with legendary distinction in North Africa, Sicily, and Salerno. At Anzio, "Darby's Rangers" were all but wiped during the first attempt at capturing Cisterna. Most members were killed or captured.

5. D'Este, *Fatal Decision*, 124.

6. Ibid., 123.

7. Roger Fazendin, *The 756th Tank Battalion at Cassino* (Lincoln, Nebraska: iUniverse Inc. 1991), 72, 111, 149.

8. Donald G. Taggart, *The History of the Third Infantry Division in World War II* (Nashville, Tennessee: The Battery Press, 1987), 164.

9. Herman Cogdell, phone conversation, June 10, 2003; "3d Infantry Division Shoulder Sleeve Insignia," http://www.army.mil/cmh-pg/matrix/3ID/3ID-Matrix.htm

10. Figure includes attached units. A World War II U.S. Army infantry division table of organization listed approximately 14,000 men.

Chapter One: L Company

1. George S. Burks, letter, September 13, 2002.
2. David Redle, phone conversation, September 15, 2000.
3. Roy Anderson, phone conversation, October 3, 2000.
4. Frank Cockerill, phone conversation, January 17, 2002.
5. Lloyd Cotter, phone conversation, May 10, 2002.
6. German rockets generally fired from six-tube banks. For maximum psychological effect, they were fitted with fin holes to create a terrible screaming sound while in flight.
7. Burks, interview, Buffalo, NY, September 13, 2002; and letter, March 5, 2003.
8. Burks, interview, Buffalo, NY, September 13, 2002.
9. Burks, letter, April 10, 2003.
10. After Action Report (AAR), U.S.S. Henrico, August 15, 1944.
11. Burks, interview, Buffalo, NY, September 13, 2002; and letter, March 5, 2003.
12. L Company (Co.) Morning Report (MR), March 15, 1944.
13. Ibid., February 2, 1944; wife of Andrew Leaming, phone conversation, January 17, 2002; Leaming was wounded February 1, 1944. Coles assumed command the same day.
14. L Co. MR, April 14, 1944.
15. Arco Ciancanelli, phone conversation, February 22 and March 8, 2002; Salvatore Fasciana, phone conversation, June 16, 2003; William Hawkins, phone conversation, July 8, 2003; Bernard Hayward, phone conversation, May 6, 2002; Fred Scarpa, tape recording, January 14, 2002; John Morris, letter, December 29, 2001; Earl V. Potter, phone conversation, August 30, 2002; Redle, phone conversation, September 15, 2000. Weight estimate ranges from 200 to 250 pounds, but all agree that Coles didn't carry any extra pounds.
16. Robert McFarland, phone conversation, June 20, 2001; John MacKinnon, letter, December 24, 2001; Dale Marker, letter, February 10, 2002; Hayward, phone conversation, May 6, 2002; Edmund Rovas, phone conversation, August 29, 2002; Homer Toman, phone conversation, August 30, 2002; Potter, phone conversation, August 30, 2002; Burks, letter, September 13, 2002; Robert Seegitz, phone conversation, October 15, 2002; Scarpa, tape recording, January 14, 2002; Lloyd Rowe, phone conversation, May 29, 2003; Cotter, phone conversation, June 4, 2003; Arthur Schrader, phone conversation, June 10, 2003; Albert Whisnant, phone conversation, June 12, 2003; James

Hunt, phone conversation, June 16, 2003; George Ferguson, phone conversation, August 16, 2003.

17. Hayward, phone conversation, May 6, 2002; Whisnant, phone conversation, June 12, 2003; Seegitz, phone conversation, October 15, 2002.

18. Burks, letters, April 13, 2004, and July 19, 2004.

19. Ibid., letters, April 13, 2004, and March 5, 2003.

20. Marilyn Wright (James Coles' daughter), phone conversation, April 21, 2004. Marilyn believes her father was sent to North Africa soon after being commissioned in 1942, but is unsure if he joined the 3rd Infantry Division (ID) immediately. Ciancanelli, phone conversation, February 22, 2002; Ciacanelli believes that Coles was in the 3rd ID prior to the Casablanca landings.

21. Wright, phone conversation, April 21, 2004.

22. Gary Dauby (Gervase Dauby son), phone conversation, April 17, 2002; Morris, letter, December 29, 2001; Sid Shaw, phone conversation, March 28, 2004.

23. Silver Star Citation, James W. Coles, 3rd ID, 1943, General Orders #94, 2.

24. Rudolph Jantz, phone conversation, May 8, 2003.

25. Max Wellfare, e-mail, April 18, 2002.

26. MacKinnon, interview, Buffalo, NY, September 13, 2002.

27. Ferguson, phone conversation, August 16, and October 15, 2003.

28. E. Rovas, phone conversation, November 20, 2002.

29. Ibid., phone conversations, August 29, and November 20, 2002.

30. Rowe, phone conversation, May 29, 2003.

31. Burks, letter, March 5, 2003.

32. John Shirley, e-mail, March 21, 2002.

33. Hawkins, phone conversation, June 18, 2003.

34. Hawkins, phone conversation, June 18, 2003; Hayward, phone conversation, May 6, 2002; Ferguson, phone conversation, October 15, 2003.

35. Technical Manual TM 11-242: Radio Set SCR-300-A, June 15, 1943; 8-9. The battery alone weighed 15 pounds!

36. Jantz, letter, May 18, 2003; and e-mail, May 12, 2004.

37. Ibid., phone conversation, May 8, 2003.

38. Ibid., letter, May 18, 2003.

39. Ibid., phone conversation, May 30, 2003.

40. Table of Organization and Equipment T/O & E 7-17: Infantry Rifle Company, February 26, 1944; 10.

41. Jantz, letter, May 18, 2003.

42. Burks, letter, March 5, 2003.

43. Ibid., letters, September 13, 2002, and April 13, 2004.

44. Jessie Hickerson, phone conversation, June 13, 2003.

45. Burks, letter, March 5, 2003.

46. Wright, phone conversation, April 21, 2004.

47. The El Paso Times, "Wounded El Pasoan Still Sees Rosy Side of Life" November 27, 1943, 5;6 1/3 c.

48. Donald B. McLean (Editor), *Company Officer's Handbook of the German Army*, (Wickenburg, Arizona: Normount Technical Publications. 1975), 50-51.

49. George Polich, e-mail, September 28, 2005.

50. Floyd Owsley, phone conversation, August 17, 2003; Robert Tyler, letter, March 16, 2003.

51. Seegitz, phone conversation, October 16, 2002.

52. Ibid.

53. Burks, letter, July 19, 2004; D'Este, *Fatal Decision*, 454-457.

54. L Co. MR, April 20, 1944.

55. Burks, letter, April 13, 2004.

56. Jantz, e-mail, November 2, 2003.

57. Robert McFarland (Editor), *The History of the 15th Infantry Regiment in World War II*. (Privately printed, early 1990s), 137.

58. D'Este, *Fatal Decision*, 357 (map). As of May 23, 1944 these divisions were aligned as follows: the British 1st and 5th Infantry Divisions on the far left, the American 1st Armored, 45th, 36th, and 34th Infantries in the middle, and the 3rd Infantry on the right. Also in the mix was a separate U.S.-Canadian Special Service Force.

59. John Shirley, *I Remember: Stories of a Combat Infantryman in World War II*. (Privately printed, 2003), 3.

60. McFarland, *15th Infantry Regiment*, 137.

61. Shirley, *I Remember*, 4-6.

62. Ibid., 8.

63. Taggart, *History of the Third Infantry Division*, 155.

64. Ibid., *History of the Third Infantry Division*, 161-162.

65. Ibid., *History of the Third Infantry Division*, 154.

66. Jantz, e-mail, May 12, 2004; Burks, letter, April 13, 2004.

67. Burks, letter, July 19, 2004.

68. Taggart, *History of the Third Infantry Division*, 161-162.

69. Schrader, phone conversation, June 10, 2003.

70. L Co. MR, May 22, 1944, declares 239, but Burks is certain the Company attacked with no more than 180. He believes the extras were replacements held near the beach and were nowhere near the front lines. Burks, letter, July 19, 2004.

71. Taggart, *History of the Third Infantry Division*, 161-162.

72. Burks, letter, April 13, 2004; L Co. MRs, May 26-29, and July 14, 1944.

73. Taggart, *History of the Third Infantry Division*, 391.

74. Jantz, e-mail, May 12, 2004.

75. Taggart, *History of the Third Infantry Division*, 161-162.

76. Ibid., 163.

77. Richard Guimond, phone conversation, May 8, 2001; Marker, phone conversation, May 23, 2001; Burks, interview, Buffalo, NY, September 13, 2002; Chester Darrah, phone conversation, June 10, and July 7, 2003.

78. Author's analysis of L Company MRs after May 23, 1944.

79. Jantz, e-mail, May 12, 2004. Jantz believes Noble was assigned as Captain's radioman this day. Noble may have been near Coles and Burks at this point. Jantz was with the HQ section.

80. Burks, letter, June 4, 2003.

81. Ibid., interview, Buffalo, NY, September 13, 2002.

82. Ibid., letter, July 19, 2004.

83. Jantz, e-mail, May 12, 2004.

84. L Co. MRs, May 30-31, 1944.

85. Burks, interview, St. Louis, MO, September 19, 2003.

86. L Co. MRs, June 1-2, 1944.

Chapter Two: Respite and Preparations

1. Burks, letter, July 19, 2004.

2. Taggart, *History of the Third Infantry Division*, 189.

3. 1930 Census and current Social Security Death Index, www.rootsweb.com.

4. Burks, interview, St. Louis, MO, September 19, 2003.

5. Ibid.

6. Hawkins, phone conversation, June 18, 2003.

7. Names are remembered by Burks and confirmed by L Company MRs, but have been withheld by the author.

8. Burks, letter, April 13, 2004.

9. Hawkins, phone conversation, June 18, 2003; Potter, interview, Holiday, FL, June 24, 2003.

10. Potter, interview, Holiday, FL, June 24, 2003.

11. Burks, letter, April 13, 2004.

12. Ibid., letter, June 27, 2003.

13. Jantz, phone conversation, May 30, 2003.

14. Potter, interview, Holiday, FL, June 24, 2003; Dauby, phone conversation, April 17, 2002.

15. Ana Miluszusky (William W. McNamara's daughter), phone conversation, July 18, 2003.

16. Darrah, phone conversation, July 7, 2003.

17. Ciancanelli, interview, Palos Park, IL, July 24, 2003.

18. Miluszusky, phone conversation, July 18, 2003.

19. Ciancanelli, phone conversation, November 19, 2002; Donna Nussbaum (Joseph Leithner's daughter), phone conversation, June 3, 2003.

20. Ciancanelli, interview, Palos Park, IL, July 24, 2003; Ciancanelli did not specifically attribute this quote to McNamara, but characterized the quote as "we said".

21. Hawkins, phone conversation, July 8, 2003.

22. Burks, letter, April 13, 2004.

23. Ibid., interview, St. Louis, MO, September 19, 2003.

24. L Co. MRs, June 15, June 21, and June 24 1944.

25. Hawkins, phone conversation, July 8, 2003.

26. Cogdell, phone conversation, December 20, 2003.

27. Bernard Greive, letter, June 22, 2003.

28. Taggart, *History of the Third Infantry Division*, 195.

29. Ibid., 195-196.

30. 15th Infantry Regiment (IR) Operations Report (OR), August 1944, 1.

31. Burks, letter, April 13, 2004.

32. 15th IR "Anvil" Field Orders, August 2, 1944.

33. Frederick Boye III (Frederick Boye's son), letter, July 20, 2004.

34. Burks, interview, Buffalo, NY, September 13, 2002.

35. Ibid., letter, July 19, 2004.

Chapter Three: Yellow Beach

1. Naval Task Force 84 AARs.

2. 2nd Battalion (Bn)/15th IR, Unit Journal (UJ) entry, August 15, 1944.

3. Patrick Heagerty, phone conversation, July 28, 2002.

4. Shirley, *I Remember*, 25.

5. Heagerty, phone conversation, July 28, 2002.

6. Hatlem, *The War in the Mediterranean*, 313.

7. Shirley, *I Remember*, Pages 25-26.

8. The "Higgins boat" was nicknamed after the designer, Andrew Higgins.

9. Hatlem, *The War in the Mediterranean*, 321.

10. Cogdell, e-mail, August 22, 2003; and phone conversation, December 20, 2003.

11. Ibid., phone conversation, June 10, 2003.

12. Burks, letter, March 5, 2003.

13. Ibid., interview, Buffalo, NY, September 13, 2002.

14. I, K, and L Companies MRs, August 15, 1944.

15. Hickerson, phone conversation, June 13, 2003; Heagerty, phone conversation, July 28, 2002.

16. Robert Tyler, "Veteran History Project Transcript" for Springfield College, July 23, 2003, 8.

17. Shirley, *I Remember*, pages 26-27.

18. Cogdell, phone conversation, May 29, 2003.

19. Cheryl Esposito, *The 756th Tank Battalion in the European Theatre*, (Privately printed, 1999), 24

20. Redle, interview, Akron, OH, January 19, 2002.

21. AAR, LCT-1015.

22. Anderson, phone conversation, January 10, 2002.

23. Redle, letter, January 3, 2001.

24. Ibid. interview, Akron, OH, January 19, 2002; "Sherman DD tank to Emerge from the deep," www.military.com

25. Anderson, interview, San Antonio, TX, September 27, 2003.

26. Redle, interview, Akron, OH, January 19, 2002.

27. 756th Tank Bn Commander's informal report on the DD-tanks, August 17, 1944.

28. B Co./756th Tank Bn MR, May 25, 1944.

29. Anderson, phone conversation, June 28, 2001; Redle, phone conversation, May 2, 2001.

30. B Co./756th Tank Bn MRs, July 2nd and August 3, 1944.

31. Anderson, phone conversation, June 28, 2001; Keith Stout (Lloyd Stout's brother), phone conversation, December 29, 2003.

32. 2nd Bn/15th IR, UJ entry, August 15, 1944 records at 06:25 "periodic artillery from our Navy." Time is approximate.

33. Samuel Eliot Morison, *History of US Naval Operations in World War II, Vol. XI*, (Edison, New Jersey: Castle Books, 1957), 256–258.

34. 2nd Bn/15th IR, UJ entry, 0710, August 15, 1944 reports this time frame and these types of planes.

35. Naval Task Force 84 AARs, Demolitions, August 30, 1944.

36. 2nd Bn/15th IR, UJ entry, 0740, August 15, 1944.

37. Naval Task Force 84 AARs, Demolitions, August 30, 1944.

38. Anderson, phone conversation, January 10, 2002.

39. AAR, LCT-1015, August 26, 1944; Redle, interview, Akron, OH, January 19, 2002; Anderson, interview, San Antonio, TX, September 27, 2003.

40. Anderson, phone conversation, January 10, 2002, and May 15, 2003.

41. Naval Task Force 84 AARs.

42. www.britannica.com/normandy/articles/landing_craft.html.

43. Rowe, letter, June 10, 2003.

44. 3rd Bn/15th IR AAR, Saint-Tropez.

45. 3rd Bn/15th IR AAR, Saint-Tropez, reports L Company landed center with I Company on right and K Company on left. M followed 10 minutes later. 2nd Bn/15th IR UJ reports their follow up wave attacked as "V.". I assume the assault wave did the same. Navy photos of assault wave also show "V" formation.

46. 15th IR Operation Anvil battle plans alignment chart for 1st wave.

47. Rowe, phone conversation, May 29, 2003.

48. Scarpa, tape recording, January 14, 2002.

49. Rowe, phone conversation, May 29, 2003.

50. Burks, letter, March 5, 2003.

51. Ibid., interview, Buffalo, NY, September 13, 2002.

52. Cogdell, phone conversation, May 29 and December 20, 2003; and e-mail, August 22, 2003.

53. Ibid., phone conversation, August 30, 2003; Heagerty, phone conversation, July 28, 2002.

54. Hunt, phone conversation, July 9, 2003.

55. Cogdell, phone conversation, May 29, 2003.

56. Hunt, phone conversation, July 9, 2003.

57. Ibid., phone conversation, June 16, 2003.

58. Cogdell, phone conversation, August 30, 2003.

59. Hunt, phone conversation, June 16, 2003.

60. Owsley, phone conversation, August 17, 2003; Ciancanelli, phone conversation, January 4, 2003; Schrader, phone conversation of June 10, 2003; and sworn written testimony of November 20, 1944. Schrader never specifically mentioned stepping into water, but others from his squad did. He did characterize his squad as "unruly."

61. Potter, interview, Holiday, FL, June 24, 2003. I don't know for certain which LCVP Potter was on. This incident may not have happened with McNamara's group.

62. John Roth, letter, March 9, 2001. This was Oliver's customary combat practice.

63. 3rd Bn/15th IR AAR, Saint-Tropez.

64. Anderson, phone conversation, January 10, 2002 and May 15, 2003; Anderson, interview, San Antonio, TX, September 27, 2003.

65. Redle, letter, January 25, 2004. Redle vaguely recalls Oliver's tank threw a track, but is uncertain. Oliver's family could not confirm this. Stout's family recalls stories from Lloyd of the landings but none that involved throwing a track. Neither Orient's family nor Anderson had information either way.

66. Rowe, letter, June 10, 2003.

67. Burks, interview, Buffalo, NY, September 13, 2002.

68. Potter, interview, Holiday, FL, June 24, 2003; and biography, March 2003, (accompanied letter of May 20, 2003).

69. Rowe, letter, June 10, 2003.

70. Heagerty, phone conversation, July 28, 2002, Heagerty was in the I Company area; 2nd Bn/15th IR AAR, Saint-Tropez.

71. Potter, biography, March 2003.

72. Schrader, sworn written testimony, November 20, 1944; DSC citation, McNamara, Seventh Army 1945 General Orders #16, pages 4 and 5.

Chapter Four: On to Saint-Tropez

1. Hawkins, phone conversation, July 8, 2003.

2. 3rd Bn/15th IR AAR, Saint-Tropez.

3. Ibid.

4. Cogdell, phone conversation, December 20, 2003.

5. 2nd Bn/15th IR AAR, Saint-Tropez.

6. Robert Nelson, phone conversation, June 17, 2003.

7. 2nd Bn/15th IR AAR, Saint-Tropez; 2nd Bn/15th IR UJ, August 15, 1944.

8. 1st Bn/15th IR AAR also reported some initial sporadic artillery.

9. 15th IR UJ, S-2 report, August 16, 1944, "Artillery" section.

10. Burks, letter, September 13, 2002.

11. McFarland, *15th Infantry Regiment*, 151.

12. Shirley, e-mails, July 25, 2002 and March 7, 2003; I Co. MR, August 15, 1994; McFarland, *15th Infantry Regiment*, 147. All sources report this casualty was 2nd Lt. Ellis F. Wheat.

13. McFarland, *15th Infantry Regiment*, 151, records that this action was led by T/Sgt. Lawrence N. Majewski. 3rd Bn/15th IR HQ Co. MR, August 15, 1944,

records that the AT platoon leader, 1st Lt. Herbert Bardes, stepped on a land mine just prior to this event.

14. Hunt, phone conversation, June 16 and July 9, 2003.

15. 15th IR UJ, S-2 report, August 16, 1944.

16. Morris, phone conversation, January 14, 2002.

17. Ralph Walburn, phone conversation, June 11, 2003.

18. Owsley, phone conversation, August 17, 2003.

19. Patrick Rodger, phone conversations, June 17 and October 7, 2003.

20. Rowe, letter, June 10, 2003.

21. 15th IR UJ, 1230 entry, August 15, 1944.

22. 2nd Bn/15th IR UJ, 1515 entry, August 15, 1944.

23. 2nd Bn/15th IR AAR, Saint-Tropez.

24. 2nd Bn/15th IR UJ, August 15, 1944.

25. Jacques Robichon, *The Second D-Day* (New York, New York: 1962), 212-214.

26. 2nd Bn/15th IR UJ,1620 entry, August 15, 1944.

27. 15th IR UJ, 1742 entry, August 15, 1944.

28. McFarland, *15th Infantry Regiment*, 152.

29. 15th IR UJ, 1836 entry, August 15, 1944.

30. Redle, letter, June 24, 2002.

31. Henry Sanislow, phone conversation, December 1, 2003.

32. Redle, phone conversation, March 17, 2003.

33. Ibid., phone conversation, July 19, 2004.

34. Ibid., letter, January 6, 2005.

35. Kenneth Macksey, *Tank Versus Tank: The Illustrated History of Armored Battlefield Conflict in the Twentieth Century*. (Reprint. New York: Barnes & Noble Books, 1999), 107 (chart.)

36. Redle, phone conversation, September 15, 2000.

37. Fazendin, *756th Tank Battalion at Cassino*, xxix.

38. Lee Mudd, "History of the 756th Tank Battalion and the Development of the Tank-Infantry Team in World War II," (Thesis, Johns Hopkins University, 2000), 11.

39. Redle, letter, January 6, 2005.

40. Fazendin, *756th Tank Battalion at Cassino*, xxxiv. 2nd Lt. Roger Fazendin was seriously wounded when his jeep ran over a mine in November 1943. He was the 756th Tank Battalion's maintenance officer at the time. Redle and Fazendin served in B Company together the two years prior to that incident. Dave was Roger's best man at his wedding.

41. Fazendin, *756th Tank Battalion at Cassino*, 115.

42. Redle, letter, June 24, 2002.

43. Ibid., letter, June 24, 2002 and January 6, 2005.

44. 1st Bn/15th IR AAR, Saint-Tropez.

45. Audie Murphy was later awarded the Distinguished Service Cross for his involvement in this action. For further reading see Chapter 14 of Audie Murphy's classic autobiography: *To Hell and Back.*

46. Isadore Valenti, *Combat Medic*, (Tarentum, PA: Word Association Publishers, 1998), 107.

47. Esposito, *756th Tank Battalion in Europe*, 29; A Co./756th Tank Bn MR, August 15, 1944. Tank commander was Sgt. George A. Boutilier.

48. Redle, interview, Akron, OH, January 19, 2002.

49. This is circumstantial speculation based on conversations with Redle and Anderson.

50. 15th IR UJ, 1940 entry, August 15, 1944.

51. McFarland, *15th Infantry Regiment*, 152.

52. Jeffrey J. Clarke and Robert Ross Smith, *Riviera to the Rhine*, (Washington, D.C.: Center for Military History, 1993), 104.

53. Taggart, *History of the Third Infantry Division*, 211. The officer is unidentified.

54. McFarland, *15th Infantry Regiment*, 153.

Chapter Five: Across Southern France

1. Hawkins, phone conversation, June 18, 2003; Rodger, phone conversation, October 7, 2003.

2. Marker, phone conversation, May 23, 2001; McFarland, *15th Infantry Regiment*, 18.

3. Burks, letter, September 13, 2002.

4. Nelson, phone conversation, May 8, 2003.

5. Shirley, *I Remember*, 28-29.

6. Anderson, phone conversation, May 15, 2003.

7. Ibid., phone conversation, June 28, 2001; Gene Palumbo, phone conversation, December 14, 2000; Redle, letter, October 5, 2000; Mary Davis (George Davis' widow), phone conversation, May 8, 2003.

8. Redle, letter, October 5, 2000; Randolph Perdue, phone conversation, December 28, 2001.

9. Anderson, phone conversation, June 28, 2001.

10. Redle, letter, October 5, 2000.

11. Alfreda Sadowski (Ed Sadowski's widow), phone conversations, January 25, 2001 and May 12, 2003.

12. Anderson, phone conversation, June 28, 2001.

13. Frank Cockerill and Bud Fink interview, San Antonio, TX, September 26, 2003.

14. Fazendin, *756th Tank Battalion at Cassino*, 125-127; Anderson, phone conversation, June 28, 2001.

15. Esposito, *756th Tank Battalion in the European Theatre*, 58.

16. Burks, letter, March 5, 2003.

17. Ibid., interview, Buffalo, NY on September 13, 2002.

18. Potter, letter, October 2, 2002.

19. Ibid., biography, March 2003.

20. L Co. MR, July 15, 1944 records that he joined the Company on May 29, 1944.

21. Potter, interview, Holiday, FL, June 24, 2003.

22. Ibid., biography, March 2003; and interview, Holiday, FL, June 24, 2003. This incident may have taken place the day before near Saint-Tropez.

23. Cogdell, phone conversation, December 20, 2003. This particular incident may not have happened this day. Cogdell only recalls it happened sometime in southern France.

24. 15th IR UJ, August 16, 1944; McFarland, *15th Infantry Regiment*, 153.

25. 15th IR UJ, August 17, 1944; McFarland, *15th Infantry Regiment*, 154.

26. Shirley, letter, December 8, 2001.

27. Robert Tyler, "World War II Experience 1943-1945" memoirs, 2002, 8.

28. Clarke and Smith, *Riviera to the Rhine*, 60 and 63.

29. Redle, interview, Akron, OH, January 19, 2002. La Marseillaise is the 200-year-old French National Anthem. The platoon leader was 2nd Lt. Bert Gilden of the 2nd Platoon.

30. 15th IR UJ, 0200 and 0400 entries, August 17, 1944.

31. Ibid., 1022 entry, August 17, 1944; 2nd Bn/15th IR UJ, 0600 entry, August 17, 1944; McFarland, *15th Infantry Regiment*, 154. These two men returned three days later and reported that the Germans had water and food supply problems (2nd Bn/15th IR UJ, 1420 entry, August 20, 1944.)

32. 15th IR UJ, 1740 entry, August 17, 1944.

33. 2nd Bn/15th IR UJ, 2100 entry, August 17, 1944; 601st Tank Destroyer (TD) Bn UJ, August 17, 1944.

34. 15th IR UJ, 1800 and subsequent entries, August 17, 1944.

35. Clarke and Smith, *Riviera to the Rhine*, 67-68.

36. 3rd ID G-2 report, August 30, 1944, prisoner interrogations, 3.

37. Clarke and Smith, *Riviera to the Rhine*, 128-131.

38. Scarpa, tape recording, January 14, 2002.

39. Rowe, phone conversation, May 29, 2003. This incident may not have occurred at this exact time and place, but occurred in the days immediately following the landings.

40. Taggart, *History of the Third Infantry Division*, 214; McFarland, *15th Infantry Regiment*, 154;

41. 15th IR UJ, 2037 entry, August 17, 1944.

42. 3rd ID G3 report, August 17-18, 1944; McFarland, *15th Infantry Regiment*, 155; 15th IR UJ, August 17-18, 1944.

43. 3rd ID G-2 report, August 17-18, 1944.

44. Clarke and Smith, *Riviera to the Rhine*, 132. This force included 117th Cavalry Reconnaissance Squadron, two medium tank companies from 753rd Tank Bn, C Co./636th TD Bn, 59th Armored Field Artillery Bn, and 2nd Bn/143rd Inf Reg.

45. Jeffrey J. Clarke, *Southern France*, (The U.S. Army Campaigns of World War II series CMH pub 72-31), 16.

46. Alan F. Wilt, *The French Riviera Campaign of August 1944*, (Carbondale, Illinois: Southern Illinois University Press, 1981), 113-114; Clarke, *Southern France*, 16.

47. Earlier in the war, the British had broken the "unbreakable" German military communications code. This super-secret program (codenamed 'ULTRA") was such a strategic advantage that only the highest-ranking Allied officers were privy to intelligence gained through it.

48. Wilt, *The French Riviera Campaign of August 1944*, 115; Clarke, *Southern France*, 17.

Chapter Six: Toward Marseille

1. 3rd ID G-3 report, August 18-19, 1944, 4.

2. 15th IR UJ, 1230 entry, August 18, 1944.

3. McFarland, *15th Infantry Regiment*, 15.

4. 15th IR UJ, various entries, August 18, 1944.

5. I Co. MRs, August 18, 20, and 26, 1944. Pfc. Raymond L. Smith was killed in action. Five others were wounded in action and transferred out for medical care: Pfcs. James A Campbell, Anastacio Batres, Nickolas M Gomich, Fred A Ruby, and Albert V Lacher Jr.

6. 15th IR UJ, 1945 entry, August 18, 1944; S-2 report, August 19, 1944. Identified both as an "88" and an "SP" gun.

7. McFarland, *15th Infantry Regiment*, 156.

8. 2nd Bn/15th IR, UJ 2000 entry, August 18, 1944.

9. Ibid., 0818 entry, August 19, 1944 reports tank knocked out by "bazooka or artillery." It's not 100% clear that T/5 Jaksys and Pvt. Smith were members of S/Sgt. Smith's tank. However, only one 2nd Platoon tank was lost in this battle, so chances are strong they were of the same crew. It is highly unlikely and out of character for S/Sgt. Smith and Cpl. LaDue to have bailed on a tank that was not knocked out at the time. B Co. /756th MRs, August 18 and 19, 1944 records fates of these four men.

10. Redle, phone conversation, December 16, 2002; Sanislow, phone conversation, December 1, 2003.

11. Redle, letter, May 2, 2002.

12. Randall Nusz (Alvin Nusz's son), phone conversation, July 15, 2002.

13. Ibid., phone conversation, July 15, 2002.

14. Redle, letter, June 24, 2002; R. Nusz interview, Ft. Knox, KY, September 18, 2002.

15. Redle, letter, June 24, 2002.

16. Rovas recalls being sent on a contact patrol to "right" side of L Company to locate the adjacent company. This would have been the 2nd Battalion area of operation.

17. Greive, phone conversations, June 4 and 30, 2003; First name believed to have been Robert or "Bob," but many remember him as simply "Doc" Lefevre. The 15th IR roster in Taggart's *History of the Third Infantry Division* lists a Pvt. Robert C Lefevre.

18. E. Rovas, phone conversation, August 29, 2002; Bill Rovas (Edmund Rovas's son) phone conversation, March 3, 2003; B. Rovas, e-mail, April 2, 2003. The name "Farmer" could be Pvt. Lonnie E. Farmer, or it may be another person altogether. According to the MRs, Pvt. Lonnie E. Farmer was absent from L Company August 15-21, 1944.

19. 2nd Bn/15th IR UJ, various entries, August 19, 1944; 3rd ID G-3 Reports, August 18-19, 1944, 2; 15th IR UJ, 1205 entry, August 19, 1944; McFarland, *15th Infantry Regiment*, 157.

20. Coles' demeanor is speculative, based on Albert Whisnant recollections (see August 20, 1944 story to follow.)

21. 15th IR UJ, 1106 entry, August 19, 1944.

22. The book by Arthur Funk, *Hidden Ally:The French Resistance, Special Operations, and the Landings in Southern France, 1944,* (Greenwood Press,

1992), provides in-depth account of the Resistance activities of Major Francis Cammaerts and others in southeastern France.

23. 15th IR UJ, 1140 entry, August 19, 1944.

24. 756th Tank Bn UJ, 1000 entry, August 19, 1944.

25. 601st TD UJ, S-3 report, August 19, 1944.

26. 3rd ID, G-3 Report, August 19-20, 1944, 2; McFarland, *15th Infantry Regiment*, 157, characterized the 45 minute march as "free sailing"; Potter, biography, March 2003, 2, recalls more time-consuming resistance at Tourves; L Co. MR, August 19, 1944, reports: "Co as advance party advanced to NE Tourves. Light enemy opposition."

27. 15th IR UJ, 1330 entry, August 19, 1944.

28. "Swarmed with happy townspeople" is speculative for Tourves, but the veterans of L Company recall that whenever the Germans weren't around, virtually every town they passed through would celebrate the arrival of U.S. soldiers.

29. 15th IR UJ, various entries, August 19, 1944; 15th IR S-3 Report, August 19-20, 1944.

30. 2nd Bn/15th IR UJ, 1920 entry, August 19, 1944.

31. Jantz, phone conversation, May 30, 2003; Shirley, *I Remember*, 19-20.

32. Shirley, letter, December 8, 2001. This was a likely place for this incident, but may not have necessarily happened here.

33. 15th IR UJ, 1530 and 1730 entries, August 19, 1944.

34. Ibid., 1550 entry, August 19, 1944; 3rd ID G-3 Report, August 19-20, 1944, 2; 15th IR S-3 Report, August 19-20, 1944. General coordinate position given for Saint-Maximin is 85*33*, Position for "La Defenos" is 860310. This puts the 3rd Bn approximately 1 km south and 2 kms east of Saint-Maximin.

35. 3rd ID G-3 Report, August 19-20, 1944, 2, for trucks reference; 2nd Bn/15th IR UJ, August 19, 1944 for time (between 1915 and 1930).

36. 756th Tank Bn UJ, 1800 entry, August 19, 1944.

37. Analysis of MRs included the 3rd Bn HQ, I, K, L Companies. M Company was not included, so the casualty totals may be higher.

38. Pvts. Pleasant O. Adkins and John Rook of I Company KIA on August 15, 1944. Pfc. Raymond L. Smith of I Company KIA on August 18, 1944. (I Co. MRs, August 26, 31, and September 13 1944; www.abmc.gov.)

39. Pvt. Edward D. Livermore of I Co. MRs, August 17, 1944; Taggart, *History of the Third Infantry Division*, 493, (According to 15th IR roster, Livermore survived the war.)

40. One of these 26 men was actually classified as "Injured in Action." (Pfc. Clement J. Warner, K Co. MRs, August 15, 1944.)

41. Whisnant, phone conversations, June 12 and July 9, 2003.

42. The exact date of this incident is not clear. Whisnant recalls it occurred a few days after the landings. The 3rd ID G-2 Report, August 19-20, 1944, 2, has an interesting note: "By-passed SP or AT gun south of St. Maximin fired four rounds toward Brignoles at 192030B (August 19 at 8:30 P.M.), then apparently withdrew." This may have been the same gun that Coles' patrol encountered.

43. 2nd Bn/15th IR UJ, 1940 entry, August 19, 1944.

44. Ibid., 1955, 2240, and 2250 entries, August 19, 1944; 15th IR UJ, 1935 entry, August 19, 1944.

45. 2nd Bn/15th IR UJ, 2130 entry, August 19, 1944.

46. 15th IR S-2 report, August 20 1944, (August 19, 1944, 0000 to 2400 cycle).

47. 3rd ID G-2 report, August 20, 1944, signed by 1st Lt. Robert Thompson. Both accounts were attributed to "ground sources."

48. 15th IR S-2 Report, August 19, 1944 (180001 to 1824000 cycle).

49. 2nd Bn/15th IR UJ, 0810 entry, August 20, 1944; 15th IR S-2 Report, August 21, 1944.

50. 15th IR S-2 Report, August 21, 1944 (200001 to 202400 cycle).

51. 15th IR UJ, 0930 entry August 20, 1944.

52. 2nd Bn/15th IR UJ, 1547 entry, August 20, 1944; 601st TD UJ and S-3 Report, August 21, 1944 (201100 to 211100 cycle).

53. 15th IR UJ, 1455 entry, August 20, 1944.

54. 15th IR S-2 Report, August 21, 1944 (200001-202400 cycle); McFarland, *15th Infantry Regiment*, 158; Taggart, *History of the Third Infantry Division*, 216; 3rd ID G-3 Report dated August 21, 1944 (201201-211200 cycle), 2.

55. 2nd Bn/15th IR UJ, 2140 entry, August 20, 1944.

56. 15th IR UJ, 0420, 0615, 0656 entries, August 20, 1944.

57. 15th IR S-2 Report, August 21, 1944 (200001-202400 cycle); McFarland, *15th Infantry Regiment*, 157-158; Taggart, *History of the Third Infantry Division*, 216;

58. 756th Tank Bn UJ, August 20, 1944 indicates the orders from General O'Daniel to move Bn to Pourcieux occurred at 10:00 am. Bn closed at Pourcieux at 4:00 pm. B Company closed at Trets later at 8:15 pm.

59. Redle originally believed the jeep driver at this incident was Cpl. Raymond Getz, however the B Company MRs show that Getz was sick and excused from duty from July 14 to September 14, 1944. In light of this, Redle now believes the driver was probably Pfc Gene Palumbo—the only other jeep driver assigned to his Company.

60. Esposito, *756th Tank Battalion in the European Theatre*, 55-56; Redle, letter, April 29, 2003; and phone conversation, March 17, 2003; Redle believes this may have been near St. Maximin.

61. 756th Tank Bn UJ, 2015 and 2330 entries, August 20, 1944.

62. This transfer date is speculation but appears to be the likely time. Anderson, phone conversation, May 15, 2003, recalls Oliver still had his DD tank a few days after the invasion.

63. McFarland, *15th Infantry Regiment*, 158.

64. Ibid., 158.

65. Location is approximate. Ciancanelli recalled this happened at a roadblock a few days after the landings. Ciancanelli, phone conversation, March 8, 2002 and January 4, 2003.

66. 15th IR UJ, 2016 entry, August 21, 1944; McFarland, *15th Infantry Regiment*, 159.

67. Hawkins, phone conversation, July 8, 2003.

68. 3rd ID G-2 Report, August 22, 1944, 2; McFarland, *15th Infantry Regiment*, 159.

69. 3rd ID G-3 dated August 22, 1944 (201201 - 211200 cycle), 2; 3rd ID G-2 report, August 22, 1944 (201201 - 211200 cycle), 2.

70. Taggart, *History of the Third Infantry Division*, 216.

71. 3rd ID G-3 Report, August 22, 1944 (201201 - 211200 cycle), 1.

72. Taggart, *History of the Third Infantry Division*, 216.

73. 3rd ID G-3 Report, August 22, 1944 (201201 - 211200 cycle), 2.

74. 3rd ID G-3 Reports, August 21-22, 1944, page 1 for both.

75. Clarke and Smith, *Riviera to the Rhine*, 149.

76. 3rd ID G-2 Report, August 22, 1944, 2. Initial reports identified the tanks as "Mark VIs" (Tigers), but even the Divisional G-2 officer noted that these were probably "Mark V" Panthers. He did note that the tanks left "very wide tank track" markings on Route 7—indicating that they were either "Vs or VIs."

77. 3rd ID G-2 Report, August 22, 1944, 2.

78. 15th IR UJ, 2242 entry, August 21, 1944.

79. O'Daniel letter (filed in 15th IR UJ near August 22, 1944), August 22, 1944 and signed by O'Daniel. Also supplemental letter of the same date signed by Col Thomas.

Chapter Seven: Roadblock

1. 2nd Bn/15th IR UJ, 0500 entry, August 22, 1944.

2. 15th IR UJ, 0645 entry, August 22, 1944.

3. Ibid., 1620 entry, August 22, 1944.

4. Ibid., 1507 entry, August 22, 1944, quotes General O'Daniel orders; the 601st TD Bn UJ, August 1944 has a copy of these August 21, 1944 orders; McFarland, *15th Infantry Regiment*, 159, reports the Regimental defensive line was approximately 22 miles long.

5. 15th IR UJ, 1445 entry, August 22, 1944.

6. Ibid., 1940 entry, August 22, 1944.

7. Ibid., 2215 entry, August 22, 1944.

8. Ibid., 1745 entry, August 22, 1944. 1st Platoon identified through process of elimination. (3rd Platoon was sent to Marignane. 2nd Platoon remained at Luxembourg.)

9. 15th IR S-2 Report dated August 23, 1944 (220001-222400 cycle), reports that 2nd and 3rd Battalions reported no enemy contact for the cycle. 15th IR UJ, 2315 and 2358 entries, August 22, 1944.

10. "Ducks..." quote from McFarland, *15th Infantry Regiment*, 161.

11. 15th IR UJ, 1000 entry, August 23, 1944.

12. Whisnant, phone conversation, June 12 and July 9, 2003; Potter, biography, March 2003, 2; and phone conversation, April 16, 2004. Both men were 3rd platoon members at the time. Potter was sent north to airport. Whisnant recalls quiet where he was, but had heard of others being hit with an artillery barrage.

13. 15th IR UJ, 2045 entry, August 22, 1944.

14. Ibid., 2145 entry, August 22, 1944.

15. Potter, biography, March 2003; 15th IR UJ, 0800 entry, August 23, 1944; 3rd ID G-3 Report, August 24, 1944; 15th IR S-3 Report, August 23, 1944;

16. Robert Ramirez, letter and photos, June 23, 2004, (Includes interview with the Chevilotte family and terrain photos.)

17. Walburn, phone conversation, June 11, 2003.

18. Owsley, phone conversation, August 17, 2003.

19. R. Ramirez, letter, June 23, 2004.

20. Ibid., Montvallon Castle was built in 1697.

21. 39th FA OR, August 1944, entry 23; Sophia Ramirez e-mail, April 23, 2004.

22. http://www.provenceweb.fr/e/bouches/vitrolles/vitrolles.htm.

23. R. Ramirez, letter and photos, June 23, 2004; and author's visit, August 21, 2004.

24. La Provence, "La famille Olive à Montvallon: 'On s'est réfugié entre deux murs pour se protéger des obus allemands'," August 22, 2004, 3.

25. Author's visit, August 21, 2004.

26. R. Ramirez e-mail, April 23, 2004; and interview, Vitrolles, August 21, 2004.

27. 15th IR UJ, 1105 entry, August 23, 1944; 3rd ID G-3 report, August 24, 1944, 2; R. Ramirez, letter and photos, June 23, 2004, (Includes interview of M. Coulon.)

28. K Co. MR, August 23, 1944.

29. 756th Tank Bn UJ, 601st TD UJ, and 3rd ID G-3 reports, August 23, 1944.

30. Estimates range between 5:00 to 6:00 PM according to the unit journals and eyewitnesses. R. Ramirez e-mail, April 23, 2004.

31. Rowe, phone conversation, June 14, 2003. This unit was federalized into the 26th Inf. Div. When replacements sorely needed, Rowe was reassigned to L Company.

32. Rowe, letter, September 16, 2005.

33. Ibid., phone conversations, May 29 and June 14, 2003; letter, June 10, 2003. Rowe believes he was wounded closer to noon on August 23. The official record indicates this artillery attack took place closer to 6:00 PM. It is possible that an attack occurred earlier in the day, but the official record only records the later one.

34. Owsley, phone conversation, August 17, 2003.

35. La Provence, "La famille Olive à Montvallon: 'On s'est réfugié entre deux murs pour se protéger des obus allemands'," August 22, 2004, 3.

36. 39th FA Journal, Battery C, August 23, 1944 entry; also interview at Montvallon of Mme. Chevilotte through R. Ramirez, August 21, 2004.

37. R. Ramirez, letter and photos, June 23, 2004 letter; Author's visit, August 21, 2004; La Provence, "La famille Olive à Montvallon: 'On s'est réfugié entre deux murs pour se protéger des obus allemands'," August 22, 2004, 3.

38. 39th FA Summary of Operations, August 1944, August 23 entry; 39th FA Journal, Battery C, August 23, 1944 entry.

39. R. Ramirez, letter and photos, June 23, 2004, (Interview with M. Coulon).

40. Ibid., letter and photos, June 23, 1944; and interview, Vitrolles, August 21, 1944.

41. 15th IR UJ, 1900 entry, August 23, 1944; 15th IR S-2 and S-3 reports, August 23, 1944; 3rd ID G-3 Report, August 23, 1944.

42. Last reported position 3rd ID G-3 report as of 1200, August 23, 1944.

43. 15th IR UJ, 1950 entry, August 23, 1944; McFarland, *15th Infantry Regiment*, 161; S-2, S-3 and G-3 Reports of same day.

44. Owsley, phone conversation, August 17, 2003.

45. Location at Montvallon is speculation. Rowe recalls he was taken into "a house" and attended to by a doctor.

46. Rowe, letter, June 10, 2003; and phone conversation, June 14, 2003.

47. 15th IR UJ, 2150 entry, August 23, 1944.

48. R. Ramirez e-mail, April 23, 2004; and interview, Vitrolles, August 21, 2004.

49. This position is speculation. However, both Greive and Rowe recall very similar terrain. Greive recalls that he had just been placed there—so the "redeployment" is also speculation. Perhaps the arrival of A Company reinforcements necessitated this move.

50. Mrs. Winsome Enzor, phone conversation, May 29, 2003; Greive, phone conversation, June 4, 2003.

51. Hunt, phone conversations, June 16 and July 9, 2003; Redle, letter, August 22, 2003; R. Ramirez, interview, Vitrolles, August 21, 2004. (Ramirez recounted an interview with M. Milles, a citizen of Le Griffon, who witnessed Orient being pulled from the tank). Andrew Orient, Individual Deceased Personnel File (IDPF). Some conjecture added to these events.

52. R. Ramirez, letter and photos, June 23, 2004 letter; Author's visit, August 21, 2004.

53. Ibid., interview, Vitrolles, August 21, 2004. (M. Milles's recollection.)

54. Andrew Orient, IDPF file.

55. Bernard Grieve, phone conversation, June 30, 2003.

56. B Co/756th Tank Bn MR, August 24, 1944.

57. L Co. MR, August 24, 1944.

58. 3rd Medical Bn OR, August 1944, B Company Report, August 23, 1944. The numbers are not broken down further. These casualties may include all wounded in the 15th IR that day.

59. 15th IR UJ, 2150 entry, August 23, 1944.

60. 39th FA Summary of Operations, August 1944, August 23 entry; 39th FA Battery C Journal, August 23, 1944 entry.

61. L Co. MR, August 24, 1944.

62. Clarke and Smith, *Riviera to the Rhine*, pages 153-154.

63. Ibid., 142.

64. Greive, phone conversation, June 4, 2003; and letter, June 22, 2003.

65. Esposito, *756th Tank Battalion in Europe*, 58. (Redle's recollection.)

Chapter Eight: Pursuit North

1. Edgar Danby, letter to his wife, August 22, 1944.
2. Anderson, Arthur Abrahamson, and Redle all recognize Danby's face by photo, but remember him as clean-shaven. However, a photo of Danby taken earlier in August shows him with a moustache. The timing and reasoning behind his shaving is speculation.
3. Arthur Abrahamson letter, May 2, 2002; and phone conversations, May 6, 2002 and May 12, 2003.
4. 756th Tank Battalion 1944 history summary, 20.
5. McFarland, *15th Infantry Regiment*, 161-162.
6. 3rd ID G-2 and G-3 reports, August 25, 1944.
7. McFarland, *15th Infantry Regiment*, 162.
8. 15th IR UJ, 1510 entry, August 23, 1944; McFarland, *15th Infantry Regiment*, 161.
9. 15th IR UJ, 0901 entry, August 24, 1944.
10. 601st TD Bn UJ, August 24, 1944.
11. 15th IR UJ, 0840 entry, August 24, 1944.
12. Ibid., 1015 and 1130 entries, August 24, 1944.
13. Ibid., 1620 entry, August 24, 1944.
14. Ibid., 1758 entry, August 24, 1944; Description of Goums from L Company veterans; Paul Gaujac, *August 15, 1944: Dragoon – The Other Invasion of France*, (Paris, France: Histoire & Collections, 2004), 172.
15. 15th IR UJ, 2230 entry, August 24, 1944.
16. 3rd ID G-3 Report, August 25, 1944, 1.
17. 15th IR UJ, 1825 and 2000 entries, August 24, 1944.
18. Ibid., 1750 entry, August 24, 1944.
19. McFarland, *15th Infantry Regiment*, 162.
20. Ibid, 162; 2nd Bn/15th IR UJ, August 25, 1944. Arrival time is an estimate. Only the 2nd Battalion gives a concrete arrival time of 10:10 AM in their unit journal, and the 2nd Battalion set out roughly four hours after 1st and 3rd Battalion departures.
21. Cannon Co. 15th IR MR, August 25, 1944; Polich, George, *Cannons Roar*, 112.
22. 15th IR UJ, 1136 entry, August 25, 1944; 601st TD Bn UJ, August 25, 1944, describes weather as "warm and fair."

23. 756th Tank Bn UJ, 1200 entry, August 25, 1944.

24. 15th IR UJ, 1715 entry, August 25, 1944.

25. 756th Tank Bn UJ, August 25, 1944.

26. French Lewis, letter, December 10, 2002; Redle, letter, March 2, 2001; and interview, Akron, OH, January 19, 2002; Perdue, phone conversation, January 31, 2004.

27. Funk, Arthur, *Hidden Ally*, 155.

28. Clarke and Smith, *Riviera to the Rhine*, 153-154.

29. 15th IR UJ, 1930 entry, August 25, 1944.

30. Ibid., 2230 entry, August 25, 1944.

31. Ibid., 2220 entry, August 25, 1944.

32. 2nd Bn/15th IR UJ, August 26, 1944. The 2nd Bn/15th IR could not depart Apt until 07:55 AM the next morning.

33. 3rd ID G-2 Report, August 26, 1944.

34. 3rd ID G-3 reports, August 24, 25, and 26, 1944. As of 12 noon on August 26, the 756th Tank Battalion had 35 operational M4s, with 13 estimated to be fit in 24 hours, 4 in 48 hours, and one evacuated as unrepairable by battalion mechanics to Ordinance.

35. Redle, phone conversation, December 5, 2000; and letters, January 3rd and March 2, 2001.

36. Anderson, phone conversation, October 3, 2000.

37. Staiger, Jörg. *Rückzug durchs Rhôntal*, (Neckargemund, Kurt Vowinckel, 1965), 75; Onno Onneken, e-mail, November 13, 2002, (Interpretation aid.)

38. 15th IR UJ, 0600 entry, August 26, 1944; 2nd Bn/15th IR, August 26, 1944 reports that battalion could not move due to lack of gasoline.

39. 15th IR UJ, August 26, 1944.

40. Ibid.; 601st TD Bn UJ, August 26, 1944.

41. Both Cotter and Polich recall their platoon was short an M8 during this time.

42. 15th IR UJ, 1045 entry, August 26, 1944. Location determined through the coordinates provided.

43. Ibid., 1730 entry, August 26, 1944.

44. 756th Tank Bn UJ, August 26, 1944, reports that the 1st Platoon was sent to the 1st Battalion to help man roadblocks near Pierrelotte at 2100.

45. 15th IR UJ, 1718 entry, August 26, 1944.

46. 2nd Bn/15th IR UJ, August 26, 1944.

47. 15th IR UJ, 1230 and 1256 entries, August 26, 1944; 2nd Bn/15th IR UJ, August 26, 1944.

48. 15th IR UJ, 1652 entry, August 26, 1944.

49. Ibid., 0415 entry, August 26, 1944.

50. Ibid., 1050 entry, August 26, 1944.

51. Ibid., 1024 entry, August 26, 1944. Location determined through the coordinates.

52. Ibid., 1333 entry, August 26, 1944.

53. Cogdell, phone conversation, September 5, 2003.

54. 15th IR UJ, 1311 entry, August 26, 1944.

55. Ibid., 1700 entry, August 26, 1944 indentifies this unit as the 2nd Platoon (B Co./3rd Chemical Mortar Battalion.)

56. Ibid., 1552 entry, August 26, 1944.

57. Ibid., 1758 entry, August 26, 1944.

58. Ibid., 2050 entry, August 26, 1944, records a specific communication from O'Daniel to Thomas specifying these times and expectations.

59. Ibid., 2140 entry, August 26, 1944; L Co. MR, August 26, 1944; Photos by Francisco Biamino taken on August 26, 1944 at Rochegude (copies obtained through Laurent Gensonnet.)

60. 15th IR UJ, 2140 entry, August 26, 1944. TD status is speculation, as they are not specifically mentioned in the 15th IR UJ. However, the 601st TD Bn UJ S-3 Report filed at 1100 on August 27, 1944, records the 3rd Platoon/B Co. TDs at coordinates 036193 near Cairanne.

61. 15th IR UJ, 0220 entry, August 27, 1944; George Polich, *Cannons Roar*, (Privately printed, 1994), 109-110.

62. Polich, letter, June 10, 2002; Jean Mathieu, letter, May 13, 2002. Mathieu recalls Americans arriving at night south of Suze with tanks. These were likely Polich's M8s.

63. K Co. MR, August 26, 1944. It is possible some or all these prisoners were taken earlier in the day. According to K Company MR, August 27, 1944, the Company suffered one casualty on the 26th: Sgt Rudy Stout was wounded by GSW and was evacuated.

64. 15th IR UJ, 1800 and 1915 entries, August 26, 1944.

65. Cockerill and Fink interview, San Antonio, TX, September 26, 2003. The rounds consisted of HE, AP (or "shot") and "Smoke." The most common was HE. The crews preferred to adjust the fuse from the "Super Quick" factory setting to the highest "Delay" possible. The change represented only a fraction of a second in timing, but was the difference between an HE round exploding outside a vehicle or structure on impact or penetrating the object and going off inside with more destructive effects. Most battlefield situations called for a delayed explosion.

66. 756th Tank Bn UJ, 2000 entry, August 26, 1944 records that B Company "reserviced" at Sérignan.

67. Redle remembers first seeing Danby in the early evening, but there is a reference in the 756th Tank Bn UJ at 1000, August 26, 1944 of the executive officer (Major Edwin Arnold) departing for B Company. Danby may have accompanied him, as it was customary for the Bn XO to personally introduce a new lieutenant to the Company Commander.

68. Redle, phone conversation, September 15, 2000; interview, Akron, OH, January 19, 2002; and letter, March 2, 2001.

69. 756th Tank Bn UJ, 2100 entry, August 26, 1944.

70. Edgar Danby, letter to his wife, August 26, 1944.

Chapter Nine: Armor Column

1. 15th IR UJ, 0330 and 0402 entries, August 27, 1944.

2. 601st TD Bn UJ, August 26-27, 1944 records the 3rd Platoon moved with 3rd Bn. Mathieu, letter, May 13, 2002, recalls that American 'tanks' were stationed just south of the entrance of Sainte-Cécile during the night of August 26.

3. The precise route is not reported, but this way clearly would have been the most direct.

4. Hickerson, phone conversation, November 14, 2003.

5. 15th IR UJ, 0430 entry, August 27, 1944.

6. Mathieu, letter, May 13, 2002.

7. 756th Tank Bn UJ, 0500 entry, August 27, 1944.

8. 15th IR UJ, 0614 entry, August 27, 1944; 756th Tank Bn UJ, 0500 entry, August 27, 1944 reports the 3rd Platoon passed through Sainte-Cécile on the way to Suze. The trip covers approximately 5 miles. Why it took over an hour is a mystery. Perhaps they got a later start, or there was a delay in reporting their arrival at the 3rd Battalion.

9. Speculation. I Company should have reached this point on foot by this time.

10. Mathieu, letter, May 13, 2002.

11. Henry Tillman, phone conversation, June 10, 2003.

12. Burks, interview, Buffalo, NY, September 13, 2002.

13. 15th IR UJ, 0614 entry, August 27, 1944.

14. Ibid., 0855 entry, August 27, 1944.

15. Cogdell, phone conversation, August 30, 2003. Cogdell distinctly remembers the name of town as "St. Paul." However, his recollection of the boy's use of "Tedeschi" may be in error. This was actually the Italian word for

"Germans." The French at the time generally used a more derogatory term "Les Boches"—slang for "brutes" or "rascals."

16. E. Rovas, phone conversation, November 20, 2002.

17. Hickerson, phone conversation, November 14, 2003. Hickerson witnessed this exchange and believes this may have happened the morning they attacked Allan.

18. Speculation based on Anderson's recollection of the incident, and practices at the time.

19. Driver was likely Jesse Rickerson. Redle recalls Rickerson was Orient's driver previously.

20. Anderson, phone conversation, October 3, 2000.

21. Both Cotter and Polich believe that the overturned M8 at Petruis may have been theirs, but neither can be 100% certain. No M8 had been lost in battle yet during the campaign, so the reason for the missing M8 was likely due to a mechanical problem.

22. Polich recalls being assigned only to Battle Patrol from the landings at Saint-Tropez on up to the fight at Allan. He thought his M8 platoon didn't team up with L Company until after both units arrived at Allan. The 3rd Bn AAR by Captain Virgil Laughlin, however, indicates that the M8s were attached to the 3rd Battalion as early as St. Paul.

23. Cotter, phone conversation, May 10, 2002.

24. Ibid.

25. Jim Mesko, *U.S. Self-Propelled Guns in Action*, (Carrollton, Texas: Squadron/Signal Publications inc., 1999), 23; George Forty, *U.S. Army Handbook 1939-1945*, (Reprint. New York: Barnes & Noble Books, 1998), 58 & 127. 60mm M2 light mortars had a range up to 1,985 yards. 81 mm M1 mortars had range up to 3,290 yards. Both mortar types were incorporated within the rifle companies (60 mm) and heavy weapons companies (81 mm) of a WWII U.S. Army infantry battalion. The 4.2" mortars had ranges up to 5,000 yards and were organized into a separate "Chemical Mortar Battalion" under the command of the division.

26. Burks, interview, Buffalo, NY, September 13, 2002.

27. Cotter, phone conversation, June 4, 2003.

28. Ibid.

29. Ibid.

30. Ibid., phone conversation, May 10, 2002.

31. Polich, *Cannons Roar*, 173.

32. Ibid., 9.

33. Ibid., 62.

34. These are the known vehicles involved. One or two additional jeeps may have been in the formation.

35. Polich recalls this was the purpose of the mission. "With all haste" is conjecture based upon O'Daniel's orders.

36. Jean Haremboure, interview, Allan, August 18, 2004.

37. 15th IR UJ, 1030 entry (signed 0940), August 27, 1944.

38. B. Rovas, e-mail, December 31, 2002, quoting his father.

39. 3rd Bn AAR, Allan, 1; Polich, *Cannons Roar*, 110; Polich, phone conversation, January 17, 2002; Whisnant, phone conversation, July 9, 2003; Fr. Girardo, "Libération de La Garde Adhémar - Août 1944" memoir, (transcribed by Bernard Hernadez).

40. The material captured is a best guess. A substantial discrepancy exists in the official documentation. The 3rd Bn AAR for the day credits L Company with capturing "7 tanks and 3 SP guns" at this roadblock, and the 15th IR UJ, 1235 entry, August 27, 1944, credits L Company with destroying "1-88mm gun, 1 AT gun, 1 MG, and 4 trucks" and capturing "3 trucks in vicinity of 920370 at approximately 1100," but no tanks are mentioned. (920370 are the coordinates for the Chatroussas position.) Since no other mention could be found of "7 tanks" being captured by L Company in any other sources, this AAR detail has been ignored. Also, the 15th IR UJ, 1235 entry, seems to be combining two incidents into one. About 1 hour after this roadblock incident, L Company destroyed several trucks in a convoy several miles further to the north. This is reported as a separate incident in the AAR and is also recalled as a separate incident by Polich.

41. Number of German dead is reported in the 3rd Bn AAR, Allan, 1. The number of Germans encountered is estimated at thirty by the 3rd ID G-3 report, August 27, 1944.

42. Staiger, *Rückzug durchs Rhôntal*, 75 (map).

43. 3rd ID G-2 report "Interrogation Report" annex, August 29, 1944, 2-3.

44. Staiger, *Rückzug durchs Rhôntal*, 75 (map).

45. German Nineteenth Army Journal, 1105 entry, August 27, 1944.

46. Departure time is an estimate base upon the entries in the 15th IR UJ.

47. 15th IR UJ, 1030 entry, August 27, 1944.

48. 756th Tank Bn UJ, 1230 entry, August 27, 1944 reports the B Company CP moving near St Paul.

49. Redle, interview, Akron, OH, January 19, 2002. Redle describes this as the way his CP typically operated at the time.

50. Fazendin, *756th Tank Battalion at Cassino*, 13, 28-29, 102-105.

Chapter Ten: Allan

1. Except where noted otherwise, the remainder of this chapter draws heavily from the 1947 book by Maurice Martel, *Allan: Mon Village,* (Privately printed, 1947). Martel was a citizen of Allan and an eyewitness and participant to many wartime events in his village.

2. Author's visit to Allan and photographs of August 2001.

3. Funk, *Hidden Ally,* 21-25; Francis Cammaerts, letters, March 24 and April 22, 2002, March 18, and June 8, 2003.

4. The reason for the journey is presumed from the circumstances.

5. Eugene Rozel, interview, Allan, August 16, 2004; Lucien Martel (Maurice Martel's son) e-mail, June 10, 2005.

6. Rozel, letter, December 16, 2004; L. Martel, e-mail, April 5, 2005

7. Girardo, "Libération de La Garde Adhémar - Août 1944".

8. Rozel, letter, January 10, 2003.

9. Ibid.

10. German Ninteenth Army Journal, 1300 entry, August 27, 1944. This entry does not specifically record when these guns were assigned to the Korps. However, Staiger reports in his book, *Rückzug durchs Rhôntal,* (77), that the LXXXV Korps expected and prepared for a massive Allied tank attack on August 25, 1944. That attack never materialized.

11. Robert Borne and Jean Dessalles, interview, Allan, early August 2001.

12. Borne and Dessalles, interview, Allan, early August 2001; Haremboure, letter, September 26, 2001; George Almoric, interview, Allan, July 31, 2001 (translated and edited by Michel Seigle.)

Chapter Eleven: Reconnaissance

1. This was most likely an American P-47. By August 25, 1944, three fighter groups (the 27th, 79th, and 324th) from the Twelfth Air Force had moved from bases on Corsica to the coast of Southern France—extending their patrol range north beyond Montélimar. Each of these three groups was comprised exclusively of P-47s—all silver. Kenn Rust, *Twelfth Air Force Story,* (Temple City, California: Historical Aviation Album, 1975), 4, 17, 35.

2. Polich, phone conversations, January 3 and 6, 2002; e-mail, February 5, 2002; letter, April 11, 2003; Polich, *Cannons Roar,* 110; Morris, phone conversation, January 14, 2002.

3. Polich, *Cannons Roar,* 110; and letter, June 10, 2002.

4. 3rd Bn AAR, Allan, 1.

5. Redle, phone conversation, September 15, 2000; Polich, letter, January 14, 2002.

6. Potter, biography, March 2003, 2; and interview, Holiday, FL, June 24, 2003. Potter is fairly certain this was passed just south of Allan before the attack, but the exact location is unknown. Perhaps these were soldiers killed earlier by the FTP.

7. Rozel, letter, January 10, 2003.

8. Ibid., letter, December 16, 2005.

9. Ibid., interview (with drawing by Rozel), Allan, early August 2001; and letters, January 10 and December 15, 2005. The nature of the conversation is speculative, but it is hard to imagine Rozel, a former French elite soldier, risking his life before his family's eyes for a simple wine delivery. Danby's placement of the bottle is also speculation. An ammo ring on the interior of the turret, however, would have been an ideal location.

10. Martel doesn't specifically record this, but the 1/25,000 US Army 1944 map of the area shows a field path connecting both roads at this location.

11. According to Martel, the approaching American force concentrated "artillery" first upon suspected German gun positions in the nearby woods, ditches and farms (41). The connection between this action and Rozel's communication with Danby is speculative.

12. Cotter, phone conversation, May 10, 2002.

13. Arnold Mackowsky, U.S. Army discharge papers.

14. L Co. MR, June 7, 1944.

15. Darrah, phone conversation, July 7, 2003.

16. Whisnant, phone conversation, July 9, 2003.

17. Matt Mackowsky (Arnold Mackowsky's grandson), e-mail, August 19, 2003.

18. Shelly Mackowsky (Arnold Mackowsky's widow), phone conversation, March 1, 2003.

19. Jantz, letter, May 18, 2003. Coles' orders to Mackowsky are speculative based upon circumstances recalled by Jantz.

20. Henri-Paul Enjames, *Government Issue: U.S. Army European Theater of Operations Collector Guide*, (Paris, France: Histoire & Collections, 2004), 205.

21. Burks, letter, December 11, 2002.

22. U.S. Seventh Army General Orders #118 (March 1945) for James Coles' DSC. (Size of German forces was provided.)

23. Jantz, phone conversation, May 8 and May 30, 2003; and letter, May 18, 2003. The Mackowsky's motivations are conjecture, and the account of Mackowsky seeing Germans encircling town is also speculative.

24. M. Mackowsky, e-mail, April 9, 2004; S. Mackowsky, phone conversations on August 29 and September 26, 2002.

25. Jantz, phone conversation, May 8, 2003.

26. This is speculation. Jantz recalls others on the patrol, but does not remember what happened to them aside from Shook. The three other prisoners, including Tyler, were taken at the time from a field outside of town. The German Nineteenth Army UJ also records that only five American prisoners were taken this early in the day.

27. The platoon's level of knowledge at this time is speculative.

28. Tyler vividly recalls the circumstances of his capture but does not remember the names of the two others with him. The identities of Bonnett and Cardelli are deduced from the L Co. MRs of August 27, and August 31, 1944, and from the recollections of Earl V. Potter who was taken captive with a later group.

29. Jantz, letter, May 18, 2003.

30. Ibid., phone conversation, May 30, 2003.

31. Ibid., letter, May 18, 2003.

32. Ibid.

33. Tyler, phone conversation, January 13, 2004.

34. Ibid., letter, May 18, 2003.

35. Onneken, e-mail, September 15, 2003. (Likely reason.)

36. Jantz is not exactly sure when they were divided in pairs. This may have occurred earlier.

37. Jantz, letter, May 18, 2003.

Chapter Twelve: The Crossroads

1. Speculation based on 15th IR UJ entries, August 27, 1944. The Bn CP was not established on the south base of Montchamp until 4:20 PM (1710 entry).

2. 756th Tank Bn UJ, August 27, 1944 reports the B Company CP 4 miles west of Saint Paul (1230 entry) and later 4 miles N of St Paul (1500 entry).

3. 2nd Bn/15th IR UJ, 1100 entry, reports the 2nd Bn/15th IR CP at Saint-Paul.

4. 15th IR UJ, 1140 entry, August 27, 1944.

5. Time estimate based on the unit journals, the recollections of Eugene Rozel, and the time line described in Martel's book. Martel reports the American tanks and infantry advance on Allan began at 1:30 PM.

6. Although Martel's description of the move on town shows coordination and strongly suggests a deliberate command, the specific reasons for American attack are speculative. Nevertheless, Jantz and Tyler recall the Germans scrambling to secure the town. From his CP five hundred yards south of Allan, Coles would have certainly heard the gunfire and the Marder engines manuevering among the buildings.

7. Martel describes U.S. forces dividing into two sections, but the exact composition is uncertain. Danby's tank was likely in the lead. Both M4s would have certainly been dispatched ahead of the TDs and M8s. The distribution of the TDs is speculative. The 2nd Platoon was held back in reserve at the Constant Farm while 1st and 3rd Platoons moved further into the village. This was determined by interviewing the surviving L Company veterans, matching names with platoon assignments and comparing them with their memories of the action.

8. Macksey, *Tank Versus Tank*, 107 (chart).

9. Staiger, *Rückzug durchs Rhôntal*, 83. The precise location of the German korps HQ at this point is not recorded—perhaps near the Borne farm or in tents to the northwest of town.

10. Haremboure, letter, September 26, 2001. Probably a Marder III. The hasty departure of a small tank and a large "Tiger" tank were witnessed by Robert Borne, a child at the time.

11. Macksey, *Tank Versus Tank*, 107 (chart); Horst Scheibert, *Marder III*, (Atglen, Pennsylvania: Schiffer Publishing Ltd., 1998), 47.

12. Borne, Dessalles, and Michel Imbert, interview, Allan, July 31, 2001; Michel Imbert interview, Allan, early August 2001. The French (particularly Imbert) recall a fresh gouge hit on tank on port side of turret front. Imbert believed the round ricocheted into Martel home. No one from Allan actually saw this happen however.

13. Martel, *Allan: Mon Village*, 41; Whisnant, phone conversation, July 9, 2003. Whisnant recalls terrain and circumstances very similar to Martel's description.

14. Martel, *Allan: Mon Village*, 41; Whisnant, phone conversation, July 9, 2003. The exact location of this van incident has been forgotten.

15. 15th IR UJ, 1430 and 1437 entries, August 27, 1944.

16. Martel writes that German artillery rained down upon the Mourier house and caused this destruction, but the Americans reported no artillery at this time. The damage to the stone walls on the southeast upper floor appear to be the work

of a flat trajectory cannon (Lucien Martel 1944 photo), for this reason I believe an American TD was responsible.

17. The term "sniper" is used as loosely here as it was in Leithner's Silver Star citation. These were not likely to be Germans with scoped rifles, but regular riflemen shooting from hidden positions. U.S Army records at the time tended to describe any enemy soldier shooting from a hidden position a "sniper."

18. Haremboure, e-mail, December 17, 2001; From Lucien Martel's 1944 photo, the vehicle is identified as a Pjgr 38(t) Marder III H-type with 75mm PAK 40/3 gun.

19. Joseph W. Leithner Silver Star Citation from an unknown newspaper (photocopy from his family). Whether this Marder III is the same one photographed later on the lane can't be determined with 100% certainty, but the circumstances, location, and timing of events strongly match those of Martel's book.

20. This communication with the TDs south of town is speculation. Lucien Martel saw the ashen remains of two individuals inside the Marder III the following day. (L. Martel, memoirs, 34.)

21. This tactical change is speculative, but explains the reason why the column moved north rather than northwest toward Montélimar.

22. Potter, biography, March 2003, 2; Potter interview, Holiday, FL, June 24, 2003.

23. Whisnant, phone conversation, July 9, 2003.

24. Potter, phone conversation, August 30, 2002; Potter, biography, March 2003, 3; Potter, interview, Holiday, FL, June 24, 2003; Martel, *Allan: Mon Village*, 42.

25. Schrader, phone conversation, June 10, 2003. In this initial conversation, Schrader thought Mackowsky had been riding the tank with him at the time. This would have been impossible, as the lieutenant had been captured two hours earlier. Schrader fell ill and passed away before this detail could be further clarified.

26. A major unresolved mystery in this history is the motivation behind Danby's decision to move his tanks north of town. Maurice Martel believed this was "to undoubtedly aid the patrol" of the fifteen or so men who went beyond the bridge and failed to report back. Whisnant thought the tanks moved to support a fierce small arms battle occurring at the time, but his memories may not be as strong as those of Potter, who recalls absolute calm at the time. Rodger also recalls calm at the time. Redle vividly remembers the radio conversation between Danby and Oliver, but not the reasons behind Danby's decision. He remembers the tanks were moving out of town at the time, but does not know if they were under fire or moving at the request of Coles. Nothing in Danby's

behavior throughout the day indicated anything other than a simple desire to do a competent job. The Unit Journals, the AAR, and the account in McFarland's book, *The Fifteenth Infantry Regiment in World War II,* describe the event but are also silent on the motivations. Polich recalls that the armor column was reconstituted just prior to the move—suggesting the advance was planned and either set to move at a predetermined time or dependent on an "all clear" from Coles. (The entire force at Allan was, after all, under his skilled command.) Captain Coles' DSC citation does not mention the tanks at all, nor can his surviving family shed any light on the incident. Despite the pressures to fulfill the day's mission, the men who fought with Coles (Redle, Jantz, Burks, and others) unanimously agree that Coles would not have called the tanks forward unless he was fully satisfied that the area was clear. Based upon the testimony and the sketchy record, this author concludes that the column was likely set to move at a predetermined time—providing that Potter's patrol did not run in any difficulties. As the lead tank and the ranking officer at the fore, Danby may have been given this standing order by Coles, without Oliver, Polich and others being aware of it.

27. Esposito, *756th Tank Battalion in Europe*, 59. (Redle's recollection.)

28. L Co. MR, February 7, 1944.

29. Scarpa, tape recording, January 14, 2002.

30. The explosive charge appears to be that of a PzGr. 39/42 round—commonly used by Panthers at that time. Http://geocities.com/desertfox1891/pzpanther/pzpanther-Charakteristics.html?200513.

31. Scarpa, phone conversations, May 11 and 23, 2001; L. Martel, memoirs, 33-34;

32. Potter, interview, Holiday, FL, June 24, 2003; Rodger, phone conversation, June 17 and October 7, 2003; Schrader, phone conversation, June 10, 2003.

33. 756th Tank Bn UJ, 1530 entry, August 27, 1944, reports three dead and two lightly wounded from the tank; 2nd Bn/15th IR UJ, 1600 entry, August 27, 1944, records destruction of tank with three dead; Scarpa, phone conversations, May 11 and 23, 2001. Scarpa is the only witness who saw the bow gunner escape in this manner. All other witnesses only recall seeing only Tikannen escape through the top hatch. The identity of the bow gunner is not known for certain.

34. Schrader, phone conversation, June 10, 2003.

35. Scarpa, phone conversations, of May 11 and 23, 2001.

36. Rodger, phone conversation, June 17 and October 7, 2003; Potter, phone conversation, August 30, 2002; and interview, Holiday, FL, June 24, 2003; Earl Whipple, phone conversation, June 11, 2003; Perdue, phone

conversation, December 28, 2001; Scarpa, phone conversations, May 11 and 23, 2001.

37. Whipple, phone conversation, June 11, 2003.

38. Rodger, phone conversation, June 17, 2003.

39. Potter, interview, Holiday, FL, June 24, 2003.

40. Michel Seigle, e-mail, September 21, 2000; Borne, Dessalles, and Imbert, interview, Allan, July 31, 2001; Whipple, phone conversation, June 11, 2003; Whisnant, phone conversation, July 9, 2003. The surviving French who lived in Allan during the war remain split as to whether the smaller (Marder-type) tank or the much larger German tank was directly responsible for knocking out Lt. Danby's Sherman. The larger "Tiger" tank is remembered as "much bigger than a Sherman." The 11th Panzer Division, however, did not have Tiger tanks. They had mostly Panthers—which fit the description of a "big" tank. Both Whisnant and Whipple saw the same German tank soon after Danby's tank was knocked out and also identify it as "big." The unit journals identify it as a "Mark VI"—which was generally used to describe a Tiger tank. The French also say the tank was covered in camouflage, which would easily blur the visual differences between Panther and a Tiger.

41. Potter, interview, Holiday, FL, June 24, 2003.

42. Ibid.; and biography, March 2003, 3.

43. Ibid., phone conversation, April 16, 2004; L Co. MR, September 2, 1944, record that these four men returned together.

44. Potter, phone conversation, April 16, 2004.

45. Ibid., biography, March 2003, 3; and interview, Holiday, FL, June 24, 2003.

46. Ibid., phone conversation, April 16, 2004.

47. Schrader, phone conversation, June 10, 2003; Polich, letter, January 14, 2002 (TD description).

48. Redle, phone conversation, May 2, 2001; 15th IR UJ, 1710 entry (signed 1620), August 27, 1944. The Regiment's message from Boye is recorded in a rather curious way: "Fwd elements at 949470. Meeting heavy resistance. CP at 925426. Tks ran back." The first coordinates are of L Company at Allan. The second coordinates are of the 3rd Bn CP on the south side of Monthchamp. Neither the destruction of Danby's tank nor the appearance of the German Panther are mentioned—which would explain why the "tanks ran back." Perhaps the battalion typist left out these details, or perhaps this was the raw message that came in from L Company's radio as the incident unfolded and Coles was not immediately aware that Danby's tank had been hit.

49. Macksey, *Tank Versus Tank*, 107 (chart).

50. Esposito, 756th *Tank Battalion in Europe*, 59. (Redle recollection.)

51. Redle, interview, Akron, OH, January 19, 2002; 756th Tank Bn UJ, 1530 entry, August 27, 1944.

52. Seigle, e-mails, September 21 and October 14, 2000.

53. Seegitz, phone conversations, October 15-16, 2002.

54. Scarpa, phone conversations, May 11 and 23, 2001.

55. Whisnant, phone conversation, July 9, 2003; Rodger, phone conversation, June 17, 2003.

56. Cogdell, phone conversation, June 10, 2003, and March 20, 2004.

57. 15th IR UJ, 1710 entry, August 27, 1944;

58. Esposito, *756th Tank Battalion in Europe*, 60. Redle recalls that L Company's radio was destroyed by shell fire. Whisnant, phone conversation, July 9, 2003, recalls Coles' jeep was abandoned just before a large German tank crushed it with a track, and that Coles was limping from a wound to the backside. 2nd Bn/15th IR UJ, 2045 entry, August 27, 1944, records "Mark 6 overran jeep and trailer destroying radio and killing 2 or 3 men." 3rd Bn AAR, Allan, 4, reports "The radio at "L" Company had been destroyed by enemy fire." 15th IR UJ, 2245 entry, August 27, 1944, records that L Company "Lost jeep with radio and code."

59. Seventh U.S. Army General Orders #118 (March 22, 1945) for James Coles' DSC citation.

60. Opinion, as discussed with Jantz, phone conversation, May 8, 2003.

61. Seventh U.S. Army General Orders #118 (March 22, 1945) for James Coles' DSC citation. Described as a "full battalion" of attackers.

62. Arnold Peterson, phone conversation, January 30, 2002; This was Peterson's observation of after reading my summary.

63. 2nd Bn/15th IR UJ, 2045 entry, August 27, 1945; 15th IR UJ, 2245 entry, August 27, 1944; Whisnant, phone conversation, July 9, 2003.

64. Redle, letter, September 18, 2000.

Chapter Thirteen: Trouble in the Rear

1. Polich, phone conversation, January 17, 2002.

2. Ibid. phone conversation, January 3, 2002; and letter, June 10, 2002.

3. Polich, *Cannons Roar*, 110; Polich, phone conversation, January 17, 2002.

4. Cotter, phone conversation, May 10, 2002. Cotter doesn't specifically recall where he was at the time. He knows for certain that he was not at the head of the column or fighting in the fields north of town, and has always assumed he

was back with his platoon. Polich does not remember Cotter being with them until later. To rectify these differing recollections, I assume here that Cotter was somewhere out of view ahead of his M8s and had to call in over the radio to check with Polich.

5. Ibid., phone conversation, May 10, 2002.

6. The particular TD involved is speculation. Polich recalls the "last" TD in the column was on the south bridge. If this memory is correct, it would have been in the best position for fire.

7. Polich, *Cannons Roar*, 110; Polich letter, January 14, 2002; Cotter, phone conversation, May 10, 2002.

8. Polich, *Cannons Roar*, 110.

9. Polich, letter, June 10, 2002.

10. Ibid., letters, January 14 and June 10, 2002.

11. Polich, *Cannons Roar*, 110-111.

12. Martel, *Allan: Mon Village*, 43. There is some chance that this "TD" may have actually been Oliver's tank. Martel places this action around the time when Oliver's antenna was severed. However, Martel describes this "tank" and infantry as moving up the street from the Constant Farm south of town. Under the circumstances, it is unlikely that Oliver's tank would have retreated back so far. Therefore, the TD's involvement is supposed.

13. Jantz, letter, May 18, 2003; and phone conversation, May 30, 2003; Jantz does not know for certain when Shook returned—only that he was rescued after L Company took the town. His repatriation may have been earlier or later than recorded here.

14. 3rd Bn AAR, Allan, 3, (misidentified as 2nd Bn/15th IR forces); 15th IR UJ, 1601, 1635, and 1738 entries, August 27, 1944.

15. 15th IR UJ, 1635 and 1737 entries, August 27, 1944, describe artillery; 2nd Bn/15th IR UJ, 1340 entry, August 27, 1944, also describes artillery; M. Carret, interview (with the help of interpretation by Jean Haremboure), Donzère, August 20, 1944.

16. 2nd Bn/15th IR UJ, 1600 entry, August 27, 1944.

17. 15th IR UJ, 1736 entry, August 27, 1944.

18. Redle originally thought Ray Getz drove him but the B Company MRs show that Getz was out sick. Palumbo was his other driver.

19. Esposito, *756th Tank Battalion in Europe*, 60; Redle, phone conversation, September 15, 2000; and interview, Akron, OH, January 19, 2002.

20. Burks, interview, Buffalo, NY, September 13, 2002; and letters, December 11, 2002 and March 5, 2003.

Chapter Fourteen: The Gauntlet

1. 15th IR UJ, 1850 entry (signed at 17:30), August 27, 1944. "947473" are the coordinates for Allan.

2. Ibid., 1850 entry, August 27, 1944; 3rd Bn AAR, Allan, 3-4. The location is an estimate. The map referenced in the AAR was not with it in the NARA file.

3. 3rd Bn AAR, Allan, 4; AAR reports this team was dispatched, but under the circumstances it is difficult to imagine they reached Allan any earlier than midnight.

4. U.S. Seventh Army General Orders #85 (March 9, 1945) for Dominick Delmonico's DSC citation; Hawkins, phone conversation, July 8, 2003; Rodger, phone conversation, June 17, 2003; Shirley, e-mail, February 24, 2003.

5. Philip Delmonico (Dominick Delmonico's brother), phone conversation, January 31, 2006.

6. McFarland, *15th Infantry Regiment*, 163; U.S. Seventh Army General Orders #85 (March 9, 1945) for Dominick Delmonico's DSC citation.

7. The Altoona (Pennsylvania) Mirror, (all articles listed in bibliography.)

8. Ibid., May 9, 1945, page unknown.

9. Ibid., "Bronze Star is Presented Posthumously," October 19, 1945, (Bronze Star language is quoted in the article.) Ordinarily, a rifleman would have taken cover while reloading. The newspaper article relates that Sigrist "stood completely exposed and fired two clips…into a German machine gun nest." Either this detail was left out or Sigrist remained standing while exchanging clips. According to George Burks (phone conversation, November 6, 2005), a man on an adrenaline kick would often do things that he would later reflect upon as "crazy."

10. 3rd Infantry Division General Orders #66 (February 25, 1945) for Cedric Porter's Bronze Star. The wounded man was likely Pfc. Scott V. Szurley, the only wounded man listed on the K Co. MR, August 28, 1944.

11. German Nineteenth Army Journal, August 1944 entry, 94.

12. Martel, *Allan: Mon Village*, 44.

13. 15th IR UJ, 2245 entry, August 27, 1944.

14. This number is an estimate. Burks HQ section broke down, and the supply and mess sections were with the Battalion.

15. L Co. MRs (See appendix chart, this book.) One of those seriously wounded later died. Therefore, overall total was six killed in action.

16. Donald Bowman, IDPF file.

17. L Co. MR abstract for the entire 1944 year (created by the author.)

18. James Doolin, IDPF file.

19. MacKinnon, letter, December 24, 2001; Cotter, phone conversation, May 10, 2002. MacKinnon witnessed Coles leave for town with the wounded man, and Cotter was there to receive them.

20. Cotter, phone conversation, May 10, 2002.

21. B Co. /756th Tank Bn MRs, August 28, and September 5, 14, and 19, 1944; Redle, letter, January 3, 2001, and phone conversation, July 15, 2002. Redle believes Oliver's crew (S/Sgt. Haskell Oliver, T5 Ed Sadowski, Pfc. George Davis, and Pvt. Bert Bulen) were likely wounded from shellfire of some sort but has no clear recollection of it. All four men have since passed on, and none of their families know for certain either.

22. Esposito, *756th Tank Battalion in Europe*, 60; Redle interview, Akron, OH, January 19, 2002. Redle believes Lt. Col. Davis was there but "couldn't sign and affidavit to that."

23. 2nd Bn/15th IR UJ, 1805 entry, August 27, 1944, gives assembly point south of "Grenier." This was a farm near Chartroussas according to 1944 1/25,000 scale maps obtained from NARA.

24. 15th IR UJ, 2245 entry, August 27, 1944.

25. Esposito, *756th Tank Battalion in Europe*, 60.

26. Ibid., 60.

27. Cotter, phone conversation, May 10, 2002.

28. Martel, *Allan: Mon Village*, 44.

29. Cotter, phone conversation, May 10, 2002.

30. Redle, interview, Akron, OH, January 19, 2002.

31. According to Redle, a Continental radial engine had to be kept running between 1600 and 2200 RPMs. (1850-2200 RPMS, according to Ralph Donley, interview, Fond-du-Lac, WI, September 16, 2005.) The engine would stall below this range, and lose power above this range. Consequently, the radial engine demanded particular tachometer vigilance and fancy gear shifting by the driver.

32. Esposito, *756th Tank Battalion in Europe*, 61. Redle recalls Coles telling him this. However, Cotter does not recall grazing the tank.

33. Polich, letter, January 14, 2002.

34. MacKinnon, letter, December 24, 2001.

35. Martel, *Allan: Mon Village*, 44.

36. Fasciana, phone conversation, June 16, 2003.

37. Cotter, phone conversations, May 10, 2002 and June 4, 2003; Polich, *Cannons Roar*, 111. Polich thinks this happened closer to 2:00 AM.

38. Polich, *Cannons Roar*, 111.

39. Ibid., 111; Whisnant, phone conversation, July 9, 2003.

40. 15th IR UJ, 0047 entry, August 28, 1944; 3rd BN AAR, Allan, 4.

Chapter Fifteen: A Small Revenge

1. 2nd Bn/15th IR UJ, 0530 entry, August 28, 1944.
2. Rozel, letter, January 10, 2003.
3. Ibid.
4. Polich, letter, January 14, 2002.
5. Martel, *Allan: Mon Village*, 44; Haremboure, letter, September 26, 2001.
6. Borne and Dessalles, interview, Allan, early August 2001.
7. 15th IR UJ, 0825 entry, August 28, 1944.
8. 2nd Bn/15th IR UJ, 0940 entry, August 28, 1944.
9. Peterson, phone conversation, January 30, 2002.
10. 2nd Bn/15th IR UJ, 1400 entry, August 28, 1944; H Company was commanded by Lt King. Reported 12 horse drawn carts destroyed.
11. Walter Tardy, phone conversation, December 18, 2001.
12. 15th IR UJ, 1220 entry, August 28, 1944.
13. L. Martel, memoirs, 33.
14. At least no incident that the author could find in the written records or the memories of the participants.
15. Shirley, letter, December 8, 2001; Stuart customarily rode in his jeep in these situations.
16. Esposito, *756th Tank Battalion in Europe*, 61. (Redle recollection.)
17. Redle, letter, June 1, 2001; Tominac may not have been the platoon leader involved, but Redle believes that it was Tominac who told him about this incident sometime after it happened. Redle originally thought the story involved a towed gun poking out of the brush, but he now recognizes the similarities between his recollection and the written record are too coincidental.
18. Esposito, *756th Tank Battalion in Europe*, 61; Redle, phone conversation, May 2, 2001; and letter, June 1, 2001. Redle is fairly certain that Froneberger was the gunner, but does not recall the identity of the tank commander involved.
19. Esposito, *756th Tank Battalion in Europe*, 61; Redle, letter, June 1, 2001; McFarland, *15th Infantry Regiment*, 170-171; 3rd Bn AAR, Allan, 4; Both the UJ and the AAR report the barrel of a "Mark VI tank" (not a towed gun) was severed,.
20. 3rd Bn AAR, Allan, 4; McFarland, *15th Infantry Regiment*, 170-171.

Epilogue

1. 756th Tank Bn UJ, 1300 entry, August 28, 1944.
2. 15th IR UJ, 1100 entry, August 28, 1944.
3. Ibid., various morning entries for August 28, 1944.
4. Esposito, *756th Tank Battalion in Europe*, 60.
5. Polich, *Cannons Roar*, 111.
6. James Doolin's IDPF file reports that he expired at the 3rd Bn Aid Station on August 27, 1944.
7. 2nd Bn/15th IR UJ, 1515 and 1540 entries, August 28, 1944.
8. 15th IR UJ, 2207 entry, August 28, 1944.
9. Ibid., 0250 entry, August 29, 1944.
10. Taggart, *History of the Third Infantry Division*, 221; McFarland, *15th Infantry Regiment*, pages 171-172.
11. Taggart, *History of the Third Infantry Division*, 221.
12. Ibid., 222; Polich, *Cannons Roar*, 111; Sherman Pratt, *Autobahn to Berchtesgaden*, (Baltimore, MD: Gateway Press, Inc., 1992), 430; Audie Murphy, *To Hell and Back*, (Reprint. New York, New York: Henry Holt and Company LLC, 2002), 187-188.
13. Pratt, *Autobahn to Berchtesgaden*, 437 (photo); Valenti, *Combat Medic*, 115.
14. Valenti, *Combat Medic*, 119.
15. Clarke and Smith, *Riviera to the Rhine*, 167-168.
16. Ibid., 167. PWs are an estimate off the 365 MIA number listed.
17. Ibid., 167-168.
18. Grossjohann, Georg. *Four Years, Five Fronts*. (Reprint, New York: Presidio Press, 2005), 147. Grossjohann commanded the 2nd Bn/308th Grenadier Regiment of the 198th Infantry Division.
19. Clarke and Smith, *Riviera to the Rhine*, 159-160.
20. Neither Jantz nor Tyler specifically recalls the names of the other three men. Mackowsky was separated from them probably because of his rank and because he needed medical attention. Tyler recalls being with two others during the 2-3 day bus journey, and Jantz recalls being with one other. When they escaped, both groups teamed up again to reach American lines. Both believe this group included five, but not with absolute certainty. According to the L Co. MR, only two other men (Cardelli, Bonnet) returned to duty with Jantz and Tyler on August 31, 1944. I must assume that the fifth man was from another unit.
21. Jantz, phone conversations of May 8 and 30, 2003; and letter, May 18, 2003; Tyler, phone conversations, March 5, 2003 and January 13, 2004; and

"Veteran History Project Transcript", July 23, 2003, 4; and "World War II Experience 1943-1945", May 2002, 11.

22. S. Mackowsky, phone conversation, August 29, 2002.

23. L Co. MR, August 29, 1944.

24. Potter, phone conversation, August 30, 2002; and interview, Holiday, FL, June 24, 2003; Potter, biography, March 2003, 3.

25. The L Co. MR, September 2, 1944, lists Potter, Evans, Mangina, and Engel as returned for duty, but Potter believes their physical arrival with the Company was not until after the battle of Besançon—which lasted September 4-8. One possible explanation of this discrepancy is that Works listed the men on the duty roll before they actually arrived.

26. T/5 Melvin E. Heaton, and Pfcs. Raymond LeClair, Kenneth D. Lynch, James A. McLaughlin, Dallas P. Taylor, and Homer R. Toman were captured during the evening of September 4-5. Most were from Weapons Platoon's machine gun section and were manning an outpost at the time.

27. Pfcs. Nicholas Massow and William F. Hawkins were lightly wounded on September 7, Pfc. James W. Morrow was wounded on September 8, and Pfcs. Dorris J Barton, Walter N. Harmon, and Clarence Nagle were wounded on September 10.

28. Pvt.Virgil L Reed was listed as MIA on September 12. At the end of the war his status was changed to an "FOD" (Finding of Death) per the West Virginia war dead record. FOD's were generally given to those MIAs believed dead but where no body was ever recovered. An FOD enabled the family to collect death benefits.

29. Rovas returned on September 14, 1944 according to the L Co. MRs.

30. B. Rovas, phone conversation, March 3, 2003.

31. Taggart, *History of the Third Infantry Division*, 280.

32. Captain Carroll F. Gates. Several L Company veterans who wish anonymity have told me that this man was a very bad fit for the unit. The MRs show Gates was wounded on October 26, 1944, but a subordinate recalls that Gates' wounds were minor and should not have precluded him from returning to his assignment. Gates may not have been a bad officer or person—just a bad fit for L Company. Some officers are more suited to non-combat roles. Other officers are fine combat leaders but just don't gel into the chemistry of certain units. Gates had big shoes to fill after the loss of Coles.

33. Burks, interview, Buffalo, NY, September 13, 2002.

34. Redle, phone conversation, August 15, 2005.

35. Stanton, Shelby L. *Order of Battle U.S. Army, World War II.* (Novato, California: Presidio Press, 1984) 79.

36. Numbers based on totals taken from Taggart, *History of the Third Infantry Division*. Figures provided for each campaign on pages 34, 76, 102, 150, 188, 234, 280, 324, and 373 were totaled by the author and converted into percentages.

37. Stanton, *Order of Battle U.S. Army, World War II*. Conclusion after comparing all casualty figures listed in this book for each U.S. Army division.

38. L. Martel, "Memoirs," 33-35; L. Martel, e-mails, May 2005.

39. Imbert, interview, Allan, early August 2004.

40. 1st platoon, 46th Quartermaster Graves Registration Company, according to all the IDPF files. Each American killed at Allan has an August 29, 1944, collection date. Not all remains were in town. Some had already been collected and were held by the 3rd Battalion.

41. All the Americans killed at Allan were eventually buried at Luyens near Aix. The tank crew was buried at the cemetery north of Allan. The German dead were handled in a variety of ways. In some instances the French buried them.

42. The tank number was W-3067828 according to Dual Dishner's IDPF file. Sadly, the Graves Registration officer also noted that nothing remained of Dishner to recover.

43. L. Martel, "Memoirs," 33-35.

44. Rozel described this entire ceremony in a school essay written at the time. (He was then 11 years old.) Rozel included a copy of this essay along with his January 23, 2002 letter.

45. December 4, 1944, according to the IDPF files for Danby, Dishner and Vargo.

46. Martel, *Allan: Mon Village*, pages 8-9.

47. Almoric, interview and tape recording, Allan, July 31, 2001 (translated by Michel Seigle). Almoric recalled that the bloodstain on the ground remained visible "for years" after the war.

Postscript

1. Abrahamson, letter, May 2, 2002; and phone conversations, May 6 and 12, 2003.

2. Anderson, phone conversations, October 3, 2000 and June 28, 2001. Unfortunately, Anderson cannot recall the name of the bow-gunner.

3. Ibid., phone conversation, October 3rd 2000 and June 28, 2001.

4. Page Boye (Frederic Boye's wife) phone conversation, October 27, 2003; Jerome Sapiro letter, December 17, 2001.

5. Burks, letter, April 13, 2004.

6. Ibid., interview, Buffalo, NY, September 13, 2002; and letters, December 11, 2002, March 5, and June 27, 2003.

7. Rodger, phone conversation, October 7, 2003; Ciancanelli, phone conversation, March 8, 2002.

8. McFarland, *15th Infantry Regiment*, 185.

9. L Co. MR, October 24, 1944.

10. Ciancanelli, interview, Palos Park, IL, July 24, 2003.

11. Ibid.

12. Anthony Ciancanelli (Arco Ciancanelli's son), phone conversation, December 11, 2005.

13. Cogdell, phone conversation, June 6, 2004.

14. L Co. MR, September 17, 1944.

15. Morris, letter, December 29, 2001; Hunt, phone conversation, June 16, 2003; Scarpa, tape recording, January 14, 2002; Wellfare, e-mail, April 17, 2002.

16. L Co. MR, October 3, 1944.

17. McFarland, phone conversation, June 20, 2001; Hayward, letter, April 21, 2002; Burks, letter, December 11, 2002; Scarpa, tape recording, January 14, 2002; Heagerty, letter, April 23, 2002; Redle, phone conversation, September 15, 2000; and interview, Akron, OH, January 19, 2002; Redle, Hayward, and McFarland recall that Coles and Sullivan escaped. Prisoner of War searchable database, http://aad.archives.gov/aad/.

18. Morris, letter, December 29, 2001; Morris wrote Caspian Sea. Redle remembers Black Sea. The Black Sea was more likely, as the Caspian Sea is land-locked and further east.

19. Redle, phone conversation, September 15, 2000.

20. Scarpa, tape recording, January 14, 2002; Heagerty, letter, April 23, 2002.

21. Heagerty, letter, April 23, 2002.

22. Ibid., letter, April 23, 2002; Redle, interview, Akron, OH, January 19, 2002.

23. Darrah, phone conversation, July 7, 2003; Redle, interview, Akron, OH, January 19, 2002.

24. Redle, interview, Akron, OH, January 19, 2002.

25. Divorce records for James Coles, Superior Court of California, San Diego County.

26. Wright, phone conversation of April 21, 2004; Barbara Willis (James Coles' daughter), letter, May 4, 2006; James W. Coles death certificate,

November 5, 1963; The El Paso Times, "James Coles Dies Sunday" October 30, 1968, (page unknown).

27. Cotter, phone conversations, May 10, 2002, and June 4, 2003; Lloyd Cotter obituary (provided by his family), letter, May 12, 2004.

28. Sapiro, letter, December 17, 2001.

29. Cotter, phone conversation, June 4, 2003.

30. Darrah, phone conversation, July 7, 2003; Potter, phone conversation, August 30, 2002; Rodger, phone conversation, June 17, 2003; Scarpa, tape recording, January 17, 2003; Shirley, e-mail, August 30 and November 16, 2001; P. Delmonico, phone conversation, January 31, 2006; The Cincinnati Times-Star, "Holder of Army's Second High Award Killed in Germany" September 24, 1945, 9:7.

31. The Cincinnati Times-Star, "Holder of Army's Second High Award Killed in Germany" September 24, 1945, 9:7.

32. Redle, letter, June 1, 2001; Perdue, phone conversation, December 28, 2001.

33. Redle, letters, October 30, 2000, and June 1, 2001.

34. Perdue, phone conversation, January 7, 2004.

35. Greive, phone conversations, June 4 and 30, 2003.

36. Jantz, phone conversations of May 8 and 30, 2003; and letter, May 18, 2003.

37. Jantz, letter, May 18, 2003.

38. Nussbaum, phone conversation, June 3, 2003; and letter, June 19, 2003.

39. Cockerill, phone conversation, January 17, 2002.

40. B Co./756th Tank Bn MR, November 6, 1944.

41. Anderson, phone conversation, May 15, 2003.

42. Carol Standifer and June Moorhead (Haskell Oliver's daughters), phone conversation, May 13, 2001.

43. L Co. MRs, September 30, 1944.

44. Owsley, phone conversations, August 17 and October 6, 2003, and May 12, 2004.

45. Arnold Mackowsky, U.S. Army discharge papers.

46. S. Mackowsky, phone conversation, March 1, 2003.

47. Social Security Death Index, www.rootsweb.com.

48. A. Miluszusky, phone conversations, July 18 and 21, 2003; and letter, August 10, 2003.

49. Redle, letter, June 24, 2002; R. Nusz, undated obituary copy.

50. Polich, *Cannons Roar*, pages 172-176.

51. Potter, biography, March 2003; and phone conversation, May 15, 2003.

52. Ibid., interview, Holiday, FL, June 24, 2003.

53. Anderson, phone conversation, October 3, 2000; Cockerill, phone conversation, January 17, 2002; Clyde Guild, letter, January 15, 2002; Perdue, phone conversation, December 28, 2001.

54. Redle, letter, October 30, 2000.

55. Ibid., letter, February 13, 2001.

56. Ibid., letter, January 3, 2001.

57. L Co. MR, October 26, 1944.

58. B. Rovas, phone conversation, March 3, 2003; and e-mail, April 2, 2003.

59. E. Rovas, phone conversation, November 20, 2002.

60. B. Rovas, e-mail, December 31, 2002.

61. Rowe, letter, June 10, 2003; and phone conversation, June 14, 2003.

62. Rowe, phone conversation, July 21, 2004.

63. Scarpa, phone conversation, May 14, 2003.

64. Schrader, phone conversation, July 1, 2003; Richer Castner (Arthur Schrader's friend), letter, June 1st 2004, with obituary.

65. Harry Halenda, phone conversation, June 14, 2003; The Altoona Mirror, "Is Promoted." October 31, 1944; "Altoonan in Battle Zone Badly Wounded." November 18, 1944; "Sgt Donald R. Sigrist." February 17, 1945; "Was Missing, Local Sergeant Reported Dead." May 9, 1945; "Funeral Mass for Veteran." May 29, 1945; "Bronze Star is Presented Posthumously." October 19, 1945; (Page numbers unknown to all articles); WWII overseas graves listing, www.abmc.gov.

66. K. Stout, phone conversation, December 29, 2003.

67. Perdue, phone conversation, December 28, 2001; Butch Westcomb (Emil Tikkanen's son-in-law), phone conversation, December 30, 2001; Carol Westcomb and Nancy Tikkanen, (Emil Tikkanen's daughters) phone conversation, July 17, 2002; C. Westcomb, e-mail, January 15, 2002.

68. Tyler, "Veteran History Project Transcript", July 23, 2003; Tyler, "World War II Experience 1943-1945", 2002; Tyler, letter, February 25, 2003.

69. A Co./756th Tank Bn MR, August 29, 1944.

70. Taggart, *History of the Third Infantry Division*, 388.

71. Abrahamson, phone conversations, May 6 and 12, 2003.

72. Names compared against *15th Infantry Regiment* Roster listed in Taggart, *History of the Third Infantry Division*, 478-506. All KIAs, MIAs, DOWs, and PWs are marked on this list.

73. Taggart, *History of the Third Infantry Division*, 399. Bronze Star list.

74. Lane Hodgdon (Fred Hodgdon's son), phone conversation, June 19, 2003.

75. Rheinhold Bonnett, IDPF file; L Co. MRs, September 17, 21, and 22, 1944.

76. Jantz, letter, May 18, 2003.

77. Prisoner of War searchable database, http://aad.archives.gov/aad/.

78. Taggart, *History of the Third Infantry Division*, 421, Bronze Star list and roster.

79. Robert Maynard, letter, January 30, 2002.

80. WWII overseas graves listing, www.abmc.gov.

81. Pfcs. James J. Lovascio, Norval A. Monroe, and Louis Polonsky IDPF files.

82. Author.

83. Onneken, e-mail, December 18, 2002.

84. Fasciana, phone conversation, June 16, 2003; Kenneth Lynch, phone conversation, November 17, 2002; Marker, letter, February 10, 2002; Scarpa, tape recordings, January 14, 2002, and November 17, 2003.

Bibliography

Interviews, Contacts and Contributors:(Army ranks shown as of August 1944. Some are approximate)

15th Infantry Regiment

L Company:

George Burks (1st Lt. & XO); Pat Cardelli family (Pfc.); Arco Ciancanelli (Pfc.); John R. Clifford (Pfc.); Herman Cogdell (T/5); James W. Coles family (Capt.); Chester Darrah (Pvt.); Gervase Dauby (S/Sgt.); Dominick Delmonico family (Cpl.); Winsome Enzor family (Pfc.); Salvatore Fasciana (Pfc.); Bernard Greive (Pvt.); Richard Guimond (Pfc.); Harry Halenda (Pvt.); William Hawkins (Pvt.); Jessie Hickerson (S/Sgt.); Fred Hodgdon family (2nd Lt.); James Hunt (Pfc.); Rudolph Jantz (Pfc.); Richard Kirschner (Pfc.); Joseph Leithner family (Pfc.); George Loudermilk family (Pfc.); James Lovascio family (Pfc.); Kenneth Lynch (Pfc.); John MacKinnon (Pvt.); Arnold Mackowski family (2nd Lt.); Dale Marker (Pfc.); William McNamara family (Pfc.); Floyd Owsley (Pfc.); Edward Perlson family (Pvt.); Earl Potter (Pfc.); Patrick Rodger (Pfc.); Edmund Rovas (Sgt.); Lloyd Rowe (Pfc.); Roy Sanders family (Sgt.); Fred Scarpa (Pfc.); Earl Schick family (Pfc.); Arthur Schrader (Pfc.); Robert Seegitz (Pfc.); Donald Sigrist family (Pfc.); Henry Tillman (Cpl.); Homer Toman (Pfc.); Richard Totte family (Pfc.); Robert Tyler (Pfc.); Ralph Walburn (Pfc.); Max Wellfare (Cpl.); Earl Whipple (Pfc.); Albert Whisnant (Pfc.); Burleigh Whitney (Pfc.)

I, K, M, and 3rd Battalion HQ Companies:

Patrick Heagerty (Pfc.); John Shirley (S/Sgt.); Earl Ravenscroft (Sgt.); Robert McFarland (2nd Lt.); John Morris (2nd Lt.); Robert Nelson (2nd Lt.) Frederick W. Boye family (Lt. Col.), Russell M. Comrie (Maj.)

Cannon Company:

Lloyd Cotter (1st Lt.); George Polich (T/Sgt.), Joseph Ranke (Pfc.)

756th Tank Battalion:

B Company:

Roy Anderson (Sgt.), Bert Bulen family (Pvt.); Frank Cockerill (Pvt., joined later); George Davis family (Pfc.); Dual Dishner family (Pvt.), Roger Fazendin family (2nd Lt., served prior); Bud Fink (Pvt., joined later), Clyde Guild (Cpl.); Karl Kincaid (Pvt., joined later); Alfred Mancini (Sgt.); Anthony Melfi family (2nd Lt., joined later); Alvin Nusz family (1st Sgt.); Haskell Oliver family (S/Sgt.); Andrew Orient family (2nd Lt.); Gene Palumbo (Pvt.); Randolph Perdue (Pfc.); David Redle (Capt.); Jesse Rickerson family (T/5); John Roth (T/4); Ed Sadowski family (T/5); Henry Sanislow (Sgt.); Paul Taylor (Pvt., joined later); Emil Tikkanen family (T/5); Steve Vargo family (Cpl.); Charles Wilkinson (Capt., served prior); Richard Young (Pvt., joined later)

A Company:

Arthur Abrahamson (1st Lt.); Arthur Richter (2nd Lt.)

Other 756th Tank Battalion:

French Lewis (Capt.), Oscar Long family (Maj.), Ed Olson (Capt.); Jeff Malsam (researcher, and grandson of Tony Malsam of C Company/ 756th Tank Battalion.)

601st Tank Destroyer Battalion:

B Company:

Charles Colprit (Sgt.); Albert Donaldson (Pfc.); Bill Harper (S/Sgt.), Robert Maynard (Capt., later); W.B. Nesmith (Sgt., served prior); Arnold Petersen (Pvt.); Ambrose Salfen (Capt.)

Staff:

Walter Tardy (Lt. Col. and Bn CO)

Other soldiers from 3rd Infantry Division:

George Ferguson (1st Lt., H Co./15th IR), Bernard Hayward (S/Sgt. in HQ 1st Bn/15th IR, postwar); Glenn Rathbun (Maj. and XO of 3rd Bn/7th IR); Jerome Sapiro (Capt., 3rd ID HQ)

Contributors from France

Allan:

Georges Almoric (town mayor in 1944 and witness); Robert Borne (witness); Pascal Delaire; Jean Dessalles (witness); Jean and Dhanya Haremboure; Michel Imbert (witness); Rene Lapierre; Lucien Martel (witness & photos); Jean Pic (tank photo); Jean Rozel (witness); Michel and Marie-Thérèse Seigle

Other:

Olivier Blanc-Brude; Francis Cammaerts (Maj., British SOE); M. Carret (Donzère witness); Chevilotte family (Montvallon witnesses); Michel de la Torre; Laurent Gensonnet; Bernard Hernandez; Jean Mathieu (Suze-la-Rousse witness); Philippe Planel; Robert & Sophia Ramirez

Other Contributors:

Steve Bell; Russell & Ruby Danby-Jones; Ed Dojutrek (veteran and historian Society of the 3rd Infantry Division); Arthur Funk (professor and author); A. Harding Ganz (professor of history at The Ohio State University); Gale Kramer; Capt. Lee Mudd (U.S. Army historian); Lloyd O'Connell (Encinitas Historical Society); Fr. Carl Subler; Alfred & Maxine Tumminia; George Wilkins (citizen of Del Mar, California)

If I omitted anyone from this list, I apologize. If you served during these times—particularly with L Company of the 15th Infantry Regiment, or the 3rd Platoons of B Company in either 756th Tank Battalion or 601st Tank Destroyer Battalion—and I could not locate you for an interview, please know that I tried everything I could think of to locate you! —Jeff

Primary Source Official Documents:

National Archives and Records Administration (College Park, Maryland)

Army and Air Force (Record Groups 407 and 18):

15th Infantry Regiment:

Operation Reports for August 1944; Anvil Plans and Field Orders; 1st, 2nd and 3rd Battalion After Action Reports for Saint-Tropez and Montélimar; Daily Journal for August 1944 (also includes Daily S-2 and S-3 Reports); 2nd Battalion Daily Journal for August 1944 (Note: Unit Journals for 1st and 3rd Battalions missing.)

601st Tank Destroyer Battalion:

Commander's Narrative for August 1944; Daily Journal and S-3 Reports for August 1944.

756th Tank Battalion:

1943 and 1944 Unit Histories [includes 34th ID General Order #29 (April 1944) for Haskell Oliver's Bronze Star]; Daily Journal for August and September 1944; Operations Reports/Commander's narratives for August (including assessment of DD-tank performance at Saint-Tropez) and September 1944.

30th Infantry Regiment:

Operations Reports for August 1944; Daily Journal from August 22 to 30, 1944.

39th Field Artillery Battalion:

Operation Reports for August 1944; Daily Journal August 24 to 31, 1944; Battery C Daily Journal for August 1944.

3rd Medical Battalion:

Operations Report for August 1944.

3rd Quartermaster Battalion:

Operation Report for August 1944.

46th QM Grave Registration:

Operations Report for September 1944 (August is missing).

7th Infantry Regiment:

2nd and 3rd Battalion After Action Reports for Montélimar; Operation Report for August 1944; Daily Journal and S-3 Reports for August 25 to 31, 1944.

3rd Infantry Division:

G-2 Daily Reports for August and September 1944; G-3 Daily Reports for August 1944; G-3 Map for August 28, 1944; "Map of Enemy Reaction to Operation Dragoon;" "Map of French Forces in Marseille;" "Map of German Withdrawal Up the Rhône;" "Map of Operation Dragoon Division Landings;" "Map of Operation Dragoon Division Maneuvers;" "Map of Third Division Assault on Saint-Tropez;" "Fact Sheet;" Biography of General O'Daniel; General Orders #94 (December 1943) for James Coles' Silver Star; #175 (August 1944) for Oliver's Silver Star; General Orders #66 (February 1945) for Cedric Porter's Bronze Star; General Orders #90 (March 1945) for DD-tank crews' Bronze Star.

Seventh U.S. Army:

G-3 Preliminary Report of South France Landings; Lessons Learned August 15 to October 15, 1944; General Orders #118 (March 1945) for James Coles' DSC; General Orders #85 (March 1945) for Dominick Delmonico's DSC; General Orders #16 (January 1945) for William McNamara's DSC (January 1945); General Orders #77 (March 1945) for Lloyd Cotter's DSC.

27th Fighter Group:

Operation Reports for August 1944.

314th Fighter Squadron:
Sortie Reports August 23 to 31, 1944.

316th Fighter Squadron:

Sortie Reports August 22 to 31, 1944.

War Department:

War College: memos on "Tank Infantry teams" and the "Panther Tank"; observer memos on the Seventh U.S. Army October 21, 1944, and October 25, 1944.

War Department Attaché Reports: #41 Sherman Tank (August 7, 1944); #112 Medium and Light Tank equipment (August 22, 1944); #118 Combat Psychology, (September 8, 1944); #130 Comments on Operation of the M4 tank (September 8, 1944); #161 Infantry Operations (September 2, 1944); #465 Combat Lessons Discussed by Casualties (June 6, 1944.)

Navy Records (Records Group 38):

Task Force 84:

Eighth Amphibious Force Reports; Preliminary After Acton Report of Operation Dragoon; After Action Reports for the U.S.S. Chase, U.S.S. Henrico, U.S.S. Thurston, and LCT-1015.

Cartography Records (Records Group 77):

AFHQ 1/25,000 Scale Maps for the South of France (August 1944): Montelimar 1&2, 3&4, 5&6; Valreas 1&2, 5&6; Orange 1&2, 5&6; Martigues 5&6, 7&8.

AFHQ 1/25,000 Map Baie de Pampelonne (July 1944).

"Official Road Map for Allied Forces, Europe: South-East France" (1/500,000 Scale)

AFHQ 1/10,000 Aerial Photo Baie de Pampelonne June 1944, Mosaic 4 and 5.

AFHQ Panoramic Beach Sketches South and North of Beach 261 (July 1944.)

Captured German Records (Records Group 242):

German LXXXV Armeekorps HQ documents (on microfilm roll T-314)

National Personnel Records Center (St. Louis, Missouri):

15th Infantry Regiment "Morning Reports": Companies I, K, 3rd Bn HQ, and Cannon from August 15 to September 15, 1944. Company L from January 1944 to December 1944.
756th Tank Battalion "Morning Reports": Company A for August 1944; Company B from January 1944 to April 1945.
601st Tank Destroyer Battalion "Morning Reports": Company B for August 1944.

U. S. Total Army Personnel Command (Alexandria, Virginia):

Individual Deceased Personnel Files (Graves Registration) for T/Sgt. Donald M. Bowman; 1st Lt. Edgar R. Danby; Pvt. Dual Dishner; Pfc. James T. Doolin; Cpl. William F. Leaman; Pfc. James J. Lovascio; Pfc. Norval A. Monroe; 2nd Lt. Andrew Orient, Pfc. Louis Polonsky; Cpl. Steve Vargo.

Veterans Affairs, Records Management Center (St. Louis, Missouri):

Veteran Affairs file for Edgar Danby.

Superior Court of California, County of San Diego:

Divorce Records for James Coles.

German Military Records (Bundesarchiv-Militärarchiv in Freiburg, Germany.):

Daily Journal and surviving reports of the Nineteenth German Army (August 25-28, 1944).

Letters, Memoirs, and Miscellaneous Primary Documents

Danby, Edgar. Wartime letters to his wife dated from 1942 through 1944. (In the author's possession.)
Danby, Septimus (Edgar Danby's father). Letters to Russell Danby (grandson) dated from the 1950s. (In the author's possession.)
Girardo, Fr. "Libération de La Garde Adhémar - Août 1944." Journal account of combat eyewitness. (Electronic copy from Bernard Hernandez.)
Joseph W. Leithner Silver Star Citation from unknown newspaper. (Photocopy from his family.)

Arnold Mackowsky U.S. Army discharge papers. (Photocopies from his family.)

Martel, Lucien, Wartime memoirs written for his family. (Photoscans from Lucien Martel.)

Potter, Earl V. "Earl V. Potter Momentos of World War II" undated biography (5 pages). (Electronic copy from Earl V. Potter.)

Rozel, Eugene. School essay written in November 1944 on the All Saints Day memorial at Allan, France. (Photocopies from Eugene Rozel.)

Schrader, Arthur. Sworn eyewitness statement signed November 20th, 1944 on the actions of William McNamara at Saint-Tropez for DSC consideration. (Photocopies from McNamara family.)

Tyler, Robert V. "Robert V. Tyler's World War II Experience 1943-1945" dated May 2002 (30 pages), and testimony for the Veteran History Project of Springfield College, Massachusetts dated April 2003 (9 pages). (Photocopies from Robert V. Tyler.)

Newspapers

The Altoona (Pennsylvania) *Mirror*, "Is Promoted." October 31, 1944; "Altoonan in Battle Zone Badly Wounded." November 18, 1944; "Sgt Donald R. Sigrist." February 17, 1945; "Was Missing, Local Sergeant Reported Dead." May 9, 1945; "Funeral Mass for Veteran." May 29, 1945; "Bronze Star is Presented Posthumously." October 19, 1945; (Page numbers unknown to all articles.)

The El Paso Times, "Wounded El Pasoan Still Sees Rosy Side of Life" November 27, 1943; "James Coles War Fatality in Europe" October 11, 1944; "J Walter Coles." January 11, 1945, "James Coles Dies Sunday" October 30, 1968. (Page numbers to articles unknown.)

La Provence (Marseille, France), "La Famille Olive à Montvallon." August 22, 2004, page 3.

Motion Pictures and Photographs

Aerial photos taken in 1947 of Montvallon and Chartroussas areas. (Obtained from the Institut Géographique National, France.)

Photos of the liberation of Rochegude on August 26th, 1944. (Photographer: Francisco Biamino, photoscans obtained by Laurent Gensonnet.)

Invasion of Riviera; Invasion of Southern France. 1944. Pathé Films newsreels downloaded via Internet from the website: www.britishpathe.com. (Each film is 3 to 4 minutes.)

Operation: Dragoon—The Allied Invasion of the South of France. Los Angeles, CA: OnDeck Home Entertainment, 30 min. 1996. Video cassette.

U.S. Army Signal Corps and U.S. Navy movies kept at the National Archives in College Park, Maryland: 3rd Division pushes on Montelimar France; Invasion Southern France, Bay of Pampelonne; Celebration of Liberation, Marseilles France; French rebuild bridge near Avignon, France; 3rd Division push Le Ganet; 15th Inf. Reg activities at camp; Riviera landings; U.S. troops advance inland; Southern France missions Twelfth Air Force; Expansion of Southern France Beachhead; (Film reels taken in August 1944 and vary in length from a few minutes to 12 minutes.)

War Department Field Manuals, Training Manuals, Regulations, and Organizational Tables: (All originated from the U.S. Government Printing Office in Washington D.C. during World War II.)

Armored Force Field Manual FM 17-3: Tank Platoon - October 22, 1942.

Armored Force Field Manual FM 17-12: Tank Gunnery - April 22, 1943.

Army Regulations AR 850-150: Authorized Abbreviations and Symbols - November 13, 1943 and September 18, 1944, with supplements.

Field Manual FM 17-32: American Tank Company Tactics - November 8, 1944.

Field Manual FM 17-36: Employment of Tanks with Infantry - March 13, 1944.

Infantry Field Manual FM 7-10: Rifle Company, Rifle Regiment - June 2, 1942.

Technical Manual TM 11-242: Radio Set SCR-300-A - June 15, 1943.

Technical Manual TM 12-427: Military Occupational Classifications of Enlisted Personnel - July 12, 1944.

Table of Organization and Equipment T/O & E 18-27: Tank Destroyer Gun Company, Tank Destroyer Battalion, Self-Propelled - March 15, 1944.

Table of Organization and Equipment T/O & E 17-27: Medium Tank Company Tank Battalion - November 18, 1944.

Table of Organization and Equipment T/O & E 7-17: Infantry Rifle Company - February 26, 1944.

Table of Organization and Equipment T/O & E 7-14: Infantry Cannon Company - February 26, 1944.

Table of Organization and Equipment T/O & E 7-16: Headquarters and Headquarters Company, Infantry Battalion - February 26, 1944.

Studies and Materials from the U.S. Army Military History Institute:
(Located in the Foreign Military Studies and Unit Histories catalogs at the
Carlisle Barracks in Carlisle, Pennsylvania.)

"11th Panzer Division in Southern France (15th Aug to 14th Sept 1944)."
Postwar interview of Generalleutnant Wend von Wietersheim
"A Brief History of the 15th Infantry Regiment."
"Battle Record of the 3rd Infantry Division."
CMH preliminary notes for period after 15 Aug 1944 by L.A. Nowak.
(Generaloberst Johannes Blaskowitz interrogation on German reaction to the
Invasion of Southern France – dated 23 July 1945.)
"Nineteenth Army (Jun 43 – Sept 44)." Commentary by Generalleutnant
Walter Botsch.
"Nineteenth German Army in Southern France from 1 July to 15 Sept 1944"
Postwar interview of General Freidrich Wiese.
"Opinions relative to the History of the U.S. 7th Army (As seen by the
German 19th Army)." Postwar interview of Generalleutnant Walter Botsch. Pgs
25-39.

Published Books

Adleman, Robert H., and Colonel George Walton. *The Champaign
Campaign*. Boston, Massachusetts: Little, Brown, and Company, 1969.

Barr, Dr. Niall, and Dr. Russell Hart. Panzer: *An Illustrated History of
German Armour in WWII*. London, United Kingdom: Aurum Press Ltd., 1999.

Bonn, Keith E. *When the Odds were Even: The Vosges Mountains
Campaign, October 1944-January 1945*. Novata, California: Presidio Press Inc.,
1994.

Breuer, William B. *Operation Dragoon*. Novato, California: Presidio Press,
1987.

Chamberlain, Peter, and Chris Ellis. *The Sherman: An Illustrated History of
the M4 Medium Tank*. 2nd printing, New York, New York: Arco Publishing
Company Inc., 1978.

Clark, Jeffrey J., and Robert Ross Smith. *Riviera to the Rhine*. Washington
D.C.: Center for Military History, 1993.

Cooper, Belton Y. *Death Traps*. Novato, California: Presidio Press Inc.,
2000.

D'Este, Carlo. *Fatal Decision: Anzio and the Battle for Rome*. New York,
New York: HarperPerennial, 1992.

De Trez, Michel. *First Airborne Task Force: Pictorial History of the Allied
Paratroopers in the Invasion of Southern France*. Belgium: D-Day Publishing,
1998.

Donnhauser, Anton J., and Generalmajor Werner Drews. *Der Weg der 11.Panzer-Division*. Bad Wörishofen, 1982.

Eisenhower, Dwight D. *Crusade in Europe*. Reprint. Garden City, NY: Doubleday and Co. Inc., 1961.

Ellis, Chris. *The German Army 1933-45*. Hersham, Surrey, United Kingdom: Ian Allan Publishing, 1993.

Enjames, Henri-Paul. *Government Issue: U.S. Army European Theater of Operations Collector Guide*. Paris, France: Histoire & Collections, 2004.

Fazendin, Roger. *The 756th Tank Battalion at Cassino*. Lincoln, Nebraska: iUniverse Inc. 1991.

Fisher, Ernest F. *U.S. Army in World War II: Cassino to the Alps- The Mediterranean Theatre*. Reprint. Minnetonka, Minnesota: National Historical Society, 1995.

Ford, Roger. *The Sherman Tank*. London: Brown Packaging Books Ltd., 1999.

Forty, George. *U.S. Army Handbook 1939-1945*. Reprint. New York: Barnes & Noble Books. 1998.

Funk, Arthur L. *Hidden Ally: The French Resistance, Special Operations, and the Landings in Southern France, 1944*. Greenwood Press, 1992.

Gaujac, Paul. *August 15, 1944: Dragoon – The Other Invasion of France*. Paris, France: Histoire & Collections, 2004.

Gill, Lonnie. *Tank Destroyer Forces WWII*. Paducah, KY: Turner Publishing Co., 1992.

Green, Michael & Gladys. *Weapons of Patton's Armies*. Osceola, Wisconsin: MBI Publishing Co., Inc., 2000.

Green, Michael. M4 Sherman: *Combat and Development History of the Sherman Tank and All Sherman Variants*. Osceola, Wisconsin: Motorbooks International, 1993.

Green, Michael. *Patton's Tank Drive: D-Day to Victory*. Osceola, Wisconsin: MBI Publishing Company, 1995.

Greer, Don. *Walk Around M4 Sherman*. Carrollton, TX: Squadron/Signal Publications Inc. 2000.

Grossjohann, Georg. *Four Years, Five Fronts*. Reprint, New York: Presidio Press, 2005.

Hart, Stephen A. *Panther Medium Tank 1942-45*. Oxford, United Kingdom: Osprey Publishing, Ltd., 2003.

Hatlem, John C., and Kenneth E. Hunter. *A WWII Pictorial History: The War in the Mediterranean*. Herndon, Virginia: Brassey's, Inc, 1998.

Hearn, Chester G. *The American Soldier in World War II*. London, United Kingdom: Salamander Books, Ltd., 2000.

Henry, Mark R. *The U.S. Army in World War II.* Oxford, United Kingdom: Osprey Publishing, 2001.

Jensen, Marvin. *Strike Swiftly! The 70th Tank Battalion from North Africa to Normandy to Germany.* Novato, California: Presidio Press, 1997.

Macksey, Kenneth. *Tank Versus Tank: The Illustrated History of Armored Battlefield Conflict in the Twentieth Century.* Reprint. New York: Barnes & Noble Books, 1999.

Madej, W. Victor. *U.S. Army Order of Battle: European Theater of Operations 1943-1945.* Allentown, Pennsylvania: Game Publishing Company., 1983.

McLean, Donald B., ed. *Company Officer's Handbook of the German Army.* Wickenburg, Arizona: Normount Technical Publications, 1975.

Mesko, Jim. *U.S. Self-Propelled Guns in Action.* Carrollton, Texas: Squadron/Signal Publications Inc., 1999.

Messenger, Charles. *The Second World War in the West.* London, United Kingdom: Cassell, 1999.

Morison, Samuel Eliot. *History of the United States Naval Operations in World War II. Vol. XI, The Invasion of France and Germany 1944-1945.* 1957. Reprint, Edison, New Jersey: Castle Books, 2001.

Murphy, Audie. *To Hell and Back.* Reprint. New York, New York: Henry Holt and Company LLC, 2002.

Parada, George, Wojciech Styrna and Stanistaw Jabtonski. *Marder III.* Lublin, Poland: Kagero, 2002.

Pratt, Lt Col. Sherman W. *Autobahn to Berchtesgaden.* Baltimore, MD: Gateway Press Inc., 1992.

Prohme, Rupert. *History of the 30th Infantry Regiment in World War II.* Washington: Infantry Journal Press, 1947.

Robichon, Jacques. *The Second D-Day.* New York, New York: Walker and Company, 1969.

Rottman, Gordon L., and Leroy Wilson, eds. *Battle Experiences: World War II European Theater.* De Ridder, Los Angeles: Brown Mouse Publishing Co., 1998.

Rust, Kenn. *Twelfth Air Force Story*, Temple City, California: Historical Aviation Album, 1975.

Sawicki, James A. *Tank Battalions of the U.S. Army.* Dumfries, Virginia: Wyvern Publications, 1983.

Scheibert, Horst. *Marder III.* Atglen, Pennsylvania: Schiffer Publishing Ltd., 1998.

Schrodek, Gustave W. *Die 11. Panzerdivision "Gespensterdivision" Bilddokumente 1940-1945.* Friedberg, 1984.

Schrodek, Gustave W. *Ihr Glaube Galt Dem Vaterland*: Geschichte Des Panzer-Regiments 15 (11. Panzer-Division). Munich: Schild Verlag, 1976.

Scutts, Jerry. *Republic P-47 Thunderbolt: The Operational Record.* Osceola, Wisconsin: Motorbooks International, 1998.

Staiger, Jörg. *Rückzug durchs Rhôntal: Abwehr und Verzögerungskampf der 19. Armee im Herbst 1944 unter besonderer Berücksichtigung des Einsatzes der 11. Panzer-Division.* Neckargemünd: Kurt Vowinckel, 1965.

Stanton, Shelby L. *Order of Battle U.S. Army, World War II.* Novato, California: Presidio Press, 1984.

Taggart, Donald G. *The History of the Third Infantry Division in World War II.* 1946. Reprint, Nashville, Tennessee: The Battery Press, 1987.

The Seventh United States Army Report of Operations: France and Germany 1944-1945. 1946. 2 vols. Reprint, Nashville, Tennessee: The Battery Press, 1988.

Valentie, Isadore. *Combat Medic*, 2nd Edition, Tarentum, Pennsylvania: Word Association Publishers, 1998.

Whiting, Charles. *America's Forgotten Army: The Story of the U.S. Seventh.* Rockville Centre, New York: Sarpedon, 1999.

Williamson, Gordon. Panzer Crewman 1939-45. Oxford, United Kingdom: Osprey Publishing Ltd., 2002.

Wilt, Alan F. *The French Riviera Campaign of August 1944.* Carbondale, Illinois: Southern Illinois University Press, 1981.

Winchester, Jim. *The World War II Tank Guide.* Edison, New Jersey: Chartwell Books Inc., 2000.

Wright, Michael, ed. *The Readers Digest Illustrated History of World War II.* Pleasantville, New York: Readers Digest Association, Inc., 1989.

Zaloga, Steven J. *M10 and M36 Tank Destroyers 1942-53.* Oxford, United Kingdom: Osprey Publishing Ltd., 2002.

Zaloga, Steven J. *Sherman Medium Tank 1942-45.* 1978. Reprint, Oxford, United Kingdom: Osprey Publishing Ltd., 2001.

Unpublished or Self-Published Books and Dissertations

Esposito, Cheryl. *The 756th Tank Battalion in the European Theatre.* Privately printed, 1999.

Josowitz, 1st Lt Edward L. *An Informal History of the 601st Tank Destroyer Battalion.* Privately printed, late 1940s.

Kosanke, Roy. "756th Tank Battalion Reunion Book". By the author, late 1980s. Photoscanned.

Martel, Maurice. *Allan: Mon Village.* Privately printed, 1947.

McFarland, Robert, ed. *The History of the 15th Infantry Regiment in World War II.* Privately printed, Early 1990s. Photocopied. (This book is transcription of the 15th Infantry Regiment's unpublished 1945 collaborative historical manuscript.)

Mudd, Lee. "History of the 756th Tank Battalion and the Development of the Tank-Infantry Team in World War II." Thesis, Johns Hopkins University, 2000.

Polich, George B. *Cannon's Roar*. Privately printed, 1995. Photoscanned.

Shirley, John. *I Remember: Stories of a Combat Infantryman in World War II*. Privately Printed, 2003.

Periodicals and Pamphlets

Clarke, Jeffrey J. *Southern France*. The U.S. Army Campaigns of World War II series CMH Pub 72-31.

Gabel, Dr. Christopher R. *Leavenworth Papers #12—Seek, Strike, and Destroy: U.S. Army Tank Destroyer Doctrine in World War II*. Fort Leavenworth, Kansas: Combat Studies Institute, September 1985.

Ganz, A. Harding. "The 11th Panzers in the Defense, 1944" Armor Magazine, March-April 1994, Pages 26-37.

Mudd, Capt. J. L. "Development of the American Tank-Infantry Team During World War II in Africa and Europe" Armor Magazine, Sept-Oct. 1999, Pages 15-22.

Internet

"Sherman DD Tank to Emerge From the Deep" article at webpage: www.military.com/Content/MoreContent/1,12044,NLtankrecovery,00.html.

1930 U.S. Census, and Social Security Death Index. See website: www.rootsweb.com.

Normandy 1944 Landing Craft. See webpage: www.britannica.com/dday/article-9344596.

Profiles of the town of Saint-Maximin and Tourves. See website: www.provenceweb.fr.

"Panther Characteristics." See webpage: www.geocities.com/ desertfox 1891/pzpanther/pzpanther-Charakteristics.html?200513.

Prisoner of War and War Casualties by State databases at the website: www.archives.gov

WWII U.S. Army overseas graves database at the website: www.abmc.gov. "3d Infantry Division Shoulder Sleeve Insignia" See webpage: http://www.army.mil/cmh-pg/matrix/3ID/3ID-Matrix.htm

INDEX